LOUIS GIANNETTI

Case Western Reserve University

fifth edition

UNDERSTANDING MOVIES

PRENTICE HALL, Englewood Cliffs, New Jersey 07632

Library of Congress Cataloging-in-Publication Data

GIANNETTI, LOUIS D.
  Understanding movies / Louis Giannetti.—5th ed.
  p.   cm.
  Includes bibliographies and index.
  ISBN 0-13-945585-X
  1. Motion pictures. I. Title.
PN1994.G47 1990
791.43—dc20   89-15951
                     CIP

Editorial/production supervision
  and interior design: F. Hubert

Page layout: Karen Noferi
Manufacturing buyer: Ray Keating/MaryAnn Gloriande
Cover design: Diane Saxe
Cover photo: From *Who Framed Roger Rabbit*.
  A Walt Disney Production. © 1988
  Touchstone Pictures and Amblin
  Entertainment, Inc.

© 1990, 1987, 1982, 1976, 1972 by Prentice-Hall, Inc.
A Division of Simon & Schuster
Englewood Cliffs, New Jersey 07632

Printed in the United States of America

10 9 8 7 6 5 4 3 2 1

ISBN 0-13-945585-X

PRENTICE-HALL INTERNATIONAL (UK) LIMITED, *London*
PRENTICE-HALL OF AUSTRALIA PTY. LIMITED, *Sydney*
PRENTICE-HALL CANADA INC., *Toronto*
PRENTICE-HALL HISPANOAMERICANA, S.A., *Mexico*
PRENTICE-HALL OF INDIA PRIVATE LIMITED, *New Delhi*
PRENTICE-HALL OF JAPAN, INC., *Tokyo*
SIMON & SCHUSTER ASIA PTE. LTD., *Singapore*
EDITORA PRENTICE-HALL DO BRASIL, LTDA., *Rio de Janeiro*

CONTENTS

The illiterate of the 20th century will be as ignorant of the camera as of the pen.

—LÁSZLÓ MOHOLY-NAGY, *photographer*

PREFACE

Cineliteracy is long overdue in American education, and not just on the college level. The average American watches about seven hours of television each day. That's a lot of time watching moving images. Yet, for the most part, we watch them uncritically, passively, allowing them to wash over us, rarely analyzing how they work on us, how they can shape our values. The following chapters may be of use in understanding how television and movies communicate, the complex network of language systems they employ. I entertain no grand pretense at teaching viewers how to respond to moving images; rather, I am concerned with suggesting some of the reasons people respond as they do.

In this fifth edition I have retained the same principle of organization as the earlier editions, structuring the chapters around the realism–formalism dichotomy. Each chapter isolates the various language systems and spectrum of techniques used by filmmakers in conveying meaning. Naturally, the chapters don't pretend to be exhaustive: They're essentially starting points. They progress from the most narrow and specific aspects of cinema (photography) to the most abstract and comprehensive (theory). The chapters are not tightly interdependent: They can be read out of sequence. Inevitably, such a looseness of organization involves a certain amount of overlapping, but I have tried to keep this to a minimum. Technical terms are **boldfaced** the first time they are, used in each chapter, meaning they are defined in the Glossary.

Each chapter has been updated to reflect recent developments in the field. I have also included many new photos and captions, most of them from recently released movies.

The final chapter, "Synthesis: *Citizen Kane,*" is a recapitulation of the main ideas of the previous chapters, only applied to a single movie. The chapter can also serve as a rough model for a term paper. The VCR revolution has allowed film analysis to be much more systematic, since a movie in cassette form can be repeated many times. In my own courses, I require my students to select a scene—preferably under three minutes—and analyze all its components according to the chapters of the book. Of course, a term paper is not likely to be as detailed as the *Citizen Kane* analysis, but the same methodology can be applied. If the chapters are read in a different sequence, the term paper can be organized in a corresponding manner. For example, many people would prefer to begin an analysis with story or theme, then proceed to matters of style and technique. *Citizen Kane* is an ideal choice because it includes virtually every technique the medium is capable of, in addition to being one of the most critically admired films in history and a popular favorite among students.

A word about the photos in this book. Most of the illustrations are publicity photos, taken with a 35mm still camera. They are not frame enlargements from the movie itself, for such enlargements reproduce poorly. They are generally too harshly contrasting and lacking in detail compared to the moving image on a large screen. When exactitude was necessary, as in the series from *The Seven Samurai* (9–15) or the edited sequence from *Potemkin* (4–18), I included actual blowups from the movies themselves. Most of the time, however, I preferred to use publicity photos because of their superior technical resolution.

Acknowledgments

A number of people have helped me in the writing of this book. I would like to thank the following friends for their help, advice, and criticism: Charles Haddad, Sheldon Wigod, Scott Eyman, Keith Joseph, Jeff Johnson, Bill Nichols, Jon Forman, Dave Wittkowsky, *The Cleveland Edition,* the Case Western Reserve University Film Society, and my students at C.W.R.U. I'm grateful to Ingmar Bergman, who was kind enough to allow me to use the frame enlargements from *Persona;* and Akira Kurosawa, who graciously consented to my using enlargements from *The Seven Samurai.* The following scholars have helped me with their insightful critiques: Mark Busby, Texas A&M University; Cynthia Contreras, Brooklyn College; Thomas L. Erskine, Salisbury State University; Perry F. Mills, Western Washington University; David J. Popowski, Mankato State University.

I would also like to acknowledge and thank the following individuals and institutions for their assistance in allowing me to use materials under their copyright. Andrew Sarris, for permission to quote from "The Fall and Rise of the Film Director," in *Interviews with Film Directors* (New York: Avon Books, 1967); Kurosawa Productions, Toho International Co., Ltd., and Audio-Brandon Films for permission to use the frame enlargements from *The Seven Samurai;* from *North by Northwest,* The MGM Library of Film Scripts, written by Earnest Lehman (Copyright © 1959 by Loews Incorporated. Reprinted by permission of The Viking Press, Inc.); Albert J. LaValley, *Focus on Hitchcock* (© 1972. Reprinted by permission of Prentice-Hall, Inc., Englewood Cliffs, New Jersey); Albert Maysles, in *Documentary Explorations,* edited by G. Roy Levin (Garden City: Doubleday & Company, Inc., 1971); Vladimir Nilsen, *The Cinema as a Graphic Art* (New York: Hill and Wang, a Division of Farrar, Straus and Giroux); Maya Deren, "Cinematography: The Creative Use of Reality," in *The Visual Arts Today,* edited by Gyorgy Kepes (Middletown, Conn.: Wesleyan

University Press, 1960); Marcel Carné, from *The French Cinema,* by Roy Armes (San Diego, Cal.: A. S. Barnes & Co., 1966); Richard Dyer MacCann, "Intro-duction," *Film: A Montage of Theories* (New York: E. P. Dutton & Co., Inc.), copyright © 1966 by Richard Dyer MacCann, reprinted with permission: V. I. Pudovkin, *Film Technique* (London: Vision, 1954); André Bazin, *What Is Cin-ema?* (Berkeley: University of California Press, 1967); Michelangelo Antonioni, "Two Statements," in *Film Makers on Film Making,* edited by Harry M. Geduld (Bloomington: Indiana University Press, 1969); Alexandre Astruc, from *The New Wave,* edited by Peter Graham (London: Secker & Warburg, 1968, and New York: Doubleday & Co.); Akira Kurosawa, from *The Movies as Medium,* edited by Lewis Jacobs (New York: Farrar, Straus and Giroux, 1970); Pauline Kael, *I Lost It at the Movies* (New York: Bantam Books, 1966).

LOUIS GIANNETTI
Cleveland, Ohio

Take him and cut him out in little stars,
And he will make the face of heav'n so fine
That all the world will be in love with Night
And pay no worship to the garish Sun.

—WILLIAM SHAKESPEARE

PHOTOGRAPHY | 1

A photograph is by no means a complete and whole reflection of reality: the photographic picture represents only one or another selection from the sum of physical attributes of the object photographed.

—VLADIMIR NILSEN

Realism and Formalism

Even before the turn of the last century, movies began to develop in two major directions: the **realistic** and the **formalistic.** In the mid-1890s in France, the Lumière brothers delighted audiences with their short movies dealing with everyday occurrences. Such films as *The Arrival of a Train* fascinated viewers precisely because they seemed to capture the flux and spontaneity of events as they were viewed in real life. At about the same time, Georges Méliès was creating a number of fantasy films that emphasized purely imagined events. Such movies as *A Trip to the Moon* were typical mixtures of whimsical narrative and trick photography. In many respects, the Lumières can be regarded as the founders of the realist tradition of cinema, and Méliès of the formalist tradition.

Realism and formalism are general rather than absolute terms. When used to suggest a tendency toward either polarity, such labels can be helpful, but in the end they're just labels. Few films are exclusively formalist in style, and fewer yet are completely realist. There is also an important difference between realism and reality, although this distinction is often forgotten. Realism is a particular *style,* whereas physical reality is the source of all the raw materials of film, both realistic and formalistic. Virtually all movie directors go to the photographable world for their subject matter, but what they do with this material—how they shape and manipulate it—is what determines their stylistic emphasis.

Generally speaking, realistic films attempt to reproduce the surface of reality with a minimum of distortion. In photographing objects and events, the filmmaker tries to suggest the copiousness of life itself. Both realist and formalist

1–1. Classification chart of styles and types of film.
Critics and scholars categorize movies according to a variety of criteria, few of them definitive. Two of the most common methods of classification are by style and by type. The three principal styles—realism, classicism, and formalism—might be regarded as a continuous spectrum of possibilities, rather than airtight categories. Similarly, the three types of movies—documentaries, fiction, and avant-garde films—are also terms of convenience, for they often overlap. Realistic films like *Distant Thunder* can shade into the documentary; formalist movies like *The Seventh Seal* have a personal quality suggesting the traditional domain of the avant-garde. Most fiction films, especially those produced in America, tend to conform to the classical paradigm. Classical cinema can be viewed as an intermediate style that avoids the extremes of realism and formalism—though most movies in the classical form lean toward one or the other style.

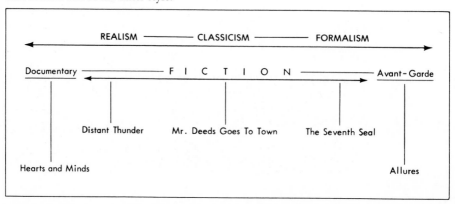

film directors must select (and hence, emphasize) certain details from the chaotic sprawl of reality. But the element of selectivity in realistic films is less obvious. Realists, in short, try to preserve the illusion that their film world is un-manipulated, an objective mirror of the actual world. Formalists, on the other hand, make no such pretense. They deliberately stylize and distort their raw materials so that only the very naive would mistake a manipulated image of an object or event for the real thing.

We rarely notice the style in a realistic movie; the artist tends to be self-effacing. Such filmmakers are more concerned with *what's* being shown rather than how it's manipulated. The camera is used conservatively. It's essentially a recording mechanism that reproduces the surface of tangible objects with as little

1–2. *Hearts and Minds* (U.S.A., 1975), *directed by Peter Davis.*
The emotional impact of a documentary image usually derives from its truth rather than its beauty. Davis's indictment of America's devastation of Vietnam consists primarily of TV newsreel footage. This photo shows some Vietnamese children running from an accidental bombing raid on their community, their clothes literally burned off their bodies by napalm. "First they bomb as much as they please," a Vietnamese observes, "then they film it." It was images such as these that eventually turned the majority of Americans against the war. Fernando Solanas and Octavio Gettino, Third World filmmakers, have pointed out: "Every image that documents, bears witness to, refutes or deepens the truth of a situation is something more than a film image or purely artistic fact; it becomes something which the System finds indigestible." Paradoxically, in no country except the United States would such self-damning footage be allowed on the public airwaves—which are controlled, or at least regulated, by governments. No other country has a First Amendment.   *(Warner Bros.)*

commentary as possible. Some realists aim for a rough look in their images, one that doesn't prettify the materials with a self-conscious beauty of form. "If it's too pretty, it's false," is an implicit assumption. A high premium is placed on simplicity, spontaneity, and directness. This is not to suggest that these movies lack artistry, however, for at its best, the realistic cinema specializes in art that conceals art.

Formalist movies are stylistically flamboyant. Their directors are concerned with expressing their unabashedly subjective experience of reality, not how other people might see it. Formalists are often referred to as **expressionists** because their self-expression is at least as important as the subject matter itself. Expressionists are often concerned with spiritual and psychological truths, which they feel can be conveyed best by distorting the surface of the material world. The camera is used as a method of commenting on the subject matter, a way of emphasizing its essential rather than its objective nature. There is a high degree of manipulation, of re-forming of reality, in formalist movies. But it's precisely this "deformed" imagery that can be so artistically striking in such films.

Most realists would claim that their major concern is with *content* rather than *form* or technique. The subject matter is always supreme, and anything that distracts from the content is viewed with suspicion. In its most extreme form, the

1–3. *Distant Thunder* **(India, 1973),** *directed by Satyajit Ray.*
In most realistic films, there is a close correspondence of the images to everyday reality. This criterion of value necessarily involves a comparison between the internal world of the movie with the external milieu that the filmmaker has chosen to explore. The realistic cinema tends to deal with people from the lower social echelons and often explores moral issues. The artist rarely intrudes on the materials, however, preferring to let them speak for themselves. Rather than focusing on extraordinary events, realism tends to emphasize the basic experiences of life. It is a style that excels in making us feel the humanity of others. Beauty of form is often sacrificed in order to capture the texture of reality as it's ordinarily perceived. Realistic images often seem unmanipulated, haphazard in their design. They frequently convey an intimate snapshot quality—people caught unawares. Generally, the story materials are loosely organized and include many details that don't necessarily forward the plot but are offered for their own sake, to heighten the sense of authenticity. (*Cinema 5*)

realistic cinema tends toward documentary, with its emphasis on photographing actual events and people (1–2). The formalist cinema, on the other hand, tends to emphasize technique and expressiveness. The most extreme example of this style of filmmaking is found in the avant-garde cinema (1–6). Some of these movies are totally abstract; pure forms (that is, nonrepresentational colors, lines, and shapes) constitute the only content. Most fiction films fall somewhere between these two extremes, in a mode critics refer to as **classical cinema** (1–4).

Even the terms *form* and *content* aren't so clear-cut as they may sometimes seem. In fact, in many respects the terms are synonymous, although they can certainly be useful in suggesting a degree of emphasis. The form of a shot—the way in which a subject is photographed—is its true content, not necessarily what the subject is perceived to be in reality. The communications theorist Marshall McLuhan pointed out that the content of one medium is actually another medium. For example, a photograph (visual image) depicting a man eating an apple (taste) involves two different mediums: Each communicates information—content—in a different way. A verbal description of the photograph of the man eating the apple would involve yet another medium (language), which communicates information in yet another manner. In each case, the precise information is determined by the medium, although superficially all three have the same content.

1–4. *Mr. Deeds Goes to Town* (U.S.A., 1936), *with Gary Cooper (with tuba), directed by Frank Capra.*

Classical cinema avoids the extremes of realism and formalism in favor of a slightly stylized presentation that has at least a surface plausibility. Movies in this form are often handsomely mounted, but the style rarely calls attention to itself. The images are determined by their relevance to the story and characters, rather than a desire for authenticity or formal beauty alone. The implicit ideal is a functional, invisible style: The pictorial elements are subordinated to the presentation of characters in action. Classical cinema is story oriented. The narrative line is seldom allowed to wander, nor is it broken up by authorial intrusions. A high premium is placed on the entertainment values of the story, which is often shaped to conform to the conventions of a popular genre. Often the characters are played by stars rather than unknown players, and their roles are sometimes tailored to showcase their personal charms. The human materials are paramount in the classical cinema. The characters are generally appealing and slightly romanticized. The audience is encouraged to identify with their values and goals. *(Columbia Pictures)*

1–5. *The Seventh Seal* **(Sweden, 1957),** *with Max von Sydow (right) and Bengt Ekerot, cinematography by Gunnar Fischer, directed by Ingmar Bergman.*

The formalist cinema is largely a director's cinema: Authorial intrusions are common. There is a high degree of manipulation in the narrative materials, and the visual presentation is stylized. The story is exploited as a vehicle for the filmmaker's personal obsessions. Fidelity to objective reality is rarely a relevant criterion of value. The most artificial genres—musicals, sci-fi, fantasy films—are generally classified as formalist. Most movies of this sort deal with extraordinary characters and events—such as this mortal game of chess between a medieval knight and the figure of Death. This style of cinema excels in dealing with ideas—political, religious, philosophical—and is often the chosen medium of propagandistic artists. Its texture is densely symbolic: Feelings are expressed through forms, like the dramatic high-contrast lighting of this shot. Most of the great stylists of the cinema are formalists.   *(Janus Films)*

In literature, the naive separation of form and content is called "the heresy of paraphrase." For example, the content of *Hamlet* can be found in a college outline, yet no one would seriously suggest that the play and outline are the same "except in form." To paraphrase artistic information is inevitably to change its content as well as its form. Artistry can never be gauged by subject matter alone. The manner of its presentation—its forms—is the true content of paintings, literature, and plays. The same applies to movies.

The great French critic André Bazin noted: "One way of understanding better what a film is trying to say is to know how it is saying it." Bazin was putting forth the theory of organic form—the belief that form and content are mutually dependent in film as well as any other kind of art. The American critic Herman G. Weinberg expressed the matter succinctly: "The way a story is told is part of that story. You can tell the same story badly or well; you can also tell it well enough or magnificently. It depends on who is telling the story."

Form and content are best used as relative terms. They are useful concepts for temporarily isolating specific aspects of art for the purposes of closer examination. Such a separation is artificial, of course, yet this technique can yield more detailed insights into the work of art as a whole. By beginning with an understanding of the basic components of the film medium—its various language systems, as it were—we will see how form and content in the cinema, as in the other arts, are ultimately the same.

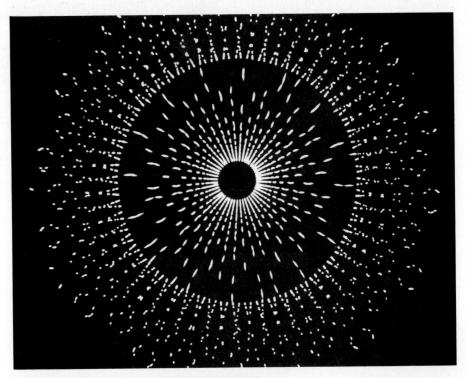

1–6. ***Allures*** **(U.S.A., 1961),** *directed by Jordan Belson.*
In the avant-garde cinema, subject matter is often suppressed in favor of abstraction and an emphasis on formal beauty for its own sake. Like many artists in this idiom, Belson began as a painter and was attracted to film because of its temporal and kinetic dimensions. He was strongly influenced by such European avant-garde artists as Hans Richter, who championed the "absolute film"—a graphic cinema of pure forms divorced from a recognizable subject matter. Belson's works are inspired by philosophical concepts derived primarily from Oriental religions, but these are essentially private sources and are rarely presented explicitly in the films themselves. Form is the true content of Belson's movies. His animated images are mostly geometrical shapes, dissolving and contracting circles of light, and kinetic swirls. His patterns expand, congeal, flicker, and split off into other shapes, only to reform and explode again. It is a cinema of uncompromising self-expression—personal, often inaccessible, and iconoclastic. *(Pyramid Films)*

The Shots

The different cinematic **shots** are defined by the amount of subject matter that's included within the **frame** of the screen. In actual practice, however, shot designations vary considerably. A **medium shot** for one director might be considered a **close-up** by another. Furthermore, the longer the shot, the less precise are the designations. In general, shots are determined on the basis of how much of the human figure is in view. The shot is not necessarily defined by the distance between the camera and the object photographed, for in some instances certain lenses distort distances. For example, a **telephoto lens** can produce a close-up on the screen, yet the camera in such shots is generally quite distant from the subject matter.

Although there are many different kinds of shots in the cinema, most of them are subsumed under the six basic categories: **(1)** the **extreme long shot, (2)** the **long shot, (3)** the **full shot, (4)** the medium shot, **(5)** the close-up, and **(6)** the **extreme close-up.** The **deep-focus shot** is usually a variation of the long or extreme long shot.

The *extreme long shot* is taken from a great distance, sometimes as far as a quarter of a mile away. It's almost always an exterior shot and shows much of the locale. Extreme long shots also serve as spatial frames of reference for the closer shots, and for this reason are sometimes called **establishing shots.** If people are included in extreme long shots, they usually appear as mere specks on the screen. The most effective use of these shots is often found in **epic** films, where locale plays an important role: westerns, war films, samurai films, and historical movies. Not surprisingly, the greatest masters of the extreme long shot are those directors associated with epic **genres:** D. W. Griffith, Sergei Eisenstein, John Ford, Akira Kurosawa, and Steven Spielberg.

The *long shot* is perhaps the most complex in the cinema, and the term itself one of the most imprecise. Usually long-shot ranges correspond approxi-

1–7. Twentieth Century–Fox publicity photo of Marilyn Monroe (1953).
Cinematographers often comment that the camera "likes" certain individuals, and "doesn't like" others, even though these others might be good-looking people in real life. Highly photogenic performers like Marilyn Monroe are rarely uncomfortable in front of the camera. Indeed, they often play to it, ensnaring our attention. Photographer Richard Avedon said of Marilyn: "She understood photography, and she also understood what makes a great photograph—not the technique, but the content. She was more comfortable in front of the camera than away from it." Philippe Halsman went even further, pointing out that her open mouth and frequently open décolletage were frankly invitational: "She would try to seduce the camera as if it were a human being. . . . She knew that the camera lens was not just a glass eye but a symbol for the eyes of millions of men, so the camera stimulated her strongly." (*Twentieth Century–Fox*)

1–8. *Doctor Zhivago* (Great Britain, 1965), *cinematography by Freddie Young, directed by David Lean.*
Deep-focus photography preserves a sharpness of image on all distance planes, encouraging the viewer to analyze the interrelationships between them. The technique tends to be more objective than soft focus, preserving the cohesiveness of real time and space. *(MGM)*

mately to the distance between the audience and the stage in the live theater. The closest range within this category is the *full shot,* which just barely includes the human body in full, with the head near the top of the frame and the feet near the bottom. Charles Chaplin and other slapstick comedians favored the full shot because it was best suited to the art of pantomime, yet was close enough to capture at least gross facial expressions.

The *medium shot* contains a figure from the knees or waist up. A functional shot, it's useful for shooting exposition scenes, for carrying movement, and for dialogue. There are several variations of the medium shot. The *two shot* contains two figures from the waist up. The *three shot* contains three figures; beyond three, the shot tends to become a full shot, unless the other figures are in the background. The **over-the-shoulder shot** usually contains two figures, one with part of his or her back to the camera, the other facing the camera.

The *close-up* shows very little if any locale, and concentrates on a relatively small object—the human face, for example. Since the close-up magnifies the size of an object, it tends to elevate the importance of things, often suggesting a symbolic significance. The *extreme close-up* is a variation of this shot. Thus, instead of a face, the extreme close-up might show only a person's eyes or mouth.

The *deep-focus shot* is usually a long shot, consisting of a number of focal distances, and photographed in depth (1–8). Sometimes called a *wide-angle shot* because it requires a **wide-angle lens** to photograph, this type of shot captures objects at close, medium, and long ranges simultaneously, all of them in sharp focus. The objects in a deep-focus shot are carefully arranged in a succession of planes. By using this layering technique, the director can guide the viewer's eye from one distance to another. Generally, the eye travels from a close range to a medium to a long.

The Angles

The **angle** from which an object is photographed can often serve as an authorial commentary on the subject matter. If the angle is slight, it can serve as a subtle form of emotional coloration. If the angle is extreme, it can represent the major meaning of an image. A picture of a person photographed from a high angle actually suggests an opposite interpretation from an image of the same person photographed from a low angle. The subject matter can be identical in the two images, yet in terms of the information we derive from both, it's clear that the form is the content, the content the form.

Filmmakers in the realistic tradition tend to avoid extreme angles. Most of their scenes are photographed from eye level, roughly five to six feet off the ground—approximately the way an actual observer might view a scene. Usually these directors attempt to capture the clearest view of an object. **Eye-level shots** are seldom intrinsically dramatic, since they tend to be the norm. Virtually all directors use some eye-level shots, particularly in routine expository scenes.

Formalist directors are not always concerned with the clearest image of an object, but with the image that best captures an object's expressive essence.

1–9. *Bonnie and Clyde* (U.S.A., 1967), *with Warren Beatty and Faye Dunaway, directed by Arthur Penn.*
High angles tend to suggest entrapment, powerlessness, or assailability. The higher the angle, the more it tends to imply fatality. The camera's angle can be inferred by the background of a shot: High angles usually show the ground or floor; low angles the sky or ceiling. *(Warner Bros.)*

Extreme angles involve distortions. Yet many filmmakers feel that by distorting the surface realism of an object, a greater truth is achieved—a symbolic truth. Both realist and formalist directors know that the viewer tends to identify with the camera's lens (1–10). The realist wishes to make the audience forget that there's a camera at all. The formalist is constantly calling attention to it.

There are five basic angles in the cinema: (**1**) the **bird's-eye view,** (**2**) the high angle, (**3**) the eye-level shot, (**4**) the low angle, and (**5**) the oblique angle. As in the case of shot designations, there are many intermediate kinds of angles. For example, there can be a considerable difference between a low and extreme low angle—although usually, of course, such differences tend to be matters of degree. Generally speaking, the more extreme the angle, the more distracting and conspicuous it is in terms of the subject matter being photographed.

The *bird's-eye view* is perhaps the most disorienting angle of all, for it involves photographing a scene from directly overhead. Since we seldom view events from this perspective, the subject matter of such shots might initially seem unrecognizable and abstract, like the kaleidoscopic arrangements of choreographer Busby Berkeley (3–4). For this reason, filmmakers tend to avoid this type of camera **setup.** In certain contexts, however, this angle can be highly expressive. In effect, bird's-eye shots permit us to hover above a scene like all-powerful gods. The people photographed seem antlike and insignificant. Directors whose themes revolve around the idea of fate—Hitchcock and Fritz Lang, for example—tend to favor high angles.

Ordinary *high-angle shots* are not so extreme, and therefore not so disorienting. The camera is placed on a **crane,** or some natural high promontory, but the sense of audience omnipotence is not overwhelming. High angles give a viewer a

1–10. *Nosferatu* (**Germany, 1922**), *with Max Schreck, cinematography by Fritz Arno Wagner, directed by F. W. Murnau.*
When an extreme low angle is combined with a perspective-distorting wide-angle lens, a character can seem threatening, for he looms above the camera—and us—like a towering giant. (*Janus Films*)

sense of a general overview, but not necessarily one implying destiny or fate. In terms of the object photographed, high angles reduce the height of objects, and usually include the ground or floor as background. Movement is slowed down: This angle tends to be ineffective for conveying a sense of speed, useful for suggesting tediousness. The importance of setting or environment is increased: The locale often seems to swallow people. High angles reduce the importance of a subject. A person seems harmless and insignificant photographed from above. This angle is also effective for conveying a character's self-contempt.

There are some filmmakers who avoid angles because they are too manipulative and judgmental. In the movies of the Japanese master Yasujiro Ozu, the camera is usually placed four feet from the floor—as if an observer were viewing the events seated Japanese style. Ozu treated his characters as equals; his approach discourages us from viewing them either condescendingly or sentimentally. For the most part, they are ordinary people, neither very virtuous nor very corrupt. But Ozu lets them reveal themselves. He believed that value judgments are implied through the use of angles, and kept his camera neutral and dispassion-

1–11. *The Lady from Shanghai* **(U.S.A., 1947),** *with Rita Hayworth, Orson Welles, and Everett Sloane; cinematography by Charles Lawton, Jr.; directed by Welles.*
Lyricism is a vague but indispensable critical term suggesting emotional subjectivity and a sensual richness of expression. Derived from the word *lyre,* a harplike stringed instrument, lyricism is most often associated with music and poetry. Lyricism in movies also suggests a rhapsodic exuberance. Though lyrical qualities can be independent of subject matter, at its best lyricism is a stylistic externalization of a film's basic concept. For example, this shootout in an abandoned fun house takes place in the hall of mirrors—a perfect visual analogue of Welles's themes: the fragmentation of personality and the treacherous allure of beauty. (*Columbia Pictures*)

ate. Eye-level shots permit us to make up our own minds about what kind of people are being presented.

Low angles have the opposite effect of high. They increase height and thus are useful for suggesting verticality. More practically, they increase a short actor's height. Motion is speeded up, and in scenes of violence especially, low angles capture a sense of confusion. Environment is usually minimized in low angle, and often the sky or a ceiling is the only background. Psychologically, low angles heighten the importance of a subject. The figure looms threateningly over the spectator, who is made to feel insecure and dominated. A person photo-

1–12. ***Double Indemnity*** **(U.S.A., 1944),** *with Barbara Stanwyck and Fred MacMurray, directed by Billy Wilder.*
Film noir (literally, black cinema) is a style defined primarily in terms of light—or the lack of it. This style typified a variety of American genres in the 1940s and early 1950s. Noir is a world of night and shadows. Its milieu is almost exclusively urban. The style is profuse in images of dark streets, cigarette smoke swirling in dimly lit cocktail lounges, and symbols of fragility, such as window panes, sheer clothing, glasses, and mirrors. Motifs of entrapment abound: alleys, tunnels, subways, elevators, and train cars. Often the settings are locations of transience, like grubby rented rooms, piers, bus terminals, and railroad yards. The images are rich in sensuous textures, like neon-lit streets, windshields streaked with mud, and shafts of light streaming through windows of lonely rooms. Characters are imprisoned behind ornate lattices, grillwork, drifting fog and smoke. Visual designs emphasize harsh lighting contrasts, jagged shapes, and violated surfaces. The tone of film noir is fatalistic and paranoid. It's suffused with pessimism, emphasizing the darker aspects of the human condition. Its themes characteristically revolve around violence, lust, greed, betrayal, and depravity. *(Paramount Pictures)*

graphed from below inspires fear, awe, and respect. For this reason, low angles are often used in propaganda films or in scenes depicting heroism.

An *oblique angle* involves a lateral tilt of the camera. When the image is projected, the horizon is skewed. A man photographed at an oblique angle will look as though he's about to fall to one side. This angle is sometimes used for **point-of-view shots**—to suggest the imbalance of a drunk, for example. Psychologically, oblique angles suggest tension, transition, and impending movement. The natural horizontal and vertical lines of a scene are converted into unstable diagonals. Oblique angles are not used often, for they can disorient a viewer. In scenes depicting violence, however, they can be effective in capturing precisely this sense of visual anxiety.

Light and Dark

Generally speaking, the cinematographer (who is also known as the director of photography or D.P.) is responsible for arranging and controlling the lighting of a film and the quality of the photography. Usually the cinematographer executes the specific or general instructions of the director. The illumination of most movies is seldom a casual matter, for lights can be used with pinpoint accuracy. Through the use of spotlights, which are highly selective in their focus and intensity, a director can guide the viewer's eyes to any area of the photographed image. Motion picture lighting is seldom static, for even the slightest movement of the camera or the subject can cause the lighting to shift. Movies take so long to complete, in part because of the enormous complexities involved in lighting each new shot. The cinematographer must make allowances for every movement within a continuous **take**. Each different color, shape, and texture reflects or absorbs differing amounts of light. If an image is photographed in depth, an even greater complication is involved, for the lighting must also be in depth. Furthermore, cinematographers don't have at their disposal most of the darkroom techniques of a still photographer: variable paper, dodging, airbrushing, choice of development, enlarger filters, etc. In a color film, the subtle effects of lights and darks are often obscured, for color tends to obliterate shadings and flatten images: Depth is negated.

There are a number of different styles of lighting. Usually designated as a lighting *key,* the style is geared to the theme and mood of a film, as well as its genre. Comedies and musicals, for example, tend to be lit in **high key,** with bright, even illumination and few conspicuous shadows. Tragedies and melodramas are usually lit in **high contrast,** with harsh shafts of lights and dramatic streaks of blackness (1–18). Mysteries and thrillers are generally in **low key,** with diffused shadows and atmospheric pools of light (1–14). Each lighting key is only an approximation, and some images consist of a combination of lighting styles—a low-key background with a few high-contrast elements in the foreground, for example. Movies shot in studios are generally more stylized and theatrical, whereas location photography tends to use available illumination, with a more natural style of lighting.

Lights and darks have had symbolic connotations since the dawn of humanity. The Bible is filled with light–dark symbolism. Rembrandt and Caravaggio

(a)   **(b)**   **(c)**   **(d)**

1–13. Four lighting sources on the same subject.
The lighting of a subject can be of greater importance than the subject itself. Here are four examples of how form (light) can determine content. Lighting from above **(a)** tends to create a romantic halo effect, suggesting spirituality. A face half-plunged in darkness **(b)** can symbolize self-division and ambivalence. Lighting from below **(c)** generally makes the subject's face appear sinister, eerie. When the subject blocks out the source of light **(d)**, viewers can be made to feel threatened, for we tend to associate light with safety. *(Photos by Evelyn Hayes)*

used light–dark contrasts for psychological purposes as well. In general, artists have used darkness to suggest fear, evil, the unknown. Light usually suggests security, virtue, truth, joy. Because of these conventional symbolic associations, some filmmakers deliberately reverse light–dark expectations. Hitchcock's movies attempt to jolt the viewers by exposing their shallow sense of security. He stages many of his most violent scenes in the glaring light.

Lighting can also be used to subvert subject matter. Paul Brickman's *Risky Business* is a coming-of-age comedy, and like most examples of its genre, the adolescent hero triumphs over the System and its hypocritical morality. But in this movie, the naive hero learns to play the game and becomes a winner by

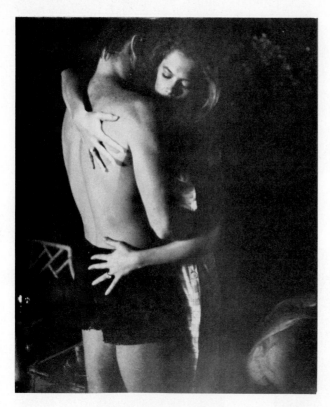

1–14. *Body Heat* **(U.S.A., 1981),** *with William Hurt and Kathleen Turner, directed by Lawrence Kasdan.*
Low-key lighting is especially evocative in romantic scenes, and in such genres as crime films, thrillers, and mysteries, in which the lack of light symbolizes the unknown, deceptive surfaces, evil itself.   (*The Ladd Company*)

being even more hypocritical than the upholders of the System. Most of the film is shot in low-key lighting—unusual for any comedy—which darkens the tone of the comic scenes. By the conclusion of the film, we're not entirely sure if the hero's "success" is ironic or straight. The movie would probably have been funnier if it had been shot in the usual high key, but the low-key photography makes it a more serious comedy—ironic and paradoxical.

Lighting can be used realistically or expressionistically. The realist tends to favor available lighting, at least in exterior scenes. Even out of doors, however, most filmmakers use some lamps and reflectors, either to augment the natural light or, on bright days, to soften the harsh contrasts produced by the sun. With the aid of special **lenses** and more light-sensitive film stocks, some directors have managed to dispense with artificial lighting completely. Available lighting tends to produce a documentary look in the film image, a hard-edged quality and an absence of smooth modeling. Not all exterior shooting is necessarily hard-edged, however. Through the use of special lenses and additional lighting, John Ford and Akira Kurosawa were able to evoke a nostalgic romantic past while still using actual locations. For interior shots, realists tend to prefer images with an obvious light source—a window or a lamp. Or they often use a diffused kind of lighting with no artificial, strong contrasts. In short, the realist doesn't use conspicuous lighting unless its source is dictated by the context.

Formalists use light less literally. They are guided by its symbolic implications and will often stress these qualities by deliberately distorting natural light

1–15. ***Barry Lyndon*** **(U.S.A./Great Britain, 1975),** *with Marisa Berenson and Murray Melvin, cinematography by John Alcott, directed by Stanley Kubrick.*

"What I'm after is a majestic visual experience," Kubrick has said of his movies. The visual style of *Barry Lyndon* is modeled on the paintings of the eighteenth-century masters, especially Gainsborough and Watteau. Kubrick is a fanatic about authenticity. Since candlelight was the main source of interior illumination in the eighteenth century, he wanted no other source of light. He has always preferred available lighting. The lamps in his contemporary stories are not just decorative, but are equipped to provide the major illumination for a scene. He believes that the glare from a recognizable light source can produce dramatic contrasts, or wash out an image in a striking manner. In order to shoot by candlelight in this film, he asked the Zeiss Corporation to adapt a very fast (f 0.7) 50 mm still camera lens for the motion picture camera. The Zeiss Lens is the fastest in existence, and Kubrick had to have a special movie camera built to allow for its use. But he got what he wanted: The glowing interiors of *Barry Lyndon* are stunning in their beauty. *(Warner Bros.)*

patterns. A face lighted from below almost always appears sinister, even if the actor assumes a totally neutral expression. Similarly, an obstruction placed in front of a light source can assume frightening implications, for it tends to threaten our sense of safety. On the other hand, in some contexts, especially in exterior shots, a silhouette effect can be soft and romantic.

When a face is obviously lighted from above, a certain angelic quality, known as the halo effect, is the result. "Spiritual" lighting of this type tends to border on the cliché, however. **Backlighting,** which is a kind of semisilhouetting, is soft and ethereal. Love scenes are often photographed with a halo effect around the heads of the lovers to give them a romantic aura (1–20). Backlighting is especially evocative when used to highlight blonde hair.

Through the use of spotlights, an image can be composed of violent contrasts of lights and darks. The surface of such images seems disfigured, torn up. The formalist director uses such severe contrasts for psychological and thematic purposes (1–16 and 1–18).

By deliberately permitting too much light to enter the aperture of the camera, a filmmaker can **overexpose** an image—producing a blanching flood of light over the entire surface of the picture. Overexposure has been most effec-

1–16. *Pennies from Heaven* (**U.S.A., 1981**), *cinematography by Gordon Willis, directed by Herbert Ross.*
High-contrast lighting is boldly theatrical, infusing the photographed materials with a sense of visual anguish. Even this static image—a striking re-creation of Edward Hopper's famous painting *Nighthawks*—is rendered more dynamic by the jagged knifeblades of light that pierce the pervasive darkness. *(MGM)*

tively used in nightmare and fantasy sequences. Sometimes this technique can suggest a kind of horrible glaring publicity, a sense of emotional exaggeration.

Color

Color in film didn't become commercially widespread until the 1940s. There were many experiments in color before this period, however. Some of Méliès's movies, for example, were painted by hand in assembly line fashion, with each

1–17. *Eraserhead* (**U.S.A., 1978**), *with Jack Nance, directed by David Lynch.*
Ordinarily the halo effect created by backlighting is romantic, but here it suggests an electrifying shriek. The effect is wholly appropriate, given the character's unique hair style and the murderous insects that swarm ferociously in this "dream of dark and troubling things," as Lynch referred to his audacious cult classic. *(Libra Films)*

painter responsible for coloring a minute area of the filmstrip. The original version of *The Birth of a Nation* (1915) was printed on various tinted stocks to suggest different moods: The burning of Atlanta was tinted red, the night scenes blue, the exterior love scenes pale yellow. Many silent filmmakers used this tinting technique to suggest different moods.

Sophisticated film color was developed in the 1930s, but for many years a major problem was its tendency to prettify everything. If color enhanced a sense of beauty—in a musical or a historical extravaganza—the effects were often appropriate. Thus, the best feature films of the early years of color were usually those with artificial or exotic settings. Realistic dramas were thought to be unsuitable vehicles for color. The earliest color processes tended also to emphasize garishness, and often special consultants had to be called in to harmonize the color schemes of costumes, makeup, and decor.

Furthermore, each color process tended to specialize in a certain base hue—red, blue, or yellow, usually—while other colors of the spectrum were somewhat distorted. It was well into the 1950s before these problems were resolved. Compared with the subtle color perceptions of the human eye, however, and despite the apparent precision of most present-day color processing, cinematic color is still a relatively crude approximation.

The most famous color films tend to be expressionistic. Michelangelo Antonioni's attitude is fairly typical: "It is necessary to intervene in a color film, to take away the usual reality and replace it with the reality of the moment." In *Red Desert* (photographed by Carlo Di Palma), Antonioni spray-painted natural locales to emphasize internal, psychological states. Industrial wastes, river pollution, marshes, and large stretches of terrain were painted gray to suggest the ugliness of contemporary industrial society and the heroine's drab, wasted exis-

1–18. *Wifemistress* (**Italy, 1977**), *with Marcello Mastroianni (right), directed by Marco Vicario.* High-contrast lighting (combined here with a telephoto lens) can create an abstract canvas of lights warring with darks—a visual analogue of the character's psychological turmoil. (*Quartet Films*)

tence. Whenever red appears in the movie, it suggests sexual passion. Yet the red—like the loveless sexuality—is an ineffective coverup of the pervasive gray.

Color tends to be a subconscious element in film. It's strongly emotional in its appeal, expressive and atmospheric rather than conspicuous or intellectual. Psychologists have discovered that most people actively attempt to interpret the lines of a composition, but they tend to accept color passively, permitting it to suggest moods rather than objects. Lines are associated with nouns; color with adjectives. Line is sometimes thought to be masculine; color feminine. Both lines and colors suggest meanings, then, but in somewhat different ways.

Since earliest times, visual artists have used color for symbolic purposes. Color symbolism is probably culturally acquired, though its implications are surprisingly similar in otherwise differing societies. In general, cool colors (blue, green, violet) tend to suggest tranquility, aloofness, and serenity. Cool colors also have a tendency to recede in an image. Warm colors (red, yellow, orange) suggest aggressiveness, violence, and stimulation. They tend to come forward in most images.

Some filmmakers deliberately exploit color's natural tendency to garishness. Fellini's *Juliet of the Spirits* features many bizarre costumes and settings to suggest the tawdry but fascinating glamor of the world of show business. Bob Fosse's *Cabaret* is set in Germany and shows the early rise of the Nazi party. The colors are somewhat neurotic, with emphasis on such 1930s favorites as plum, acid green, purple, and florid combinations, like gold, black, and pink.

Black and white photography in a color film is sometimes used for symbolic purposes. Some filmmakers alternate whole episodes in black and white with entire sequences in color. The problem with this technique is its facile symbolism. The jolting black and white sequences are too obviously "significant" in the most arty sense. A more effective variation is simply not to use too much color, to let black and white predominate. In De Sica's *The Garden of the Finzi-Continis,* which is set in Fascist Italy, the early portions of the movie are richly resplendent in shimmering golds, reds, and almost every shade of green. As political repression becomes more brutal, these colors almost imperceptibly begin to wash out, until near the end of the film the images are dominated by whites, blacks, and blue-grays.

In the color photo section following page 22, we can see that film color functions in a variety of ways. In *The Year of Living Dangerously* (Color Plate 1), red is used as a warning signal, suggesting danger, suppressed violence, impending revolution. On the other hand, in realistic movies like *The Flaxfield* (C.P. 2), the color palette is restricted to monochromatic variations of brown, the color of soil. In *Juliet of the Spirits* (C.P. 3), Fellini uses red to suggest sexuality, white to symbolize purity and innocence. In the sequence pictured, the main character is trapped in a sexual dream; she is worried about the glowing pink sky. She remains transfixed in anxiety, lost, scared.

In stories dealing with the darker side of the human condition, filmmakers generally avoid bright colors, which are incongruously cheerful. The persecuted Jews of *Bittersweet* (C.P. 4) are smothered in darkness and shadows—a symbol of the Holocaust that will soon envelop them. In epic genres like war films, confusing military clashes can be clarified visually by the color coding of the

1—19. *Crime and Punishment* (U.S.A., 1935), *with Peter Lorre, cinematography by Lucien Ballard, directed by Josef von Sternberg.*
Sternberg was a master of atmospheric lighting effects and closely supervised the photography of his films. His stories are unfolded primarily in terms of light and shade, rather than conventional dramatic means. "Every light has a point where it is brightest, and a point toward which it wanders to lose itself completely," he explained. "The journey of rays from that central core to the outposts of blackness is the adventure and drama of light." Note how the closed form of the mise en scène and the light encircling the protagonist (Lorre) produce an accusatory effect, a sense of entrapment.   *(Paramount Pictures)*

soldiers' banners and uniforms—a technique Kurosawa uses extensively in his masterpiece, *Ran* (C.P. 5).

The futuristic *Road Warrior* (C.P. 6) is whimsical in its use of color, combining incongruous elements like studded black leather, shoulder pads, bare midriff, and fluffy feathers for a soupçon of elegance. Expressionistic fantasy-oriented movies like *Little Shop of Horrors* (C.P. 16) are usually electric in bright pop colors—the colors of the imagination, not reality.

In the 1980s, a new computer technology was developed, allowing black and white movies to be "colorized"—a process that provoked a howl of protest from most film artists and critics. The colorized versions of some genres, like period films, musicals, and other forms of light entertainment, are not damaged too seriously by this process, but the technique is a disaster in carefully photographed black and white films, like *Citizen Kane,* with its **film noir** lighting style and brilliant deep-focus photography (see Chapter 11, Synthesis: *Citizen Kane*).

Colorization also throws off the compositional balance of some shots, creating new **dominants.** In the shot from *Dark Victory* (C.P. 8), for example, the dominant is Brent's blue suit, which is irrelevant to the dramatic context. In the

1–20. *An Unmarried Woman* (**U.S.A.,** **1978**), *with Jill Clayburgh and Alan Bates, cinematography by Arthur Ornitz, directed by Paul Mazursky.*
Even within a single film, lighting styles can vary considerably, depending on the mood of a given scene. Most of the earlier portions of this movie are photographed in a documentary style. After the protagonist (Clayburgh) falls in love, the photographic style becomes more romantic. The city's lights are etherealized by the shimmering soft-focus photography. The halo effect around the lovers' heads reinforces the air of enchantment—these are not just lovers, these are soulmates. (*Twentieth Century–Fox*)

original black and white version, Davis is the dominant, her dark outfit contrasting with the white fireplace that frames her figure. Distracting visual dominants undercut the dramatic impact of such scenes. We keep thinking Brent's suit *must* be important. It is, but only to the computer.

Lenses, Filters, Stocks, Opticals, and Gauges

Because the camera's lens is a crude mechanism when compared to the human eye, some of the most striking effects in a movie image can be achieved through the distortions of the photographic process itself. Particularly with regard to size and distance, the camera lens doesn't make mental adjustments, but records things literally. For example, whatever is placed closest to the camera's lens will appear larger than an object at a greater distance. Hence, a coffee cup can totally obliterate a human being if the cup is in front of the lens and the human is standing at long-shot range.

Realist filmmakers tend to use normal, or standard, lenses in order to produce a minimum of distortion. These lenses photograph subjects more or less as they are perceived by the human eye. Formalist filmmakers often prefer lenses and **filters** that intensify given qualities and suppress others. Cloud formations, for example, can be exaggerated threateningly or softly diffused, depending on what kind of lens or filter is used. Different shapes, colors, and lighting intensities can be radically altered through the use of specific optical modifiers. There are literally dozens of different lenses, but most of them are subsumed under three major categories: those in the standard (nondistorted) range, the telephoto lenses, and the wide-angles.

Color Plate 1. *The Year of Living Dangerously* **(Australia, 1983),** *with Mel Gibson, directed by Peter Weir.*
Drenched in moody hues and eerie shadows, this film often uses expressionistic splashes of color to convey symbolic ideas and underlying emotions.
(MGM/UA)

Color Plate 2. *The Flaxfield* **(Belgium, 1983),** *directed by Jan Gruyaert.*
This study of Belgian peasant life at the turn of the last century appropriately emphasizes earth colors, the browns predominating, but with muted blues providing a delicate foil. *(Mort Wax)*

Color Plate 3. *Juliet of the Spirits* **(Italy, 1965),** *with Giulietta Masina, directed by Federico Fellini.*
Throughout this movie, Fellini contrasts the surrealistic locales and costumes of the other characters with the childlike simplicity and purity of his heroine, a lost innocent. *(Rizzoli Films)*

Color Plate 4. *Bittersweet* **(Holland, 1985),** *with Ester Spitz, directed by Kees van Oostrum.*
In films dealing with somber subjects, color is generally suppressed or smothered by darkness. *Bittersweet* deals with the Nazi persecution of Dutch Jews during World War II. *(Netherlands Consulate General)*

Color Plate 5. *Ran* (Japan, 1985), *directed by Akira Kurosawa.*
An epic tale of social upheaval and warfare (the title means Chaos). *Ran* features many shots in which the clashing armies are color-coded (red, yellow, or blue), thus allowing us to see who is winning and losing. *(Orion Classics)*

Color Plate 6. *The Road Warrior* (Australia, 1982), *with Vernon Welles, directed by George Miller.*
Black is often the color of villainy. In this movie, the villainy is wittily undercut by such campy touches as the off-the-shoulder feathers and a red-tinged Mohawk mane. *(Warner Bros.)*

Color Plate 7. *Who Framed Roger Rabbit* (U.S.A., 1988), *with Bob Hoskins and friend, directed by Robert Zemeckis, animation directed by Richard Williams.*
This film combines the washed-out browns of the 1940s Los Angeles setting with the pop colors of the world of "Toons." *(Touchstone Pictures/Amblin Entertainment)*

Color Plate 8. *Dark Victory* (U.S.A., 1939), *with Bette Davis and George Brent, directed by Edmund Goulding.*
"Tell me the truth now. Do you think this suit is *too* blue?" *(Warner Bros.)*

Color Plate 9. *Radio Days* **(U.S.A., 1987),** *with Mia Farrow (center) and Danny Aiello, directed by Woody Allen.*
This nostalgic re-creation of radio's golden age—the late 1930s and early 40s—is heightened by the amber filters and warm glowing colors of most of the scenes.   *(Orion Pictures)*

Color Plate 10. *Hope and Glory* **(Great Britain, 1987),** *directed by John Boorman.*
Like Woody Allen's *Radio Days, Hope and Glory* is a re-creation of the early World War II era, but Boorman's movie is more realistic, less stylized. Hence, the colors are subdued, less saturated.   *(Columbia Pictures)*

Color Plate 11. *Bagdad Cafe* **(West Germany, 1987),** *with C. C. H. Pounder and Marianne Sagebrecht, directed by Percy Adlon.*
German filmmakers, in keeping with their tradition of expressionism, tend to favor symbolically distorted colors that are audaciously nonrealistic. *(Island Pictures)*

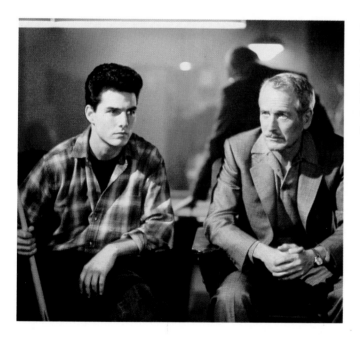

Color Plate 12. *The Color of Money* **(U.S.A., 1986),** *with Tom Cruise and Paul Newman, directed by Martin Scorsese.*
The sunless world of dank, smoke-filled pool halls provides the settings for most of the scenes in this movie—a fluorescent world of pale complexions and drained colors. *(Touchstone Films)*

Color Plate 13. *The Running Man (U.S.A., 1987), with Richard Dawson and Arnold Schwarzenegger, directed by Paul Michael Glazer.*
This futuristic portrayal of life as a game show features many sets that look like giant pinball machines, with flashing gaudy colors. *(Taft Entertainment/Keith Barish Productions)*

Color Plate 14. *The Last Emperor* (Italy/U.S.A./Great Britain/China, 1987), *directed by Bernardo Bertolucci.*
Bertolucci was the first western filmmaker ever allowed to shoot in China's legendary Forbidden City, with its brilliant colors and garish decorations. *(Nelson Entertainment)*

Color Plate 15. *Blue Velvet (U.S.A., 1986), with Isabella Rossellini and Kyle MacLachlan, directed by David Lynch.*
Because of this film's title and theme song, Rossellini's blue velvet robe becomes an erotic fetish, mysterious and charged with forbidden sexuality.
(DeLaurentiis Entertainment Group)

Color Plate 16. *Little Shop of Horrors (U.S.A., 1986), with Rick Moranis, directed by Frank Oz.*
In keeping with the skid-row setting of this musical, the colors and special effects are a bit tacky—a poor person's idea of colorful. *(The Geffen Film Co.)*

1–21. Filmstrips of the four principal gauges used in movies, expressed in millimeters wide.

Photographic quality depends in part on the gauge of the film used to photograph and project the images. (1) Suitable for projecting in an average-sized room, 8 mm and Super 8 mm are primarily for home use. (2) The gauge ordinarily used in schools and museums is 16 mm; if projected in extremely large halls, 16-mm images tend to grow fuzzy and the color tends to fade. (3) The standard gauge for the vast majority of movie theaters is 35 mm. (4) For epic subjects requiring a huge screen, 70 mm is generally used; the images retain their linear sharpness and color saturation even in enormous theaters.

The *telephoto lens* is often used to get close-ups of objects from extreme distances. For example, no cinematographer is likely to want to get close enough to a lion to photograph a close-up with a standard lens. In cases such as these, the telephoto is used, thus guaranteeing the safety of the cinematographer while still

1–22. *The Garden of the Finzi-Continis* **(Italy, 1970),** *with Dominique Sanda, cinematography by Ennio Guarnieri, directed by Vittorio De Sica.* De Sica wanted this movie to be ravishingly photographed—a visual correlative to the fragile beauty of the characters and their world. He also wanted the movie to be realistic because the story deals with a shameful chapter of history—the deportation of Italian Jews to Nazi Germany. Guarnieri's cinematography triumphantly fuses these somewhat disparate needs. Even the close-ups—which offer few possibilities in the art of composition—are exquisitely designed, almost abstract. Yet they were photographed primarily with available lighting, in actual locations. The photography is beautiful as well as authentic; it is also organic to the dramatic context and to the character's enigmatic nature. Such is the art of a great cinematographer. *(Cinema 5)*

1–23. *Aliens* (U.S.A., **1987**), *with Sigourney Weaver and Carrie Henn, directed by James Cameron.*
Soft-focus photography blurs the background into a hazy neutrality, forcing us to concentrate on those elements that remain in sharp focus. The technique can produce a sense of privileged intimacy, a private moment temporarily wrested from its context. *(Twentieth Century–Fox)*

producing the necessary close-up. Telephotos also allow them to work discreetly. In crowded city locations, for example, passersby are likely to stare at a movie camera. The telephoto permits the cinematographer to remain hidden—in a truck, for example—while he or she shoots close shots through the windshield or back window of the truck. In effect, the lens works like a telescope, and because of its long focal length, it is sometimes called a *long lens.*

Telephoto lenses produce a number of side effects that are sometimes exploited by directors for symbolic use. Most long lenses are in sharp focus on one distance plane only. Objects placed before or beyond that distance blur, go out of focus—an expressive technique, especially to the formalist filmmaker (1–18). The longer the lens, the more sensitive it is to distances; in the case of extremely long lenses, objects placed a mere few inches away from the selected focal plane can be out of focus. This deliberate blurring of planes in the background, foreground, or both can produce some striking photographic and atmospheric effects.

The focal distance of long lenses can usually be adjusted while one is actually shooting, and thus the director is able to neutralize planes and guide the viewer's eye to various distances in a sequence—a technique called "rack focusing," or **selective focusing.** In *The Graduate,* director Mike Nichols used a slight focus shift instead of a cut when he wanted the viewer to look first at the young heroine, who then blurs out of focus, then at her mother, who is standing a few feet off in a doorway. The focus-shifting technique suggests a cause–effect relationship and parallels the heroine's sudden realization that her boyfriend's secret mistress is her own mother. In *The French Connection,* William Friedkin used selective focus in a sequence showing a criminal under surveillance. He remains in sharp focus while the city crowds of his environment are an undifferentiated blur. At strategic moments in the sequence, Friedkin shifted the focus plane from the criminal to the dogged detective who is tailing him in the crowd.

Long lenses also flatten images, decreasing the sense of distance between depth planes. Two people standing yards apart might look inches away when photographed with a telephoto lens. With very long lenses, distance planes are so compressed that the image can resemble a flat surface of abstract patterns. When anything moves toward or away from the camera in such shots, the mobile object doesn't seem to be moving at all. In *Marathon Man,* the hero (Dustin Hoffman) runs desperately toward the camera, but because of the flattening of the long lens, he seems almost to be running in place rather than moving toward his destination.

1–24. *Breathless* (France, 1959), *with Jean-Paul Belmondo (back to camera), cinematography by Raoul Coutard, directed by Jean-Luc Godard.*
Prior to 1959, most fiction movies were photographed with heavy cameras, lots of lights, and large technical crews. The French New Wave changed all that. In order to capture the spontaneity of the moment, Godard and others preferred the newly perfected hand-held camera, with its vastly increased mobility and flexibility. The New Wave directors also preferred fast film stock so they could shoot with available lighting. Coutard was one of the first masters of the hand-held camera. He was also able to produce striking images using only available lighting. "A film cameraman ought never to let himself forget that the eye of the spectator is naturally tuned to full daylight," he observed. *(Contemporary Films)*

The *wide-angle lenses,* also called "short lenses," have short focal lengths and wide angles of view. These are the lenses used in deep-focus shots, for they preserve a sharpness of focus on virtually all distance planes. The distortions involved in short lenses are both linear and spatial. The wider the angle, the more lines and shapes tend to warp, especially at the edges of the image. Distances between various depth planes are also exaggerated with these lenses: Two people standing a foot away from each other can appear yards apart in a wide-angle image. Orson Welles's films are filled with wide-angle shots. In *The Trial,* for example, he used such lenses to emphasize the vast, vacuous distance between people. In close-up ranges, wide-angle lenses tend to make huge bulbs of people's noses and slanting, sinister slits of their eyes. Welles used several such shots in *Touch of Evil.*

Movement toward or away from the camera is exaggerated when photographed with a short lens. Two or three ordinary steps can seem like inhumanly lengthy strides—an effective technique when a director wants to emphasize a character's strength, dominance, or ruthlessness. The **fish-eye lens** is the most extreme wide-angle modifier; it creates such severe distortions that the lateral portions of the screen seem reflected in a sphere, as though we were looking through a crystal ball (5–10).

Lenses and filters can be used for purely cosmetic purposes—to make an actor or actress taller, slimmer, younger, or older. Josef von Sternberg sometimes covered his lens with a translucent silk stocking to give his images a gauzy, romantic aura. A few glamor actresses beyond a certain age even had clauses in their contracts stipulating that only beautifying soft-focus lenses could be used for their close-ups. These optical modifiers eliminate small facial wrinkles and skin blemishes.

There are even more filters than there are lenses. Some trap light and refract it in such a way as to produce a diamondlike sparkle in the image. Many filters are used to suppress or heighten certain colors. Color filters can be especially striking in exterior scenes. Robert Altman's *McCabe and Mrs. Miller* (photographed by Vilmos Zsigmond) used green and blue filters for many of the exterior scenes, yellow and orange for interiors. These filters emphasized the bitter cold of the winter setting, and the communal warmth of the rooms inside the primitive buildings.

Though there are a number of different kinds of film stocks, most of them fall within the two basic categories: fast and slow. **Fast stock** is highly sensitive to light, and in some cases can register images with no illumination except what's available on location, even in nighttime sequences. **Slow stock** is relatively insensitive to light and requires as much as ten times more illumination than fast stocks. Traditionally, slow stocks are capable of capturing colors with precision, without washing them out.

Fast stocks were commonly associated with documentary movies, for with their great sensitivity to light, these stocks can reproduce images of events while they're actually occurring. The documentarist is able to photograph people and places without having to set up cumbersome lights. Because of this light sensitivity, fast stocks produce a grainy image in which lines tend to be fuzzy and colors tend to wash out. In a black and white film, lights and darks contrast sharply and many variations of gray can be lost (1–26).

1–25. *Dog Star Man* (U.S.A., 1959–1964), *directed by Stan Brakhage.*
Avant-garde filmmakers are often anti-illusionist—they attempt to break down the realism of an image by calling attention to its artificiality and its material properties. A movie image is printed on a strip of celluloid, which can be manipulated, even violated. In this sequence, a baby emerges from the mouth of another baby. Brakhage is playing with the idea of what's "behind" a film image.   *(Anthology Film Archives)*

1–26. ***The Battle of Algiers*** **(Italy/Algeria, 1967),** *directed by Gillo Pontecorvo.*
Fast film stocks are highly sensitive to light and can record images with no additional
illumination except what's available on a set or location. These stocks tend to produce harsh
light–dark contrasts and grainy images. Many of its original audiences thought that *The
Battle of Algiers* was a documentary compilation of authentic revolutionary footage. Its
grainy images and shaky camera work produce a gripping sense of immediacy. Pontecorvo
eventually added a title at the beginning of the movie, stating that all the images were created
specially for the film and no documentary footage was intercut with his own.   *(Rizzoli Film)*

Ordinarily, technical considerations such as these would have no place in a
book of this sort, but the choice of stock can produce considerable psychological
and aesthetic differences in a movie. Since the early 1960s, many fiction filmmakers have switched to fast stocks in order to give their images a documentary sense
of urgency. Jean-Luc Godard particularly favored the use of fast film, and his
usual cinematographer Raoul Coutard created some striking effects, notwithstanding the presumed limitations of these stocks (1–24).

The **optical printer** is an elaborate machine that produces many special
effects in the cinema. It includes a camera and projector precisely aligned, and
permits the operator to rephotograph all or a portion of an existing frame of a
film. **Double exposure,** or the superimposition of two images, is one of the most
important of these effects, for it permits the director to portray two levels of
reality simultaneously. For this reason, the technique is often used in fantasy and
dream sequences, as well as in scenes dealing with the supernatural. The optical
printer can also produce **multiple exposures,** or the superimposition of many
images simultaneously. Multiple exposures are useful for suggesting mood, time
lapses, and any sense of mixture—of time, places, objects, events. The optical
printer can combine one actor with moving images of others in a different time
and place.

1–27. *Pas De Deux* **(Canada, 1968),** *directed by Norman McLaren.*
The optical printer is an invaluable piece of equipment, particularly to the formalist filmmaker for, among other things, it allows the superimposition of two or more realities within a unified space. This film employs a technique called chronophotography in which the movements of two dancers are staggered and overlayed by the optical printer to produce a stroboscopic effect: As the dancers move, they leave a ghostly imprint on the screen.   *(National Film Board of Canada)*

The Cinematographer

The cinema is a collaborative enterprise, the result of the combined efforts of many artists, technicians, and businesspeople. Because the contributions of these individuals vary from film to film, it's hard to determine who's responsible for what in a movie. Most sophisticated viewers agree that the director is generally the dominant artist in the best movies. The principal collaborators—actors, writers, cinematographers—perform according to the director's unifying sensibility. But directorial dominance is an act of faith. Many films are stamped by the personalities of others—a prestigious **star,** for example, or a skillful editor who manages to make sense out of a director's botched **footage.**

Cinematographers sometimes chuckle sardonically when a director's visual style is praised by critics. Some directors don't even bother looking through the viewfinder, and leave such matters as composition, angles, and lenses up to the cinematographer. When directors ignore these important formal elements, they throw away some of their most expressive pictorial opportunities and function more like stage directors, who are concerned with dramatic rather than visual values—that is, with the script and the acting rather than the photographic quality of the image itself.

On the other hand, a few cinematographers have been praised for their artistry when in fact the effectiveness of a film's images is largely due to the director's pictorial skills (1–28). Hitchcock provided individual frame drawings for most of the shots in his films, a technique called **storyboarding.** His cinematographers framed up according to Hitchcock's precise sketches. Hence, when he claimed that he never looked through the viewfinder, he meant that he assumed his cinematographer had followed instructions.

Sweeping statements about the role of the cinematographer are impossible to make, for it varies widely from film to film and from director to director. In actual practice, virtually all cinematographers agree that the style of the photography should be geared to the story, theme, and mood of the film. William Daniels had a prestigious reputation as a glamor photographer at MGM and for many years was known as "Greta Garbo's cameraman." Yet Daniels also shot Erich von Stroheim's harshly realistic *Greed,* and the cinematographer won an Academy Award for his work in Jules Dassin's *Naked City,* which is virtually a

1–28. *Metropolis* **(Germany, 1926),** *cinematography by Karl Freund and Günther Rittau, directed by Fritz Lang.*

Like many German filmmakers of his generation, Lang controlled all aspects of the visual style in his movies. He considered himself a formalist, and planned almost every detail in advance. Each night before shooting he worked at least two hours planning his angles, lenses, and lighting effects. He always had exact sketches of his sets, and sometimes even small-scale models to work out his shots. "Every picture has a certain rhythm which only one man can give it," Lang explained. "That man is the director. He has to be like the captain of a ship." *(Janus Films)*

semidocumentary. In the films of Antonioni (*La Notte, Il Grido, Eclipse*) the cinematography of Gianni Di Venanzo is austere and realistic. But in the works of Fellini (*8½, Juliet of the Spirits*) it's extravagantly romantic. Most of Coutard's work for Godard is relatively documentarylike, but Coutard's camerawork for François Truffaut is noticeably more lyrical, as in *Jules and Jim*.

Great directors tend to prefer artists, not mere technicians, as their cinematographers. The names of some cameramen are inextricably linked with specific directors: Billy Bitzer with D. W. Griffith, Edouard Tissé with Sergei Eisenstein, Freddie Young with David Lean, Gregg Toland with William Wyler, Gordon Willis with Woody Allen, and Sven Nykvist with Ingmar Bergman, among many others. Some cinematographers have eventually become directors, most notably Jan Troell (1-29), George Stevens, Nicholas Roeg, Jack Cardiff, and Haskell Wexler. Directors John Cassavetes and Stanley Kubrick shot a lot of their own footage, as do a number of other filmmakers.

1–29. *The Emigrants* (Sweden, 1972), *with Liv Ullmann and Max von Sydow, photographed and directed by Jan Troell.*
If we were to view a scene similar to this in real life, we would probably concentrate most of our attention on the people in the wagon. But there are considerable differences between reality and cinematic realism. Realism is an artistic style. In selecting materials from the chaotic sprawl of reality, the realist filmmaker necessarily eliminates some details and emphasizes others into a structured hierarchy of visual significance. For example, the stone wall in the foreground of this shot occupies more space than the humans. Visually, this dominance suggests that the rocks are more important than the people. The unyielding stone wall symbolizes divisiveness and exclusion—ideas that are appropriate to the dramatic context. If the wall were irrelevant to the theme, Troell would have eliminated it and selected other details from the copiousness of reality—details that would be more pertinent to the dramatic context.   (*Warner Bros.*)

During the halcyon years of the Hollywood studio stystem—roughly the 1930s and 1940s—some of the best cinematographers were associated with a specific studio and helped establish the semiofficial style of that studio. Each of the major studios had a characteristic "look" during this period, and it was created in part by its lighting cameramen. MGM—the most prosperous studio—was proud of its roster of cinematographers, which included Hal Rosson, William Daniels, and Ray June. At Paramount, Lee Garmes, Karl Struss, Charles B. Lang, and John F. Seitz were the big names. Warner Brothers specialized in moody low-key styles, popularized by Tony Gaudio and Sol Polito, who was generally regarded as Hollywood's most gifted cinematographer of mobile camera work. For many years Twentieth Century–Fox was the employer of Arthur

1–30. *How Green Was My Valley* **(U.S.A., 1941),** *cinematography by Arthur Miller, directed by John Ford.*
Ford was one of the supreme masters of the big studio era, a visual lyricist of the first rank. He disliked overt emotions in his movies. He preferred conveying feelings through form. Stylized lighting effects and formal compositions such as this invariably embody intense emotions. Of all his collaborators, Ford was most generous in his praise of his cinematographers. The roster of great directors of photography that he worked with reads like a Who's Who of American Cinematography: Joseph MacDonald, Gregg Toland, Joseph August, Arthur Miller, Bert Glennon, Archie Stout, William Clothier, and Winton Hoch.   *(Twentieth Century–Fox)*

C. Miller and Leon Shamroy—the first to explore Fox's new widescreen process, CinemaScope. Even the smaller studios could boast a few great cameramen, like Columbia's Joseph L. Walker. Lowly Universal had under contract two of the finest artists of the period, Russell Metty and Stanley Cortez. Independent producer Sam Goldwyn gave Gregg Toland virtual carte blanche to carry on his elaborate experiments in lighting.

Many filmmakers understand the technology of cinematography very well. Others are totally ignorant of such matters and require impossible results. Astonishingly, these artists often manage to deliver. Cinematographers have to be extraordinarily hearty, flexible, and resourceful. Daniels, for example, was required to work in 132° heat for the Death Valley sequences of *Greed*. Often cameramen must work underwater, in deep, dark, narrow pits, high overhead on precarious ledges, and in almost every kind of dangerous situation (1–31).

There are some great movies that are photographed competently, but without distinction. Realist directors are especially likely to prefer an unobtrusive style. Many of the works of Buñuel, for example, can only be described as "professional" in their cinematography. Buñuel was rarely interested in formal beauty—except occasionally to mock it. Rollie Totheroh, who photographed most of Chaplin's works, merely set up his camera and let Chaplin the actor take over. Photographically speaking, there are few memorable shots in his films. What makes the images compelling is the genius of Chaplin's acting. This photographic austerity—some would consider it poverty—is especially apparent in those rare scenes when Chaplin is off camera.

But there are far more films in which the *only* interesting or artistic quality is the cinematography. For every great work like Fritz Lang's *You Only Live Once*, Leon Shamroy had to photograph four or five bombs of the ilk of *Snow White and the Three Stooges*. Lee Garmes photographed several of von Sternberg's visually opulent films, but he also was required to shoot *My Friend Irma Goes West*. Some of James Wong Howe's most brilliant innovations—including

1–31. Production photo of *Deliverance* (U.S.A., 1972), *cinematography by Vilmos Zsigmond (in rubber suit), directed by John Boorman.*

Cinematographers are expected to work under the most dangerous conditions, with cumbersome equipment. Zsigmond and his crew had to work from a rubber raft which swirled precariously in the currents of the wild Chattooga River in Georgia. A superlative stylist, Zsigmond has photographed such visually striking films as *McCabe and Mrs. Miller, The Long Goodbye, Scarecrow, Deliverance, The Deer Hunter,* and *Heaven's Gate.*   (*Warner Bros.*)

1–32. Days of Heaven (U.S.A., 1978), *cinematography by Nestor Almendros, directed by Terrence Malick.*

The Spanish-born Almendros has worked primarily in France, especially with Truffaut and Eric Rohmer. *Days of Heaven* was his first American assignment and won him an Academy Award. Malick wanted the setting to suggest a lush Garden of Eden. He encouraged Almendros to make his cinematography as visually seductive as possible. Whether focusing on a close-up of a locust munching on a stalk of wheat or an extreme long shot of a rural sunrise, the images are ravishing in their lyricism.   *(Paramount Pictures)*

deep-focus interior photography and ceilinged sets—were wasted on a potboiler entitled *Transatlantic,* which was made ten years before *Citizen Kane,* the film often cited as the first movie to use interior deep-focus and ceilinged sets.

In this chapter, we've been concerned with visual images largely as they relate to the art and technology of cinematography. But the camera must have materials to photograph—objects, people, settings. Through the manipulation of these materials, the director is able to convey a multitude of ideas and emotions spatially. This arrangement of objects in space is referred to as a director's *mise en scène*—the subject of the following chapter.

FURTHER READING

ALTON, JOHN, *Painting with Light* (New York: Macmillan, 1962).

CLARKE, CHARLES, *Professional Cinematography* (Hollywood, Cal.: American Society of Cinematographers, 1964). A practical manual.

EYMAN, SCOTT, *Five American Cinematographers* (Metuchen, N.J. & London: Scarecrow Press, 1987). Interviews with Karl Struss, Joseph Ruttenberg, James Wong Howe, Linwood Dunn, and William Clothier.

FIELDING, RAYMOND, *The Techniques of Special Effects Cinematography* (New York: Hastings House, 1965).

HIGHAM, CHARLES, ed., *Hollywood Cameramen* (Bloomington: Indiana University Press, 1970). Interviews with cinematographers, including Shamroy, Garmes, Daniels, Howe, Cortez, Miller, and Struss.

MALTIN, LEONARD, *The Art of the Cinematographer* (New York: Dover, 1978).

———, ED., *Behind the Camera: The Cinematographer's Art* (New York: New American Library, 1971). Interviews with Miller, Ballard, Hal Mohr, Hal Rosson, and Conrad Hall.

MASCELLI, JOSEPH, *The Five C's of Cinematography* (Hollywood, Cal.: Cine/Graphics, 1965). A practical manual.

ROVIN, JEFF, *Movie Special Effects* (San Diego, Cal.: A. S. Barnes, 1977).

YOUNG, FREDDIE, *The Work of the Motion Picture Cameraman* (New York: Hastings House, 1972). Technical emphasis.

MISE EN SCÈNE | 2

One must compose images as the old masters did their canvases,
with the same preoccupation with effect and expression.

—MARCEL CARNÉ

Mise en scène (pronounced meez on sen, with the second syllable nasalized) was originally a French theatrical term, meaning "placing on stage." The phrase refers to the arrangement of all the visual elements of a theatrical production within a given playing area—the stage. This area can be defined by the proscenium arch, which encloses the stage in a kind of picture frame; or the acting area can be more fluid, extending even into the auditorium. No matter what the confines of the stage may be, its mise en scène is always in three dimensions. Objects and people are arranged in actual space, which has depth as well as height and width. This space is also a continuation of the same space that the audience occupies, no matter how much a theater director tries to suggest a separate "world" on the stage.

In movies, mise en scène is somewhat more complicated, a blend of the visual conventions of the live theater with those of the plastic arts. Like the stage director, the filmmaker arranges objects and people within a given three-dimensional space. But once this arrangement is photographed, it's converted into a two-dimensional *image* of the real thing. The space in the "world" of the movie is not the same as that occupied by the audience. Only the image exists in the same physical area, like a picture in an art gallery. Mise en scène in the movies resembles the art of painting in that an image of formal patterns and

2–1. *Manhattan* **(U.S.A. 1979),** *with Woody Allen and Diane Keaton, directed by Allen.*
Mise en scène is a complex analytical term, encompassing four distinct formal elements: (1) the staging of the action, (2) the physical setting and decor, (3) the manner in which these materials are framed, and (4) the manner in which they are photographed. The art of mise en scène is indissolubly linked with the art of cinematography. In this shot, for example, the story content is simple: The characters are conversing, getting to know each other, becoming attracted. Gordon Willis's tender, low-key lighting, combined with the beauty of the setting—the sculpture garden of the Museum of Modern Art—provides the scene with an intensely romantic atmosphere. (*United Artists*)

shapes is presented on a flat surface and enclosed within a **frame.** But because of its theatrical heritage, cinematic mise en scène is also a fluid choreographing of visual elements that correspond to a dramatic idea, or complex of ideas.

The Frame

Each movie image is enclosed by the frame of the screen, which defines the world of the film, separating it from the actual world of the darkened auditorium. Unlike the painter or still photographer, the filmmaker doesn't conceive of the framed compositions as self-sufficient statements. Like drama, film is a temporal as well as spatial art, and consequently the visuals are constantly in

2–2. *Notorious* **(U.S.A., 1946),** *with Ingrid Bergman, Claude Rains, and Leopoldine Konstantine, directed by Alfred Hitchcock.*

Hitchcock always regarded himself as a formalist, calculating his effects with an extraordinary degree of precision. He believed that an unmanipulated reality is filled with irrelevancies: "I do not follow the geography of a set, I follow the geography of the screen," he said. The space around actors must be orchestrated from shot to shot. "I think only of that white screen that has to be filled up the way you fill up a canvas. That's why I draw rough setups for the cameraman." Here, the mise en scène is a perfect analogue of the heroine's sense of entrapment, without violating the civilized veneer demanded by the dramatic context. The dialogue in such instances can be perfectly neutral, for the psychological tensions are conveyed by the placement of the camera and the way the characters are arranged in space.   *(RKO)*

flux. The compositions are broken down, redefined, and reassembled before our eyes. A single-frame image from a movie, then, is necessarily an artificially frozen moment that was never intended to be yanked from its context in time and motion. For critical purposes, it's sometimes necessary to analyze a still frame in isolation, but the viewer ought to make due allowances for the dramatic context.

The frame functions as the basis of composition in a movie image. Unlike the painter or still photographer, however, the filmmaker fits not the frame to the composition, but the compositions to a single-sized frame. The ratio of the frame's horizontal and vertical dimensions—known as the **aspect ratio**—remains constant throughout the movie. Screens come in a variety of aspect ratios, especially since the introduction of **widescreen** in the early 1950s. Prior to this time, most movies were shot in a 1.33:1 aspect ratio, though even in the silent era filmmakers were constantly experimenting with different-sized screens (2–3).

Today, most movies are projected in one of two aspect ratios: the 1.85:1 (standard) and the 2.35:1 (widescreen). Some films originally photographed in widescreen are cropped down to a conventional aspect ratio after their initial commercial release. This appalling practice is commonplace in movies that are reduced from 35 mm to 16 mm, the standard gauge used in most noncommercial exhibitions like those at colleges and museums. The more imaginatively the widescreen is used, the more a movie is likely to suffer when its aspect ratio is violated in this manner. Generally, at least a third of the image is hacked away by lopping off the edges of the frame. This kind of cropping can result in many visual absurdities: A speaker at the edge of the frame might be totally absent in the "revised" composition, or an actor might react in horror at something that never even comes into view. When shown on television—which has an aspect ratio of approximately 1.33:1—some of the greatest widescreen films can actually seem clumsy and poorly composed.

In the traditional visual arts, frame dimensions are governed by the nature of the subject matter. Thus, a painting of a skyscraper is likely to be vertical in shape and would be framed accordingly. A vast panoramic scene would probably be more horizontal in its dimensions. But in movies the frame ratio is imposed from without and isn't necessarily governed by the nature of the materials being photographed. This is not to say that all film images are therefore inorganic, however, for in this regard the filmmaker can be likened to a sonneteer, who chooses a rigid form precisely because of the technical challenges it presents. Much of the enjoyment we derive in reading a sonnet results from the tension between the content and the form, which consists of fourteen intricately rhymed lines. When technique and subject matter are fused in this way, aesthetic pleasure is heightened. The same principle can be applied to framing in film.

The constant size of the movie frame is especially hard to overcome in vertical compositions. A sense of height must be conveyed in spite of the dominantly horizontal shape of the screen. One method of overcoming the problem is through **masking.** In his 1916 masterpiece, *Intolerance,* D. W. Griffith blocked out portions of his images through the use of black masks, which in effect connected the darkened portions of the screen with the darkness of the auditorium. To emphasize the steep fall of a soldier from a wall, the sides of the image were masked out. To stress the vast horizon of a location, Griffith masked out

2-3. *Napoleon* (France, 1926), *directed by Abel Gance.*
Napoleon is the most famous widescreen experiment of the silent era. Its triptych sequences—such as the French army's march into Italy (pictured)—were shot in what Gance called "Polyvision." The process involved the coordination of three cameras so as to photograph a 160° panorama—three times wider than the conventional aspect ratio. (*Universal Pictures*)

(a)

(b)

2–4. *2001: A Space Odyssey* (U.S.A./ Great Britain, 1968), *directed by Stanley Kubrick.*

The widescreen is particularly suited to capturing the vastness of a locale. If this image were cropped to a conventional aspect ratio **(b)**, much of the feel of the infinity of space would be sacrificed. We tend to scan an image from left to right, and therefore, in Kubrick's composition **(a)**, the astronaut seems to be in danger of slipping off into the endlessness of space. If the composition is turned upside down, however **(c)**, the astronaut seems to be coming home into the safety of the spacecraft. *(MGM)*

(c)

the lower third of the image—thus creating a widescreen effect. Many kinds of masks are used in this movie, including diagonal, circular, and oval shapes. Some years later, the Soviet director Eisenstein urged the adoption of a square screen, on which masked images could be projected in whatever shape was appropriate to the subject matter.

In the silent movie era, the **iris** (a circular or oval mask that can open up or close in on a subject) was rather overused. In the hands of a master, however, the iris can be a powerful dramatic statement. In *The Wild Child,* François Truffaut used an iris to suggest the intense concentration of a young boy: The surrounding blackness is a metaphor of how the youngster "blocks out" his social environment while focusing on an object immediately in front of him.

As an aesthetic device, the frame performs in several ways. The sensitive director is just as concerned with what's left out of the frame as with what's included. The frame selects and delimits the subject, editing out all irrelevancies and presenting us with only a "piece" of reality. The materials included within a shot are unified by the frame, which in effect imposes an order on them—the order that art carves out of the chaos of reality. The frame is thus essentially an isolating device, a technique that permits the director to confer special attention on what might be overlooked in a wider context.

The movie frame can function as a metaphor for other types of enclosures. Some directors use the frame voyeuristically. In many of the films of Hitchcock, for example, the frame is likened to a window through which the audience may satisfy its impulse to pry into the intimate details of the characters' lives. In fact, *Psycho* and *Rear Window* employ this peeping technique literally. Other directors use the frame in a less snooping manner. In Jean Renoir's *The Golden Coach,* for instance, the frame suggests the proscenium arch of the live theater, and appropriately so, since the controlling symbol of the movie centers on the idea of life as a stage.

2–5. *The Incredible Shrinking Man* (U.S.A., 1957), *with Grant Williams, directed by Jack Arnold.*
The mise en scène of the live theater is scaled in proportion to the human figure. Cinematic mise en scène can be microscopic or cosmic (2–4) with equal ease, thanks to the magic of special effects. In this photo, for example, the mise en scène represents only a few inches of space: Its scale is defined not by the human figure, but by the box of matches and the size of the common pin which the dwindling hero is attempting to convert into a weapon.   (*Universal Pictures*)

2–6. *Tokyo Story* (**Japan, 1953**), *directed by Yasujiro Ozu.*
Ozu's mise en scène is usually formal, its compositional weights balanced with exquisite delicacy. Note how the diagonal thrust of the tree branches (in an image otherwise composed of stately verticals and horizontals) counteracts the weight of the three figures on the right. The scene is staged within a prosceniumlike enclosure—a frame within a frame—reinforcing its ceremonial dignity. Ozu exploits these formal compositions as ironic foils to the human materials: The intense emotions of the characters are often at odds with the decorum prescribed by such social rituals. "The Ozu scene is balanced, asymmetrical, pleasing to the eye; it is at the same time rigid and uncompromising, as all empty compositions are," Donald Richie has pointed out. "When the actor enters and behaves in a way contrary to the expectations created by such a formal decor, the result is an often touching spontaneity. This composition, then, exists but to be broken."   (*New Yorker Films*)

Certain areas within the frame can suggest symbolic ideas. By placing an object or actor within a particular section of the frame, the filmmaker can radically alter his or her comment on that object or character. Placement within the frame is another instance of how form is actually content. Each of the major sections of the frame—center, top, bottom, and edges—can be exploited for such symbolic and metaphoric purposes.

The central portions of the screen are generally reserved for the most important visual elements. This area is instinctively regarded by most people as the intrinsic center of interest. When we take a snapshot of a friend, we generally center his figure within the confines of the viewfinder. Since childhood, we have been taught that a drawing must be balanced, with the middle serving as the focal point. The center, then, is a kind of norm: We *expect* dominant visual elements to be placed there. Precisely because of this expectation, objects placed in the center tend to be visually undramatic. Central dominance is generally favored when the subject matter is intrinsically compelling. Realist filmmakers prefer

2–7. *Greed* **(U.S.A., 1924),** *with Gibson Gowland (right) and Jean Hersholt, directed by Erich von Stroheim.*

Highly symmetrical designs are generally employed when a director wishes to stress stability and harmony. In this photo, for example, the carefully balanced weights of the design reinforce these (temporary) qualities. The visual elements are neatly juxtaposed in units of twos, with the two beer-filled glasses forming the focal point. The main figures balance each other, as do the two converging brick walls, the two pairs of curtains, the two windows, the two people in each window, the shape of the picture above the men, and the shape of the resting dog below them. *(MGM)*

central dominance because formally it's the most unobtrusive kind of framing. The viewer is allowed to concentrate on the subject matter without being distracted by visual elements that seem off center. However, even **formalists** use the middle of the screen for dominance in routine expository shots.

The area near the top of the frame can suggest ideas dealing with power, authority, and aspiration. A person placed here seems to control all the visual elements below, and for this reason, authority figures are often photographed in this manner. In images suggesting spirituality, often the top of the frame is exploited to convey a godlike splendor. This grandeur can also apply to objects— a palace, the top of a mountain. If an unattractive character is placed near the top of the screen, he or she can seem threatening and dangerous, superior to the other figures within the frame. However, these generalizations are true only when the other figures are approximately the same size or smaller than the dominating figure.

The top of the frame is not always used in this symbolic manner. In some instances, this is simply the most sensible area to place an object. In a medium shot of a figure, for example, the person's head is logically going to be near the top of the screen, but obviously this kind of framing isn't meant to be symbolic. It's merely reasonable, since that's where we'd *expect* the head to appear in medium shots. Indeed, mise en scène is essentially an art of the long and extreme long shot, for when the subject matter is detailed in a closer shot, the director has fewer choices concerning the distribution of visual elements.

The areas near the bottom of the frame tend to suggest opposite meanings from the top: subservience, vulnerability, and powerlessness. Objects and figures placed in these positions seem to be in danger of slipping out of the frame entirely. For this reason, these areas are often exploited symbolically to suggest danger. When there are two or more figures in the frame and they are approximately the same size, the figure nearer the bottom of the screen tends to be dominated by those above.

The left and right edges of the frame tend to suggest insignificance, since these are the areas farthest removed from the center of the screen. Objects and figures placed near the edges are literally close to the darkness outside the frame. Many directors use this darkness to suggest those symbolic ideas traditionally associated with the lack of light—the unknown, the unseen, and the fearful. In some instances, the blackness outside the frame can symbolize oblivion or even death. In movies about people who want to remain anonymous and unnoticed,

2–8. *Midnight Express* (**U.S.A., 1978**), *with Brad Davis (hands raised), directed by Alan Parker.*
All of the compositional elements in this shot contribute to a sense of entrapment. The protagonist is totally surrounded, not only by the ring of soldiers who have their guns poised for a kill, but also by an outer ring of compositional weights—the airplane above, the stairs and railing to the left, the bench and huddled bystanders at the lower portions of the frame, and the three gunmen sealing off the right. The high angle and the gridlike lines of the concrete runway reinforce the sense of entrapment. The image might almost be entitled *No Exit.* (*Columbia Pictures*)

the director sometimes deliberately places them off center, near the "insignificant" edges of the screen.

Finally, there are some instances when a director places the most important visual elements completely off frame. Especially when a character is associated with darkness, mystery, or death, this technique can be highly effective, for the audience is most fearful of what it can't see. In the early portions of Fritz Lang's *M,* for example, the psychotic child-killer is never seen directly. We can only sense his presence, for he lurks in the darkness outside the light of the frame. Occasionally, we catch a glimpse of his shadow streaking across the set, and we're aware of his presence by the eerie tune he whistles when he's emotionally excited or upset.

There are two other off-frame areas that can be exploited for symbolic purposes: the space behind the set and the space in front of the camera. By not showing us what is happening behind a closed door, the filmmaker can provoke the viewer's curiosity, creating an unsettling effect, for we tend to fill in such vacuums with vivid imaginings. The final shot from Hitchcock's *Notorious* is a

2–9. *The General* (U.S.A., 1926), *with Buster Keaton, directed by Keaton and Clyde Bruckman.*

Keaton was a master of classical composition. His visual style is sophisticated and elegant, yet at the same time functional, simple, direct. His comedy is essentially spatial, and derives its humor from the way in which Buster masters—or is mastered by—objects in a unified space. Keaton's visual gags are impeccably framed, without an inch of wasted space. Almost any random shot demonstrates an acute sensitivity to how much—or how little—visual information is necessary to maximize the shot's impact.   (*Audio-Brandon Films*)

good example. The hero helps the groggy heroine past a group of Nazi agents to a waiting auto. The rather sympathetic villain (Claude Rains) escorts the two, hoping his colleagues won't become suspicious. In a **deep-focus long shot,** we see the three principals in the foreground while the Nazi agents remain near the open door of the house in the upper background—watching, wondering. The hero maliciously locks the villain out of the car, then drives out of frame, leaving the villain stranded without an explanation. His colleagues call out his name, and he is forced to return to the house, dreading the worst. He climbs the stairs and reenters the house with the suspicious agents, who then close the door behind them. Hitchcock never does show us what happens behind the door.

The area in front of the camera can also create unsettling effects of this sort. In John Huston's *The Maltese Falcon,* for example, we witness a murder without ever seeing the killer. The victim is photographed in a **medium shot** as a gun enters the frame just in front of the camera. Not until the end of the movie do we discover the identity of the off-frame killer.

Composition and Design

Although the photographable materials of movies exist in three dimensions, one of the primary problems facing the filmmaker is much like that confronting the painter: the arrangement of shapes, colors, lines, and textures on a flat rectangular surface. In the classical cinema, this arrangement is generally held in some kind of balance, or harmonious equilibrium. The desire for balance is analogous to people balancing on their feet, and indeed to most manufactured structures, which are balanced on the surface of the earth. Instinctively, we assume that balance is the norm in most human enterprises.

In movies, however, there are some important exceptions to this rule. When a visual artist wishes to stress a *lack* of equilibrium, many of the standard conventions of **classical** composition are deliberately violated. In movies, the dramatic context is usually the determining factor in composition. What is superficially a bad composition might actually be highly effective, depending on its psychological context. Many films are concerned with neurotic characters or events that are out of joint. In such cases, the director might well ignore the conventions of classical composition. Instead of centering a character in the image, his or her spiritual maladjustment can be conveyed symbolically by photographing the subject at the edge of the frame. In this manner, the filmmaker throws off the visual balance and presents us with an image that's psychologically more appropriate to the dramatic context.

There are no set rules about these matters. A classical filmmaker like Buster Keaton uses mostly balanced compositions. Filmmakers outside the classical tradition tend to favor compositions that are asymmetrical or off center. In movies there are a variety of techniques to convey the same ideas and emotions. Some filmmakers favor visual methods, others favor dialogue, still others editing or acting. Ultimately, whatever works is right (2–10).

The human eye automatically attempts to harmonize the formal elements of a composition into a unified whole. The eye can detect as many as seven or

(a)

2–10a. *Macbeth* **(U.S.A./Great Britain, 1971),** *with Francesca Annis and Jon Finch, directed by Roman Polanski.*

Movie images are generally scanned in a structured sequence of eye-stops. The eye is first attracted to a dominant contrast that compels our most immediate attention by virtue of its conspicuousness, and then travels to the subsidiary areas of interest within the frame. In this photo, for example, the eye is initially attracted to the face of Lady Macbeth, which is lit in high contrast and is surrounded by darkness. We then scan the brightly lit "empty" space between her and her husband. The third area of interest is Macbeth's thoughtful face, which is lit in a more subdued manner. The visual interest of this photo corresponds to the dramatic context of the film, for Lady Macbeth is slowly descending into madness and feels spiritually alienated and isolated from her husband.   *(Columbia Pictures)*

(b)

2–10b. *Macbeth* **(U.S.A., 1948),** *with Peggy Webber, directed by Orson Welles.*

Realists and formalists solve problems in different ways, with different visual techniques. Polanski's presentation of Lady Macbeth's madness is conveyed in a relatively realistic manner, with emphasis on acting and subtle lighting effects. Welles employs a more formalistic approach, using physical correlatives to convey interior states, such as the iron fence's knifelike blades, which almost seem to pierce Webber's body. The fence is not particularly realistic or even functional: Welles exploits it primarily as a symbolic analogue of her inner torment. Neither approach is better or worse. It all depends on how well it's done.   *(Republic Pictures)*

2–11. *Big* **(U.S.A., 1988),** *with Tom Hanks and Jared Rushton, directed by Penny Marshall.* In shots emphasizing disorder or confusion, the film director sometimes deliberately overloads the composition to produce a sense of visual chaos. In this photo, for example, the lines, shapes, and compositional weights form no discernible design. *(Twentieth Century–Fox)*

eight major elements of a composition simultaneously. In most cases, however, the eye doesn't wander promiscuously over the surface of an image, but is guided to specific areas in sequence. The director accomplishes this through the use of a **dominant contrast,** also known as the **dominant.** The dominant is that area of an image that immediately attracts our attention because of a conspicuous and compelling contrast. It stands out in some kind of isolation from the other elements within the image. In black and white movies, the dominant contrast is generally achieved through a juxtaposition of lights and darks. For example, if the director wishes the viewer to look first at an actor's hand rather than his face, the lighting of the hand would be harsher than that of the face, which would be lit in a more subdued manner. In color films, the dominant is often achieved by having one color stand out from the others. Virtually any formal element can be used as a dominant: a shape, a line, a texture, and so on.

After we take in the dominant, our eye then scans the **subsidiary contrasts** which the artist has arranged to act as counterbalancing devices. Our eyes are seldom at rest with visual compositions, then, even with paintings or still photographs. We look somewhere first, then we look at those areas of diminishing interest. None of this is accidental, for visual artists deliberately structure their images so that a specific sequence is followed. In short, movement in film isn't confined only to objects and people that are literally in motion.

In most cases, the visual interest of the dominant corresponds with the

2–12. *Superman* (**U.S.A./Great Britain**, **1978**), *with Glenn Ford, directed by Richard Donner.*
Because the top half of the frame tends to be intrinsically heavier than the bottom, directors usually keep their horizon well above the middle of the composition. They also place most of the visual weights in the lower portions of the screen. When a filmmaker wishes to emphasize the vulnerability of the characters, however, the horizon is often lowered, and sometimes the heaviest visual elements are placed above the characters. In this witty shot, for example, the parents of little Clark Kent are astonished—and visually imperilled—by the superhuman strength of their adopted son. (*Warner Bros.*)

dramatic interest of the image. Since films have temporal and dramatic contexts, however, the dominant is often movement itself, and what some aestheticians call **intrinsic interest.** Intrinsic interest simply means that the audience, through the context of a story, knows that an object is more important dramatically than it appears to be visually. Thus, despite the fact that a gun might occupy only a small portion of the surface of an image, if we know that the gun is *dramatically* important, it will assume dominance in the picture despite its visual insignificance. In *The Pawnbroker,* for example, director Sidney Lumet wanted to show the relative indifference of city dwellers to a murder that has just taken place. A youth's body lies bleeding on the sidewalk, while people pass by or stare impassively. In a number of shots, his body isn't even visible to the viewer, but because of its intrinsic interest, it takes over as the dominant contrast as we strain to locate the body behind the obstruction of the gawking crowd.

Movement is almost always an automatic dominant contrast, providing the other elements in the image are stationary. Even a third-rate director can guide the viewer's eyes through the use of motion. For this reason, lazy filmmakers ignore the potential richness of their images and rely solely on movement as a means of capturing the viewer's attention. On the other hand, most directors will vary their dominants, sometimes emphasizing motion, other times using movement as a subsidiary contrast only. The importance of motion varies with the kind of shot used. Movement tends to be less distracting in the longer shots and highly conspicuous in the closer ranges.

Unless the viewer has time to explore the surface of an image at leisure, visual confusion can result when there are more than eight or nine major compositional elements. If visual confusion is the deliberate intention of an image—as in a battle scene, for example—the director will sometimes overload the composi-

2–13. *Jules and Jim* **(France, 1961),** *with Henri Serre, Jeanne Moreau, and Oskar Werner, directed by François Truffaut.*
Compositions grouped into units of three, five, and seven tend to suggest dynamic, unstable relationships. Those organized in units of two, four, or six, on the other hand, tend to imply fixed, harmonious relationships. This triangular composition is organically related to the theme of the movie, which deals with the shifting love relationships between the three characters. The woman is almost invariably at the apex of the triangle: She likes it that way.   *(Janus Films)*

tion in order to produce this effect (2–11). In general, the eye struggles to unify various elements into an ordered pattern. For example, even in a complex design, the eye will connect similar shapes, colors, textures, etc. The very repetition of a formal element can suggest the repetition of an experience. These connections form a visual rhythm, forcing the eye to leap over the surface of the design in order to perceive the overall balance. Visual artists often refer to compositional elements as *weights*. In most cases, especially in classical cinema, the artist distributes these weights harmoniously over the surface of the image. In a totally symmetrical design—almost never found in fiction movies—the visual weights are distributed evenly, with the center of the composition as the axis point. Since most compositions are asymmetrical, however, the weight of one element is counterpoised with another. A shape, for example, counteracts the weight of a color. Psychologists and art theorists have discovered that certain portions of a composition are intrinsically weighted. The German art historian Wölfflin, for instance, pointed out that we tend to scan pictures from left to right, all other compositional elements being equal. Especially in classical compo-

2–14. *The 400 Blows* **(France, 1959),** *with Jean-Pierre Léaud, directed by François Truffaut.*
Often the context of a scene does not permit a director to express emotions dramatically.
Here, the boy's anxiety and tenseness are expressed in purely visual terms. His inward
agitation is conveyed by the diagonal lines of the fence. His sense of entrapment is suggested
by the tight framing (sides, top, bottom), the shallow focus (rear), and the obstruction of the
fence itself (foreground).   *(Janus Films)*

sitions, the image is often more heavily weighted on the left to counteract the
intrinsic heaviness of the right.

The upper part of the composition is heavier than the lower. For this
reason, skyscrapers, columns, and obelisks taper upward or they would appear
top-heavy. Images seem more balanced when the center of gravity is kept low,
with most of the weights in the lower portions of the screen. A landscape is
seldom divided horizontally at the midpoint of a composition, or the sky would
appear to oppress the earth. Epic filmmakers like Eisenstein and Ford create
some of their most disquieting effects with precisely this technique: They let the
sky dominate through its intrinsic heaviness. The terrain and its inhabitants seem
overwhelmed from above.

Isolated figures and objects tend to be heavier than those in a cluster.
Sometimes one object—merely by virtue of its isolation—can balance a whole
group of otherwise equal objects. In many movies, the protagonist is shown
apart from a hostile group, yet the two seem evenly matched despite the arith-
metical differences. This effect is conveyed through the visual weight of the hero
in isolation (3–11).

Psychological experiments have revealed that certain lines suggest directional movements. Although vertical and horizontal lines seem to be visually at rest, if movement *is* perceived, horizontal lines tend to move from left to right, vertical lines from bottom to top. Diagonal or oblique lines are more dynamic—that is, in transition. They tend to sweep upward. These psychological phenomena are important to the visual artist, especially the filmmaker, for the dramatic context is not always conducive to an overt expression of emotion (2–14). For example, if a director wishes to show a character's inward agitation within a calm context, this quality can be conveyed through the dynamic use of line: An image composed of tense diagonals can suggest the character's inner turmoil, despite the apparent lack of drama in the action. Some of the most expressive cinematic effects can be achieved precisely through this tension between the compositional elements of an image and its dramatic context.

A skeletal structure underlies most visual compositions. Throughout the

2–15. ***Last Tango in Paris*** (**Italy/France, 1973**), *with Marlon Brando and Maria Schneider, directed by Bernardo Bertolucci.*
Visual motifs, like symbols, derive their significance from the dramatic context of a film. In this movie, Bertolucci associates circular light globes with sexual fantasies. The motif is found in a number of scenes and is associated with various characters in different locations. The motif first appears in the lobby of the apartment house where the two lovers (Brando and Schneider) meet for their sexual trysts. A similar light globe is found in the lobby of the hotel of Brando's deceased wife. Her lover also has a circular globe in his room where he and his mistress met for their liaisons. The same type of light fixture is found in the apartment belonging to Schneider's mother: Both of these women use the military gear which once belonged to the *pater familias* as sexual fetishes. The globe motif proliferates lyrically on the screen in the famous tango sequence, shown here. (Almost all of Bertolucci's movies contain dance scenes.)   (*United Artists*)

ages, artists have especially favored S and X shapes, triangular designs, and circles. These designs are often employed simply because they are thought to be inherently beautiful. Design is generally fused with a thematic idea, at least in the best movies. In *Jules and Jim,* for example, Truffaut consistently uses triangular designs, for the film deals with a trio of characters whose relationships are constantly shifting, yet always interrelated. The form of the images in this case is a symbolic representation of the romantic triangle of the dramatic content. These triangular designs dynamize the visuals, keeping them off balance, subject to change (2–13). Generally, designs consisting of units of three, five, and seven tend to produce these effects. Designs composed of two, four, or six units seem more static, stable, and balanced (2–7).

The design of a composition is not usually meaningful in itself, but derives its meaning from the dramatic situation. Form is an organic extension of content. In most westerns, for example, the circle formed by wagon trains when attacked

2–16. *The Graduate* (U.S.A., 1967), *with Anne Bancroft and Dustin Hoffman, directed by Mike Nichols.*

Viewers can be made to feel insecure or isolated when a hostile foreground element (Bancroft) comes between us and a figure we identify with. In this scene, our hero, Benjamin Braddock, college graduate, feels threatened. An older woman, a friend of his parents, tries to seduce him—he thinks. He's not sure. His feelings of entrapment and imminent violation are conveyed not by his words, which are stammering and embarrassed, but by the mise en scène. Blocked off in front by her seminude body, he is also visually confined at his rear by the window frame—an enclosure within an enclosure (the room) within the enclosure of the movie frame.   *(Avco Embassy Pictures)*

2–17. *Missing* **(U.S.A., 1982),** *with Sissy Spacek and Jack Lemmon, directed by Costa-Gavras.* Backgrounds are rarely neutral territory, especially in realistic films. Backgrounds contain information that helps characterize the foreground elements. The setting of this movie is the fascist police state of Chile. In a city morgue, the Spacek character has accidentally discovered the dead body of a friend. *(University City Studios)*

by Indians suggests ideas dealing with security and unity. In another context, such as *Last Tango in Paris,* circular shapes can have totally different implications (2–15).

Territorial Space

So far we have been concerned with the art of mise en scène primarily as it relates to the structuring of patterns on a two-dimensional surface. But since most movie images deal with the illusion of volume and depth, the film director must keep these theatrical considerations in mind while composing the visuals. It's one thing to construct a pleasing arrangement of shapes, lines, colors, and textures; but movie images must also tell a story in time, a story that generally involves human beings and their problems. Unlike notes of music, then, forms in film are not usually pure—they refer specifically to objects in reality.

Directors generally emphasize volume in their images precisely because they wish to avoid an abstract, flat look in their compositions. In most cases, filmmakers compose on three visual planes: the midground, the foreground, and the background. Not only does this technique suggest a sense of depth, it can also radically alter the dominant contrast of an image, serving as a kind of qualifying characteristic, either subtle or conspicuous. For example, a figure is often placed in the midground of a composition. Whatever is placed in the

55

foreground will comment on the figure in some way (2–14). Some foliage, for instance, is likely to suggest a naturalness and blending with the environment of nature. A gauzy curtain in the foreground can suggest mystery, eroticism, and femininity. The crosshatching of a window frame can suggest self-division. And so on, with as many foreground qualifiers as the director and cinematographer can think of. These same principles apply to backgrounds, although objects placed in these areas tend to yield in dominance to mid- and foreground ranges.

One of the most elementary, yet crucial, decisions the film director makes is what shot to employ vis-à-vis the materials photographed. That is, how much detail should be included within the frame? How close should the camera get to the subject—which is another way of saying how close should *we* get to the subject, since the viewer's eye tends to identify with the camera's lens. These are not minor problems, for the amount of space included within the frame can radically affect our response to the photographed materials. With any given subject, the filmmaker can employ a variety of shots, each of which includes or excludes a given amount of surrounding space. But how much space is just right in a shot? What's too much or too little?

Space is a medium of communication, and the way we respond to objects and people within a given area is a constant source of information in life as well as movies. In virtually any social situation, we receive and give off signals relat-

2–18. *A Night at the Opera* (U.S.A., 1935), *with Groucho, Chico, and Harpo Marx, directed by Sam Wood.*
The Marx Brothers were among the foremost **surrealists** of their era, subverting even the most commonplace assumptions—about space, for example. In this famous scene, people keep entering this tiny stateroom and going about their business as though it were the most natural thing in the world to remain packed into such a confined area.   *(MGM)*

2–19. *Grand Illusion* (France, 1938), *with (center to right) Erich von Stroheim, Pierre Fresnay, and Jean Gabin; directed by Jean Renoir.*
Tight framing allows for relatively little freedom of movement. The frame, in effect, becomes a symbolic prison, a useful technique in films dealing with entrapment, confinement, or literal imprisonment, like Renoir's World War I masterpiece.   (*Janus Films*)

ing to our use of space and those people who share it. Most of us aren't particularly conscious of this medium, but we instinctively become alerted whenever we feel that certain social conventions about space are being violated. For example, when people enter a movie theater, they tend to seat themselves at appropriate intervals from each other. But what's appropriate? And who or what defines it? Why do we feel threatened when someone takes a seat next to us in a nearly empty theater? After all, the seat isn't ours, and the other person has paid for the privilege of sitting wherever he wishes. Is it paranoid to feel anxiety in such a situation, or is it a normal instinctive response?

A number of psychologists and anthropologists—including Konrad Lorenz, Robert Sommers, and Edward T. Hall—have explored these and related questions. Their findings are especially revealing in terms of how space is used in cinema. In his study *On Aggression,* for example, Lorenz discusses how most animals—including humans—are territorial. That is, they lay claim to a given area and defend it from outsiders. This territory is a kind of personal haven of safety and is regarded by the organism as an extension of itself. When living creatures are too tightly packed into a given space, the result can be stress, tension, and anxiety. In many cases, when this territorial imperative is violated, the intrusion can provoke aggressive and violent behavior, and sometimes a battle for dominance ensues over control of the territory.

Territories also have a spatial hierarchy of power. That is, the most dominant organism of a community is literally given more space, whereas the less dominant are crowded together. The amount of space an organism occupies is generally proportioned to the degree of control it enjoys within a given territory. These spatial principles can be seen in many human communities as well. A classroom, for example, is usually divided into a teaching area and a student seating area, but the proportion of space allotted to the authority figure is greater than that alloted to each of those being instructed. The spatial structure of virtually any kind of territory used by humans betrays a discernible concept of authority. No matter how egalitarian we like to think ourselves, most of us conform to these spatial conventions. When a distinguished person enters a crowded room, for example, most people instinctively make room for him. In fact, they're giving him far more room than they themselves occupy.

But what has all this got to do with movies? A great deal, for space is one of the principal mediums of communication in film. The way that people are arranged in space can tell us a lot about their social and psychological relationships. In film, dominant characters are almost always given more space to occupy than others—unless the film deals with the loss of power or the social insignificance of a character. The amount of space taken up by a character in a movie doesn't necessarily relate to that person's actual social dominance, but to his or her dramatic importance. Authoritarian figures like kings generally occupy a larger amount of space than peasants; but if a film is primarily about peasants, they will dominate spatially. In short, dominance is defined contextually in film—not necessarily the way it's perceived in real life.

The movie frame is also a kind of territory, though a temporary one, existing only for the duration of the shot. The way space is shared within the frame is one of the major tools of the **metteur en scène,** who can define, adjust, and redefine human relationships by exploiting spatial conventions. Furthermore, once a relationship has been established, the director can go on to other matters simply by changing the camera **setup.** The film director, in other words, is not confined to a spatial area that is permanent throughout the scene. A master of mise en scène can express shifting psychological and social nuances with a single shot—by exploiting the space between characters, the depth planes

2–20. *Sons of the Desert* (U.S.A., 1933), *with Stan Laurel and Oliver Hardy, directed by William Seiter.*
Whenever Stan does something really dumb, which usually results in a loss of dignity for his partner, Ollie turns to the camera—to us—trying to restrain his exasperation, appealing to our sympathy as fellow superior beings. Only we can truly appreciate the profound depths of his patience. The dim-witted Stanley, totally puzzled as usual, is standing in a quarter-turn position, absorbed by other matters entirely, wondering how he'll defend himself against Ollie's inevitable another-fine-mess accusation. *(MGM)*

2–21. *Ironweed* **(U.S.A., 1987),** *with Jack Nicholson (right), directed by Hector Babenco.*
The profile position catches characters unaware as they look off frame left or right. We are allowed unimpeded freedom to stare, to analyze. Less intimate than the full-front or quarter-turn position, the profile view is also less emotionally involving. We view the characters from a detached, neutral perspective. *(Tri-Star Pictures)*

within the image, the intrinsically weighted areas of the frame, and the direction the characters are facing vis-à-vis the camera.

An actor can be photographed in any of five basic positions, each conveying different psychological undertones: (**1**) *full front*—facing the camera; (**2**) the *quarter turn;* (**3**) *profile*—looking off frame left or right; (**4**) the *three-quarter turn;* and (**5**) *back to camera.* Since the viewer identifies with the camera's lens, the positioning of the actor vis-à-vis the camera will determine many of our reactions. The more we see of his face, the greater our sense of privileged intimacy; the less we see, the more mysterious and inaccessible he will seem.

The full-front position is the most intimate—the character is looking in our direction, inviting our complicity. In most cases, of course, the actor ignores the camera—ignores us—yet our privileged position allows us to observe him without his defenses up, his vulnerabilities exposed. On those rare occasions when a character acknowledges our presence by addressing the camera, the sense of intimacy is vastly increased, for in effect we agree to become his chosen confidants. One of the greatest masters of this technique was Oliver Hardy, whose famous slow burn was a direct plea for sympathy and understanding (2–20).

The quarter turn is the favored position of most filmmakers, for it provides a high degree of intimacy but with less emotional involvement than the full-front position. The profile position is more remote. The character seems unaware of being observed, lost in his or her own thoughts (2–21). The three-quarter turn is more anonymous. This position is useful for conveying a character's unfriendly or antisocial feelings, for in effect, he is partially turning his back on us, rejecting our interest (2–22). When a character has his or her back to the camera, we can

2–22. *Night Moves* (U.S.A., 1975), *with Gene Hackman (extreme right, in three-quarter-turn position), directed by Arthur Penn.*
The three-quarter-turn position is a virtual rejection of the camera, a refusal to cooperate with our desire to see more. This type of staging tends to make us feel like voyeurs prying into the private affairs of the character, who seems to wish we'd go away. In this shot, Penn's mise en scène embodies a sense of alienation: Each character is imprisoned in his or her own space cubicle. They look buried alive.   *(Warner Bros.)*

only guess what's taking place internally. This postition is often used to suggest a character's alienation from the world. It is also useful in conveying a sense of concealment, mystery. We want to see more (2–23).

The amount of open space within the territory of the frame can be exploited for symbolic purposes. Generally speaking, the closer the shot, the more confined the photographed figures appear to be. Such shots are usually referred to as **tightly framed.** Conversely, the longer, **loosely framed** shots tend to suggest freedom. Prison films often employ tightly framed **close-ups** and medium shots because the frame functions as a kind of symbolic prison. In *A Condemned Man Escapes,* for example, Robert Bresson begins the movie with a close-up of the hero's hands, which are bound by a pair of handcuffs. Throughout the film, the prisoner makes elaborate preparations to escape, and Bresson preserves the tight framing to emphasize the sense of claustrophobia that the hero finds unendurable. This spatial tension is not released until the end of the movie when the protagonist disappears into the freedom of the darkness outside the prison walls. His triumphant escape is photographed in a loosely framed long shot—the only one in the film—which also symbolizes his sense of spiritual release. Framing and spatial metaphors of this kind are common in films dealing with the theme of confinement—either literal, as in Renoir's *Grand Illusion* (2–19), or psychological, as in *The Graduate* (2–16).

Often a director can suggest ideas of entrapment by exploiting perfectly neutral objects and lines on the set. In such cases, the formal characteristics of these literal objects tend to close in on a figure, at least when viewed on the flat screen (2--22). Michelangelo Antonioni is a supreme master of this technique. In

2–23. *Red Desert* **(Italy, 1964),** *with Monica Vitti and Richard Harris, directed by Michelangelo Antonioni.*
When characters turn their backs to the camera, they seem to reject us outright or to be totally unaware of our existence. We long to see and analyze their facial expressions, but we're not permitted this privilege. The character remains an enigma. If we identify with the character, as in this scene, we can be made to fear for her safety, for she is unprotected from the rear, too preoccupied with the danger in front of her. This is a position of maximum vulnerability. *(Rizzoli Film)*

Red Desert, for example, the heroine (Monica Vitti) describes a mental breakdown suffered by a friend she once knew. The audience suspects she's speaking of her own breakdown, however, for the surface of the image implies constriction: While she talks, she's riveted to one position, her figure framed by the lines of a doorway behind her, suggesting a coffinlike enclosure. When figures are framed within a frame in this manner, a sense of confinement is usually emphasized.

Territorial space within the frame can be manipulated with considerable psychological complexity. When a figure leaves the frame, for example, the camera can adjust to this sudden vacuum in the composition by **panning** slightly to make allowances for a new balance of weights. Or the camera can remain stationary, thus suggesting a sense of loss symbolized by the empty space that the character formerly occupied. Hostility and suspicion between two characters can be conveyed by keeping them at the edges of the composition, with a maximum of space between them (2–10a), or by having an intrusive character force his or her physical presence into the other character's territory, which is temporarily defined by the confines of the frame.

Proxemic Patterns

Spatial conventions vary from culture to culture, as anthropologist Edward T. Hall has demonstrated in such studies as *The Hidden Dimension* and *The Silent Language.* Hall discovered that **proxemic** patterns—the relationships of organ-

2–24. *The Golden Positions* **(U.S.A., 1970),** *directed by James Broughton.*
In stylized genres such as musicals, fantasy films, and, shown here, avant-garde movies, the proxemic conventions of everyday life are often violated in favor of a striking visual effect. Space, in such instances, functions as an abstract ground for the figures. Broughton takes impish delight in lampooning human absurdities. In this shot, he zaps the prim correctness of his two ladies by presenting them in the buff. Ironically, their sagging, vulnerable flesh is the main source of their humanity. *(Anthology Film Archives)*

isms within a given space—can be influenced by external considerations. Climate, noise level, and the degree of light all tend to alter the space between individuals. People in Anglo-Saxon and Northern European cultures tend to use more space than those in warmer climates. Noise, danger, and lack of light tend to make people move closer together. Taking these cultural and contextual considerations into account, Hall subdivides the way people use space into four major proxemic patterns: **(1)** the *intimate,* **(2)** the *personal,* **(3)** the *social,* and **(4)** the *public* distances.

Intimate distances range from skin contact to about eighteen inches away. This is the distance of physical involvement—of love, comfort, and tenderness between individuals. With strangers, such distances would be regarded as intrusive—most people would react with suspicion and hostility if their space were invaded by someone they didn't know very well. In many cultures, maintaining an intimate distance in public is considered bad taste.

The personal distance ranges roughly from eighteen inches away to about four feet away. Individuals can touch if necessary, since they are literally an arm's-length apart. These distances tend to be reserved for friends and acquaintances rather than lovers or members of a family. Personal distances preserve the privacy between individuals, yet these ranges don't necessarily suggest exclusion, as intimate distances almost always do.

Social distances range from four feet to about twelve feet. These are the distances usually reserved for impersonal business and casual social gatherings. It's a friendly range in most cases, yet somewhat more formal than the personal distance. Ordinarily, social distances are necessary when there are more than three members of a group. In some cases, it would be considered rude for two individuals to preserve an intimate or personal distance within a social situation. Such behavior might be interpreted as standoffish.

Public distances extend from twelve feet to twenty-five feet and more. This range tends to be formal and rather detached. Displays of emotion are consid-

2–25. *Persona* **(Sweden, 1966),** *with Liv Ullmann, directed by Ingmar Bergman.*
Throughout this scene, which contains no dialogue, Bergman uses space to communicate his ideas—space within the frame and the space implied between the camera (us) and the subject. The character is in a hospital room watching the news on television (a). Suddenly, she sees a horrifying scene of a Buddhist monk setting himself on fire to protest the war in Vietnam. She retreats to the corner of the room, to the very edge of the frame (b). Bergman then cuts to a closer shot (c), intensifying our emotional involvement. The full horror of her reaction is conveyed by the extreme close-up (d), bringing us into an intimate proximity with her.　*(United Artists)*

(a)　　　　　　　　　　　　　　　　　　　　(b)

(c)　　　　　　　　　　　　　　　　　　　　(d)

ered bad form at these distances. Important public figures are generally seen in the public range, and because a considerable amount of space is involved, people generally must exaggerate their gestures and raise their voices in order to be understood clearly.

Most people adjust to proxemic patterns instinctively. We don't usually say to ourselves, "This guy is invading my intimate space" when a stranger happens to stand eighteen inches away from us. However, unless we're in a combative mood, we involuntarily tend to step away in such circumstances. Obviously, social context is also a determining factor in proxemic patterns. In a crowded subway car, for example, virtually everyone is in an intimate range, yet we generally preserve a public attitude by not speaking to the person whose body is literally pressed against our own.

Proxemic patterns are perfectly obvious to anyone who has bothered to observe the way people obey certain spatial conventions in actual life. But in movies, these patterns are also related to the **shots** and their distance ranges. Although shots are not always defined by the literal space between the camera and the object photographed, in terms of psychological effect, shots tend to suggest physical distances.

Usually filmmakers have a number of options concerning what kind of shot to use to convey the action of a scene. What determines their choice—though usually instinctively rather than consciously—is the emotional impact of the different proxemic ranges. Each proxemic pattern has an approximate camera equivalent. The intimate distances, for example, can be likened to the close and **extreme close shot** ranges. The personal distance is approximately a medium close range. The social distances correspond to the medium and **full shot** ranges. And the public distances are roughly within the long and **extreme long shot** ranges. Since our eyes identify with the camera's lens, in effect we are placed within these ranges vis-à-vis the subject matter. When we are offered a close-up of a character, for example, in a sense we feel that we're in an intimate relationship with that character. In some instances, this technique can bind us to the character, forcing us to care about him, and to identify with his problems. If the character is a villain, the close-up can produce an emotional revulsion in us; in effect, a threatening character seems to be invading our space.

In general, the greater the distance between the camera and the subject, the more emotionally neutral we remain. Public proxemic ranges tend to encourage a certain detachment. Conversely, the closer we are to a character, the more we feel that we're in proximity with him, and hence, the greater our emotional involvement. "Long shot for comedy, close-up for tragedy" was one of Chaplin's most famous pronouncements. The proxemic principles are sound, for when we are close to an action—a person slipping on a banana peel, for example—it's seldom funny, because we are concerned for the person's safety. If we see the same event from a greater distance, however, it often strikes us as comical. Chaplin used close-ups sparingly for this very reason. So long as Charlie remains in long shots, we tend to be amused by his antics and absurd predicaments. In scenes of greater emotional impact, however, Chaplin resorted to closer shots, and their effect is often devastating on the audience. We suddenly realize that the situation we've been laughing at is no longer funny.

Perhaps the most famous instance of the power of Chaplin's close-ups is

found at the conclusion of *City Lights*. Charlie has fallen in love with an impoverished flower vendor who is blind. She believes him to be an eccentric millionaire,
and out of vanity he allows her to continue in this delusion. By engaging in a
series of monumental labors—love has reduced him to work—he manages to
scrape together enough money for her to receive an operation that will restore
her sight. But he is dragged off to jail before she can scarcely thank him for the
money. The final scene takes place several months later. The young woman can
now see and owns her own modest flower shop. Charlie is released from prison,
and disheveled and dispirited, he meanders past her shop window. She sees him
gazing at her wistfully and jokes to an assistant that she's apparently made a new
conquest. Out of pity she goes out to the street and offers him a flower and a
small coin. Instantly she recognizes his touch. Hardly able to believe her eyes,

(a)

2–26a. *The Gold Rush* (U.S.A., 1925),
*with Charles Chaplin and Georgia Hale,
directed by Chaplin.*

2–26b. *City Lights* (U.S.A., 1931), *with
Charles Chaplin, directed by Chaplin.*

Both these scenes involve a fear of rejection by a woman Charlie holds in awe.
The scene from *The Gold Rush* is predominantly comical. The tramp has belted his
baggy pants with a piece of rope, but he
doesn't realize it is also a dog's leash, and
while dancing with the saloon girl, Charlie is yanked to the floor by the jittery
dog at the other end of the rope. Because
the camera remains relatively distant
from the action, we tend to be more objective and detached and to laugh at his
futile attempts to preserve his dignity.
On the other hand, the famous final shot
from *City Lights* isn't funny at all, and
produces a powerful emotional effect. Because the camera is in close, *we* get close
to the situation. The proxemic distance
between the camera and the subject
forces us to identify more with his feelings, which we can't ignore at this
range. (*rbc Films*)

(b)

she can only stammer, "You?" In a series of alternating close-ups, their embarrassment is unbearably prolonged (2–26b). Clearly he is not the idol of her romantic fantasies, and he is painfully aware of her disappointment. Finally he stares at her with an expression of shocking emotional nakedness. The film ends on this image of sublime vulnerability.

   The choice of a shot is generally determined by practical considerations. Usually the director selects the shot that most clearly conveys the dramatic action of a scene. If there is a conflict between the effect of certain proxemic ranges and the clarity needed to convey what's going on, most filmmakers will opt for clarity and gain their emotional impact through some other means. But there are many times when shot choice isn't necessarily determined by functional considerations. For example, if a scene calls for a shot of a man reading alone at a table, the director has a number of options, determined at least in part by proxemic considerations. A functional stylist like Howard Hawks would probably have photographed the scene in a medium shot, showing the upper part of the man's body and the table top. A comic realist like Chaplin would probably have used a full or long shot to prevent the audience from identifying too much with the character and to permit us to see the social context. A predominantly formalist filmmaker like Hitchcock usually wanted the audience to identify with his protagonists, and he probably would have offered us a number of close-ups of the man's face and the objects on the table to emphasize an emotional sequence

2–27. Fatal Attraction (U.S.A., 1987), *with Glenn Close and Michael Douglas, directed by Adrian Lyne.*

The most powerful scenes in this psychological thriller have to do with the invasion of space. Douglas plays a married man who has a one-night stand with the Close character. Feeling used, she tries to reestablish contact, but he rebuffs her. However, she will not be ignored. She invades his workplace. Again, he rejects her—after all, he's a happily married man. The scorned woman becomes obsessed, and in revenge, she throws acid on his car. Still no response. Like an avenging fury, she finally invades his home—threatening his doubly wronged wife and their small child. *(Paramount Pictures)* of ideas. A director like Antonioni might portray the scene in an extreme long shot to suggest the man's loneliness and alienation. As with virtually every other cinematic technique, then, the dramatic context determines the choice of shot and its proxemic effects.

Open and Closed Forms

The concepts of **open** and **closed forms** are generally employed by art historians and critics, but these terms can also be useful in film analysis. Like most theoretical constructs, they are best employed in a relative rather than absolute sense. There are no movies that are completely open or closed in form, only those that tend toward these polarities. Like other critical terms, these should be applied only when they are relevant and helpful in understanding what actually exists in a movie. If the concepts don't seem relevant, they should be discarded and replaced with something that is. Criticism is the handmaiden of art, not vice versa.

Open and closed forms are two distinct attitudes about reality. Each has its own stylistic and technical characteristics. The two terms are loosely related to

2–28. *The Garden of the Finzi-Continis* (Italy, 1970), *with Dominique Sanda (center), directed by Vittorio De Sica.*

Realist directors are more likely to prefer open forms, which tend to suggest fragments of a larger external reality. Design and composition are generally informal. Influenced by the aesthetic of the documentary, open form images seem to have been discovered rather than arranged. Excessive balance and calculated symmetry are avoided in favor of an intimate and spontaneous effect. Still photos in open form are seldom picturesque or obviously artful. Instead, they suggest a frozen instant of truth—a snapshot wrested from the fluctuations of time. *(Cinema 5)*

the concepts of realism and formalism as they have been defined in these chapters. In general, realist filmmakers tend to employ open forms, while formalists lean toward closed. Open forms tend to be stylistically recessive, whereas closed forms are generally self-conscious and conspicuous.

In terms of visual design, open form emphasizes informal, unobtrusive compositions. Often such images seem to have no discernible structure, and suggest a random form of organization. Objects and figures seem to have been found, rather than deliberately arranged (2–28). Closed form emphasizes a more stylized design. While such images can suggest a superficial realism, seldom do they have that accidental, discovered look that typifies open forms. Objects and figures are more precisely placed within the frame, and the balance of weights is elaborately worked out.

Open forms stress apparently simple techniques because with these unself-conscious methods the filmmaker is able to emphasize the immediate, the famil-

2–29. *Joseph Andrews* **(Great Britain, 1976),** *with John Bull (in sedan chair), Ann-Margret, and Peter Firth, directed by Tony Richardson.*
Good movies employ open and closed forms organically, depending on the nature of the subject matter. Like its companion piece *Tom Jones* (which is also based on a classic novel by Henry Fielding), Richardson's movie often employs open forms to suggest the tumultuous sprawl of its eighteenth-century setting. People stream in and out of the frame, obscuring our view of the main characters. The images are in constant flux, too hurried and haphazardly composed to settle down into a prettily arranged picture. Many of these scenes were photographed with a hand-held camera, to suggest an impromptu documentary recording. *(Paramount Pictures)*

2–30. ***Another Country*** **(Great Britain, 1984),** *with Rupert Everett (center doorway), directed by Marek Kanievska.*
In closed form, the frame is a self-sufficient miniature universe with all the formal elements held in careful balance. Though there may be more information outside the frame, for the duration of any given shot this information is visually irrelevant. Closed forms are often employed in scenes dealing with entrapment or confinement, such as this shot in which the protagonist is about to be disciplined by his boarding school superiors.   (*Orion Classics*)

iar, the intimate aspects of reality. Sometimes such images are photographed in only partially controlled situations, and these **aleatory** conditions can produce a sense of spontaneity and directness that would be difficult to capture in a rigidly controlled context (2–29). Closed forms are more likely to emphasize the unfamiliar. The images are rich in textural contrasts and compelling visual effects. Because the mise en scène is more precisely controlled and stylized, there is often a deliberate artificiality in these images—a sense of visual improbability, of being one remove from reality. Closed forms also tend to be more densely saturated with visual information; richness of form takes precedence over considerations of surface realism. If a conflict should arise, formal beauty is sacrificed for truth in open forms; in closed forms, on the other hand, literal truth is sacrificed for beauty.

Compositions in open and closed forms exploit the frame differently. In open-form images, the frame tends to be deemphasized. It suggests a window, a temporary masking, and implies that more important information lies outside the edges of the composition. Space is continuous in these shots, and to emphasize its continuity outside the frame, directors often favor panning their camera across the locale. The shot seems inadequate, too narrow in its confines to contain the copiousness of the subject matter. Like many of the paintings of Edgar Degas (who usually favored open forms), objects and even figures are arbitrarily cut off by the frame to reinforce the continuity of the subject matter beyond the formal edges of the composition. In closed forms, the shot represents a miniature proscenium arch, with all the necessary information carefully structured within the confines of the frame. Space seems enclosed and self-contained rather than continuous. Elements outside the frame are irrelevant, at least in terms of the formal properties of the individual shot, which is isolated from its context in space and time (2–30).

For these reasons, still photos taken from movies that are predominantly in open form are not usually very pretty. There is nothing intrinsically striking or eye-catching about them. Books about movies tend to favor photos in closed form because they are usually more obviously beautiful, more "composed." The beauty of an open-form image, on the other hand, is more elusive. It can be likened to a snapshot that miraculously preserves some candid rare expression, a kind of haphazard instant of truth. Open form also tends to value a certain visual ambiguity. Often the charm of such images lies precisely in their impenetrability—a mysterious half smile on the face of a character, an evocative shadow that casts a strange pattern across the set.

In open-form movies, the dramatic action generally leads the camera. In such movies as *Faces* and *Husbands,* for example, John Cassavetes emphasized the fluidity of the camera as it dutifully follows the actors wherever they wish to go, seemingly placed at their disposal. Such films suggest that chance plays an important role in determining visual effects. Needless to say, it's not what actually happens on a set that's important, but what *seems* to be happening on the screen. In fact, many of the simplest effects in an open-form movie are achieved after much painstaking labor and manipulation.

In closed-form films, on the other hand, the camera often anticipates the dramatic action. Objects and actors are visually blocked out within the confines of a predetermined camera setup. **Anticipatory setups** tend to imply fatality or determinism, for in effect, the camera seems to know what will happen even before it occurs. In the films of Fritz Lang, for example, the camera often seems to be waiting in an empty room: The door opens, the characters enter, and the action then begins. In some of Hitchcock's movies, a character is seen at the edge of the composition, and the camera seems to be placed in a disadvantageous position, too far removed from where the action is apparently going to occur. But then the character decides to return to that area where the camera has been waiting. When such setups are used, the audience also tends to anticipate actions. Instinctively, we expect something or someone to fill in the visual vacuum of the shot. Philosophically, open forms tend to suggest freedom of choice, a multiplicity of options open to the characters. Closed forms, conversely, tend to imply destiny and the futility of the will: The characters don't seem to make the important decisions, the camera does—and in advance.

Needless to say, open and closed forms are most effective in movies where these techniques are appropriate to the subject matter. A prison film employing mostly open forms is not likely to be emotionally convincing. Most movies employ both open and closed forms, depending on the specific dramatic context. Renoir's *Grand Illusion,* for example, uses closed forms for the prison camp scenes, and open forms after two of the prisoners escape.

Like most cinematic techniques, open and closed forms have certain limitations as well as advantages. When used to excess, open forms can seem sloppy

(a)

2–31a & b. *Full Metal Jacket* (Great Britain/U.S.A., 1988), directed by Stanley Kubrick.
Even within a single scene, filmmakers will switch from open to closed forms, depending on
the feelings or ideas that are being stressed in each individual shot. For example, both of
these shots take place during a battle scene in the Vietnamese city of Hue. In 2–31a, the
characters are under fire, and the wounded soldier's head is not even in the frame. The form
is appropriately open. The frame functions as a temporary masking device that's too narrow
in its scope to include all the relevant information. Often the frame seems to cut figures off in
an arbitrary manner in open form, suggesting that the action is continued off screen, like
newsreel footage that was fortuitously photographed by a cameraman who was unable to
superimpose an artistic form over his runaway materials. In 2–31b, the form is closed, as four
soldiers rush to their wounded comrade, providing a protective buffer from the outside
world. Open and closed forms aren't intrinsically meaningful, then, but derive their significance from the dramatic context. In some cases, closed forms can suggest entrapment (2–
30); in other cases, such as 2–31b, closed form implies security, camaraderie.   *(Warner Bros.)*

(b)

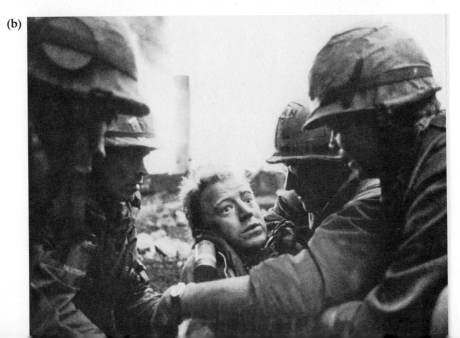

and naive, like an artless home movie. Too often open forms can seem uncontrolled, unfocused, and even visually ugly. Occasionally, these techniques are so blandly unobtrusive that the visuals are boring. On the other hand, closed forms can seem arty and pretentious. The images are so unspontaneous that their visual elements look computer-programmed. Many viewers are turned off by the stagey flamboyance of some closed-form films. At their worst, these movies can seem decadently overwrought—all icing and no cake.

A systematic mise en scène analysis of any given shot includes the following twelve elements:

1. *Shot and camera proxemics.* What type of shot? How far away from the action is the camera?

2–32. *The Little Foxes* (U.S.A., 1941), *with Bette Davis (center), directed by William Wyler.* Space is ideologically charged: How people are arranged in space can suggest power. In this shot, for example, Wyler places the most ruthless character (Davis) in the center of the image—a position of dominance. She is also the highest in the frame, towering above the other two figures, whom she regards with contempt. She also takes up the most space, even though she is a small woman. *(RKO)*

2. *Angle.* Are we looking up or down on the subject, or is the camera neutral (eye-level)?

3. *Lens and/or filter.* How do these distort or comment on the photographed materials?

4. *Lighting style.* High or low key? High contrast? Some combination of these?

5. *Dominant.* Where is our eye attracted first?

6. *Subsidiaries.* Where does our eye travel after taking in the dominant?

7. *Composition.* How is the two-dimensional space segmented and organized? What is the underlying design?

8. *Form.* Open or closed? Does the image suggest a window that arbitrarily isolates a fragment of the scene? Or a proscenium arch, in which the visual elements are carefully arranged and held in balance?

9. *Framing.* Tight or loose? Do the characters have no room to move around in, or can they move freely without impediments?

10. *Depth.* On how many planes is the image composed? Does the background or foreground comment in any way on the midground?

11. *Staging positions.* Which way do the characters look vis-à-vis the camera?

12. *Character proxemics.* How much space is there between the characters?

In these first two chapters, we have been concerned with the most important source of meaning in the cinema—the visual image. But of course movies exist in time and have many other ways of communicating information. Photography and mise en scène are merely two language systems of many. For this reason, a film image must sometimes be restrained or less saturated with meanings than a painting or still photo, in which all the necessary information is contained within a single image. The principles of variation and restraint exist in all temporal arts. In movies, these principles can be seen in those images that seem rather uninteresting, usually because the dominant is found elsewhere—in the music, for example, or the **editing.** In a sense, these images are visual rest areas.

A filmmaker has literally hundreds of different ways to convey meanings. Like the painter or still photographer, the movie director can emphasize visual dominants. In a scene portraying violence, for example, he or she can use diagonal and zigzagging lines, aggressive colors, close-ups, extreme angles, harsh lighting contrasts, unbalanced compositions, large shapes, and so on. Unlike most other visual artists, the filmmaker can also suggest violence through movement, either of the subject itself or of the camera. The film artist can suggest violence through editing, by having one shot collide with another in a kaleidoscopic explosion of different perspectives. Furthermore, through the use of the sound track, violence can be conveyed by loud or rapid dialogue, harsh sound effects, or strident music. Precisely because there are so many ways to convey a given effect, the filmmaker will vary the emphasis, sometimes stressing image, sometimes movement, other times sound. Occasionally, especially in climactic scenes, all three are employed at the same time.

2–33. *M* **(Germany, 1931),** *directed by Fritz Lang.*

A mise en scène analysis involves a breakdown of the major components of a film image in relation to its dramatic context. This shot takes place near the end of the movie. A psychotic child-killer (Peter Lorre, extreme right) has been hunted down by the members of the underworld. These "normal" criminals have taken him to an abandoned warehouse where they intend to try and execute the psychopath for his heinous crimes—in order to take the police heat off themselves. In this scene, the killer is confronted by a witness (center) who holds an incriminating piece of evidence—a balloon. The components of the shot include: (1) The *shot* is slightly more distant than a full shot. The *camera's proxemic range* from the protagonist and his accusor is personal; from the two guards on the stairs, social. (2) The *angle* is slightly high, suggesting an air of fatality. (3) A standard *lens* is used, with no apparent *filters.* (4) The *lighting* is in murky low key, with high-contrast spotlights on the balloon and the four main figures. (5) The *dominant* is the balloon, the brightest object in the frame (when the photo is turned upside down and converted to a pattern of abstract shapes, its dominance is more readily discernible). (6) The principal *subsidiary contrasts* are the figures of the killer, the witness, and the two criminals in the upper left. (7) The *composition* is divided into three general areas—left, center, and right—suggesting instability. (8) The *form* is definitely closed, the frame suggesting a constricting cell. (9) The *framing* is tight: The killer is trapped in the same territory with his threatening accusors; they tower above him, sealing off any avenue of escape, while he cowers below at the extreme right edge, almost falling into the symbolic blackness outside the frame. (10) The image is composed on three *depth* planes: the two figures in the foreground, the two figures on the stairs in the midground, and the brick wall of the back-ground. (11) The accusors stand in a quarter-turn *position,* implying a greater intimacy with us than the protagonist, who is in the profile position, totally unaware of anything but his own terror. (12) The *character proxemics* are personal between the foreground characters and intimate between the men on the stairs. The range between the two pairs is social.   *(Janus Films)*

FURTHER READING

ARNHEIM, RUDOLF, *Art and Visual Perception: A Psychology of the Creative Eye* (Berkeley: University of California Press, 1954). Primarily about paintings and drawings.

———, *Towards a Psychology of Art* (Berkeley: University of California Press, 1966). A theoretical discussion emphasizing a gestalt approach.

BORDWELL, DAVID, JANET STAIGER, and KRISTIN THOMPSON, *The Classical Hollywood Cinema: Film Style and Mode of Production to 1960* (New York: Columbia University Press, 1985). Scholarly study.

BRAUDY, LEO, *The World in a Frame* (Garden City, N.Y.: Doubleday, 1976). Filled with intelligent insights.

DONDIS, DONIS A., *A Primer of Visual Literacy* (Cambridge, Mass., and London, England: The M.I.T. Press, 1974). Primarily on design and composition.

FREEBURG, VICTOR O., *Pictoral Beauty on the Screen* (New York: Macmillan, 1923). A discussion of the conventions of classical composition.

HALL, EDWARD T., *The Hidden Dimension* (Garden City, N.Y.: Doubleday, 1969). How humans and other animals use space.

NILSEN, VLADIMIR, *The Cinema as a Graphic Art* (New York: Hill and Wang, 1959). How reality is shaped by form, with major emphasis on classical composition.

RUESCH, JURGEN, and WELDON KEES, *Nonverbal Communication* (Berkeley: University of California Press, 1966).

SOMMERS, ROBERT, *Personal Space* (Englewood Cliffs, N.J.: Prentice-Hall, 1969). How individuals use and abuse space.

MOVEMENT | 3

*The opening of a door, a hand, or an eye can bring about a climax
as thrilling as a crash of locomotives on the screen.*

—RICHARD DYER MACCANN

"Movies," "motion pictures," "moving pictures"—all these phrases suggest the central importance of motion in the art of film. *Cinema* derives from the Greek word for "movement," as do the words *kinetic, kinesthesia,* and *choreography*—terms usually associated with the art of dance. Yet oddly enough, filmgoers and critics give surprisingly little consideration to movement per se as a medium of communication, as a language system. Like the image itself, motion is usually thought of in terms of gross subject matter. We tend to remember "what happens" only in a general sense. If we were to describe a sequence from a ballet in such vague terms, our discussion would certainly strike the sophisticated dance enthusiast as naive. Yet cinematic sequences—which can be choreographed with just as much or even greater complexity—are seldom appreciated for their kinetic richness and beauty.

Kinetics

Like images, motion can be literal and concrete or highly stylized and **lyrical.** In the kinetic arts—pantomime, mime, ballet, modern dance—we find a wide variety of movements, ranging from the realistic to the formally abstract. This stylistic spectrum can also be seen in movies. For example, a naturalistic actor like Spencer Tracy employed only realistic movements, the same sort that could be observed in actual life. Tracy moves so simply in his films that he hardly seems to be acting. Pantomimists are more stylized in their movements. Chaplin, for example, tended to employ motion more balletically, more symbolically. A swag-

3-1. *Le Bal* (France/Italy), *directed by Ettore Scola.*
This feature-length movie traces the manners and mores of the World War II era in France entirely through dance. Each sketch is choreographed in a different dance style. *(Almi Classics)*

gering gait and a twirling cane symbolized Charlie's (usually fleeting) arrogance and conceit.

Even more stylized are the movements of performers in a musical. In this **genre,** characters express their most intense emotions through song and dance. A dance number is seldom meant to be taken literally: It's a stylized **convention** that we accept as a symbolic expression of certain feelings and ideas. In *Singin' in the Rain,* for example, Gene Kelly does an elaborate dance routine in a downpour (3–2). He twirls around lampposts, splashes through puddles like a happy idiot, and leaps ecstatically through a pelting rain—literally nothing can dampen the exhilaration of his love. A wide gamut of emotions is expressed in this sequence, with each kinetic variation symbolizing the character's feelings about his girl. She can make him feel dreamy, childlike, erotically stimulated, brave and forthright, dopey and moonstruck, and finally wild with joy. In some kinds of action genres, physical contests are stylized in a similar manner. Samurai and kung-fu films, for example, often feature elaborately choreographed sequences.

Ballet and mime are even more abstract and stylized. A great mime like Marcel Marceau is not so much concerned with expressing literal ideas (which is more properly the province of pantomime) as the *essence* of an idea, stripped of superfluities. A twisted torso can suggest an ancient tree, bent elbows its crooked branches, fluttering fingers the rippling of its leaves. In ballet, movements can be so stylized that we can't always assign a discernible content to them, though the narrative context generally provides us with at least a vague sense of what the movements are supposed to represent. On this level of abstraction, however, movements acquire self-justifying characteristics. They are lyri-

3–2. *Singin' in the Rain* (U.S.A., 1952), *with Gene Kelly, choreography by Kelly, directed by Kelly and Stanley Donen.*
Kelly worked in a broad range of dancing styles—tap, ballroom, modern dance, and ballet. He was usually at his best in muscular, gymnastic styles, with an emphasis on virile trajectories and bravura leaps. But he was also charming in nonchalant styles, to which he usually added a characteristic swagger. He often incorporated lengthy ballet sequences in his films, generally a dream sequence or a fantasy. Above all, Kelly's dancing is sexy, with an emphasis on pelvic movements, tensed loins, twisting torsos, and erotic, close-to-the-floor gyrations. He usually wore close-fitting clothes to emphasize his well-muscled body. He also allowed his personality to shine through, breaking the formality of the choreography with a cocky grin or an ecstatic smile that's as hammy as it is irresistible. (*MGM*)

3-3. *Roxanne* (U.S.A., 1987), *with Steve Martin and Kevin Nealon, directed by Fred Schepisi.* Physical contests such as brawls, swordfights, and Oriental self-defense methods can be choreographed with considerable kinetic force. Steve Martin's graceful script is a loose adaptation of Rostand's famous play, *Cyrano de Bergerac.* The period swordfights of the play are comically transposed into contemporary feats of physical agility. *(Columbia Pictures)*

cal: That is, we respond to them more for their own beauty than for their function as symbolic expressions of ideas.

This concern with kinetic beauty for its own sake can be seen in certain schools of modern dance. Many of the choreographies of Merce Cunningham and Erick Hawkins, for example, aren't meant to symbolize anything of a narrative nature. Abstract motion is presented for its own sake, somewhat in the same manner that pure colors, shapes, and lines are offered for their own sakes in nonrepresentational painting. In movies, nonrepresentational movements are most often found in **avant-garde** films, which seldom tell stories.

In dance, movements are defined by the space that encloses the choreography—a three-dimensional stage. In film, the **frame** performs a similar function. However, with each **setup** change, the cinematic "stage" is redefined. The intrinsic meanings associated with various portions of the frame are closely related to the significance of certain kinds of movements. For example, with vertical movements, an upward motion seems soaring and free because it conforms to the eye's natural tendency to move upward over a composition. Movements in this direction often suggest aspiration, joy, power, and authority—those ideas associated with the superior portions of the frame. Downward movements suggest opposite ideas: grief, death, insignificance, depression, weakness, and so on.

Since the eye tends to read a picture from left to right, physical movement in this direction seems psychologically natural, whereas movement from the right to left often seems inexplicably tense and uncomfortable. The sensitive filmmaker exploits these psychological phenomena to reinforce the dramatic ideas. Frequently the protagonists of a movie travel toward the right of the screen,

3–4. *Dames* (U.S.A., 1934), *choreographed by Busby Berkeley, directed by Ray Enright.*
Berkeley liberated the camera from the tyranny of the proscenium arch. He often photographed his dancers from unusual angles, like this **bird's-eye shot.** His style was the most abstract of all American choreographers. He sometimes didn't even bother to use dancers, preferring a uniform contingent of comely maidens who are used as camera material, like bits of glass in a shifting kaleidoscope of formal patterns.   (*Warner Bros.*)

while the villains move toward the left. In John Huston's *The Red Badge of Courage,* the hero moves from right to left when he runs away from a battle in fear. Later, when he courageously joins an infantry charge, his movements are from left to right.

Movement can be directed toward or away from the camera. Since we identify with the camera's lens, the effect of such movements is somewhat like a character moving toward or away from us. If the character is a villain, walking toward the camera can seem aggressive, hostile, and threatening, for in effect, he's invading our space. If the character is attractive, movement toward the camera seems friendly, inviting, sometimes seductive. In either case, movement toward the audience is generally strong and assertive, suggesting confidence on the part of the moving character.

Movement away from the camera tends to imply opposite meanings. Intensity is decreased and the character seems to grow remote as he or she withdraws from us. Audiences feel safer when a villain moves away in this manner, for he thereby increases the protective distance between us and him. In some contexts, such movements can seem weak, fearful, and suspicious. Most movies end with a withdrawal of some sort, either of the camera from the locale or of the characters from the camera.

There are considerable psychological differences between lateral movements on the screen and depth movements—that is, movements toward or away from the camera. A script might simply call for a character to move from one place to another, but *how* the director chooses to photograph this movement will determine much of its psychological implications. Generally speaking, if the character moves from right to left (or vice versa), he or she will seem determined and efficient, a person of action (3–5). Unless the camera is at **extreme long shot** range, these movements are necessarily photographed in brief **takes**—shots last-

3–5. *White Nights* **(U.S.A., 1986),** *with Gregory Hines and Mikhail Baryshnikov, directed by Taylor Hackford.*
Lateral movements tend to emphasize speed, decisiveness, and excitement. Such shots are usually brief, for the amount of time required to move from one side of the frame to the other is minimal.   *(Columbia Pictures)*

ing only a few seconds. Since lateral movements tend to emphasize speed and efficiency, they are often used in action movies.

On the other hand, when a character moves in or out of the depth of a scene, the effect is often one of slowness. Unless the camera is at close range or an extreme **wide-angle lens** is used, movements toward or away from the camera take longer to photograph than lateral movements. With a **telephoto lens,** such movements can seem hopelessly dragged out. Furthermore, when depth movement is photographed in an uninterrupted lengthy take, the audience tends to anticipate the conclusion of the movement, thus intensifying the sense of tedium while we wait for the character to arrive at his destination. Especially when a character's physical goal is apparent—the length of a long corridor, for example—audiences generally grow restless if they are forced to view the entire movement (3–6).

Most classical filmmakers would photograph the action in several different setups, thus compressing the time and space from the inception of the movement to its conclusion. Classical filmmakers also tend to stage movement diagonally, to create a more dynamic trajectory of motion.

The distance and **angle** from which movement is photographed determine much of its meaning. In general, the longer and higher the shot, the slower the movement tends to appear. If movement is recorded from close and low angles, it seems more intense, speeded up. A director can photograph the same subject—a running man, for example—in two different setups and produce oppo-

(a)

(b)

3–6. *L'Avventura* **(Italy, 1960),** *with Monica Vitti, directed by Michelangelo Antonioni.*
Psychological films often employ movements in and out of the depth of an image, especially
to create a sense of tediousness and exhaustion. Shots of this sort require **anticipatory
setups** that reinforce these qualities, for we see the destination of a character's movement
long before it's completed. Here, the heroine's search for her lover in the corridors of a hotel
suggests the futility of her love affair. The endless succession of doors, fixtures, and hallways
implies, among other things, the repetition of the frustration she is now experiencing. Much
of the meaning of shots such as these lies in their duration: Space is used to suggest time.
Needless to say, Antonioni's movies are among the slowest paced of the contemporary
cinema: Long after the viewer has had time to absorb the visual information of a shot, it
continues on the screen. When this film was originally shown at the Cannes Film Festival, an
audience of hostile critics kept shouting "Cut! Cut!" at the screen. The shots were so lengthy
and the pace so slow that viewers assumed the director was inept at editing. But like many of
Antonioni's works, *L'Avventura* is about spiritual erosion, and the movie's slow rhythm is
organically related to this theme. *(Janus Films)*

site meanings. If the man is photographed in an extreme long shot from a high angle, he will seem ineffectual and impotent. If he's photographed from a low angle in a **medium shot,** he will seem a dynamo of energy. Despite the fact that the subject matter in each setup is absolutely identical, the true content of each shot is its form.

Even film critics (who should know better) are often ignorant of these perceptual differences, thinking of movement only in terms of story and gross physical action. The result has been a good deal of naive theorizing on what is "intrinsically cinematic." The more movement is perceived as extravagant in real life, they argue, the more "filmic" it becomes. **Epic** events and exterior locations are presumed to be fundamentally more suited to the medium than intimate, restricted, or interior subjects. Such views are based on a misunderstanding of movement in film. True, one can use the terms epic and psychological in describing the general emphasis of a movie. Even on this general level, however, arguments about intrinsically cinematic subjects are usually crude. No sensible person would claim that Tolstoy's *War and Peace* is intrinsically more novelistic than Dostoyevsky's *Crime and Punishment,* although we may refer to one as an epic and the other as a psychological novel. In a similar vein, only a naive viewer would claim that Michelangelo's *Sistine Ceiling* is intrinsically more visual than a Vermeer painting of a domestic scene. It is different, yes, but not necessarily better or worse, and certainly not through any intrinsic quality. In short, there are some good and bad epic works of art, and some good and bad psychological works. It's the treatment that counts, not the material per se.

Movement in film is a subtle issue, for it's necessarily dependent on the kind of shot employed. The cinematic close-up can convey as much movement as the most sweeping vistas in an extreme long shot. In fact, in terms of the area covered on the screen's surface, there is actually more movement in a close-up showing tears running down a person's face than there is in an extreme long shot of a parachutist drifting fifty feet (3–7).

Epic and psychological movies employ movement in different ways, with emphasis on different shots. Epic movies usually depend on the longer shots for their effects, whereas psychological films tend to employ the closer shots. Epics are concerned with a sense of sweep and breadth, psychological movies with depth and detail. Epics often emphasize events, psychological films the implications of events. One stresses action, the other reaction.

Two filmmakers can approach the same story and produce totally different results. *Hamlet* is a good example. Laurence Olivier's film version of this play is essentially an epic, with emphasis on the longer shots. Tony Richardson's version is primarily a psychological study, dominated by close and medium shots. Olivier's movie emphasizes setting. There are many **long shots,** especially of the brooding castle of Elsinore. Much is made of Hamlet's interaction with this moody locale. We are informed at the beginning of the film that the story is about "a man who could not make up his mind." The long shots are used to emphasize this interpretation visually. Most of them are **loosely framed,** suggesting that Hamlet (played by Olivier) has considerable freedom of movement, freedom to act. But he refuses to use this freedom, preferring to sulk in dark corners, paralyzed with indecision. When he does move, the motion is generally

(a)

(b)

3–7a. *The Stunt Man* (U.S.A., 1980), *directed by Richard Rush.* (*Twentieth Century–Fox*)

3–7b. *The Wild Child* (France, 1970), *with Jean-Pierre Cargol, directed by François Truffaut.* (*United Artists*)

Unlike movement in the dance or the live theater, cinematic movement is always relative. Only gross movements are likely to be perceived in an extreme long shot, whereas the flicker of an eye can rivet our attention in a close-up. In these photos, for example, the path of the boy's tear covers more screen space than the pilot's fall from the sky.

recorded from long distances, thus reinforcing the impotence of the protagonist in relationship to his environment.

Richardson's *Hamlet* is relatively unconcerned with costumes and decor. The protagonist (Nicol Williamson) is almost always seen in **tightly framed** close and medium shots. Unlike Olivier's indecisive and contemplative Hamlet, Williamson's is impulsive and rash, a man who often acts before he thinks. Imprisoned by the confining close shots, the tortured hero virtually spills off the edges of the frame into oblivion. The unstable hand-held camera can barely keep up with him as he lunges hyperkinetically from place to place. If the same movements were photographed from a long-shot range, of course, the character would seem to move more normally.

In the live theater, these two interpretations would have to be achieved through other means. Although the drama is in part a visual medium, the "frame" size (the confines of the set or the proscenium arch) remains the same for the duration of the play. The live theater, in short, is restricted to "long shots," where such distortions of movement are virtually impossible.

3–8. *Top Hat* **(U.S.A., 1935),** *with Fred Astaire and Ginger Rogers, choreography by Astaire and Hermes Pan, directed by Mark Sandrich.*

Astaire's dancing style is the epitome of cool—elegant, debonair, effortless. He influenced such classical choreographers as Jerome Robbins and George Balanchine, and such dancers as Rudolf Nureyev, who described Astaire as "the greatest dancer in American history." His range was extraordinarily broad, encompassing the wit and speed of tap, the airy romanticism of ballroom styles, and later in his career, the ethereal lyricism of modern dance. He insisted on artistic control over his dance numbers. A perfectionist, he also insisted on a six-week rehearsal period before production began. In his nine RKO musicals, he and Hermes Pan worked out the choreography, then taught the steps to Ginger Rogers, who usually came in shortly before production. The camera is essentially functional: It records the movements of the dancers in lengthy takes, at full shot range, panning and tilting after them as unobtrusively as possible. Their dance numbers are actually love scenes: He woos his lady kinetically. In fact, they rarely even kiss on screen. She is usually reluctant, cool to his verbal advances, but once the music begins, their bodies undulate and sway in rhythmic syncopation, and soon she's a lost creature, yielding completely to her kinesthetic destiny. *(RKO)*

3–9. *Two Tars* **(U.S.A., 1928),** *with Stan Laurel and Oliver Hardy, directed by James Parrott.* The comedy of Laurel and Hardy—like that of most slapstick comedians—is quintessentially kinetic. They were unrivalled in their ability to swell a tiny gesture into an apocalyptic orgy of destruction. Their comedies are filled with rituals of revenge and slow escalations of hostility, snowballing finally into total mass demolition—a story formula they employed many times with brilliant results. *(MGM)*

If there is a great deal of movement in the closer shots, its effect on the screen will be exaggerated. For this reason, filmmakers tend to employ these ranges for relatively static scenes. The animation of two people talking and gesturing, for example, has enough movement to prevent most medium shots from appearing static.

Close-ups are even more subtle in their recording of movement. Robert Bresson and Carl Dreyer often highlighted subtle movements by photographing an expressive face in close-up. In fact, these two filmmakers referred to the human face as a spiritual "landscape." In Dreyer's *Passion of Joan Arc,* for instance, one of the most powerful scenes is a close shot of Joan as a tear slowly trickles down her face. Expanded thousands of times by the close-up, the path of the tear represents a cataclysmic movement on the screen, far more powerful than the inane cavalry charges and clashing armies of routine epic films.

Hackneyed techniques are almost invariably the sign of a second-rate film-maker. Certain emotions and ideas—like joy, love, hatred—are so prevalent in the cinema that serious artists are constantly searching for new methods of presentation, methods that confer uniqueness to the commonplace, that transform the familiar into something fresh and unexpected. For example, death scenes are common in movies. But because of their frequency, they are often presented tritely. Of course, death remains a universal concern, one that can still move audiences if handled with any degree of originality and imagination.

One method of avoiding staleness is to convey emotions through kinetic symbolism. Like the choreographer, the filmmaker can exploit the meanings inherent in certain types of movements. Even so-called abstract motions tend to suggest ideas and feelings. Some movements strike us as soft and yielding, for example, while others seem harsh and aggressive. Curved and swaying motions are generally graceful and feminine. Those that are straight and direct strike us as intense, stimulating, and powerful. Furthermore, unlike the choreographer, the filmmaker can exploit these symbolic movements even without having people perform them.

If a dancer were to convey a sense of grief at the loss of a loved one, his or her movements would probably be implosive, withdrawn, with an emphasis on slow, solemn, downward movements. A film director might use this same kinetic principle but in a totally different physical context. For instance, in Walter Lang's *The King and I,* we realize that the seriously ailing King (Yul Brynner) has died when we see a close-up of his hand slowly slipping toward the bottom of the frame, disappearing finally off the lower edge into darkness.

In Eisenstein's *Old and New* (also known as *The General Line*), a valuable stud bull dies, and its death has disastrous consequences for the agricultural commune that has purchased the animal. These consequences are expressed through two parallel shots emphasizing the same kinetic symbolism. First Eisenstein shows us an **extreme close-up** of the dying bull's-eye as it slowly closes. The mournful lowering of the eyelid is magnified many times by the closeness of the shot. Eisenstein then cuts to a shot of the sun lowering on the horizon, its streaming shafts of light slowly retracting as the sun sinks below the earth's rim. Trivial as a bull's death might seem, to the hardworking members of the commune it suggests an almost cosmic significance. Their hopes for a better future die with the animal.

Of course, context is everything in movies. The kind of symbolism in *Old and New* would probably seem pretentious and arty in a more realistic movie. However, the same kinetic *principle* can be used in almost any kind of context. In Norman Jewison's *In the Heat of the Night,* for example, a police officer

3–10. *Lightning Swords of Death* (Japan, 1973), *with Tomisaburo Wakayama, directed by Kenji Misumi.*
Film directors often exploit empty or "negative space" to suggest ideas dealing with loss, both physical and psychological. In this image, the decapitated victim's sudden death is viscerally reinforced by the empty space that fills his half of the screen. The symmetrical balance of the composition is destroyed with the victim's fall, releasing the tensions of the tight frame and creating a sudden vacuum that accompanies the protagonist's victory over his enemy. (*Columbia Pictures*)

3–11. *Yojimbo* **(Japan, 1961),** *directed by Akira Kurosawa.*
Kurosawa's movies are rich in symbolic kinetic techniques. He often creates dramatic tensions by juxtaposing static visual elements with a small but dynamic whirlpool of motion. In this scene, for example, the greatly outnumbered protagonist (Toshiro Mifune) prepares to do battle with a group of vicious hoodlums. In static visual terms, the samurai hero seems trapped by the enclosing walls and the human wall of thugs that blocks off his space. But surrounding the protagonist is a furious whipping wind (the dominant contrast of the shot), which symbolizes his fury and physical power. *(Janus Films)*

3–12. *The French Connection* (U.S.A., 1971), *directed by William Friedkin.*

Expansive outward movements and sunburst effects are generally associated with explosive emotions, like joy or terror. In this shot, however, the symbolism is more complex. The scene occurs at the climax of a furious chase sequence in which the much despised protagonist (Gene Hackman, with gun) finally triumphs over a vicious killer by shooting him—just as he seems on the verge of eluding the dogged police officer once again. This kinetic outburst on the screen symbolizes not only the bullet exploding in the victim's body, but a joyous climax for the protagonist after his humiliating and dangerous pursuit. The kinetic "ecstasy of death" also releases the dramatic tension that has built up in the audience during the chase sequence: In effect, we are seduced into sharing the protagonist's joy in the kill. (*Twentieth Century–Fox*)

(Sidney Poitier) must inform a woman (Lee Grant) that her husband has been brutally murdered. When she hears the news, the woman shields her body with her arms in a kind of shrivelling, implosive gesture. In effect, she withdraws into herself, her body withering as the news sinks in. She will not permit even the sympathetic officer to touch or comfort her in any way.

In Charles Vidor's *Ladies in Retirement,* these same kinetic principles are used in a totally different context. An impoverished housekeeper (Ida Lupino) has asked her aging employer for financial assistance to prevent the housekeeper's two retarded sisters from being put away in an asylum. The employer, a vain, selfish woman who acquired her wealth as the mistress of a rich man, refuses to help her employee. As a last resort, the desperate housekeeper decides to kill the old woman and use her isolated cottage as a refuge for the good-naturedly dotty sisters. The murder scene itself is conveyed through kinetic

(a)

(b)

3–13. *High Noon* (U.S.A., 1952), *with Gary Cooper, directed by Fred Zinnemann.* The closer and tighter the shot, the more the motion dominates. In longer, more loosely framed shots, movement tends to recede in importance, usually in direct proportion to the distance of the kinetic action from the camera. Even the slightest alterations in framing can affect our reactions. The two fight sequences portrayed here, for example, imply subtle differences. The closer, more tightly framed shot **(a)** suggests more danger and desperation because the antagonist (Lloyd Bridges) almost manages to pull the protagonist off screen right. In the somewhat longer, looser shot **(b),** the protagonist's control over his adversary is reinforced by the amount of space allowed for the hero's movements. By allowing more space and distance, the director is able to present the fight scene with a greater degree of stylization and objectivity. The control of the visual elements within the frame becomes a spatial metaphor for the protagonist's control over his antagonist. *(United Artists)* symbolism. We see the overdressed dowager playing a ditty at her piano. The housekeeper, who plans to strangle the woman from behind, slowly creeps up while she is singing. But instead of showing us the actual strangulation, Vidor cuts to a medium close shot of the floor, where, one by one, the dowager's pearls drop to the floor. Suddenly a whole clump of pearls splatters near the old lady's now motionless feet. The symbolism of the dropping pearls is appropriate to the context, for they embody not only the woman's superfluous wealth, but her vanity and selfishness as well. Each falling pearl suggests an elegantly encrusted drop of blood: Drop by drop, her life ebbs away, until the remaining strands of pearls crash to the floor and the wretched creature is dead. By conveying the murder through this kinetic symbolism, Vidor prevents us from witnessing the brutal event, which probably would have lost the audience's sympathy for the housekeeper.

In each of these instances, the filmmakers—Lang, Eisenstein, Jewison, and Vidor—were faced with a similar problem: how to present a death scene with freshness and originality. Each director solved the problem by exploiting similar movements: a slow, contracting, downward motion—the same kind of movement that a dancer would employ literally on a stage.

3–14. ***Yankee Doodle Dandy*** **(U.S.A., 1943),** *with James Cagney, directed by Michael Curtiz.* Cagney liked to describe himself as "just a hoofer gone wrong." He began his career as a chorus boy on Broadway, but once he was hired by Warner Brothers in the early 1930s, he was quickly typecast as a gangster. He constantly tried to expand his artistic range, but oddly, he rarely danced in his movies except for this Oscar-winning performance as George M. Cohan. Cagney's dancing in this film is exhilarating—cocky, strutting, and funny. A quintessentially kinetic performer, he was a dynamo of motion—edgy, punctuating the air with hand gestures, prancing on the balls of his feet. "Never settle back on your heels," was his philosophy. "Never relax. If you relax, the audience relaxes." *(Warner Bros.)*

Kinetic symbolism can be used to suggest other ideas and emotions as well. For example, ecstasy and joy are often expressed by expansive motions, fear by a variety of tentative or trembling movements. Eroticism can be conveyed through the use of undulating motions. In Kurosawa's *Rashomon,* for example, the provocative sexuality of a woman is suggested by the sinuous motions of her silk veil—a movement so graceful and tantalizing that the protagonist (Toshiro Mifune) is unable to resist her erotic allure. Since most Japanese viewers regard overt sexuality in the cinema as tasteless—even kissing is rare in their movies—sexual ideas are often expressed through these symbolic methods.

Every art form has its rebels, and cinema is no exception. Because movement is almost universally regarded as basic to film art, a number of directors have experimented with the idea of stasis. In effect, these filmmakers are deliberately working against the nature of their medium, stripping it of all but the most essential motions. Such filmmakers as Bresson, Ozu, and Dreyer have been described as **minimalists** because their kinetic techniques are so austere and restrained. When virtually nothing seems to be moving in an image, even the slightest motion can take on enormous significance. In many cases, this stasis is exploited for symbolic purposes: Lack of motion can suggest spiritual or psychological paralysis, as in the movies of Antonioni, for example.

The Moving Camera

Before the 1920s, filmmakers tended to confine movements to the subject photographed. There were relatively few who moved their cameras during a shot, and then usually to keep a moving figure within the frame. In the 1920s such German filmmakers as F. W. Murnau and E. A. Dupont moved the camera within the shot not only for physical reasons but for psychological and thematic reasons as well. The German experiments permitted subsequent filmmakers to use the mobile camera to communicate subtleties previously considered impossible. True, **editing**—that is, moving the camera *between* shots—is faster, cheaper, and less distracting, but cutting is also abrupt, disconnected, and unpredictable compared to the fluid lyricism of a moving camera.

3–15. *Airplane!* (U.S.A., 1980), *with (left to right) Lloyd Bridges, Robert Stack, and Lee Terri; directed by Jim Abrahams, David Zucker, and Jerry Zucker.*
Moving the camera toward the materials is an aggressive gesture and can suggest an even greater threat off camera. In this shot, the characters look on in stunned disbelief as a huge jet airliner with a paranoid ex-pilot at the controls is about to crash into the Chicago airport terminal—where they're standing. (*Paramount Pictures*)

3–16. *Rope* (U.S.A., 1948), *with James Stewart (left), Farley Granger (right), and John Dall (second from right), directed by Alfred Hitchcock.*
An incorrigible experimenter in form, Hitchcock shot this film in a single uninterrupted take, the camera and characters choreographed so that the size of the images could be varied from close-ups to long shots. During shooting, whenever the camera had to be reloaded (every ten minutes), he devised ways to mask the cut between shots, such as having a character's back momentarily darken the screen and continuing the "uninterrupted" scene when the character moves away from the lens. The film is one of the few examples of a literal adherence to the unities of time, place, and action.   *(Warner Bros.)*

A major problem of the moving camera involves time. Films that employ this technique extensively tend to seem slow moving, since moving in or out of a scene is more time consuming than a straight cut. A director must decide whether moving the camera is worth the film time involved, and whether the movement warrants the additional technical and budgetary complications. If a filmmaker decides to move the camera, he or she must then decide how. Should it be mounted on a vehicle or simply moved around the axis of a stationary tripod? Each major type of camera movement implies different meanings, some obvious, others subtle. There are seven basic moving camera shots: **(1) pans, (2) tilts, (3) crane shots, (4) dolly shots, (5) zoom shots, (6) hand-held shots,** and **(7) aerial shots.**

Panning shots—those movements of the camera that scan a scene horizontally—are taken from a stationary axis point, with the camera mounted on a tripod. Such shots are time consuming since the camera's movement must

3-17. *Die Hard* **(U.S.A., 1988),** *with Bruce Willis, directed by John McTiernan.*
Action and adventure films are among the most kinetic of genres, stressing physical movement above all other qualities. *(Twentieth Century–Fox)*

ordinarily be smooth and slow to permit the images to be recorded clearly. Pans are also unnatural in a sense, for when the human eye pans a scene, it jumps from one point to another, skipping over the intervals between points. The most common use of a pan is to keep the subject within frame. If a person moves from one position to another, the camera moves horizontally to keep him in the center of the composition. Pans in extreme long shots are especially effective in epic films where an audience can experience the vastness of a locale. But pans can be just as effective at medium and close ranges. The so-called **reaction pan,** for instance, is a movement of the camera away from the central attraction—usually a speaker—in order to capture the reaction of an onlooker or listener. In such cases, the pan is an effective way of preserving the cause–effect relationship between the two subjects and of emphasizing the solidarity and connectedness of people.

The **swish pan** (also known as a "flash pan" and a "zip pan") is a variation of this technique and is often used for transitions between shots—as a substitute cut. What the swish pan involves is a whirling of the camera at a speed so rapid that only blurred images are recorded. Despite the fact that they actually take more time than cuts, swish pans connect one scene to another with a greater sense of simultaneity than cuts can suggest. For this reason, flash pans are often used to connect events at different locales that might otherwise appear remote from each other.

Pan shots tend to emphasize the unity of space and the connectedness of people and objects within that space. Precisely because we expect a panning shot to emphasize the literal contiguity of people sharing the same space, these shots can surprise us when their realistic integrity is violated. In Robert Benton's

Places in the Heart, for example, the final shot of the movie connects the world of the living with the dead. The film is a celebration of the simple Christian values that bind a small Texas community together during the troubled times of the 1930s depression. The final shot takes place in church. The camera begins to pan the congregation in a long sweeping motion down each row of pews. Interspersed among the surviving characters are several that we know to be dead, including a murderer and his victim, worshipping side by side. Though the rest of the movie is realistically presented, this final shot leaps to a symbolic level, suggesting that the unified spirit of the community includes all its members, deceased as well as living.

　　Tilt shots are vertical movements of the camera around a stationary horizontal axis. Many of the same principles that apply to pans apply to tilts: They can be used to keep subjects within frame, to emphasize spatial and psychological inter-

3–18. *An American in Paris* (U.S.A., 1951), *with Gene Kelly (center), choreographed by Kelly, directed by Vincente Minnelli.*
In some respects, film choreography can be more complex than stage choreography, which is always viewed from a stationary position. In movies, however, the camera can be choreographed as well as the dancers. Kelly's choreography often features lyrical crane shots in which the camera's swirling motions are dreamily counterpointed by the motions of the dancer—a virtual pas de deux, with the camera/viewer serving as surrogate partner.　(*MGM*)

relationships, to suggest simultaneity, and to emphasize cause–effect relationships. Tilts, like pans, can also be used subjectively in **point-of-view shots:** The camera can simulate a character's looking up or down a scene, for instance. Since a tilt is a change in angle, it is often used to suggest a psychological shift within a character. When an eye-level camera tilts downward, for example, the person photographed suddenly appears more vulnerable.

Dolly shots, sometimes called trucking or tracking shots, are taken from a moving vehicle (dolly). The vehicle literally moves in, out, or alongside a moving figure or object while the action is being photographed. Tracks are sometimes laid on the set to permit the vehicle to move smoothly—hence the term *tracking shot.* If these shots involve long distances, the tracks have to be laid or withdrawn while the camera is moving in or out. Today, any vehicular movement of the camera can be referred to as a dolly shot. The camera can be mounted on a car, a train, even a bicycle.

Tracking is a useful technique in point-of-view shots to capture a sense of movement in or out of a scene. If a filmmaker wants to emphasize the *destination* of a character's movement, the director is more likely to use a straight cut between the initiation of the movement and its conclusion. If the *experience* of the movement itself is important, the director is more likely to dolly. Thus, if a

3–19. *Gone With the Wind* **(U.S.A., 1939),** *with Vivien Leigh (left, in front of boiling cauldron), directed by Victor Fleming.*
The pull-back dolly or crane shot begins with a close view of a subject, then withdraws to reveal the larger context. The contrast between the close and distant views can be funny, shocking, or sadly ironic. In this famous scene, the camera begins with a close shot of the heroine (Leigh), then slowly pulls back, revealing the wounded bodies of hundreds of soldiers, and stopping finally at a distant long-shot range, in front of a high flagpole, the tattered Confederate flag blowing in the wind like a shredded remnant.   (*MGM*)

3–20. *The Conformist* (**Italy/France, 1970**), *with Dominique Sanda, Stefania Sandrelli, and Jean-Louis Trintignant, directed by Bernardo Bertolucci.*
Bertolucci's traveling shots are personal, eccentric, even perverse. Often the camera lunges forward, sideways, or up and away—even in the middle of dialogue sequences. These spontaneous eruptions destabilize the visual materials, infusing the action with a surge of kinetic energy. In his celebrated dance scenes, however, Bertolucci's camera becomes sweepingly lyrical, almost rhapsodic. The director's favorite cinematographer, Vittorio Storaro, is regarded as an unsurpassed contemporary master of mobile camera work. (*Paramount Pictures*)

character is searching for something, the time-consuming point-of-view dolly helps to elongate the suspense of the search. Similarly, the **pull-back dolly** is an effective technique for surprising the character (and audience) with a revelation (3–19). By moving back, the camera reveals something startling, something previously off frame.

A common function of traveling shots is to provide an ironic contrast with dialogue. In Jack Clayton's *The Pumpkin Eater,* a distraught wife (Anne Bancroft) returns to an ex-husband's house where she has an adulterous liaison with him. As the two lie in bed, she asks him if he had been upset over their divorce and whether or not he missed her. He assures her that he wasn't upset, but while their voices continue on the sound track, the camera belies his words by slowly dollying through his living room, revealing pictures and mementos of the ex-wife. The shot is a kind of direct communication between the director and audience, bypassing the characters. These techniques are deliberate authorial intrusions. They are favored by filmmakers who view their characters with skepticism or irony—Lubitsch and Hitchcock, for example.

One of the most common uses of dolly shots is to emphasize psychological rather than literal revelations. By slowly tracking in on a character, the filmmaker is getting close to something crucial. The movement acts as a signal to the audience, suggesting, in effect, that we are about to witness something important. A cut to a close-up would tend to emphasize the rapidity of the discovery, but slow dolly shots suggest a more gradual revelation. For example, in Clive Donner's *The Caretaker* (also known as *The Guest*), this technique is used several times. Based on Harold Pinter's play, the movie concerns two brothers and an old tramp who tries to set one brother against the other. The dialogue, as is often the case in a Pinter script, is evasive and not very helpful in providing an understanding of the characters. The brothers are different in most respects. Mick (Alan Bates) is materialistic and aggressive. Aston (Robert Shaw) is gentle and withdrawn. Each brother has a crucial speech in which the camera slowly tracks from a long range to a close-up. Neither of the speeches is really very informative, at least not on a literal level. However, the juxtaposition of the dialogue with the implications of the dolly shot helps the audience to feel that it has finally "arrived" at an understanding of each character.

3-21. *Dirty Dancing* (**U.S.A., 1987**), *with Cynthia Rhodes, Jennifer Grey, and Patrick Swayze; choreographed by Kenny Ortega; directed by Emile Ardolino.*
"Dance is the activity where the sexual connection is most explicit," Michael Malone has pointed out, "which is why movies use it to symbolize sex and why skillful dancing is an invariable movie clue to erotic sophistication, a prerequisite for the lover." See Michael Malone, *Heroes of Eros: Male Sexuality in the Movies* (New York: E.P. Dutton, 1979).   *(Vestron Pictures)*

3–22. *The Earrings of Madame De . . .* **(France, 1954),** *with Danielle Darrieux, directed by* *Max Ophüls.*
Traveling shots consume time, and Ophüls often uses them to symbolize the forward rush of time and its irrevocability. The fluidity of Ophüls's camera hastens his heroines to their disillusioning rendezvous with reality, critic Andrew Sarris has noted. "As we follow the Ophülsian characters, step by step, up and down stairs, and up and down streets, and round and round the ballroom, we realize their imprisonment in time."   *(Franco-London Films)*

A stationary camera tends to convey a sense of stability and order, unless there is a great deal of movement within the frame. The moving camera—by its very instability—can create ideas of vitality, flux, and sometimes disorder. Orson Welles exploited the mobile camera to suggest the leading character's dynamic energy in *Othello*. Early in the movie, the confident Moor is often photographed in traveling shots. In the ramparts scene, he and Iago walk with military briskness as the camera moves with them at an equally energetic pace. When Iago tells him of his suspicions, the camera slows down, then comes to a halt. Once Othello's mind has been poisoned, he is photographed mostly from stationary setups. Not only has his confident energy drained away, but a spiritual paralysis invades his soul. In the final shots of the movie, he barely moves, even within the still frame. This paralysis motif is completed when Othello kills himself.

When the camera literally follows a character, the audience assumes that it will discover something along the way. A journey, after all, usually has a destination. But traveling shots are often symbolic rather than literal. In Federico Fellini's *8½.* for example, the moving camera is used to suggest a variety of thematic ideas. The protagonist, Guido (Marcello Mastroianni), is a film director who's trying to put together a movie near a bizarre health spa. Everywhere he turns, he's confronted by memories, fantasies, and realities more fantastic than anything he can imagine. But he is paralyzed by indecision. What, if anything, from all this copious flux will he select for his movie? He can't use it all, for it won't fit together—the materials are too sprawling. Throughout the film, the camera wanders restlessly, prowling over the fantastic locale, compulsively hoarding images of faces, textures, and shapes. All are absorbed by Guido, but he is unable to detach them from their contexts to form a meaningful artistic structure.

The film's traveling shots function on several levels. They are used to suggest Guido's increasingly desperate search for a theme, a story, or a cinematic structure of some kind. They are also analogues of Guido's passive receptivity. He is like a walking recording machine, seeking out and storing image upon image for their own sake. The traveling shots, in conjunction with the movement of people, processions, and traffic, are also analogues for the unbroken flow of experiences that comprises Guido's reality—a reality he finally refuses to simplify for the sake of producing a tidy little movie. But where Guido fails, Fellini succeeds triumphantly. The final sequence of the film (which takes place in Guido's imagination) emphasizes the continuity and coherence of *all* his experiences. The characters from his life—including those of Guido's past and fantasies—join hands and dance joyously around a circus ring, a ritual celebration of the limitlessness of the artistic imagination. The ring is a visual symbol of Fellini's conception of life's infinite flow, which has no beginning or end.

A number of film theorists have discussed the unique capacity of cinema to convert space into time and time into space. The amount of time it takes to photograph a concrete object can be the main purpose of a shot, especially a traveling shot. The acknowledged master of these types of dolly shots was Max Ophüls. In such movies as *Letter From an Unknown Woman* and *The Earrings of Madame De . . .* , the heroines throw themselves into imprudent but glorious

3–23. *The Killing Fields* **(U.S.A., 1984),** *with Haing S. Ngor (carrying child), cinematography by Chris Menges, directed by Roland Joffé.*
When the hand-held camera is used to photograph confusing or agitated events, these traits are intensified by the instability of the camera. In this movie, for example, one of the scariest sequences is the panic-stricken evacuation of Phnom Penh, the Cambodian capital, just as the barbaric Khymer Rouge guerrillas are about to enter the city. People stream in and out of the frame, scurrying to escape. The camera races with them, sweeping first in one direction, then another. Nothing is stable. (*Warner Bros.*)

3-24. *The Wizard of Oz (U.S.A., 1939), with Judy Garland and Ray Bolger, directed by Victor Fleming.*
Musical performers in the golden age of the studio system had to be versatile. Garland, a singer, could hold her own even with a superlative dancer like Bolger. He, in turn, could warble a tune in fine style. In this number, "If Only I Had a Brain," both performers acquit themselves with distinction—as singers *and* dancers.   *(MGM)*

love affairs. The camera tracks relentlessly as the women become more irrevocably involved with their lovers. As critic Andrew Sarris pointed out, Ophüls uses his dolly shots as metaphors of time's cruel prodigality. His world is one of tragic flux and instability in which love is destined to run its eventually bitter course. These lengthy tracking shots preserve the continuity of time by preserving the continuity of space. There is no time for pause and reflection "between shots" in these films. This symbolic technique can be overlooked by the casual viewer because the dolly shots are to some degree functional: They follow characters in their daily rounds of activities. But a stationary camera would be just as functional (not to mention less expensive), for the characters could move toward or away from a fixed setup.

Hand-held shots are generally less lyrical, more noticeable than vehicular shots. Hand-held cameras, which are usually mounted with a harness on the cinematographer's shoulder, were perfected in the 1950s to allow cameramen to move in or out of scenes with greater flexibility and speed. Originally used by documentarists to permit them to shoot in nearly every kind of location, these cameras were quickly adopted by many fiction film directors as well. Hand-held shots are often jumpy and ragged. The camera's rocking is hard to ignore, for the screen exaggerates these movements, especially if the shots are taken from close ranges. For this reason, filmmakers often use the hand-held camera for point-of-view shots. In Mike Nichols's *The Graduate,* for example, a hand-held shot is used to simulate the hero's attempts to maneuver through a crowded room of people. However, most cinematographers can manipulate a lightweight camera as steadily as a dolly if the situation requires.

Crane shots are essentially airborne dolly shots. A crane is a kind of mechanical arm, often more than twenty feet in length. In many respects, it resembles the cranes used by the telephone company to repair lines. It can lift a cinematographer and camera in or out of a scene. It can move in virtually any direction: up, down, diagonally, in, out, or any combination of these. Because of this flexibility, a crane shot can suggest a number of complex ideas. It can move from high, long distances to low, close ones, as it does in Hitchcock's *Notorious*, where the camera sweeps from an extreme high-angle long shot of a ballroom to an extreme close-up of the hand of the heroine (Ingrid Bergman) clasping a small key.

Zoom lenses don't usually involve the actual movement of the camera, but on the screen their effect is very much like an extremely fast tracking or crane shot. The zoom is a combination of lenses, which are continuously variable, permitting the camera to change from close wide-angle distances to extreme telephoto positions (and vice versa) almost simultaneously. The effect of the zoom is a breathtaking sense of being plunged into a scene, or an equally jolting sense of being plucked out of it. Zoom shots are used instead of dolly or crane shots for a number of reasons. They can zip in or out of a scene much faster than any vehicle. From the point of view of economy, they are cheaper than dolly or crane shots since no vehicle is necessary. In crowded locations, zoom lenses can be useful for photographing from long distances, away from the curious eyes of passersby.

There are certain psychological differences between zoom shots and those

3–25. *Mean Streets* (U.S.A., 1973), *with Robert De Niro, Amy Robinson, and Harvey Keitel, directed by Martin Scorsese.*
Especially at close ranges, the hand-held camera tends to be mercurial. In scenes of violence, such as this, a wildly lurching camera can kineticize the visual materials with a terrifying quicksilver instability. *(Warner Bros.)*

3-26. Ballet Mécanique (France, 1924), *directed by Fernand Léger.*
Best known for his cubist paintings, Léger was also an avant-garde filmmaker. One of the first to explore abstraction in the cinema, he created many striking **kinetic** effects by animating and choreographing ordinary objects like crockery, dishes, and machine gears. *(Museum of Modern Art)*

involving an actual moving camera. Dolly and crane shots tend to give the viewer a sense of entering into or withdrawing from a set: Furniture and people seem to stream by the sides of the screen, as the camera penetrates a three-dimensional space. Zoom lenses foreshorten people and flatten space. The edges of the image simply disappear at all sides. The effect is one of sudden magnification. Instead of feeling as though we are entering a scene, we feel as though a small portion of it has been thrust toward us. In shots of brief duration, these differences are not significant, but in more lengthy shots, the psychological differences can be pronounced.

Since the early 1960s, when the zoom lens became fashionable, it has been one of the most abused devices in cinema—mostly through overuse. Hack directors use zoom shots to zap up their materials—to lend dull, talky scenes a sense of urgency. Many television adventure series would be impossible without the indispensible zoom, for these programs consist mostly of predictable events that are made to seem cataclysmic by the rapid zooming in and out on essentially static scenes. A sign of a desperate director is the arbitrary and frequent use of zoom shots.

Aerial shots, usually taken from a helicopter, are really variations of the crane shot. Like a crane, the helicopter can move in virtually any direction. When a crane is impractical—usually on exterior locations—an aerial shot can duplicate the effect. The helicopter shot can be much more extravagant, of course, and for this reason, is occasionally used to suggest a swooping sense of freedom. In *Jules and Jim,* an aerial shot conveys Jim's lyrical exhilaration when, after many years, he plans to visit his friend Jules and his wife in Germany. In *Apocalypse Now,* Francis Coppola used aerial shots to produce a godlike sense of inexorability, as swirling American helicopters annihilate a Vietnamese village. The sequence is a kinetic tour de force, suffusing the action with a sense of exhilaration—and horror. Virtually every shot in this brilliantly edited sequence contains a forward rush, a sense of being swept up by events that are out of control.

Mechanical Distortions of Movement

Movement in film is not a literal phenomenon but an optical illusion. Present-day cameras record movement at 24 frames per second (fps). That is, in each second, 24 separate still pictures are photographed. When the film is shown in a

3–27. *Snow White and the Seven Dwarfs* **(U.S.A., 1937),** *by Walt Disney.*
Beginning with the "Silly Symphonies" of the early 1930s, the field of animation was dominated for many years by Disney, whose movies were ostensibly aimed at children. Disney's great feature length films—*Snow White and the Seven Dwarfs, Fantasia, Pinocchio, Bambi,* and *Dumbo*—are classics of the cinema and appeal to adults as well. See also Christopher Finch, *The Art of Walt Disney* (New York: Abrams, 1973).   (© *Walt Disney Productions*)

3–28a. *A La Votre* (Holland), *by Monique Renault.*

3–28b. *An Old Box* (Canada), *by Paul Driessen.*

3–28c. *De Facto* (Bulgaria), *by Stojan Dukov.*

3–28d. *Honeymation* (Hungary), *by Ferenc Varsanyi.*

Animation encompasses an enormous range of styles, including the erotic lyricism of Monique Renault, the crabbed linearity of Paul Driessen, the childlike cartoon figures of Stojan Dukov, and the cookie animation of Ferenc Varsanyi. All of these films and others are included in *The 12th International Tournée of Animation.* Each year, the Tournée committee selects a sampling of the finest animated films and releases them as a feature-length anthology. *(FilmWright)*

projector at the same speed, these still photographs are mixed instantaneously by the human eye, giving the illusion of movement. This phenomenon is called the *persistence of vision.* By simply manipulating the timing mechanism of the camera and/or projector, a filmmaker can distort movement on the screen. Even at the turn of the century, Méliès was experimenting with various kinds of trick photography, and although most of these experiments were just clever stunts, subsequent directors have used these discoveries with artistic results. There are five basic distortions of this kind: **(1) animation, (2) fast motion, (3) slow motion, (4) reverse motion,** and **(5) freeze frames.**

There are two fundamental differences between *animation* and live-action movies. In animation sequences, each frame is photographed separately, rather than continuously at the rate of 24 frames per second. Another difference is that animation, as the word implies, doesn't ordinarily involve the photographing of subjects that move by themselves. The subjects photographed are generally drawings or static objects. Thus, in an animated movie, thousands of frames are separately photographed. Each frame differs from its neighbor only to an infinitesimal degree. When a sequence of these frames is projected at 24 fps, the illusion is that the drawings or objects are moving, and hence, are "animated."

The common denominator of both animated and live-action film procedures is the use of the camera, the photographic process. In a sense, animation has greater affinities with the graphic arts, whereas ordinary fiction films have closer ties with the live theater. But in both cases, the recording camera acts as an intermediary between the subject and the audience. Even animated films, however, have different emphases. Many of the features of Walt Disney, for instance, are as dramatic as ordinary fiction films. In fact, a number of parents have considered Disney's *Bambi* too frightening and violent for children. On the other hand, some of the brilliant animated films of the Canadian Norman McLaren and the Yugoslavian Zagreb School are virtually abstract expressionist paintings on celluloid.

A popular misconception about animated movies is that they are intended primarily for the entertainment of children—perhaps because the field was dominated for so many years by Disney. In actuality, the gamut of sophistication in

3–29. *Heavy Traffic* **(U.S.A., 1973),** *by Ralph Bakshi.*
Many animated films are too mature or sophisticated, either in subject matter or technique, to be appreciated by young children. Bakshi's witty social satire is deliberately gross and raunchy, and was accordingly awarded an X rating.   (*American International Pictures*)

this genre is as broad as in live-action fiction films. The works of Disney and the puppet films of the Czech Jiri Trnka appeal to both children and adults. Some of the great Yugoslavian animated movies are likely to appeal primarily to adults— Ante Bajaja's *Justice,* for example. A few of these films are as sophisticated as the drawings of Paul Klee. There are even some X-rated animated films, most notably Ralph Bakshi's *Fritz the Cat* and *Heavy Traffic* (3–29). The computer-animated films of John and James Whitney are formally complex and are not likely to appeal to children.

Another popular misconception about animated movies is that they are simpler than live-action films. The contrary is more often the case. For every second of screen time, 24 separate drawings usually have to be photographed. Thus, in an average 90-minute feature, over 129,600 drawings are necessary. Furthermore, some animators use transparent plastic sheets (called **cels**), which they layer over each other in order to give the illusion of depth to their drawings. Some single frames consist of as many as three or four layers of cels. Most animated films are short precisely because of the overwhelming difficulty of producing all the necessary drawings for a longer movie. Feature-length animated movies are usually produced assembly-line fashion, with dozens of draftsmen drawing thousands of separate frames.

Technically, animated films can be as complex as live-action movies. The same techniques can be used in both forms: traveling shots, zooms, angles, various lenses, editing, **dissolves,** etc. The only difference is that animators *draw* these elements into their images. Furthermore, animators also can use most of the techniques of the painter: different kinds of paints, pens, pencils, pastels, washes, acrylics, and so on.

Some filmmakers have even combined the techniques of live-action with animation. In *Neighbors,* for example, McLaren used a technique called *pixilla-*

3–30. *King Kong* **(U.S.A., 1933),** *with Fay Wray, special effects by Willis H. O'Brien, directed by Merian C. Cooper and Ernest B. Schoedsack.*

O'Brien was a specialist in model animation, which uses stop-motion photography on miniature models with malleable parts. When animated, these models become giant prehistoric creatures. Actually, a variety of special effects were used in the film, including matte and process shots and composite shots produced by the optical printer. In this "realistic" shot, for example, a live-action print was fused with an animated print using an 18-inch model of Kong. There were six miniature models in all, plus a 20-foot bust of Kong's head and shoulders and an 8-foot-long mechanized hairy hand, which could lift the screaming Miss Wray up, down, and away. (*RKO*) *tion,* which involves photographing live actors frame by frame, a method sometimes called *stop-motion photography.* When the sequence is projected on the screen, the actors move in abrupt, jerky motions, suggesting a primitive cartoon figure. Other filmmakers have combined animation and theatrical film techniques within the same frame. This mixture is accomplished with the aid of the **optical printer.** Two film strips are superimposed—one consisting of animated frames, the other of photographs of actual people and things. **Mattes** are used to block out areas of the real scene where the animated drawings will appear in the finished print.

The most successful instance of combining live action with animation is *Who Framed Roger Rabbit,* directed by Robert Zemeckis. Richard Williams was the director of animation for the project, which involved over 320 animators. Nearly 2 million drawings were made for the movie. Some single frames were so complex that they required two dozen drawings. The integration of real details with cartoon characters is startling. A cartoon rabbit drinks from a real coffee cup, which rattles. Cartoon characters throw real shadows on the set. They bump into live people, knocking them down (see C.P. 7).

Fast motion is achieved by having events photographed at a slower rate than 24 fps. Ordinarily, the subject photographed moves at a normal pace. When the sequence is projected at 24 fps, the effect is one of acceleration. This technique is sometimes used to intensify the natural speed of a scene—one showing galloping horses, for example, or cars speeding past the camera. Early silent comedies were photographed before the standardization of cameras and projectors at 24 fps, and therefore their sense of speed is exaggerated at present-day projector speeds. Even at 16 or 20 fps, however, some of these early directors

3–31. *Koyaanisqatsi* **(U.S.A., 1982),** *directed by Godfrey Reggio.*
Reggio's nonverbal avant-garde feature includes several fast-motion sequences portraying a world gone mad with speed and technology. In this shot, ribbons of traffic stream through the streets of the city of dreadful night, like sinister meteors. *Koyaanisqatsi* (pronounced koy-yanna-scott-see) is a Hopi Indian word meaning "life out of balance."   (*New Yorker Films*)

3–32. *Chariots of Fire* **(Great Britain, 1980),** *with Ben Cross, directed by Hugh Hudson.*
Slow motion is often used in movies about athletic events. The technique can prolong the balletic grace of an athlete's movements. In other cases, like this re-creation of a 1924 Olympic track event, the slow motion heightens the agonized strain in every muscle of an athlete's body as he hurtles himself against the finish wire.   *(Warner Bros.)*

employed fast motion for comic effects. Without the use of acceleration, the comedies of Mack Sennett would lose much of their loony vitality.

According to the French aesthetician Henri Bergson, when people act mechanically rather than flexibly, comedy is the result. People, unlike machines, can think, feel, and act reasonably. A person's intelligence is measured by his or her ability to be flexible. When behavior becomes machinelike and inflexible, we find it laughable. One aspect of machinelike behavior is speed: When a person's movements are speeded up on film, he or she seems inhuman, ridiculous. Dignity is difficult in fast motion, for acceleration robs us of our humanity. The Upton Inn mixup in Richardson's *Tom Jones* is funny precisely because the fast motion captures the machinelike predictability of all the characters: Tom flies from Mrs. Waters's bed, Mr. Fitzpatrick flies off the handle, Squire Weston screams for his daughter, and the servants scream for their lives.

Slow motion sequences are achieved by photographing events at a faster rate than 24 fps and projecting the film strip at the standard speed. Slow motion tends to ritualize and solemnize movement. Even the most commonplace actions take on a choreographic gracefulness in slow motion. Where speed tends to be the natural rhythm of comedy, slow, dignified movements tend to be associated with tragedy. In *The Pawnbroker,* Sidney Lumet used slow motion in a **flashback** sequence, showing the protagonist as a young man on an idyllic country outing with his family. The scenes are lyrical and otherworldly—too perfect to last.

When violent scenes are photographed in slow motion, the effect is paradoxically beautiful. In *The Wild Bunch,* Peckinpah used slow motion to photograph the grisliest scenes of horror—flesh tearing, blood splattering, horses toppling, an almost endless variety. By aestheticizing these scenes of ugliness, Peckinpah demonstrates why the men are so addicted to a life of violence when it seems so profitless. Violence becomes almost an aesthetic credo, somewhat as it's portrayed in the fiction of Hemingway. Slow motion violence became virtually a trademark in the works of Peckinpah; but after the late 1960s, other directors reduced it to a cinematic cliché.

Reverse motion simply involves photographing an action with the film running reversed. When projected on the screen, the events run backward. Since Méliès's time, reverse motion has not progressed much beyond the gag stage. In *A Hard Day's Night,* Lester used reverse motion as a comic choreographic retake; in *The Knack,* for a quick laugh when an egg "returns" to its shell. One of the most expressive uses of reverse motion—combined with slow motion—is in Jean Cocteau's *Orpheus.* The protagonist has taken a journey into Hell to regain his lost wife. He makes a serious blunder while there and expresses a wish to return to his original point of decision to correct his mistake. Magically, he is whisked into the past before our eyes, as the previous sequence unfurls backwards in slow motion—to the physical setting where the fateful decision was made. The reverse motion in this sequence is a good instance of how space can be temporalized and time spatialized in the cinema.

A *freeze frame* suspends all movement on the screen. A single image is selected and reprinted for as many frames as is necessary to suggest the halting of motion. By interrupting a sequence with a freeze shot, the director calls attention to an image—offering it, as it were, for our delectation. Sometimes the image is a fleeting moment of poignance that is over in a fraction of a second, as in the final shot of Truffaut's *The 400 Blows.* Directors also use freeze frames for comic purposes. In *Tom Jones,* Richardson freezes the shot of Tom dangling on

3–33. *Hair* **(U.S.A., 1979),** *choreography by Twyla Tharp, directed by Milos Forman.*
Slow motion etherealizes movement, lending it a dreamy, otherworldly grace. Throughout this musical, slow motion is used in the dance numbers to emphasize the individuality rather than the uniformity of the dancers. Twyla Tharp's choreography is organic to the story, which deals with the freewheeling lifestyle of some 1960s hippies. The dance numbers are loose and spontaneous, with each dancer doing his or her own thing—like jiggling links in a chain. (*United Artists*)

3–34. *Viridiana* (**Mexico/Spain, 1961**), *directed by Luis Buñuel.*
This notorious freeze-frame parody of Leonardo's *Last Supper* is only one example of
Buñuel's savage assault on the Church, sentimental liberalism, and middle-class morality. His
sardonic wit is often shocking, blasphemous. For example, the context of this freeze frame is
a drunken orgy of beggars who pose for a group photo to the accompaniment of Handel's
Messiah. A woman reeling in boozy stupor "snaps" the picture not with a camera but her
genitals. This raucous gesture throws the "disciples" into paroxysms of laughter. Though a
nonbeliever, Buñuel was able to infuse a sense of scandal in these sacrilegious jokes. "Thank
God I am still an atheist," he once sighed.   *(Audio-Brandon Films)*

a noose while the off-screen narrator urbanely explains to the audience why Tom
should not hang until his tale is finished.

In other instances, the freeze frame can be used for thematic purposes. The
final image of Richardson's *The Loneliness of the Long Distance Runner* is
frozen to emphasize the permanence of the protagonist's status at the end of the
picture. Freeze frames are ideal metaphors for dealing with time, for in effect,
the frozen image permits no change. Near the end of *True Grit,* for example,
Henry Hathaway froze a shot of the protagonist (John Wayne) and his horse
leaping over a fence. By halting the shot at the crest of the leap, Hathaway
creates a metaphor of timeless grandeur: The image suggests a heroic equestrian
statue, immune from the ravages of time and decay. Of course, the total absence
of movement is often associated with death, and Hathaway's freeze frame also
implies this idea. Perhaps a more explicit metaphor of death can be seen in the
conclusion of George Roy Hill's *Butch Cassidy and the Sundance Kid,* where the
two heroes (Paul Newman and Robert Redford) are "frozen" just before they
are shot to death. Like Hathaway's freeze frame, Hill's suggests an ultimate
triumph over death.

Most of the mechanical distortions mentioned above were discovered by
Méliès. For many years after, they were largely ignored by the majority of
commercial filmmakers until the late 1950s, when the French New Wave direc-

tors revived them. Since then, many of these techniques have been used promiscuously. Zooms, freeze frames, and slow motion sequences became almost de rigueur in the 1960s. In many cases, they degenerated into clichés—modish flourishes that were tacked on to the materials, regardless of whether the techniques were organic to the spirit of the subject.

Movement in film is not simply a matter of "what happens." The director has dozens of ways to convey motion, and what differentiates a great director from a merely competent one is not so much a matter of what happens, but *how* things happen—how suggestive and resonant are the movements in a given dramatic context? Or, how effectively does the form of the movement embody its content?

FURTHER READING

BACHER, LUTZ, *The Mobile Mise en Scène* (New York: Arno Press, 1978). Primarily on lengthy takes and camera movements.

DEREN, MAYA, "Cinematography: The Creative Use of Reality," in *The Visual Arts Today,* Gyorgy Kepes, ed. (Middletown, Conn.: Wesleyan University Press, 1960). A discussion of dance and documentary in film.

GIANNETTI, LOUIS D., "The Aesthetic of the Mobile Camera," in *Godard and Others: Essays in Film Form* (Cranbury, N.J.: Fairleigh Dickinson University Press, 1975). Symbolism and the moving camera.

HALAS, JOHN, and ROGER MANVELL, *Design in Motion* (New York: Focal Press, 1962). Movement and mise en scène.

HOLLOWAY, RONALD, *Z is for Zagreb* (San Diego, Cal.: A. S. Barnes, 1972). A discussion of the famous Zagreb animators.

HOLMAN, BRUCE L., *Puppet Animation in the Cinema* (San Diego, Cal.: A. S. Barnes, 1975). Emphasis on Czech and Canadian animators.

JACOBS, LEWIS, et al., "Movement," in *The Movies as Medium,* Lewis Jacobs, ed. (New York: Farrar, Straus & Giroux, 1970). A collection of essays.

KNIGHT, ARTHUR, "The Street Films: Murnau and the Moving Camera," in *The Liveliest Art* (rev. ed.) (New York: Mentor, 1979). The German school of the 1920s.

LINDSAY, VACHEL, *The Art of the Moving Picture* (New York: Liveright, 1970). Reprint of an early classic study.

STEPHENSON, RALPH, *The Animated Film* (San Diego, Cal.: A. S. Barnes, 1973). Historical survey.

EDITING | 4

The foundation of film art is editing.
—V. I. PUDOVKIN

So far, we have been concerned with cinematic communication as it relates to the single shot, the basic unit of construction in movies. Except for traveling shots and **lengthy takes,** however, shots in film tend to acquire meaning when they are juxtaposed with other shots and structured into an **edited** sequence. Physically, editing is simply joining one strip of film (**shot**) with another. Shots are joined into scenes. On the most mechanical level, editing eliminates unnecessary time and space. Through the association of ideas, editing connects one shot with another, one scene with another, and so on. Simple as this may now seem, the convention of editing represents what critic Terry Ramsaye referred to as the "syntax" of cinema, its grammatical language. Like linguistic syntax, the syntax of editing must be learned. We don't possess it innately.

Continuity

In the earliest years of cinema, the late 1890s, movies were brief, consisting of short events photographed in **long shot** in a single **take.** The duration of the shot and the event were equal. Soon filmmakers began to tell stories—simple ones, it's true, but requiring more than a single shot. Scholars have traced the development of narrative to filmmakers in France, Great Britain, and the United States.

By the early twentieth century, filmmakers had already devised a functional style of editing we now call *cutting to continuity*. This type of cutting is a technique used in most fiction films even today, if only for exposition scenes. Essentially, this style of editing is a kind of shorthand, consisting of time-honored conventions. Continuity cutting tries to preserve the fluidity of an event without literally showing all of it.

For example, a continuous shot of a woman leaving work and going home

4–1. Editing styles can be classified according to how intrusive or interpretive the cutting is. The least manipulative style is found in a sequence-shot, which contains no editing. Cutting to continuity merely condenses the time and space of a completed action. Classical cutting interprets an action by emphasizing certain details over others. Thematic montage argues a thesis—the shots are connected in a relatively subjective manner. Abstract cutting is a purely formalistic style of editing, totally divorced from any recognizable subject matter.

4-2. *The Arrival of a Train* (**France, 1895**), *directed by Louis and Auguste Lumière.*
The Lumière brothers might be regarded as the godfathers of the documentary movement.
Their brief *actualités* (as they called them) are primitive documentaries shot for the most part
in single takes. These early newsreels often contained several different sequences, but rarely is
there much cutting within a sequence—hence the term sequence shot (that is, a complex
action photographed in a continuous take, without cuts). Audiences of this era were so
astonished by the novelty of a moving picture that this alone was enough to hold their
attention. *(Museum of Modern Art)*

might take forty-five minutes. Cutting to continuity condenses the action into
five or six brief shots, each of which leads by association to the next. (**1**) She
enters a corridor as she closes the door to her office. (**2**) She leaves the office
building. (**3**) She enters and starts her car. (**4**) She drives her car along a highway.
(**5**) Her car turns into her driveway at home. The entire forty-five-minute action
might take ten seconds of screen time, yet nothing essential is left out. It's an
unobtrusive condensation.

To keep the action logical and continuous, there must be no confusing
breaks in an edited sequence of this sort. Often, all the movement is carried out
in the same direction on the screen to avoid confusion. For example, if the
woman moves from right to left in one shot and her movements are from left to

right in the other shots, we might think that she is returning to her office. Cause–effect relationships must be clearly set forth. If the woman slams on her brakes, the director is generally obliged to offer us a shot of what prompted the driver to stop so suddenly.

The continuity of actual space and time is fragmented as smoothly as possible in this type of editing. Unless the audience has a clear sense of a continuous action, an editing transition can be disorienting. Hence, the term **jump-cut,** which means an editing transition that's confusing in terms of space and time. To make their transitions smooth, filmmakers generally use **establishing shots** at the beginning of their stories or at the beginning of any new scene within the narrative.

Once the location is established, filmmakers then can cut to closer shots of the action. If the events require a considerable number of cuts, the filmmaker might cut back to a **reestablishing shot**—a return to the opening long shot. In this way, the viewer is reminded of the spatial context of the closer shots. "Between" these various shots, time and space can be expanded or contracted with considerable subtlety.

By 1908, when the American genius D.W. Griffith entered the field of filmmaking, movies had already learned how to tell stories thanks to the technique of cutting to continuity. But the stories were simple and crude compared to those in more sophisticated narrative mediums like literature and drama. Nonetheless, movie storytellers already knew that by breaking up an action into different shots, the event can be contracted or expanded, depending on the number of shots. In other words, the shot, not the scene, was the basic unit of film construction.

Movies before Griffith were usually photographed in stationary long shot— roughly the position of a close observer in the live theater. But with the breakup

4–3 *A Trip to the Moon* **(France, 1902),** *directed by Georges Méliès.*
Around 1900, in America, England, and France, filmmakers began to tell stories. Their narratives were crude, but they required more than just one shot to complete. Méliès was one of the first to devise the style of cutting to continuity. The narrative segments are connected by a fade—the diminishing of the light at the conclusion of a scene. The next scene then fades in, often in a different location and at a different time, though usually with the same characters. Méliès advertised these films as stories in "arranged scenes."   *(Museum of Modern Art)*

of shots into both exterior and interior locations, the spectator is, in effect, at both places at once. Furthermore, since film time doesn't depend on the duration of the literal event, filmmakers of this era introduced a more subjective time, one that's determined by the duration of the shots (and the elapsed time implied between them), not by the actual occurrence.

D.W. Griffith and Classical Cutting

The basic elements of editing syntax were already in place when Griffith entered the field, but it was he more than any other individual who molded these elements into a language of power and subtlety. Film scholars have called this language *classical cutting*. Griffith has been called the Father of Film because he consolidated and expanded many of the techniques invented by his predecessors, and was the first to go beyond gimmickry into the realm of art. By 1915, the year

4–4. *The Birth of a Nation* (U.S.A., 1915), *directed by D.W. Griffith.*
Griffith's greatest gift to the cinema was classical cutting—a style of editing that still characterizes most of the fiction films around the world. Classical cutting allows filmmakers to inflect their narratives, to add nuances and emphasis. It also subjectivizes time. For example, in this famous last-minute rescue finale, Griffith cross-cuts to four different groups. Despite the sense of speed suggested by the brevity of the shots, the sequence actually expands time. Griffith used 255 separate shots for about twenty minutes of screen time.   *(Museum of Modern Art)*

4–5. *The Times of Harvey Milk* (U.S.A., 1984), *directed by Robert Epstein.* Documentaries are generally structured around ideas rather than plots, and for this reason, thematic montage is the most common style of editing in such films. Their degree of subjectivity is pronounced, with no pretense at neutrality. In this Academy Award-winning documentary about the political career of Harvey Milk, an assassinated gay activist and minority rights champion, the continuity of the shots is determined primarily by the voice-over narration, not the sequence of shots, which are out of chronology. Interviews with people who knew Milk personally are intercut with television newsreel footage of Milk from the past. Time is restructured to heighten Epstein's thesis: Harvey Milk was murdered by an obsessive homophobe. He was made that way by a homophobic society. *(Cinecom International Film Inc.)*

of his masterpiece *The Birth of a Nation,* classical cutting was already an editing style of great sophistication and expressiveness. Griffith had seized upon the principle of the association of ideas in the concept of editing and expanded it in a variety of ways.

Classical cutting involves editing for dramatic intensity and emotional emphasis rather than for purely physical reasons. Through the use of the **close-up** within the scene, Griffith managed to achieve a dramatic impact that was unprecedented. Close-ups had been used earlier, but Griffith was the first to use them for psychological rather than physical reasons alone. Audiences were now permitted to see the smallest details of an actor's face. No longer were performers required to flail their arms and tear their hair. The slightest arch of an eyebrow could convey a multitude of subtleties.

By splitting the action into a series of fragmentary shots, Griffith achieved not only a greater sense of detail, but a far greater degree of control over his audience's reactions. In carefully selecting and juxtaposing long, **medium,** and close shots, he constantly shifted the spectator's point of view within a scene—expanding here, excluding there, emphasizing, consolidating, connecting, contrasting, paralleling, and so on. The possibilities were far ranging. The space and time continuum of the real scene was radically altered. It was replaced by a subjective continuity—the association of ideas implicit in the connected shots.

In its most refined form, classical cutting presents a series of psychologically connected shots—shots that aren't necessarily separated by real time and space (4–11). For example, if four characters are seated in a room, a director might cut from one speaker to a second with a dialogue exchange, then cut to a **reaction shot** of one of the listeners, then to a **two shot** of the original speakers, and finally to a close-up of the fourth person. The sequence of shots represents a kind of psychological cause–effect pattern. In other words, the breakup of shots is justified on the basis of dramatic rather than literal necessity. The scene could be photographed just as functionally in a single shot, with the camera at long shot range. This type of setup is known as a **master shot** or a **sequence shot.** Classical cutting is more nuanced and more intrusive. It breaks down the unity of space, analyzes its components, and refocuses our attention to a series of details. The action is mental and emotional rather than literal.

During the golden years of the American studio system—roughly the 1930s and 1940s—directors were often urged (or forced) to adopt the master shot technique of shooting. What this method involved was shooting an entire scene in long shot without cuts. This take contained all the dramatic variables, and

4–6. *Rhythmus 21* (Germany, 1921), *directed by Hans Richter.*

In the avant-garde cinema, subject matter is often suppressed or exploited primarily as abstract data. The continuity between shots has nothing to do with a story, but is determined by purely subjective or formal considerations. Along with many other European abstract artists of his generation, Richter was a champion of the "absolute film," which consists solely of nonrepresentational forms and designs. *(Museum of Modern Art)* hence served as the basic or "master" shot for the scene. The action was then repeated a number of times with the camera photographing medium shots and close-ups of the principals in the scene. When all this footage was gathered together, the editor had a number of choices in constructing a story continuity. Often disagreements arose over the proper sequence of shots. Usually the studio director was permitted a **first cut**—that is, the sequence of shots representing his interpretation of the materials. Under this system, the studios usually had the right to a **final cut.** Many directors disliked master shot techniques precisely because, with so much footage available, a producer could construct a radically different continuity.

4–7. *Fat City* **(U.S.A., 1972),** *directed by John Huston.*
Classical cutting involves editing for dramatic emphasis, to highlight details that might otherwise be overlooked. In Huston's fight scene, for example, the entire boxing match could have been presented in a single setup (a), though such a presentation would probably strike us as unexciting. Instead, Huston breaks up his shots according to the psychological actions and reactions within the fighter protagonist (Stacy Keach), his manager (Nicholas Colosanto), and two friends in the auditorium (Jeff Bridges and Candy Clark).   (*Columbia Pictures*)

(a)   (b)

(c)   (d)

Master shots are still used by many directors. Without a master, editors often complain of inadequate footage—that the available shots won't cut smoothly. In complex battle scenes, most directors are likely to shoot many **cover shots**—that is, general shots that can be used to reestablish a sequence if the other shots won't cut. In *The Birth of a Nation*, Griffith used multiple cameras to photograph many of the battle scenes, a technique also used by Kurosawa in some sequences of *The Seven Samurai*.

Griffith and other classical filmmakers developed a variety of editing conventions that they thought made the cutting "invisible," or at least didn't call attention to itself. One of these techniques is the *eyeline match*. We see character A look off frame left. Cut to a shot—from his point of view—of character B. We assume B is to A's left. Cause–effect.

Another convention of classical cutting is *matching action*. Character A is seated but begins to rise. Cut to another shot of character A concluding the rising action and then moving away. The idea is to keep the action fluid, to mask the cut with a smooth linkage that's not noticed because the motion of the character takes precedence. The continuity of the movement conceals the suture.

The so-called *180° rule* is still observed by filmmakers, though even during the big studio era, there was nothing sacred about it. (For example, John Ford loved violating the 180° rule. He loved violating almost any rule.) This convention involves **mise en scène** as well as editing. The purpose is to stabilize the space of the playing area so that the spectator isn't confused or disoriented. An imaginary "axis of action" line is drawn through the middle of a scene, viewed from the **bird's-eye** angle (4–8). Character A is on the left, character B on the right. If

4–8. Bird's-eye view of 180° rule.

4–9. *Sisters* **(U.S.A., 1973),** *directed by Brian DePalma.*
Shot/reverse angle cutting is common in dialogue sequences, for the technique keeps the characters separated, somewhat antagonistic. (If characters were attracted to one another, they would share the same frame.) This movie, a dazzling homage to Hitchcock, is about twins and other kinds of doubles. DePalma occasionally uses a split screen to embody the idea visually. By providing us with both the shot (left) and reverse angle reaction shot (right) in the same frame, we have the eerie feeling of being in two places at once—a feeling that's appropriate to the dramatic material. Note that even in a double-image shot like this, DePalma observes the conventions of the 180° rule.   *(American International Pictures)*

the director wanted a two shot, he or she would use camera 1. If we then go to a close-up of A (camera 2), the camera must stay on the same side of the 180° line in order to keep the same background—a continuity aid for the spectator. Similarly, a close-up of character B (camera 3) would be shot on the same side of the axis of action.

In shot–**reverse angle** exchanges—common for dialogue sequences—the director takes care to fix the placement of the characters from shot to shot. If character A is on the left and character B is on the right in the first shot, they must remain that way in the reverse angle taken from over the shoulder of character B (4–9). Notice that the reverse angle is not literally 180° opposite, but we agree to accept it as such.

Even today, filmmakers rarely take the camera behind the imaginary axis line, unless their deliberate intention is to confuse the spectator. During fight scenes and other types of chaotic clashes, the filmmaker often wants the spectator to feel threatened, disoriented, anxious. This can be accomplished by violating the 180° rule.

Griffith also perfected the conventions of the chase—still very much with us. Many of his movies ended with a chase and last-minute rescue sequence. Most of them feature **parallel editing**—the alternation of shots of one scene with another at a different location. By **cross-cutting** back and forth between the two (or three or four) scenes, Griffith conveyed the idea of simultaneous time. For example, near the end of *The Birth of a Nation,* Griffith cross-cuts between four groups. In juxtaposing shots from these separate scenes, he manages to intensify the suspense by reducing the duration of the shots as the sequence reaches its climax. The sequence itself lasts twenty minutes of film time, but the psychological effect of the cross-cutting (the shots average about five seconds each) suggests speed and tension. Generally speaking, the greater the number of cuts within a scene, the greater its sense of speed. To avoid the risk of monotony during this sequence, Griffith changed his **setups** many times. There are **extreme long,** long, medium, and close shots, varied angles, lighting contrasts, even a moving camera (it was mounted on a truck).

4–10. *It's a Wonderful Life* (**U.S.A., 1946**), *with James Stewart, directed by Frank Capra.* Capra was a master of classical editing. His cutting style is fast, light, seamless. But he never displayed his editing virtuosity for its own sake. Like every other technique, editing is subordinated to the needs of the characters in action—the cardinal commandment of classical cutting. In this and other scenes, Capra included a "reactive character" who guides the viewer's response to the action. This character represents a kind of norm, the way an average person would respond to a given situation. In this scene, for example, Capra's charming fantasy takes a whimsical turn. The forlorn hero (Stewart) listens to his guardian angel (Henry Travers, left) explain why he isn't a very *distinguished* angel (he has yet to earn his wings). A casual bystander (Tom Fadden, center) happens to overhear and is totally spooked by their conversation. Capra is able to punctuate the comedy of the scene by cutting to this character's response whenever the angel says something weird.   (RKO)

If the continuity of a sequence is reasonably logical, the fragmentation of space presents no great difficulties. But the problem of time is more complex. Its treatment in film is more subjective than the treatment of space. Movies can compress years into two hours of projection time. They can also stretch a split second into many minutes. Most films condense time. There are only a handful that attempt to make screen time conform to real time: Agnès Varda's *Cleo From Five to Seven* and Zinnemann's *High Noon* are perhaps the best known examples. Both deal with about two hours of time—also the approximate length of the films. Even these movies cheat by compressing time in the expository

4–11. *The Last Picture Show* (U.S.A., 1971), *with Ellen Burstyn and Cybill Shepherd, directed by Peter Bogdanovich.*

In its subtlest form, classical cutting can break up even a confined action into smaller units of meaning. François Truffaut once observed that movies in which people tell lies require more shots than those in which they tell the truth. For example, if a young daughter tells her mother that she thinks she is in love with a boy, and the mother responds by warning the girl of some of the emotional dangers involved, there is no reason why the scene shouldn't be photographed in a single setup with both females in the same frame. Essentially, this is how Bogdanovich presents a similar scene **(a)**. However, if the mother were a lying hypocrite, and the daughter suspected that the older woman might be in love with the boy herself, a director would be forced to break the scene down into five or six shots **(b–g)** in order to give viewers emotional information they wouldn't receive from the characters themselves. (*Columbia Pictures*)

(a)

opening sequences and expanding it in the climactic scenes. In actual practice, time exists in a kind of limbo: So long as the audience is absorbed by the screen action, time is what the film says it is. The problem, then, is to absorb the viewer.

On the most mechanical level, screen time is determined by the physical length of the filmstrip containing the shot. This length is governed generally by the complexity of the image subject matter. Usually, longer shots are more densely saturated with visual information than close-ups and need to be held longer on the screen. Raymond Spottiswoode, an early film theorist, claimed that a cut must be made at the peak of the "content curve"—that is, the point in a shot at which the audience has been able to assimilate most of its information. Cutting after the peak of the content curve produces boredom and a sense of dragging time. Cutting before the peak doesn't give the audience time to assimilate the visual action. An image with a complex mise en scène requires more time to assimilate than a simple one. Once an image has been established, however, a return to it during the sequence can be considerably shorter, since it works as a reminder.

But the sensitive treatment of time in editing is largely an instinctive matter that defies mechanical rules. Most great directors have edited their own films, or at least worked in close collaboration with their editors, so crucial is this art to the success of films. The best-edited sequences are determined by mood as well as subject matter. Griffith, for example, generally edited love scenes in long **lyrical** takes, with relatively few setups. His chase and battle scenes were composed of brief shots, jammed together. Paradoxically, the love scenes actually compress real time, whereas the rapidly cut sequences elongate it.

There are no fixed rules concerning rhythm in films. Some editors cut according to musical rhythms. The march of soldiers, for example, could be edited to the beat of a military tune, as can be seen in several marching sequences in King Vidor's *The Big Parade*. This technique is also common with American avant-garde filmmakers, who feature rock music soundtracks or cut according to a mathematical or structural formula. In some cases, a director will cut before the peak of the content curve, especially in highly suspenseful sequences. In a number of movies, Hitchcock teases the audience by not providing enough time to assimilate all the meanings of a shot. Violent scenes are conventionally cut in a highly fragmented manner. On the other hand, Antonioni usually cuts long after the content curve has peaked. In *La Notte,* for example, the rhythm is languorous and even monotonous: The director attempts to create a sense of weariness in the audience, paralleling that of the characters. Antonioni's characters are usually pretty tired people—in every sense of the term.

Tact is another editing principle that's difficult to generalize about since it too depends on context. None of us likes to have the obvious pointed out to us, whether in real life or while watching a movie. Like personal tact, directorial tact is a matter of restraint, taste, and respect for the intelligence of others. Hack directors often present us with emotionally gratuitous shots, falling over themselves to make sure we haven't missed the point. In many TV dramatic series, for example, the main characters gather together at the conclusion, at which time they revel in an orgy of self-congratulation. The smugness of these scenes is offensive in long shot, insufferable when individualized in a series of cloying close-ups. Such edited sequences lack tact. They're pushy.

4–12. *The Deer Hunter* (U.S.A., 1978), *directed by Michael Cimino.*
Editing is an art as well as a craft. Like all art, it often defies mechanical formulations, taking
on a life of its own. For example, when sneak preview audiences were asked for their
reactions to this three-hour-long movie, most viewers responded enthusiastically, but felt
that the hour-long wedding sequence of the opening could have been cut down. In terms of
its plot, nothing much "happens" in this sequence. Its purpose is primarily *lyrical*—a loving
celebration of the social rituals that bind the community together. The story content of the
sequence could be condensed to a few minutes of screen time—which is exactly what its
makers did. When the shortened version was shown to audiences, reactions were negative.
Cimino and his editor, Peter Zinner, restored the cut footage. The long wedding sequence is
necessary not for its story content so much as for its experiential value. It provides the movie
with a sense of balance: The community solidarity of the sequence is what the characters
fight *for* in the subsequent battle footage of the film.   (*Universal Pictures*)

Griffith's most radical experiments in editing are found in his 1916 masterpiece, *Intolerance*. This movie was the first fiction film to explore the idea of
thematic montage. Both the film and the technique exerted an enormous influence on movie directors of the 1920s, especially in the Soviet Union. Thematic
montage stresses the association of *ideas,* irrespective of the continuity of time
and space.

Intolerance is unified by the theme of people's inhumanity to other people.
Rather than tell one story, Griffith intercut four. One takes place in ancient

Babylon. The second deals with the crucifixion of Jesus. The third concerns the massacre of the Huguenots by the Catholic royalists in sixteenth-century France. The last story takes place in America in 1916 and deals with a battle between labor and management.

The four stories are developed not separately but in parallel fashion. Scenes of one time period are intercut with scenes of another. At the conclusion of the movie, Griffith features suspenseful chase sequences in the first and last stories, a brutal scene of slaughter in the French story, and a slow tragic climax in the killing of Jesus. The concluding sequence contains literally hundreds of shots, juxtaposing images that are separated by thousands of years, and by as many miles. All these different time periods and locations are unified by the central theme of intolerance. The continuity is no longer physical, or even psychological, but conceptual—that is, thematic.

Intolerance was not a commercial success, but its influence was immense. The filmmakers of the Soviet Union were dazzled by Griffith's movie and based their own theories of montage on his practices in this film. A great many directors have profited from Griffith's experiments in the subjective treatment of time. In *The Pawnbroker,* for example, Sidney Lumet exploits the art of editing to produce a series of parallels that are thematically rather than chronologically related. He uses a kind of subliminal editing, in which some shots are held on the screen for only a fraction of a second. The central character is a middle-aged Jew

4–13. *The 4th Man* **(Holland, 1984),** *with Jeroen Krabbé, directed by Paul Verhoeven.*

Editing can shift the action from reality to fantasy in an instant. Often such shifts are accompanied by a cue—eerie music, for example, or a rippling image that suggests a different level of consciousness. At other times, the shift is undetectable, a deliberate attempt to disorient the viewer. The novelist hero of this movie often intermingles reality with fantasy. In this scene, he is trying to shave while suffering from a colossal hangover. His roommate is practicing his music, making the shaky hero even shakier. In exasperation, he walks over to the roommate and strangles him. A moment later, we see the hero shaving again and the roommate still practicing his music. The strangulation took place only in the hero's vivid imagination. Because it is presented with no transitional cue, we too confuse reality with fantasy—the theme of the film. (*International Spectrafilm Distribution*) who survived a Nazi concentration camp twenty-five years earlier; all his loved ones, however, were killed there. He tries to repress the memories of these earlier experiences, but they force their way into his consciousness. Lumet suggests this psychological process by intercutting a few frames of the memory shots during a scene that is occurring in the present. A present-tense event detonates the protagonist's memory of something similar from his past. As past contends with present, the flickering memory shots endure longer, until a **flashback** sequence eventually becomes dominant, and the present is momentarily suspended. With only a few exceptions, however, it was not until the 1960s that such unorthodox editing practices became widespread. Griffith seldom cut before the peak of the content curve, and most of his successors patterned themselves on his model.

Filmmakers can interrupt the present with shots not only of the past but of the future as well. In Sydney Pollack's *They Shoot Horses, Don't They?* short **flash-forwards** of a courtroom scene are interspersed throughout the present-tense story. The flash-forwards suggest predestination: Like the dance contest of the story proper, the future is rigged, and personal effort is equated with self-

4–14. *Flashdance* (U.S.A., 1983), *with Jennifer Beals, directed by Adrian Lyne.*
Editing is often used to deceive—to conceal rather than reveal. For example, the dance numbers in this film were performed by a double, a professional dancer whose identity is cunningly concealed by the artful lighting and the discreetly distanced camera. The dance shots were intercut with closer shots of Jennifer Beals, wearing the same costume and moving to the same music. With the musical number providing the continuity, these intercut shots create the illusion of a continuous movement, with Beals featured throughout. These editing techniques are also commonly used in such scenes as sword fights, dangerous stunts, and many other activities requiring specialized skills.   (*Paramount Pictures*)

deception. Flash-forwards are also used in Alain Resnais's *La Guerre Est Finie* and Joseph Losey's *The Go-Between.*

Griffith also restructured time and place through the use of fantasy inserts. In *Intolerance,* for example, a young woman on the verge of murdering her unfaithful boyfriend imagines a scene where she is apprehended by the police. Flashbacks, flash-forwards, and cutaways to fantasies allow filmmakers to develop ideas thematically rather than chronologically, freeing them to explore the subjective nature of time. The very flexibility of time in movies makes the theme of temporality an ideal subject for the medium.

Like Faulkner, Proust, and other novelists, filmmakers have succeeded in cracking the tyranny of mechanically measured time. One of the most complex instances of the restructuring of time is found in Stanley Donen's *Two for the Road.* The story deals with the development and gradual disintegration of a love relationship. It unfolds in a series of mixed flashbacks. That is, the flashbacks are not in chronological sequence, nor are they completed in any one scene. Rather, they are jumbled and fragmented, somewhat in the manner of a Faulkner novel. To complicate matters, most of the flashbacks take place on the road, during various trips the couple has taken in the past. If each of the time periods of the film were designated with the letters A, B, C, D, and E, its temporal structure might be charted as follows: E (present), A (most distant past), B, C, D, B, A, E, C, D, B . . . ending with E. The audience gradually learns to identify each time period through various continuity clues: the heroine's hair styles, the modes of transportation, the particular crisis during each trip, and so on.

From its crude beginnings, Griffith expanded the art of editing to include a wide variety of functions: locale changes, time lapses, shot variety, emphasis of psychological and physical details, overviews, symbolic inserts, parallels and contrasts, associations, point-of-view shifts, simultaneity, and repetition of **motifs.**

Griffith's method of editing was also more economical. Related shots could be bunched together in the shooting schedule, regardless of their positions (or

4–15. *West Side Story* (U.S.A., 1961), *choreography by Jerome Robbins, directed by Robert Wise and Robbins.*
The editing continuity of a musical number can be highly abstract. The story doesn't necessarily dictate the sequence of shots. Nor are they linked by some principle of thematic association. Rather, the shots are juxtaposed primarily for their lyrical and kinetic beauty. (*United Artists*)

"time" and "place") in the finished film. Especially in later years, in the era of high-salaried stars, directors could shoot all the star sequences in a brief period and out of cinematic continuity. Less expensive details (extreme long shots, minor actors, close-ups of objects, etc.) could be shot at a more convenient time. Later, the shots would be arranged in their proper sequence on the editor's cutting bench.

Soviet Montage and the Formalist Tradition

Griffith was a practical artist, concerned with communicating ideas and emotions in the most effective manner possible. In the 1920s, the Soviet filmmakers expanded his associational principles and established the theoretical premises for thematic editing, or *montage* as they called it (from the French, *monter,* to assemble). V.I. Pudovkin wrote the first important theoretical treatises on what he called constructive editing. Most of his statements are explanations of Griffith's practices, but he differed with the American (whom he praises lavishly) on several points. Griffith's use of the close-up, Pudovkin claimed, is too limited. It's used simply as a clarification of the long shot, which carries most of the meaning. The close-up, in effect, is merely an interruption, offering no meanings of its own. Pudovkin insisted that each shot should make a new point. Through

4–16. ***Dead Men Don't Wear Plaid*** **(U.S.A., 1981),** *with Steve Martin and Carl Reiner (bald pate), directed by Reiner.*
Reiner's comic parody of Nazi films and other noir genres of the 1940s is a tour de force of editing. A silly spy plot involving Martin is intercut with footage from such vintage 1940s movies as *Double Indemnity, Suspicion, The Bribe, Out of the Past,* and *Sorry, Wrong Number.* Pudovkin and Kuleshov would have understood perfectly. *(Universal City Studios)*

the juxtaposition of shots, new meanings can be created. The meanings, then, are in the juxtapositions, not in one shot alone.

Filmmakers in the Soviet Union were strongly influenced by the psychological theories of Pavlov, whose experiments in the association of ideas served as a basis for the editing experiments of Lev Kuleshov, Pudovkin's mentor. Kuleshov believed that ideas in cinema are created by linking together fragmentary details to produce a unified action. These details can be totally unrelated in real life. For example, he linked together a shot of Moscow's Red Square with a shot of the American White House, close-ups of two men climbing stairs with another close-up of two hands shaking. Projected as a continuous scene, the linked shots suggest that the two men are in the same place at the same time.

Kuleshov conducted another famous experiment that provided a theoretical foundation for the use of nonprofessional actors in movies. Kuleshov and many of his colleagues believed that traditional acting skills were quite unnecessary in the cinema. First, he shot a close-up of an actor with a neutral expression. He juxtaposed this with a close-up of a bowl of soup. Then he joined the close-up of the actor with a shot of a coffin containing a female corpse. Finally, he linked the actor's neutral expression with a shot of a little girl playing. When these combinations were shown to audiences, they exclaimed at the actor's expressiveness in portraying hunger, deep sorrow, and paternal pride. In each case, the meaning was conveyed by juxtaposing two shots, not by one alone. Actors can be used as raw material, as objects juxtaposed with other objects. The emotion is produced not by the actor's performance, but by associations brought about by the juxtapositions. In a sense, the *viewer* creates the emotional meanings, once the appropriate objects have been linked together by the filmmaker.

For Kuleshov and Pudovkin, a sequence was not filmed, it was constructed. Using far more close-ups than Griffith, Pudovkin built a scene from many separate shots, all juxtaposed for a unified effect. The environment of the scene is the source of the images. Long shots are rare. Instead, a barrage of close-ups (often of objects) provides the audience with the necessary associations to link together the meaning. These juxtapositions can suggest emotional and psychological states, even abstract ideas.

The Soviet theorists of this generation were criticized on several counts. This technique detracts from a scene's sense of realism, some critics complained, for the continuity of actual time and place is totally restructured. But Pudovkin and the other Soviet formalists claimed that realism captured in long shot is *too* near reality: It's theatrical rather than cinematic. Movies must capture the essence, not merely the surface, of reality, which is filled with irrelevancies. Only by juxtaposing close-ups of objects, textures, symbols, and other selected details can a filmmaker convey *expressively* the idea underlying the undifferentiated jumble of real life.

Some critics also believe that this manipulative style of editing guides the spectator too much—the choices are already made. The audience must sit back passively and accept the inevitable linking of associations presented on the screen. Political considerations are involved here, for the Soviets tended to link film with propaganda. Propaganda, no matter how artistic, doesn't usually involve free and balanced evaluations.

4–17. *Lifeboat* **(U.S.A., 1943),** *with Tullulah Bankhead (center), directed by Alfred Hitchcock.* Hitchcock was one of Pudovkin's most articulate champions. "Cinema is form," Hitchcock insisted. "The screen ought to speak its own language, freshly coined, and it can't do that unless it treats an acted scene as a piece of raw material which must be broken up, taken to bits, before it can be woven into an expressive visual pattern." He referred to the piecing together of fragmentary shots as "pure cinema," like individual notes of music that combine to produce a melody. In this movie, he confined himself entirely to nine characters adrift at sea in a small boat. In other words, this photo contains the raw material for every shot in the film. Formalists insist that the artistry lies not in the materials per se, but in the way they are taken apart and reconstructed expressively.   (*Twentieth Century-Fox*)

Like many Soviet formalists, Sergei Eisenstein was interested in exploring general principles that could be applied to a variety of apparently different forms of creative activity. He believed that these artistic principles were organically related to the basic nature of all human activity, and ultimately to the nature of the universe itself. Needless to say, only the barest outline of his complex theories can be offered here. Like the ancient Greek philosopher Heraclitus, Eisenstein believed that the essence of existence is constant change. He believed that nature's eternal fluctuation is **dialectical**—the result of the conflict and synthesis of opposites. What appears to be stationary or unified in nature is only temporary, for all phenomena are in various states of becoming. Only energy is permanent, and energy is constantly in a state of transition to other forms. Every opposite contains the seed of its own destruction in time, Eisenstein believed, and this conflict of opposites is the mother of motion and change.

The function of all artists is to capture this dynamic collision of opposites, to incorporate dialectical conflicts not only in the subject matter of art but in its techniques and forms as well. Conflict is universal in all the arts, according to Eisenstein, and therefore all art aspires to motion. Potentially, at least, the cinema is the most comprehensive of the arts because it can incorporate the visual conflicts of painting and photography, the kinetic conflicts of dance, the tonal conflicts of music, the verbal conflicts of language, and the character and action conflicts of fiction and drama.

Eisenstein placed special emphasis on the art of editing. Like Kuleshov and Pudovkin, he believed that montage was the foundation of film art. He agreed with them that each shot of a sequence ought to be incomplete, contributory rather than self-contained. However, Eisenstein criticized the concept of linked shots for being mechanical and inorganic. He believed that editing ought to be dialectical: The conflict of two shots (thesis and antithesis) produces a wholly new idea (synthesis). Thus, in film terms, the conflict between shot A and shot B is not AB (Kuleshov and Pudovkin), but a qualitatively new factor—C (Eisenstein). Transitions between shots should not be flowing, as Pudovkin suggested, but sharp, jolting, even violent. For Eisenstein, editing produces harsh collisions, not subtle linkages. A smooth transition, he claimed, was an opportunity lost.

Editing for Eisenstein was an almost mystical process. He likened it to the growth of organic cells. If each shot represents a developing cell, the cinematic cut is like the rupturing of the cell when it splits into two. Editing is done at the point that a shot "bursts"—that is, when its tensions have reached their maximum expansion. The rhythm of editing in a movie should be like the explosions of an internal combustion engine, Eisenstein claimed. A master of dynamic rhythms, his films are almost mesmerizing in this respect: Shots of contrasting volumes, durations, shapes, designs, and lighting intensities collide against each other like objects in a torrential river plunging toward their inevitable destination.

The differences between Pudovkin and Eisenstein may seem academic. In

4–18. A portion of the Odessa Steps sequence from *Potemkin* (USSR, 1925), *directed by Sergei Eisenstein.*

Perhaps the most celebrated instance of editing virtuosity in the silent cinema, the Odessa Steps sequence is an illustration of Eisenstein's theory of collision montage in practice. The director juxtaposed lights with darks, vertical lines with horizontals, lengthy shots with brief ones, close-ups with long shots, static setups with traveling shots, and so on. See also *Eisenstein's Potemkin: A Shot-by-Shot Presentation,* by David Mayer (New York: Grossman, 1972).   *(Audio-Brandon Films)*

(a)

(b)

(c)

(d)

(e)

(f)

(g)

(h)

(i)

(j)

(s)

(t)

(u)

(v)

(w)

(x)

(y)

(z)

(aa)

(bb)

(cc)

(dd)

(ee)

(ff)

(gg)

(hh)

(ii)

(jj)

(kk)

(ll)

(mm)

(nn)

(oo)

(pp)

(qq)

(rr)

(ss)

(tt)

(uu)

(vv)

(ww)

(xx)

(yy)

(zz)

(aaa)

(bbb)

(ccc)

(ddd)

(eee)

(fff)

(ggg)

(hhh)

actual practice, however, the two approaches produced sharply contrasting results. Pudovkin's movies are essentially in the classical mold. The shots tend to be additive and are directed toward an overall emotional effect, which is guided by the story. In Eisenstein's movies, the jolting images represent a series of essentially intellectual thrusts and parries, directed toward an ideological argument. The directors' narrative structures also differed. Pudovkin's stories didn't differ much from the kind Griffith used. On the other hand, Eisenstein's stories were much more loosely structured, usually a series of documentary-like episodes used as convenient vehicles for exploring ideas.

When Pudovkin wanted to express an emotion, he conveyed it in terms of physical images—objective correlatives—taken from the actual locale. Thus, the sense of anguished drudgery is conveyed through a series of shots showing details of a cart mired in the mud: Close-ups of the wheel, the mud, hands coaxing the wheel, straining faces, the muscles of an arm pulling the wheel, and so on. Eisenstein, on the other hand, wanted film to be totally free of literal continuity and context. Pudovkin's correlatives, he felt, were too restricted by realism.

Eisenstein wanted movies to be as flexible as literature, especially to make figurative comparisons without respect to time and place. Movies should include images that are thematically or metaphorically relevant, Eisenstein claimed, regardless of whether they can be found in the locale or not. Even in his first feature, *Strike* (1925), Eisenstein intercut shots of workmen being machine-gunned with images of oxen being slaughtered. The oxen are not literally on location, but are intercut purely for metaphorical purposes. A famous sequence from *Potemkin* links three shots of stone lions: one asleep, a second aroused and on the verge of rising, and a third on its feet and ready to pounce. Eisenstein considered the sequence an embodiment of a metaphor: "The very stones roar."

Ingenious as these metaphorical comparisons can be, the major problem with this kind of editing is its tendency to be obvious—or impenetrably obscure. Eisenstein saw no difficulty in overcoming the space and time differences between film and literature. But the two mediums employ metaphors in different ways. We have no difficulty in understanding what's meant by the comparison "he's timid as a sheep," or even the more abstract metaphor, "whorish time undoes us all." Both statements exist outside of time and place. The simile isn't

4–19. *Persona* (Sweden, 1966), *written and directed by Ingmar Bergman.*
In the densely symbolic prologue to the main story of this film, Bergman intercuts his motif
of hands. We see an upside-down cartoon figure washing his hands in the sea (a), followed
by a live-action shot of a pair of hands washing (b). Like the movie itself, these shots contrast
two cinematic styles in the same work. Bergman also includes a shot of a nail being driven
into a man's hand—an obvious crucifixion allusion (c). We see immobile hands dangling
lifelessly (d), suggesting a hospital, or perhaps a morgue. We also see a restless boy groping
towards us (e). Bergman then offers a reverse-angle shot (f), and we see that the boy is
reaching toward a blurry image of a woman. Or is he conjuring up her image like a magician-
artist? All of these fragmentary motifs are subsequently developed in the main body of the
story. *(United Artists)*

set in a pasture, nor is the metaphor set in a brothel. Such comparisons are not meant to be understood literally, of course. In movies, figurative devices of this kind are more difficult. Editing can produce a number of figurative comparisons, but they don't work in quite the same way that they do in literature. Eisenstein's theories of collision montage have been explored primarily in the avant-garde cinema (4–19). Most fiction filmmakers have found them too intrusive and heavy-handed.

André Bazin and the Tradition of Realism

André Bazin was not a filmmaker, but solely a critic and theorist. For a number of years, he was the editor of the influential French journal *Cahiers du Cinéma,* in which he set forth an aesthetic of film that was in sharp opposition to such formalists as Pudovkin and Eisenstein. Bazin was untainted by dogmatism. While he emphasized the realistic nature of the cinema, he was generous in his praise of movies that exploited editing effectively. Throughout his writings, however, Bazin maintained that montage was merely one of many techniques a director could employ in making movies. Furthermore, he believed that in many cases, editing could actually destroy the effectiveness of a scene (4–20 and 4–22).

Bazin's realist aesthetic is based on his belief that photography, TV, and cinema, unlike the traditional arts, produce images of reality automatically, with a minimum of human interference. This technological objectivity connects the moving image with the observable physical world. A novelist or a painter must represent reality by re-presenting it in another medium—through language and color pigments. The filmmaker's image, on the other hand, is essentially an objective recording of what actually exists. No other art, Bazin felt, can be as comprehensive in the presentation of the physical world. No other art can be as realistic, in the most elementary sense of that word.

Bazin's aesthetic had a moral as well as technological bias. He was influenced by the philosophical movement called Personalism. This school of thought emphasized the individualistic and pluralistic nature of truth. Just as most Personalists agreed that there are many truths, Bazin felt that in the cinema there are many ways of portraying the real. The essence of reality, he believed, lies in its ambiguity. Reality can even be interpreted in opposing, and equally valid, ways, depending on the sensitivities of the artist. To capture this ambiguity, the filmmaker must be modest and self-effacing, a patient observer willing to follow where reality leads. The film artists that Bazin admired most—Flaherty, Renoir, and De Sica, for example—are those whose movies reflect a sense of wonder before the ambiguous mysteries of reality.

 double meaning

Bazin believed that the distortions involved in using formalist techniques—especially thematic editing—often violate the complexities of reality. Montage superimposes a simplistic ideology over the infinite variability of actual life. Formalists tend to be too egocentric and manipulative, he felt. They are concerned with imposing their narrow view of reality, rather than allowing reality to exist in its awesome complexity. He was one of the first to point out that such

4–20. ***The Golden Age of Comedy*** **(U.S.A., 1958),** *with Mack Sennett and friend, compiled by Robert Youngston.*
Cheap science-fiction films and adventure movies often combine realistic elements with the supernatural or the very dangerous, but seldom in the same frame. It's cheaper and easier to keep the terrified people in one shot, then cut to the object of their terror in another shot. Kuleshov would applaud such a solution. But Bazin claimed that a realistic presentation—that is, *not* cutting, but keeping them both in the same frame—is far more effective, for audiences instinctively sense when a scene of this type is being faked with manipulative editing techniques.   (*Distributors Corporation of America*)

great filmmakers as Chaplin, Mizoguchi, and Murnau preserved the ambiguities of reality by minimizing editing.

Bazin even viewed classical cutting as potentially corrupting. Classical cutting breaks down a unified scene into a certain number of closer shots that correspond implicitly to a mental process. But the technique encourages us to follow the shot sequence without our being conscious of its arbitrariness. "The editor who cuts for us makes in our stead the choice which we would make in real life," Bazin pointed out. "Without thinking, we accept his analysis because it conforms to the laws of attention, but we are deprived of a privilege." He believed that classical cutting subjectivizes an event because each shot represents what the filmmaker thinks is important, not necessarily what we would think.

One of Bazin's favorite directors, the American William Wyler, reduced editing to a minimum in many of his films, substituting the use of **deep-focus** photography and lengthy takes. "His perfect clarity contributes enormously to the spectator's reassurance and leaves to him the means to observe, to choose,

(a)

4–21a. *The Sorrow and the Pity* (France/Switzerland/W. Germany, 1971), *directed by Marcel Ophüls.* *(Cinema 5)*

4–21b. *Divide and Conquer* (U.S.A., 1943), *directed by Frank Capra and Anatole Litvak.* *(Museum of Modern Art)*

Even in the world of documentary films, editing styles can range from ultra-realistic to ultra-formalistic. Like most cinéma-vérité documentarists, Marcel Ophüls keeps editing to an absolute minimum. Implicit in the art of editing is artifice—that is, the manipulation of formal elements to produce a seductive aesthetic effect. Many documentarists believe that an edited analysis of a scene shapes and aestheticizes it—compromising its authenticity. A selected sequence of shots, however factually based, extrapolates one person's truth from an event and, in so doing, infuses it with an ideology. An unedited presentation, on the other hand, preserves a multiplicity of truths.

Divide and Conquer, one of the famous *Why We Fight* series of World War II, was created on the editing bench by Capra, who did virtually no "directing" in the conventional sense. Rather, he reedited existing footage, much of it taken from captured enemy newsreels and Nazi propaganda films. By restructuring the footage and accompanying this new continuity with an anti-Nazi commentary, Capra totally reversed the significance of the original materials.

Most documentaries fall between these two extremes, as documentarist Albert Maysles has pointed out: "We can see two kinds of truth here. One is the raw material, which is the footage, the kind of truth that you get in literature in the diary form—it's immediate, no one has tampered with it. Then there's the other kind of truth that comes in extracting and juxtaposing the raw material into a more meaningful and coherent storytelling form which finally can be said to be more than just raw data. In a way, the interests of the people in shooting and the people in editing (even if it's the same individual), are in conflict with one another, because the raw material doesn't want to be shaped. It wants to maintain its truthfulness. One discipline says that if you begin to put it into another form, you're going to lose some of the veracity. The other discipline says if you don't let me put this into a form, no one is going to see it and the elements of truth in the raw material will

(b)

never reach the audience with any impact, with any artistry, or whatever. So there are
these things which are in conflict with one another and the thing is to put it all together,
deriving the best from both. It comes almost to an argument of content and form, and you
can't do one without the other."

and form an opinion," Bazin said of Wyler's austere cutting style. In such movies
as *The Little Foxes, The Best Years of Our Lives,* and *The Heiress,* Wyler
achieved an unparalleled neutrality and transparency. It would be naive to confuse this neutrality with an absence of art, Bazin insisted, for all of Wyler's effort
tends to hide itself.

Unlike some of his followers, Bazin did not advocate a simple-minded
theory of realism. He was perfectly aware, for example, that cinema—like all
art—involves a certain amount of selectivity, organization, and interpretation. In
short, a certain amount of distortion. He also recognized that the values of the
filmmaker will inevitably influence the manner in which reality is perceived.
These distortions are not only inevitable, but in most cases desirable. For Bazin,
the best films were those in which the artist's personal vision is held in delicate
balance with the objective nature of the medium. Certain aspects of reality must
be sacrificed for the sake of artistic coherence, then, but Bazin felt that abstraction and artifice ought to be kept to a minimum. The materials should be allowed
to speak for themselves. Bazinian realism is not mere newsreel objectivity—even
if there were such a thing. He believed that reality must be heightened somewhat
in the cinema, that the director must reveal the poetic implications of ordinary
people, events, and places. By poeticizing the commonplace, the cinema is neither a totally objective recording of the physical world nor a symbolic abstraction
of it. Rather, the cinema occupies a unique middle position between the sprawl
of raw life and the artificially re-created worlds of the traditional arts.

Bazin wrote many articles overtly or implicitly criticizing the art of editing, or at least pointing out its limitations. If the essence of a scene is based on the idea of division, separation, or isolation, montage can be an effective technique in conveying these ideas. But if the essence of a scene demands the simultaneous presence of two or more related elements, the filmmaker ought to preserve the continuity of real time and space (4–22). He or she can do this by including all the dramatic variables within the same **frame**—that is, by exploiting the resources of the long shot, the lengthy take, deep focus, and **widescreen.** The filmmaker can also preserve actual time and space by **panning, craning, tilting, or tracking** rather than cutting to individual shots.

John Huston's *The African Queen* contains a shot illustrating Bazin's principle. In attempting to take their boat down river to a large lake, the two protagonists (Humphrey Bogart and Katharine Hepburn) get sidetracked on a tributary of the main river. The tributary dwindles down to a stream and finally trickles into a tangle of reeds and mud, where the dilapidated boat gets hopelessly mired. The exhausted travelers resign themselves to a slow death in the suffocating reeds, and eventually fall asleep on the floor of the boat. The camera then moves upward, over the reeds, where—just a few hundred yards away—is the lake. The bitter irony of the scene is conveyed by the continuous movement of the camera, which preserves the physical proximity of the boat, the intervening reeds, and the lake. If Huston had cut to three separate shots, we wouldn't understand these spatial interrelationships, and therefore the irony would be sacrificed.

Bazin pointed out that in the evolution of movies, virtually every technical innovation pushed the medium closer to a realistic ideal: in the late 1920s, sound; in the 1930s and 1940s, color and deep-focus photography; in the 1950s, widescreen. In short, technology usually alters technique, not critics and theo-

4–22. *Safety Last* (U.S.A., 1923), *with Harold Lloyd, directed by Fred Newmeyer and Sam Taylor.*

In direct opposition to Pudovkin, Bazin believed that when the essence of a scene lies in the simultaneous presence of two or more elements, editing is ruled out. Such scenes gain their emotional impact through the unity of space, not through the juxtaposition of separate shots. In this famous sequence, for example, Lloyd's comedy of thrills is made more comic and more thrilling by the scene's realistic presentation: The dangling hero and the street below are kept in the same frame. Actually, the distance between the two is exaggerated by the cunning placement of the camera, and there was always at least a platform about three stories below him—"but who wants to fall three stories?" Lloyd asked. (*Museum of Modern Art*) rists. For example, when *The Jazz Singer* ushered in the talkie revolution in 1927, sound eclipsed virtually every advance made in the art of editing since Griffith's day. With the coming of sound, films *had* to be more realistically edited, whether their directors wished them so or not. Microphones were placed on the set itself, and sound had to be recorded while the scene was being photographed. Usually the microphones were hidden—in a vase of flowers, a wall sconce, etc. Thus, in the earliest sound movies, not only was the camera restricted, but the actors were as well. If they strayed too far from the microphone, the dialogue couldn't be recorded properly.

The effects on editing of these early talkies were disastrous. **Synchronized sound** anchored the images, so whole scenes were played with no cuts—a return to the "primitive" **sequence shot.** Most of the dramatic values were aural. Even commonplace sequences held a fascination for audiences. If someone entered a room, the camera recorded the fact, whether it was dramatically important or not, and millions of spectators thrilled to the sound of the door opening and slamming shut. Critics and filmmakers despaired: The days of the recorded stage play had apparently returned. Later these problems were solved by the invention of the **blimp,** a soundproof camera housing that permits the camera to move with relative ease, and by the practice of **dubbing** sound after the shooting is completed (see Chapter 5).

But sound also provided some distinct advantages. In fact, Bazin believed that it represented a giant leap in the evolution toward a totally realistic medium. Spoken dialogue and sound effects heightened the sense of reality. Acting styles became more sophisticated as a result of sound. No longer did performers have to exaggerate visually to compensate for the absence of voices. Talkies also permitted filmmakers to tell their stories more economically, without the intrusive titles that interspersed the visuals of silent movies. Tedious expository scenes could also be dispensed with. A few lines of dialogue easily conveyed what an audience needed to know about the premise of the story.

The use of deep-focus photography also exerted a modifying influence on editing practices. Prior to the 1930s, most cameras photographed interiors on one focal plane at a time. These cameras could capture a sharp image of an object from virtually any distance, but unless an enormous number of extra lights were set up, other elements of the picture that weren't at the same distance from the camera remained blurred, out of focus. One justification for editing, then, was purely technical: clarity of image.

The aesthetic qualities of deep-focus photography permitted composition in depth: Whole scenes could be shot in one setup, with no sacrifice of detail, for every distance appeared with equal clarity on the screen. Deep focus tends to be most effective when it adheres to the real time–space continuum. For this reason, the technique is sometimes thought to be more theatrical than cinematic, for the effects are achieved primarily through a spatially unified mise en scène rather than a fragmented juxtaposition of shots.

Bazin liked the objectivity and tact of deep focus. Details within a shot can be presented more democratically, as it were, without the special attention that a close-up inevitably confers. Thus, realist critics like Bazin felt that audiences would be more creative—less passive—in understanding the relationships between people and things. Unified space also preserves the ambiguity of life.

4–23. *Utamaro and His Five Women* (Japan, 1955), *directed by Kenji Mizoguchi.* Bazin and his disciples were enthusiastic champions of the films of Mizoguchi. The Japanese master favored the use of lengthy takes rather than editing. He generally cut within a continuous take only when there was a sharp psychological shift within the scene. Used sparingly in this way, the cut acquires a greater dramatic impact than can be found in most conventionally edited movies. (*New Yorker Films*)

Audiences aren't led to an inevitable conclusion but are forced to evaluate, sort out, and eliminate "irrelevancies" on their own.

In 1945, immediately following World War II, a movement called **neorealism** sprang up in Italy, and gradually influenced directors all over the world. Spearheaded by Roberto Rossellini and Vittorio De Sica, two of Bazin's favorite filmmakers, neorealism deemphasized editing. The directors favored deep-focus photography, long shots, lengthy takes, and an austere restraint in the use of close-ups. Rossellini's *Paisan* features a sequence shot that was much admired by realist critics. An American G.I. talks to a Sicilian young woman about his family, his life, and his dreams. Neither character understands the other's language, but they try to communicate in spite of this considerable obstacle. By refusing to condense time through the use of separate shots, Rossellini emphasizes the awkward pauses and hesitations between the two characters. Through its preservation of real time, the lengthy take forces us to experience the increasing, then relaxing, tensions that exist between them. An interruption of time through the use of a cut would have dissipated these tensions.

When asked why he deemphasized editing, Rossellini replied: "Things are there, why manipulate them?" This statement might well serve as Bazin's theoretical credo. He deeply admired Rossellini's openness to multiple interpretations, his refusal to diminish reality by making it serve an a priori thesis. "Neorealism by definition rejects analysis, whether political, moral, psychological, logical, or social, of the characters and their actions," Bazin pointed out. "It looks on reality as a whole, not incomprehensible, certainly, but inescapably one."

Sequence shots tend to produce (often unconsciously) a sense of mounting anxiety in the viewer. We expect setups to change during a scene. When they don't, we often grow restless, hardly conscious of what's producing our uneasi-

4–24. *The Makioka Sisters* (Japan, 1983), *directed by Kon Ichikawa*.
Bazin championed mise en scène and deep-focus cinematography because he believed these techniques offer us the freedom to choose what *we* think is significant. This long shot could be broken down into at least six separate close-ups. An edited sequence of such closer shots forces us to follow the filmmaker's logic. His choice and ours are not necessarily the same.   *(Rs/S8)*

ness. Jim Jarmusch's bizarre comedy, *Stranger Than Paradise,* uses sequence shots throughout. The camera inexorably waits at a predetermined location. The young characters enter the scene and play out their tawdry, comic lives, complete with boring stretches of silence, glazed expressions of torpor, and random ticks. Finally, they leave. Or they just sit there. The camera sits with them. Fade out. Very weird.

Like many technological innovations, widescreen provoked a wail of protest from many critics and directors. The new screen shape would destroy the close-up, many feared, especially of the human face. There simply was too much space to fill, even in long shots, others complained. Audiences would never be able to assimilate all the action, for they wouldn't know where to look. It was suitable only for horizontal compositions, some argued, useful for epic films, but too spacious for interior scenes and small subjects. Editing would be further minimized, the formalists complained, for there would be no need to cut to something if everything was already there, arranged in a long horizontal series.

At first, the most effective widescreen films were, in fact, westerns and

4–25. *Stranger Than Paradise* **(U.S.A., 1984),** *directed by Jim Jarmusch.*
Each scene in this movie is a sequence shot—a lengthy take without cuts. Far from being
"primitive," the sequence-shot technique produces a sophisticated, wry effect, bizarre and
funny. In this scene, the two protagonists (John Lurie and Richard Edson) eat yet another
goulash dinner while Lurie berates his stout, outspoken aunt (Cecillia Stark) for still speaking Hungarian after years of living in America. The scene's comic rhythms are accented by
the staging: The bickering relatives must bend forward to see each other, while the visitor,
caught in the crossfire, tries unsuccessfully to stay neutral.   *(Samuel Goldwyn)*

historical extravaganzas. But before long, directors began to use the new screen
with more sensitivity. Like deep-focus photography, scope meant that they had
to be more conscious of their mise en scène. More relevant details had to be
included within the frame, even at its edges. Films could be more densely saturated and—potentially at least—more effective artistically. Filmmakers discovered that the most expressive parts of a person's face were the eyes and mouth,
and consequently, close-ups that chopped off the tops and bottoms of actors'
faces weren't as disastrous as had been predicted.

Not surprisingly, the realist critics were the first to reconsider the advantages of widescreen. Bazin liked its authenticity and objectivity. Here was yet
another step away from the distorting effects of editing, he pointed out. As with
deep focus, widescreen helped to preserve spatial and temporal continuity.
Close-ups containing two or more people could now be photographed in one
setup without suggesting inequality, as deep focus often did in its variety of depth

planes. Nor were the relations between people and things fragmented as they were with edited sequences. Scope was also more realistic because the widescreen enveloped the viewer in a sense of an experience, even with its edges—a cinematic counterpart to the eye's peripheral vision. All the same advantages that had been applied to sound and deep focus were now applied to widescreen: its greater fidelity to real time and space; its detail, complexity, and density; its more objective presentation; its more coherent continuity; its greater ambiguity; and its encouragement of creative audience participation.

Interestingly, several of Bazin's protégés were responsible for a return to more flamboyant editing techniques in the following decades. Throughout the 1950s, Godard, Truffaut, and Chabrol wrote criticism for *Cahiers du Cinéma*. By the end of the decade, they turned to making their own movies. The *nouvelle vague,* or **New Wave** as this movement was called in English, was eclectic in its theory and practice. The members of this group, who were not very tightly knit, were unified by an almost obsessional enthusiasm for film culture, especially American film culture. Unlike that of most previous movements, the range of enthusiasms of these critic/filmmakers was extraordinarily broad: Hitchcock, Renoir, Eisenstein, Hawks, Bergman, Ford, and many more. While rather dogmatic in their personal tastes, the New Wave critics tended to avoid theoretical dogmatism. They believed that technique was meaningful only in terms of subject matter. In fact, it was the New Wave that popularized the idea that *what* a movie says is inextricably bound up with *how* it's said. Furthermore, editing styles ought to be determined not by fashion, the limitations of technology, or dogmatic pronouncements, but by the essence of the subject matter itself.

4–26. *The Hidden Fortress* (**Japan, 1958**), *directed by Akira Kurosawa.*
Most filmmakers bemoaned the advent of widescreen in the 1950s almost as much as they bemoaned sound in the late 1920s. Bazin and other realists embraced the innovation as yet another step away from the distorting effects of montage. Widescreen tends to deemphasize depth in favor of breadth, but Bazin believed that a horizontal presentation of the visual materials could be more democratic—less distorting even than deep focus, which tends to emphasize visual importance in terms of an object's closeness to the camera's lens.   (*Toho Films*)

4–27. *Z* (France, 1969), *directed by Costa-Gavras.*
Almost from the inception of the motion picture, chase scenes have been regarded as intrinsically cinematic, allowing the filmmaker to cut back and forth between pursuer and the pursued. The sense of urgency can be increased considerably by showing the pursuer invading the personal space of the pursued, as in this shot in which a sympathetic character is almost murdered by a speeding auto.   (*Cinema 5*)

Hitchcock's *North by Northwest:* Storyboard Version

Alfred Hitchcock is widely regarded as the greatest editor in the history of the cinema. His precut scripts were legendary. No other director worked from such precisely detailed plans. He often provided frame drawings of his shots (a technique called **storyboarding**), especially for those sequences involving complex editing. Some of his scripts contained as many as 600 setup sketches. Every shot was calculated for a precise effect. Nothing was superfluous, nothing left to chance. "I would prefer to write all this down, however tiny and however short the pieces of film are—they should be written down in just the same way a composer writes down those little black dots from which we get beautiful sound," he explained.

The following excerpt is not Hitchcock's shooting script of *North by Northwest,* but perhaps the next best thing: a reconstruction of a sequence taken directly from the movie by Albert J. LaValley, which appears in his volume, *Focus on Hitchcock*. Ernest Lehman's "literary" version of this scene is reprinted in Chapter 9.

Each number represents a separate shot; drawings identified with a letter as well represent a continuation of the previous shot, though with enough new action to warrant an additional sketch. The numbers in parentheses indicate the approximate length of the shots in seconds. The following abbreviations are used: E.L.S., extreme long shot; L.S., long shot; M.S., medium shot; C.U., close-up; P.O.V., a shot taken from Thornhill's point of view.

The premise: Roger Thornhill (Cary Grant) is a fugitive from the law. To prove his innocence, he must talk with a man named Kaplan. Roger is told to come to the scene's location, where he expects to meet Kaplan.

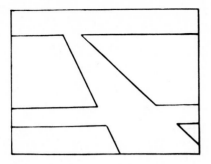

1. E.L.S., aerial. Dissolve to empty road across fields where rendezvous with KAPLAN is to take place. We see and hear bus arriving, door opening.

1b. THORNHILL emerges, bus leaves. He is alone. (52)

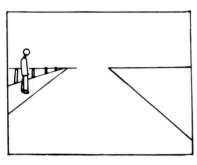

2. L.S., low angle. THORNHILL at roadside, waiting.(5)

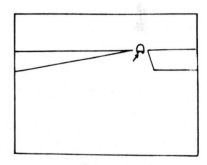

3. E.L.S., P.O.V. Looking down main road: bus going away in distance. (4)

4. M.S. THORNHILL near sign, turns left to right, looking for someone. (3 ⅔)

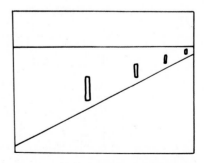

5. L.S., P.O.V. View across road, empty fields with posts. (4)

6. M.S. THORNHILL by sign, turns from right to left, looking. (3)

7. L.S., P.O.V. Across fields. (4)

8. M.S. THORNHILL by sign again, waiting, turns head and looks behind him. (3)

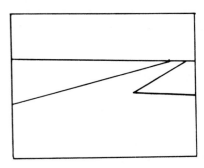

9. E.L.S., P.O.V. The field behind him, road. (4)

10. M.S. THORNHILL by sign, waiting, turning forward—long waiting feeling. (6½)

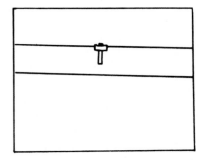

11. E.L.S. Empty landscape across road, signs, post. (3)

12. M.S. THORNHILL by sign. Turns right. (2)

13. E.L.S. Empty main road, car coming in distance. (4)

14. M.S. THORNHILL by sign, looking at car approaching. (¾)

15. L.S. Car goes by fast, whizzing sound, camera pans slightly to right. (1 ¾)

16. M.S. THORNHILL by sign, moves back to left, follows car with his eyes. (2)

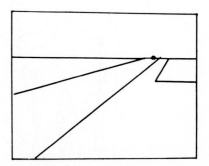

17. E.L.S., P.O.V. Road, car going, sound recedes. (4)

18. M.S. THORNHILL by sign, hands in pockets, turns from left to right. (3)

19. L.S., P.O.V. Field across road again. (3)

20. M.S. THORNHILL by sign, same pose, still looking, turns from right to left (2 ¾)

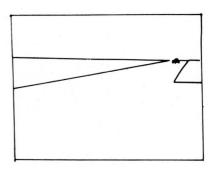

21. E.L.S. Road, car in distance, sounds begin. (3 ½)

22. M.S. THORNHILL by sign, looking at car, no movement. (2 ½)

23. E.L.S. Car coming closer, sound increasing. (3 ¾)

24. M.S. THORNHILL by sign, looking at car coming. (3)

25. L.S. Car closer, rushes past, camera pans a bit to follow it. (3)

26. M.S. THORNHILL by sign, takes hands from pockets, turns left to right to follow car. (3)

27. E.L.S. View of road, car in distance receding. (3 ¾)

28. M.S. THORNHILL by sign, waiting again. (2 ¼)

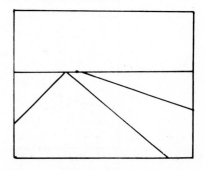

29. E.L.S. Road, truck coming; we hear its sound.(4)

30. M.S. THORNHILL by sign, sound of truck increasing. (3)

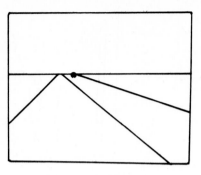

31. E.L.S. Truck coming down road, sound still increasing. (3 ¾)

32. M.S. THORNHILL by sign (2 ¼)

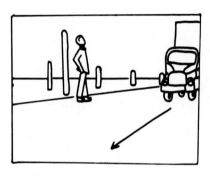

33. L.S. Truck whizzes by.

33b. Kicking up dust, obscuring THORNHILL, camera pans slightly left, and he emerges out of the dust gradually. (4)

34. M.S. THORNHILL wiping dust from his eyes, turns to right. (7)

35. E.L.S. Fields across way, car coming out behind corn. (5)

36. M.S. THORNHILL by sign puzzled by car. (5)

37. E.L.S. Car making turn on dirt road. (4)

38. M.S. THORNHILL awaiting car. (3 ⅔)

39. L.S. Car nearing main road, camera pans following it to right, a sign there. (4)

40. M.S. THORNHILL waiting to see what will happen. (3 ⅓)

41. L.S. MAN getting out of car, talking to driver, we hear the door of the car slam. (3 ½)

42. M.S. THORNHILL reacting, wondering, getting ready to meet this man. (2)

43. L.S. Sound of car turning around, dust raised, car turns around and the MAN walks towards main road opposite THORNHILL, looking back at the car leaving. (1 ⅘)

44. M.S. THORNHILL, closer than previous shots, eyeing the man. (1 ½)

45. L.S. Camera pans right slightly; the MAN goes over by the sign and turns his head to look up the road and over at THORNHILL. (4 ⅓)

46. M.S. Same as 44. THORNHILL's reaction, his head tilts and he looks across the road. (3 ⅘)

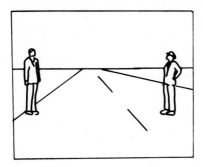

47. L.S. low angle. Road in the middle stretching to infinity, two men oddly stationed on either side of road, the other MAN looking up the road a bit. (7)

48. M.S. THORNHILL's reaction, takes hands out of pockets, opens coat, puts hands on hips, contemplates situation. (6 ⅓)

49. L.S. Same as 45, only the MAN turns his head looking the other way. (3 ½)

50. M.S. Same as 48, but THORNHILL has both hands on hips now, his head looking across. His head turns up road to see if anyone is coming; he looks back, one hand on hip, other at side, at MAN across way.

50b. Starts walking across road part way. (10)

51. L.S., P.O.V. The man on the other side of road, as THORNHILL crosses, camera tracks across road part way, acting as his eyes. (2 ⅔)

52. M.S. THORNHILL walks across road; synchronous tracking camera continuing movement begun in 50b.

53. L.S., P.O.V. Same as 49, 51 of other MAN across road, but camera tracks in on him, acting as THORNHILL's eyes, continues movement begun in 50b.

54. M.S. THORNHILL on other side of road, but camera tracks to continue movement of 50, 52.

54b. Camera continues tracking to other side of road until other man comes in view and THORNHILL begins to talk to him. THORNHILL's hands are a bit nervous in movement; he plays with his little finger; the other man has hands in pockets.

> THORNHILL (after a long wait): Hi! (a long pause follows) Hot day. (Another pause.)
> MAN: Seen worse.
> THORNHILL (after a long pause): Are you supposed to be meeting someone here?
> MAN: Waitin' for the bus. Due any minute.
> THORNHILL: Oh. (another pause)
> MAN: Some of them crop duster pilots get rich if they live long enough.
> THORNHILL: Yeah! (very softly)
> (21)

55. E.L.S. Fields with plane at great distance in far left of frame coming right. (2⅔)

56. M.S. Reaction shot of both looking at plane.

    THORNHILL: Then . . . a . . . (pause) then your name isn't Kaplan?

    MAN: Can't say that it is 'cause it ain't. (pause) Here she comes (as he looks down the road). (11)

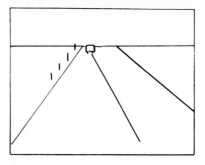

57. E.L.S. Bus coming down the road.

    MAN: (voice off) . . . right on time. (2 ⅔)

58. M.S. Same as 56, two talking then looking again across road at crop duster.

    MAN: That's funny.

    THORNHILL: (very softly) What?

    MAN: That plane's dustin' crops where there ain't no crops.

    THORNHILL turns to look (8)

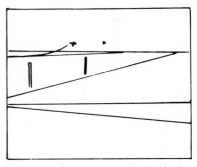

59. E.L.S. Same as 55, field with the plane over it. (4)

60. M.S. Two men off center looking at plane. THORNHILL's hands continue nervous movements; the other's are in his pockets as before. Sound of approaching bus. (3 ⅓)

61. L.S. Bus arriving and coming quite close to camera. (1 ⅘)

62. M.S. MAN gets on as door of bus opens and seems to shut THORNHILL out. The bus leaves.

62b. THORNHILL puts hands on hips and looks across, then looks at his watch. For a second he is alone in the frame as the bus goes out of sight. (2 ⅓)

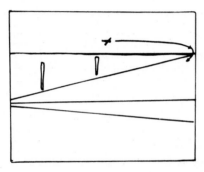

63. E.L.S., P.O.V. Same as 59, what THORNHILL sees across the road; the plane goes to end of frame and turns right, toward him. (5 ⅕)

64. M.S. THORNHILL in front of road by sign, puzzled and rather innocent looking; sound of plane approaching. (2 ⅓)

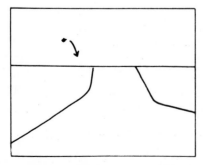

65. E.L.S. Plane coming toward camera, still far, but closer and with sound increasing. (3 ⅘)

66. M.S. Same as 64. THORNHILL reacting. (2 ¼)

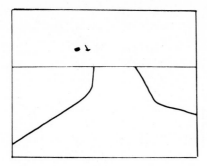

67. E.L.S. Same as 65 but plane closer and louder. (2 ⅛)

68. M.S. Closer shot of THORNHILL, still puzzled and confused as plane comes at him. (4 ½)

69. L.S. Plane clearly coming at him, filling mid-frame, very loud. (1 ⅓)

70. THORNHILL drops, a short held shot, he falls out of frame at bottom. (⅔)

71. L.S. THORNHILL falling on ground, both arms on ground, plane behind him, he in a hole. (3 ½)

72. L.S. Plane going away from him. (3)

73. L.S. THORNHILL on ground getting up, kneeling on left knee. (3 ½)

74. E.L.S. Plane going farther away and sound receding. (2 ⅘)

75. L.S. THORNHILL getting up. (2 ⅕)

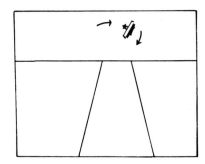

76. E.L.S. Plane in distance banking. (2 ⅓)

77. M.S. THORNHILL up and about to run. (2 ⅓)

78. L.S. Plane approaching again, sound getting louder. (2)

79. M.S. THORNHILL runs and falls in ditch. (1 ½)

80. L.S. THORNHILL in ditch, sound of plane and bullets sprayed on him, smoke; he turns head to left and faces camera to watch when plane is gone. (5 ⅓)

81. L.S. Plane getting ready again, banking. (5 ⅕)

82. M.S. THORNHILL in ditch coming up, gets up on left arm, sound of receding plane. (2 ½)

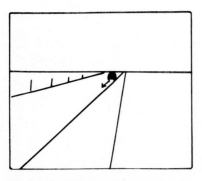

83. E.L.S., P.O.V. The road as THORNHILL sees it, car in distance. (2 ½)

84. M.S. Same as 82, THORNHILL rising from ditch, receding plane sound. (1 ½)

85. L.S., low angle. THORNHILL runs to road to try to stop car.

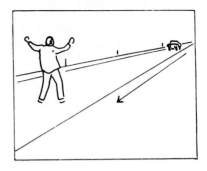

85b. He tries to flag it down. Car sounds approach and it whizzes by. (9 ½)

86. M.S. THORNHILL's back after turning left as the car whizzes by. (4 ⅔)

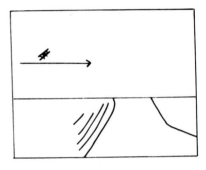

87. E.L.S. Plane in distance, sounds again. (2 ⅓)

88. L.S. THORNHILL's back with plane in distance at far left coming at him.

88b. L.S. He looks at plane, turns around looking for a place to hide, looks at plane again, turns around and runs toward camera. Camera reverse tracks.

88c. THORNHILL running toward camera, camera reverse tracking. He turns around twice while running to look at plane; it goes over his head just missing him. (13 ½)

89. M.S. THORNHILL falling, side view, legs up, bullet and plane sounds. (5)

90. L.S., P.O.V. Cornfield, a place to hide. (2 ½)

91. M.S. THORNHILL lying flat on ground, looking. (1 ⅔)

92. L.S. THORNHILL getting up, plane in distance banking again for new attack. (3)

93. M.S. THORNHILL running, turns back to look at plane, camera tracks with him as he runs to cornfield. (4 ½)

94. L.S., low angle. THORNHILL's back as he runs into cornfield; low camera angle shows lots of ground, stalks. He disappears into corn. (2 ¾)

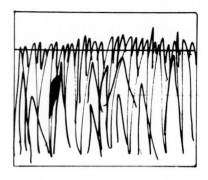

95. L.S. Picture of corn; a patch reveals where THORNHILL is hiding. The corn rustles. (2)

96. M.S. Camera follows THORNHILL down as he falls on ground inside the corn patch. He turns back to look up to see if plane is coming. A cornstalk falls; then he looks down again, up again, down again, up. (7 ¾)

97. L.S. Plane coming along edge of cornfield and over it; it gets very loud. (4 ½)

98. M.S. Same as 96. Corn rustles, wind from the plane blows over. THORN-HILL sees he's out of danger, and smiles a bit, feeling that he's outwitted his pursuers. (15 ⅘)

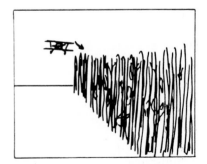

99. L.S. Plane coming in on bend, repeating pattern of 97; it gets louder. (3 ¼)

100. M.S. Same as 96, 98. THORNHILL in corn, getting up, looking around, suddenly aware of plane in new way; he's startled that it's coming back. (4 ⅘)

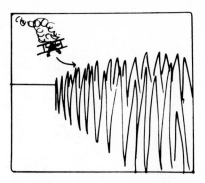

101. L.S. Plane over corn, repeating pattern of 97, only dust coming out of it; plane comes closer to camera. (7)

102. M.S. Same as 96, 98, 100; THORN-HILL's reaction to dust, which fills up screen: he coughs, takes out handkerchief, camera follows him as he raises himself up and down; coughing sounds. (12 ¼)

103. M.S. THORNHILL in corn, new shot; he runs toward camera trying to get out of corn; rustling corn, he looks out of field. (4 ½)

104. E.L.S., P.O.V. Out of cornfield, view of road as framed by corn; tiny speck on road in distance is truck. (2 ¾)

105. M.S. THORNHILL in corn, but he is standing; he moves forward, looks back up for plane, makes dash for the truck coming down road; he goes out of frame for moment at the end. (3 ½)

106. L.S. THORNHILL running toward truck, gets to road from corn; truck farther along the road, sounds of truck (4)

107. E.L.S. Plane banking over corn, getting ready to turn toward him; faint plane sounds; horn of truck. (2)

108. L.S., low angle. THORNHILL in road, truck coming, he waves at it. (1 ²/₃)

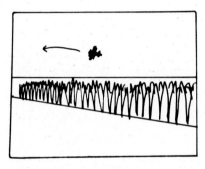

109. E.L.S. Continuation of 107, plane further left. (2)

110. M.S. THORNHILL trying to stop truck, sounds of horns, brakes. (2)

111. L.S. Truck approaching, getting bigger. (2)

112. M.S. Same as 110, but he looks at plane coming in on his left, then puts up both hands instead of one, and bites his tongue. (1 ½)

113. L.S. Truck even closer, about fifty feet in front of camera. (1)

114. M.S. Same as 112, 110. THORN-HILL waving frantically now. (1)

115. C.U. Grille of truck as it tries to halt; brake sounds. (1)

116. C.U. THORNHILL's face in anguish about to be hit.

116b. His hands go up and his head goes down. (⅘)

117. L.S. THORNHILL falls under the truck, front view. (1)

118. M.S. THORNHILL under the truck, side view. (2 ½)

119. L.S., low angle. Plane comes toward truck (and camera). (1 ¾)

120. L.S. Plane hits truck, view from across road. (1)

121. L.S. Truck bursts in flames; another angle of truck and plane; music begins and continues to end of scene. (2 ½)

122. L.S. Shot of truck in flames from in front, two men scramble hurriedly from cab.

   DRIVER: Let's get out of here. It's going to explode. (6 ½)

123. L.S. Backs of men running somewhat comically to cornfield. (2)

124. L.S. THORNHILL runs toward camera from explosions of oil truck behind him. Music tends to mute explosion sounds (2 ¾)

125. L.S. Reverse angle of THORNHILL as he now backs away from explosion. A car has just pulled to side of road, followed by a pickup truck with a refrigerator, which pulls to the side in front of it. Doors open and people get out. THORNHILL goes over and talks to them. No sounds are heard (the music continues), but we see his motions of explanation. (9)

126. L.S. View of explosion in distance with close-up of farmer's arm on right. (2)

127. L.S. THORNHILL and others watch explosion. He backs away from scene to right of frame while they all move closer to the wreck as THORNHILL retreats unnoticed by them. (11)

128. L.S. Backs of others watching explosion. (6 ⅓)

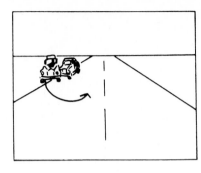

129. L.S. THORNHILL takes the pickup truck with refrigerator in back and pulls out while they are watching the explosion. (3 ⅘)

130. L.S. Same as 128, but the FARMER turns, seeing his truck being taken, and shouts "Hey." (2 ½)

131. L.S. Chase by the FARMER, bow-legged and comic; he finally stops as the truck recedes into the distance. "Come back, come back," he is shouting. Dissolve to next sequence. (15)

FURTHER READING

BARR, CHARLES, "CinemaScope: Before and After," in *Film Theory and Criticism* (3rd ed.), Gerald Mast and Marshall Cohen, eds. (New York: Oxford University Press, 1985). An attack on Eisenstein's editing theories in favor of Bazin, with emphasis on mise en scène and the widescreen.

BAZIN, ANDRÉ, *What Is Cinema?* Hugh Gray, ed. and trans. (Berkeley: University of California Press, vol. I, 1967, vol. II, 1971). A collection of essays emphasizing the realistic nature of the film medium.

DMYTRYK, EDWARD, *On Film Editing* (Boston: Focal Press, 1984). A practical handbook by a former editor turned director.

EISENSTEIN, SERGEI, *Film Form* (New York: Harcourt Brace Jovanovich, 1949). One of the classic studies of montage, written in Eisenstein's typically elliptical, difficult style.

GRAHAM, PETER, ed., *The New Wave* (London: Secker & Warburg, 1968). A collection of essays by and about Bazin, Truffaut, Godard, and others.

JACOBS, LEWIS, "Art: Edwin S. Porter and the Editing Principle," "D. W. Griffith: *The Birth of a Nation* and *Intolerance,*" in *The Rise of the American Film* (New York: Teachers College Press, 1968). A historical account of the evolution of editing in its early years.

LA VALLEY, ALBERT J., ED., *Focus on Hitchcock* (Englewood Cliffs: N.J.: Prentice-Hall, 1972).

PUDOVKIN, V.I., *Film Technique and Film Acting,* Ivor Montague, ed. and trans. (New York: Grove Press, 1960). See also *Kuleshov on Film,* Ronald Levaco, ed. and trans.

(Berkeley: University of California Press, 1974).

REISZ, KAREL, *The Technique of Film Editing* (New York: Hastings House, 1968). The standard text on the history, practice, and theory of editing.

ROSENBLUM, RALPH, and ROBERT KAREN, *When the Shooting Stops . . . The Cutting Begins* (New York: Viking, 1979). An insider's account of the art and craft of editing, by the editor of *The Pawnbroker, Annie Hall,* and many other films.

SOUND | 5

Cinematic sound is that which does not simply add to, but multiplies, two or three times, the effect of the image.

—AKIRA KUROSAWA

There are three classifications of sound in movies: sound effects, music, and spoken language. These can be employed independently or in any combination. **Realistic** sounds tend to be **synchronous.** That is, they derive their source from the images and are often recorded simultaneously with them. Many exposition scenes, for example, use synchronized sound (dialogue) with corresponding images **(two shots).** Even **long** and **extreme long shots** are sometimes shot synchronously—to capture the actual noise of traffic in an urban location, for example. **Formalists** tend to use sound **nonsynchronously.** That is, sounds are detached from their sources, often acting in contrast with the image or existing as totally separate sources of meaning.

Historical Background

In 1927, when *The Jazz Singer* ushered in the talkie era, many critics felt that sound would deal a deathblow to the art of movies. But the setbacks were temporary, and today sound is one of the richest sources of meaning in film art.

5–1. *The Jazz Singer* **(U.S.A., 1927),** *with Al Jolson, directed by Alan Crosland.*
There had been a number of experiments in synchronous sound prior to this film, but they failed to create much of a stir with the public. Significantly, Warner Brothers managed to break the sound barrier with a new genre, the musical. Actually, even this movie was mostly silent. Only Jolson's musical numbers and a few snatches of dialogue were in synch sound. See John Springer. *All Talking, All Singing, All Dancing!* (New York: Citadel, 1966). *(Warner Bros.)*

Actually, there never was a silent period, for virtually all movies prior to 1927 were accompanied by some kind of music. In the large city theaters, full orchestras provided atmospheric background to the visuals. In small towns, a piano was often used for the same purpose. In many theaters, the "Mighty Wurlitzer" organ, with its bellowing pipes, was the standard musical accompaniment. Music was played for practical as well as artistic reasons, for these sounds muffled the noises of the patrons who were occasionally rowdy, particularly when entering the theater.

Most of the early "100 percent talkies" were visually dull. The equipment of the time required the simultaneous recording of sound and image: The camera was restricted to one position, the actors couldn't move far from the microphone, and **editing** was restricted to its most minimal function—primarily scene changes. The major source of meaning was in the sound, especially dialogue. The images tended merely to illustrate the sound track. Before long, adventurous directors began experimenting. The camera was housed in a soundproof

5–2. *Modern Times* (U.S.A., 1936), *with Charles Chaplin, directed by Chaplin.*
Sound shortened the careers of many film artists, especially the great silent clowns, like Keaton, Lloyd, and Harry Langdon, who did not long survive the new aural medium. Like Laurel and Hardy, Chaplin managed to bridge the transition but in the process, he was forced to give up his Tramp character. In *Modern Times,* which was made nine years after the talkie revolution, he put up a gallant but ultimately futile battle against spoken language. It was the last appearance of the Tramp. Though the film contains sound effects and a musical score (composed by Chaplin himself) the only spoken dialogue is recited by a Big Brother figure on a TV monitor.   *(rbc Films)*

blimp, thus permitting the camera to move in and out of a scene silently. Soon, several microphones, all on separate channels, were placed on the set. Overhead sound **booms** were devised to follow an actor on a set, so that his voice was always within range, even when he moved around.

Despite these technical advances, formalist directors remained hostile to the use of realistic (synchronous) sound recording. Eisenstein was especially wary of dialogue, and he predicted an onslaught of "highly cultured dramas" that would force the cinema back to its stagey beginnings. Synchronous sound, he believed, would destroy the flexibility of editing and thus kill the very soul of film art. Synchronous sound did, in fact, require a more literal **continuity,** especially in dialogue sequences. Eisenstein's metaphoric cutting, with its leaps in time and space, wouldn't make much sense if realistic sound had to be provided with each image. Indeed, Hitchcock pointed out that the most cinematic sequences are essentially silent. Chase scenes, for example, require only some general sound effects to preserve their continuity.

Most of the talented directors of the early sound era favored nonsynchronous sound. The proper use of language in film, Eisenstein claimed, was in the **voice-over** monologue, not dramatic dialogue. The monologue would replace the expository titles of the silent film, giving the images uninterrupted dominance. This preference for the monologue reflected the Soviet bias toward documentary film, whereas dialogue tended to be associated with the live theater.

The Frenchman René Clair came to the same conclusions as the Soviets. Sound should be used selectively, not indiscriminately. The ear, he believed, is just as selective as the eye, and sound can be edited in the same way images can. Even dialogue sequences needn't be totally synchronous, Clair believed. Conversation can act as a continuity device, freeing the camera to explore contrasting information—a technique especially favored by ironists like Hitchcock and Ernst Lubitsch.

Clair made several musicals illustrating his theories. In *Le Million* (5–4), for example, music and song often replace dialogue. Language is juxtaposed ironically with nonsynchronous images. Many of the scenes were photographed without sound and later **dubbed** when the montage sequences were completed. These charming musicals are never immobilized by the stagey confinement that ruined most sound films of this era. The dubbing technique of Clair, though ahead of its time, eventually became a major approach in sound film production.

Several American directors also experimented with sound in these early years. Like Clair, Lubitsch used sound and image nonsynchronously to produce a number of witty and often cynical juxtapositions. The celebrated "Beyond the Blue Horizon" sequence from his musical *Monte Carlo* is a good example of his mastery of the new mixed medium. While the spunky heroine (Jeanette MacDonald) sings cheerily of her optimistic expectations, Lubitsch provides us with a display of technical bravura. Shots of the speeding train that carries the heroine to her destiny are intercut with **close-ups** of the whirring locomotive wheels in rhythmical syncopation with the huffing and the chugging and the tooting of the train. Unable to resist a malicious fillip, Lubitsch even has a chorus of suitably obsequious peasants chime in with the heroine in a triumphant reprise as the train plunges past their fields in the countryside. The sequence is both exhilarating and outrageously funny. Critic Gerald Mast observed: "This visual-aural

5–3. *She Done Him Wrong* (U.S.A., 1933), *with Mae West, directed by Lowell Sherman.*

Tone of voice can be far more communicative than words in revealing a person's thoughts. This is why most sophisticated moviegoers prefer written subtitles to dubbing in foreign language movies. Mae West was an expert in conveying sexual innuendos through tone of voice—so much so, in fact, that censors insisted on monitoring her scenes during production for fear that the apparently neutral dialogue in her screenplays would be delivered in a "salacious" manner. America responded enthusiastically to Mae's insolence and snappy wisecracks. In this film she's at her outspoken best: cool, lecherous, cynical. In her opening scene, she saucily proclaims herself to be "one of the finest women who ever walked the streets." West preferred playing outcasts, like showgirls and kept women. This afforded her the opportunity of satirizing sexual hypocrisies. Her one-liners are legendary, like the famous "It's not the men in my life that counts, it's the life in my men." Or "Whenever I'm caught between two evils, I take the one I've never tried." Or "I used to be Snow White, but I drifted." Again: "When I'm good, I'm very good; when I'm bad, I'm even better." When asked how tall he is, a handsome young man replies: "Ma'am, I'm six feet seven inches." Naughty Mae smiles and says: "Let's forget about the six feet and talk about the seven inches." Mae's "lewd" comic style—almost exclusively verbal—fueled the wrath of the censors, ushering in the puritanical Production Code in 1934.   *(Paramount Pictures)*

symphony of music, natural sound, composition, and cutting is as complex and perfect an example of montage-in-sound as Eisenstein's editing devices in *Potemkin* were of montage in silents."

The increased realism brought on by sound inevitably forced acting styles to become more natural, for performers no longer needed to compensate visually for the lack of dialogue. Like stage actors, film players realized that the subtlest nuances of meaning could be conveyed through the voice. The movable

5–4. *Le Million* **(France, 1931),** *directed by René Clair.*
Because Clair preferred to dub his sound after the visuals had been photographed, his early talkies have the same kinetic fluidity of his presound movies. Sound is often used in ironic counterpoint with the images, sometimes to undermine them. Like most ironists, Clair's stock-in-trade is contrast—not only between what's expected and what actually is, but also between what we see and what we hear.   (*Brandon Films*)

camera is a further advantage for the screen actor. If he is required to mutter under his breath, for example, he can do so naturally, photographed in close-up. He need not, like the stage actor, mutter in stage whisper—a necessary convention in the live theater.

In the silent cinema, directors had to use titles to communicate nonvisual information: dialogue, exposition, abstract ideas, and so on. In some films, these interruptions nearly ruined the delicate rhythm of the visuals. Dreyer's *Passion of Joan of Arc,* for example, has frequent interjections of irritating explanatory titles and dialogue. Other directors avoided titles by dramatizing visually as much as possible. This practice led to many visual clichés. Early in the story, for example, the villain might be identified by showing him kicking a dog; or a heroine could be recognized by the halo-effect lighting around her head, and so forth.

Coming from the world of radio, Orson Welles was an important innovator in the field of sound. In *The Magnificent Ambersons,* he perfected the technique of sound **montage,** in which the dialogue of one character overlaps with that of another, or several others. The effect is almost musical, for the language is exploited not necessarily for the literal information it may convey, but as pure sound orchestrated in terms of emotional tonalities. One of the most brilliant episodes employing this technique is the leave-taking scene at the final Amberson ball. The scene is shot in **deep focus,** with **expressionistic** lighting contrasts throwing most of the characters into silhouette. The dialogue of one group of characters gently overlaps with that of another, which in turn overlaps with a third group. The effect is hauntingly poetic, despite the relative simplicity of the words themselves. Each person or couple is characterized by a particular sound texture: The young people speak rapidly in a normal to loud volume, a middle-aged couple whispers intimately and slowly. The shouts of various other family members punctuate these dialogue sequences in sudden outbursts. The entire scene seems choreographed, both visually and aurally: Silhouetted figures stream in and out of the **frame** like graceful phantoms, their words floating and undulating in the shadows. The quarrels among the Amberson family are often recorded in a similar manner. Welles's actors don't wait patiently for cues: Accusations and recriminations are hurled simultaneously, as they are in life. The violent words, often irrational and disconnected, spew out in spontaneous

5–5. *The Merry Widow* (U.S.A., 1925), *with John Gilbert and Mae Murray, directed by Erich von Stroheim.*
Talkies wiped out the careers of many silent film stars, including that of John Gilbert, the most popular leading man of the late silent era. Gilbert's voice was said to be too high pitched, though in fact it wasn't. The problem was far more complex. Silent film acting was stylized and visually heightened to compensate for the lack of sound. Even by silent standards, Gilbert was known for his emotional intensity—his gestures romantically exaggerated, his ardor raised to a fever pitch. The increased realism brought on by the advent of talkies made such acting techniques seem comically overwrought. Audiences laughed at their former idols. Said critic Scott Eyman: "When a star the stature of Gilbert fell, it was like the fall of an angel, awful and irrevocable." Talkies ushered in a new era, with a new breed of actors. Young leading men like Clark Gable were more relaxed and natural in front of the camera, their style of acting more suited to the new realism of talkies.   (MGM)

eruptions of anger and frustration. As in many family quarrels, everyone shouts, but people only half listen.

Robert Altman used similar sound montage techniques in *M*A*S*H, Nashville,* and other movies. Like Welles, Altman often uses language as pure sound, particularly in *McCabe and Mrs. Miller,* in which as many as twenty different sound tracks were mixed. In several scenes, speeches are deliberately thrown away and we're able to catch only a fleeting phrase here and there; however, these phrases are sufficient to give us a sense of what's really going on in a scene. More important, they give us a sense of how language and sounds are actually heard in reality—in ambiguous, elliptical wisps that are often incongruous and funny.

5–6. *Fellini Satyricon* **(Italy, 1969),** *with Hiram Keller, Gordon Mitchell, and Martin Potter, directed by Federico Fellini.*

In Italy, live sound recording is rare. Most Italian filmmakers still prefer to record their sound after the images have been photographed, and in Fellini's case, even after they have been edited. The results have not proved salutary. Fellini's movies since the 1960s often have poor sound tracks. The voices seem disconnected, either too remote or too intimate compared to the visuals. In many cases, we are unsure of who's doing the talking, for most of the sound is nonsynchronous, even in important dialogue sequences. The English-dubbed version of this movie is filled with distracting contradictions. The dialogue rarely matches the visuals in synchronous sequences, even though the principals are native speakers of English. British "equivalents" are used for Roman speech. For example, lower-class characters speak in an incongruous cockney dialect. Much of the dialogue is in a phony nineteenth-century "literary" idiom, totally inappropriate to the earthiness of most of the scenes. Though the mise en scène is brilliantly executed, the lamentable sound track undermines the power of the visuals. The Italian-language version of the movie is somewhat superior, but still crude compared to other filmmakers of Fellini's rank and prestige. *(United Artists)*

Sound Effects

Although the function of sound effects is primarily atmospheric, they can also be precise sources of meaning in film. The pitch, volume, and tempo of sound effects can strongly affect our responses to any given noise. High-pitched sounds are generally strident and produce a sense of tension in the listener. Especially if these types of noises are prolonged, the shrillness can be totally unnerving. For this reason, high-pitched sounds (including music) are often employed in suspense sequences, particularly just before and during the climax. Low-frequency sounds, on the other hand, are heavy, full, and less tense. Often they are used to emphasize the dignity or solemnity of a scene, like the male humming chorus in *The Seven Samurai.* Low-pitched sounds can also suggest anxiety and mystery: Frequently a suspense sequence begins with such sounds, which then gradually increase in frequency as the scene moves toward its climax.

Sound volume works in much the same way. Loud sounds tend to be forceful, intense, and threatening, whereas quiet sounds strike us as delicate, hesitant, and often weak. These same principles apply to tempo. The faster the tempo of sound, the greater the tension produced in the listener. In the chase sequence of Friedkin's *The French Connection,* all of these principles are employed masterfully. As the chase reaches its climax, the screeching wheels of the

5–7. *Ran* (Japan, 1985), *with Mieko Harada, directed by Akira Kurosawa.*
Kurosawa is a master of sound. In this loose adaptation of Shakespeare's *King Lear,* the vengeful character of Lady Kaede (pictured) makes Lady Macbeth look like Mary Poppins. She is characterized by the eerie chafing sound of her silk gowns as she glides across the polished floors like a sinister apparition.   *(Orion Classics)*

pursuing auto and the crashing sound of the runaway train grow louder, faster, and higher pitched.

Off-screen sounds bring off-screen space into play: The sound expands the image beyond the confines of the **frame.** Sound effects can evoke terror in suspense films and thrillers. Since we tend to fear what we can't see, directors will sometimes use off-screen sound effects to strike a note of anxiety. The sound of a creaking door in a darkened room can be more fearful than an image of someone stealing through the door. In Lang's *M*, the child murderer is identified by a tune he whistles off screen. During the early portions of the movie, we never see him and recognize him only by his sinister tune.

In several scenes of Hitchcock's *Psycho,* Bernard Herrmann's score—consisting entirely of strings—suggests shrill bird noises. This **motif** is used as a form of characterization. A shy and appealing young man (Anthony Perkins) is associated with birds early on in the film. He stuffs birds as a hobby, and his own features are intense and rather hawklike. During a brutal murder sequence, the sound track throbs with screeching bird music. The audience assumes the murderer is the boy's mother, but birds have been associated with him, not her. One of Hitchcock's recurrent themes is the transference of guilt. In this film, the transfer is rather complex. The youth has dug up his long-dead mother's body and literally stuffed it. Often he dresses himself up in her clothing. While we think we see the mother killing two victims, we have in fact seen the schizophrenic youth as his other self—his mother. The bird music offers an early clue to this psychological transference.

Because images tend to dominate sounds while we're actually experiencing a movie, many sound effects work on a subconscious level. In *Psycho,* the heroine (Janet Leigh) drives her car through a rainstorm. On the sound track, we hear her windshield wiper blades slashing furiously against the downpour. Later, when she is taking a shower in a motel, these same sounds are repeated.

5–8. *The Exorcist* **(U.S.A., 1973),** *directed by William Friedkin.*
Sound in film is generally geared to space: When a severe discrepancy exists, the effect can be disorienting and even frightening. In this movie, the devil has possessed a young girl (Linda Blair, lying on bed). The sounds emanating from her small body echo loudly, creating a cavernous effect, as if the girl's slight figure had been spiritually expanded thousands of times in order to accommodate the demons that inhabit it.   *(Warner Bros.)*

The source of the water noise is apparent, but the slashing sounds seem to come from nowhere—until a demented killer crashes into the bathroom brandishing a knife.

Sound effects can also serve symbolic functions, which are usually determined by the dramatic context. In Luis Buñuel's *Belle de Jour,* for example, the sounds of jingling bells are associated with the heroine's sexual fantasies. Other symbolic sound effects are more universally understood. In Bergman's *Wild Strawberries,* the protagonist, an elderly professor, has a nightmare. The **surrealistic** sequence is virtually silent except for the insistent sound of a heartbeat—a *memento mori* for the professor, a reminder that his life will soon end.

In reality, there's a considerable difference between hearing and listening. Our minds automatically filter out irrelevant sounds. While talking in a noisy city location, for example, we listen to the speaker, but we barely hear the sounds of traffic. The microphone is not so selective. Most movie sound tracks are cleaned up of such extraneous noises. A sequence might include selected city noises to suggest the urban locale, but once this context is established, outside sounds are

5–9. *Our Hitler, A Film from Germany* (West Germany, 1977), *with Heinz Schubert (Hitler), directed by Hans-Jürgen Syberberg.*
In the late nineteenth century, the German composer Richard Wagner advocated a theory of a universal artwork (*Gesamtkunstwerk*) that combines music, choreography, drama, poetry, architecture, and painting. Wagner's ideal is more fully realized in the expressive possibilities of cinema than any other medium. Syberberg believes that cinema is the universal artwork of our age. In this seven-hour avant-garde feature, Syberberg combines stylized tableaux, newsreel clips, front and rear projections, theatrical sets, a subjective treatment of time and space, exaggerated acting styles, interviews, deliberate anachronisms, jokes, quotations, symbols in profusion, recordings of Nazi and Allied radio broadcasts, and the music of Richard Wagner. (*Omni Zoetrope Release*)

diminished and sometimes even eliminated in order to permit us to hear the conversation clearly.

Since the 1960s, however, a number of directors have retained these noisy sound tracks in the name of greater realism. Influenced by the documentary school of **cinéma vérité**—which tends to avoid simulated or re-created sounds—directors like Jean-Luc Godard even allowed important dialogue scenes to be partly washed out by on-location sounds. In *Masculine–Feminine,* Godard's use of sound is especially bold. His insistence on natural noises—all of them as they were recorded on the set—dismayed many critics, who complained of the "cacophonous din." The movie deals with violence and the lack of privacy, peace, and quiet. Simply by exploiting his sound track, Godard avoided the need to comment overtly on these themes—they are naggingly persistent in virtually every scene. One of the most effective sound techniques in this movie is the use of gunshots for transitions. Often the abruptness of the editing is punctuated by the shattering blast of these shots, which have no visual source. Other scenes are accompanied by the cracking of billiard and bowling balls, the clattering of pinball machines, and the nervous stamping of a typewriter—all of them suggesting gunfire shots. Important dialogue is sometimes drowned out by the noise of street traffic, an adjoining conversation, or the clatter of dishes in a cafe. Because we're accustomed to a clean sound track, we are distracted by these extraneous noises. But this is precisely Godard's point: Serenity is almost totally absent from contemporary urban life.

5–10. *A Clockwork Orange* (**U.S.A./Great Britain, 1971**), *with Miriam Karlin, directed by Stanley Kubrick.*
This film is almost consistently in the loud range. Noises are magnified and reverberating, dialogue is shouted rather than spoken. Our ears are assaulted by a barrage of relentless sounds. Kubrick uses this technique to attack the audience aurally: The volume never permits us to relax. The noise is as violent in its intensity as the dramatic events of the movie. (*Warner Bros.*)

The final scene from a movie is often the most important. Because of its privileged position, it can represent the filmmaker's summing up of the significance of the previous scenes. In Ermanno Olmi's *Il Posto* (The Job, also known as *The Sound of Trumpets*), the director undercuts the ostensible "happy ending" with an ironic sound effect. The movie deals with a shy working-class youth who struggles diligently to land a lower level clerking job with a huge, impersonal corporation in Milan. Finally, he is hired. The boy is especially pleased that he has a secure job "for life." Olmi is more ambivalent. The final scene of the film presents a picture of stupifying tedium and entrapment: A close-up of the youth's sensitive face is juxtaposed with the monotonous sound of a mimeograph machine, clacking louder and louder and louder.

Sound effects can also express internal emotions. In Robert Redford's *Ordinary People,* for example, an uptight mother (Mary Tyler Moore) has prepared French toast for her emotionally unstable son. Though it is his favorite breakfast food, the young man is too tense to eat: His ambivalent attitude toward his mother is one of his main problems. Irritated by his "selfish" indifference to her gesture of maternal concern, she swoops up his plate and carries it to

5–11. *Apocalypse Now* **(U.S.A., 1979),** *directed by Francis Ford Coppola.*
The sound mixing in Coppola's surrealistic Vietnam epic is masterful, suffused with grotesque ironies. In this sequence, American helicopters hover and swirl like huge mechanized gods, dropping napalm bombs on a jungle village to the accompaniment of Wagner's inexorable "Ride of the Valkyries" which thunders on the sound track. As terrified peasants scurry for shelter, American soldiers prepare to go surfing in the poisonous fumes of battle.   *(United Artists)*

the sink, where she stuffs the French toast into the garbage disposal, its grinding roar a symbolic embodiment of her anger and agitation.

Like absolute stasis, absolute silence in a sound film tends to call attention to itself. Any significant stretch of silence creates an eerie vacuum—a sense of something impending, about to burst. Arthur Penn exploited this phenomenon in the conclusion of *Bonnie and Clyde.* The lovers stop on a country road to help a friend (actually an informer) with his truck, which has presumably broken down. Clumsily, he scrambles under the truck. There is a long moment of silence while the two lovers exchange puzzled, then anxious, glances. Suddenly, the sound track roars with the noise of machine guns as the lovers are brutally cut down by policemen hiding in the bushes.

Like the **freeze frame,** silence in a sound film can be used to symbolize death since we tend to associate sound with the presence of ongoing life. Kurosawa uses this technique effectively in *Ikiru,* after the elderly protagonist has been informed by a doctor that he is dying of cancer. Stupified by the specter of death, the old man stumbles out on the street, the sound track totally silent. When he's almost run over by a speeding auto, the sound track suddenly roars with the noise of city traffic. The protagonist is yanked back into the world of the living.

Music

Music is a highly abstract art, tending toward pure form. It's impossible to speak of the "subject matter" of a musical phrase. When merged with lyrics, music acquires a more concrete content because words, of course, have specific references. Both words and music convey meanings, but each in a different manner. With or without lyrics, music can be more specific when juxtaposed with film images. In fact, many musicians have complained that images tend to rob music of its ambiguity by anchoring musical tones to specific ideas and emotions. For example, few moviegoers can listen to Strauss's *Thus Spake Zarathustra* without being reminded of Kubrick's *2001: A Space Odyssey.* Some music lovers have lamented that Ponchielli's elegant "Dance of the Hours" conjures images of ridiculous dancing hippos, one of Disney's most brilliant sequences in *Fantasia* (5–13).

Theories about film music are surprisingly varied. Pudovkin and Eisenstein insisted that music must never serve merely as accompaniment: It ought to retain its own integrity. The film critic Paul Rotha claimed that music must even be allowed to dominate the image on occasion. Some filmmakers insist on purely descriptive music—a practice referred to as **mickeymousing** (so-called because of Disney's early experiments with music and **animation**). This type of score employs music as a literal equivalent to the image. If a character stealthily tiptoes from a room, for example, each step has a musical note to emphasize the suspense. Other directors believe that film music shouldn't be too good or it will detract from the images. Most imaginative directors reject this notion. For them, the music of even the greatest composers can be used in movies.

The list of composers who have worked directly in film is a long and impressive one, including Darius Milhaud, Arthur Honegger, Paul Hindemith,

5–I2. Audiovisual score from *Alexander Nevsky* (USSR, I938), *music by Sergei Prokofiev, directed by Sergei Eisenstein.*

The composer need not always subordinate his talents to those of the film director. Here, two great Soviet artists aligned their contributions into a totally fused production in which the music corresponds to the movement of the images set in a row. Prokofiev avoided purely "representational" elements (mickeymousing). Instead, the two concentrated sometimes on the images first, other times on the music. The result was what Eisenstein called "vertical montage," where the notes on the staff, moving from left to right, parallel the movements or major lines of the images which, set side by side, also "move" from left to right. Thus, if the lines in a series of images move from lower left to upper right, the notes of music would move in a similar direction on the musical staff. If the lines of a composition were jagged and uneven, the notes of music would also zigzag in a corresponding manner. See Sergei Eisenstein, "Form and Content: Practice," in *Film Sense* (New York: Harvest Books, I947).

Dmitri Shostakovich, Arnold Schoenberg, Sergei Prokofiev, William Walton, Benjamin Britten, Aaron Copland, Quincy Jones, Duke Ellington, The Modern Jazz Quartet, Virgil Thomson, Kurt Weill, Bob Dylan, George Gershwin, Ralph Vaughan Williams, Richard Rodgers, Cole Porter, Leonard Bernstein, and the Beatles, to mention only a few of the best known.

A filmmaker doesn't need to have technical expertise to use music effectively. As Aaron Copland pointed out, directors must know what they want from music *dramatically:* It's the composer's business to translate these dramatic needs into musical terms. Directors and composers work in a variety of ways. Most composers begin working after they have seen the **rough cut** of a movie— that is, the major footage before the editor has tightened up the slackness between shots. Some composers don't begin until the film has been totally completed except for the music. Directors of musicals, on the other hand, usually work with the composer before shooting begins.

Beginning with the opening credits, music can serve as a kind of overture to suggest the mood or spirit of the film as a whole. John Addison's opening music in *Tom Jones* is a witty, rapidly executed harpsichord piece. The harpsichord

5–13. *Fantasia* (U.S.A., 1940), *by Walt Disney.*

Music is the most abstract of the arts. When fused with images, however, it automatically acquires more anecdotal significance—a fact which dismays many musicians. When Disney used Ponchielli's dainty "Dance of the Hours" to accompany a deliciously ludicrous dance between Hyacinth Hippo and Ben Ali Gator in this movie, many music lovers were appalled by the "vulgarization." (*Walt Disney Productions*)

itself is associated with the eighteenth century, the period of the film. The occasionally jazzy phrases in the tune suggest a sly twentieth-century overview—a musical equivalent of the blending of centuries found in the movie itself.

Certain kinds of music can suggest locales, classes, or ethnic groups. For example, John Ford's westerns feature simple folk tunes like "Red River Valley" or religious hymns like "Shall We Gather at the River," which are associated with the American frontier of the late nineteenth century. Richly nostalgic, these songs are often played on frontier instruments—a plaintive harmonica or a concertina. Similarly, many Italian movies feature lyrical, highly emotional melodies, reflecting the operatic heritage of that country (5–14). The greatest composer of this kind of film music was Nino Rota, who scored virtually all of Fellini's films, as well as such distinguished works as Zeffirelli's *Romeo and Juliet* and Coppola's two *Godfather* movies.

Music can be used as foreshadowing, particularly when the dramatic context doesn't permit a director to prepare an audience for an event. Hitchcock, for example, often accompanied an apparently casual sequence with "anxious" music—a warning to the audience to be prepared. Sometimes these musical warnings are false alarms; other times they explode into frightening crescendos. Similarly, when actors are required to assume restrained or neutral expressions, music can suggest their internal—hidden—emotions. Bernard Herrmann's music functions in both ways in *Psycho*.

Modern atonal and dissonant music generally evokes a sense of anxiety in listeners. Often such music seems to have no melodic line and can even resemble

5–14. *Once Upon a Time in the West* **(Italy, 1969),** *with Charles Bronson and Claudia Cardinale, music by Ennio Morricone, directed by Sergio Leone.*
Leone's mythic fable is perhaps the most operatic western ever made, thanks to Morricone's brilliant score, which includes a jew's-harp, harmonica, banjo, whistling, and a soprano vocal. The film's principal theme is scored for full orchestra and is almost Verdian in its rapturous lyricism.   (*Paramount Pictures*)

a series of random noises. Giovanni Fusco's music for several of Antonioni's films (*L'Avventura, Red Desert, Eclipse*) produces precisely this sense of neurosis and paranoia. Fusco's music provides a similar function in the movies of Alain Resnais: *Hiroshima Mon Amour* and *La Guerre Est Finie*.

Music can also control emotional shifts within a scene. In John Huston's *The Red Badge of Courage*, for example, the protagonist (Audie Murphy), in an irrational outburst of daring, snatches the flag from a dying comrade and charges onto a raging battlefield. To emphasize the youth's surge of patriotism, the scene is accompanied by a spirited rendering of Yankee fighting songs. The charging young soldier stumbles by a wounded Confederate standard-bearer, writhing in pain on the ground, his flag in tatters. The music shifts to an agonizing dirge and gradually transforms into a grotesque distortion of "Dixie." The kinetic excitement of the protagonist's charge might easily have overshadowed the poignancy of the wounded Confederate, but with the aid of the music, the audience as well as the protagonist are suddenly brought to a grim halt.

Music can also provide ironic contrast. In many cases, the predominant mood of a scene can be neutralized or even reversed with contrasting music. In *Bonnie and Clyde*, the robbery scenes are often accompanied by spirited banjo music, giving these sequences a jolly sense of fun. More satirically, a scene from Kenneth Anger's *Scorpio Rising* shows a Hell's Angel motorcyclist putting on his elaborate riding gear. The scene is almost solemnly ritualistic, but the young man's narcissism is satirized by the banal tune "Blue Velvet," which plays on the

5–15. *Amadeus* **(U.S.A., 1984),** *with Tom Hulce (right), music by Wolfgang Amadeus Mozart, directed by Milos Forman.*
In addition to being a fairly accurate characterization of the boorish but likable lout who was Wolfgang Amadeus Mozart, this film also explores an interesting religious paradox. Why would God torment a pious servant (Mozart's rival, Salieri) with a knowledge of his own inescapable mediocrity as a composer, while the irreverent Mozart is blessed with genius? *Amadeus* means "loved of God." (*New Yorker Films*)

sound track. The homosexual undertones of his lifestyle are emphasized by the line "she wore blooo vell-vet . . ." Contrasting music needn't always be satiric, however. In Ermanno Olmi's *The Tree of the Wooden Clogs,* for example, the organ music of Johann Sebastian Bach accompanies many of the scenes, which are virtually documentary re-creations of Italian peasant life around 1900. The music provides these simple episodes with a sense of majesty—celebrating the dignity of labor and the grandeur of the human spirit.

Characterization can be suggested through musical motifs. In Fellini's *La Strada,* the pure, sad simplicity of the heroine (Giulietta Masina) is captured by a melancholy tune she plays on a trumpet. This theme is varied and elaborated upon in Nino Rota's delicate score, suggesting that even after her death her spiritual influence is still felt. Herrmann's score for *Citizen Kane* employs motifs flamboyantly and in a more complex manner (see Chapter 11).

Characterization can be even more precise when lyrics are added to music. In *The Last Picture Show,* for instance, pop tunes of the 1950s are used in association with specific characters. The bitchy Jacy (Cybill Shepherd) is linked to "Cold, Cold Heart," while her deceived boyfriend Duane (Jeff Bridges) is characterized by "A Fool Such as I." *American Graffiti* uses pop tunes in a similar manner. Two young lovers who have just quarreled are shown dancing at a sock hop to the tune of "Smoke Gets in Your Eyes." The lyric "yet today my love has flown away" acquires particular poignancy for the girl because the boy has just told her that he intends to date others when he goes off to college. The lovers are reconciled at the end of the movie when he decides not to leave after all. On the sound track, "Only You" is appropriately intuned, its syrupy lyrics emphasizing the destiny of love.

5–16. *Pink Floyd The Wall* **(Great Britain, 1982)** *directed by Alan Parker.*
"We don't need no education. We don't need no thought control. No dark sarcasm in the classroom. Teachers, leave us kids alone . . ." When combined with the dreamlike precision of Parker's surrealistic images, Pink Floyd's music evokes a powerful emotional response. *(MGM/UA Entertainment)*

5–17. *The Yellow Submarine* **(Great Britain, 1968),** *directed by George Dunning.*
Inspired by the Beatles's revolutionary album, *Sergeant Pepper's Lonely Hearts Club Band,* this animated feature captures the youthful spirit of whimsy and charm that typified British pop culture during the 1960s. *(Apple Films)*

Stanley Kubrick is a bold—and controversial—innovator in the use of film music. In *Dr. Strangelove,* he sardonically juxtaposes Vera Lynn's sentimental World War II tune, "We'll Meet Again," with images of a global nuclear holocaust—a grim reminder that we probably *won't* meet again after World War III. In *2001,* Kubrick juxtaposed images of a twenty-first-century rocket ship gliding through the immense blueness of space with the sounds of Strauss's nineteenth-century "Blue Danube Waltz"—an aural foreshadowing of man's obsolete technology in the more advanced technological universe beyond Jupiter. In *A Clockwork Orange,* Kubrick used music as a distancing device, particularly in violent scenes. Musical incongruity undercuts the realism of an otherwise vicious gang fight that takes place to the accompaniment of Rossini's urbane and witty overture to *The Thieving Magpie.* A brutal attack and rape scene is accompanied by a grotesque song-and-dance routine set to the tune of "Singin' in the Rain."

A frequent function of film music is to underline speech, especially dialogue. A common assumption about this kind of music is that it merely acts to prop up bad dialogue or poor acting. The hundreds of mediocre love scenes performed to quivering violins have perhaps prejudiced many viewers against this kind of musical accompaniment. However, some of the most gifted actors have benefited from it. In Olivier's *Hamlet,* the composer William Walton worked out his score with painstaking precision. In the "To be or not to be" soliloquy, the music provides a counterpoint to Olivier's brilliantly modulated delivery, adding yet another dimension to this complex speech.

Musicals and Opera

One of the most enduring and popular film genres is the musical, whose principal raison d'être is song and dance. Like opera and ballet, the narrative elements of a musical are usually pretexts for the production numbers, but many musicals are exceptionally sophisticated dramatically. Musicals can be divided into the realistic and the formalistic. Realistic musicals are generally backstage stories, in which the production numbers are presented as dramatically plausible. Such musicals usually justify a song or dance with a brief bit of dialogue—"Hey kids, let's rehearse the barn number"—and the barn number is then presented to the audience. A few realistic musicals are virtually dramas with music. In George Cukor's *A Star Is Born,* for example, the narrative events would hold up without the musical numbers, although audiences would thereby be deprived of some of Judy Garland's best scenes—a documentation, as it were, of her character's talent. *New York, New York* and *Cabaret* are also dramas interspersed with music.

Formalist musicals make no pretense at realism. Characters burst out in song and dance in the middle of a scene without easing into the number with a plausible pretext. This convention must be accepted as an aesthetic premise, otherwise the entire film will strike the viewer as absurd. Everything is heightened and stylized in such works—sets, costumes, acting, etc. Most of Vincente Minnelli's musicals are of this type: *Meet Me in St. Louis, The Band Wagon, An American in Paris,* and *Gigi.*

Although musicals have been produced in several countries, the **genre** has been dominated by Americans, perhaps because it's so intimately related to the American studio system. In the 1930s, several major studios specialized in a

5–18. *The Band Wagon* **(U.S.A., 1953),** *with Fred Astaire, Nanette Fabray, and Jack Buchanan; music by Howard Dietz and Arthur Schwartz; directed by Vincente Minnelli.*

The best movie musicals are generally created directly for the screen and are seldom stage adaptations. This charming "Triplets" number would be difficult to pull off in the live theater, for the three performers were required to strap false legs and feet onto their knees, their real legs bent behind them as they execute their song and dance. *(MGM)* particular type of musical. RKO produced the charming Fred Astaire–Ginger Rogers vehicles such as *Top Hat, Shall We Dance?* and *Carefree,* all directed by Mark Sandrich. Paramount specialized in sophisticated "continental" musicals like Lubitsch's *The Love Parade, One Hour With You,* and *Monte Carlo.* At Warner Brothers, choreographer–director Busby Berkeley delighted audiences with his proletarian show-biz stories like *Gold Diggers of 1933* and *Dames.* Berkeley's stylistic signature is his fondness for abstract geometrical patterns (created with the **optical printer**) and photography of dancers from unconventional **angles** (see 3–4).

In the 1940s and 1950s, the musical was dominated by MGM, which had the finest musical directors under contract: Kelly, Donen, and Minnelli. Indeed, this prosperous studio had a virtual monopoly on the musical personalities of the day, including Garland, Kelly, Frank Sinatra, Mickey Rooney, Ann Miller, Vera-Ellen, Leslie Caron, Donald O'Connor, Cyd Charisse, Howard Keel, Mario Lanza, Kathryn Grayson, and many others. MGM also lured away Astaire, Pan, and Berkeley who, along with Michael Kidd, Bob Fosse, Gower Champion, and the ubiquitous Kelly, created most of the choreographies for the studio. Arthur Freed was the producer of most of Metro's important musicals, including the majority of Minnelli's films, as well as the stylish works of Donen: *On the Town, Singin' in the Rain* (both codirected by Kelly), and the exquisite *Funny Face.*

The combining of music with drama is a practice extending back at least to ancient Greece, but no other medium excels the expressive range of the cinema. The stage has no equivalent to the musical documentary, like *Woodstock* or *Gimme Shelter.* Movie musicals can take the form of animated fantasies, such as the Disney features *Bambi* and *Dumbo.* Musical biographies like *Amadeus* and *The Buddy Holly Story* are commonplace in film. Examples of great musicals

5–19. *New York, New York (U.S.A., 1977), with Liza Minnelli and Robert De Niro, music by John Kander and Fred Ebb, directed by Martin Scorsese.*
A number of commentators have pointed out that the most enduring genres tend to evolve toward a revisionist phase— mocking many of the genre's original values by subjecting them to skeptical scrutiny. For example, most musicals of the big studio era were essentially love stories and are concluded with the obligatory boy-wins-girl finale. Such revisionist musicals as *Cabaret* and *New York, New York,* however, end with the lovers going their separate ways, too absorbed by their own careers to submit to love's rituals of self-sacrifice. *(United Artists)*

5–20. *The Magic Flute* (Sweden, 1975), *with Josef Kostlinger, music by Wolfgang Amadeus Mozart, directed by Ingmar Bergman.*

In adapting opera to the screen, the filmmaker must adjust the style of presentation to fit the essence of the materials. For example, Mozart's *The Magic Flute* was originally created for a popular, nonsophisticated audience, and its loony storyline is based on fairy tales and the esoteric symbolism of eighteenth-century freemasonry. Bergman decided to stage it "realistically"—that is, as a straightforward presentation in the eighteenth-century manner, complete with all the wires and stage fakery in plain sight, thus creating an air of childlike enchantment. From time to time, Bergman cuts to reaction shots of present-day spectators watching the production from the opera house auditorium. *(Surrogate Release)*

5–21. *Don Giovanni* (France, 1979), *music by Wolfgang Amadeus Mozart, directed by Joseph Losey.*

The story materials of this opera are more coherent, less supernatural, than those of *The Magic Flute,* and Losey accordingly staged the action in real locations in Italy. Instead of concentrating exclusively on images of the singers, Losey often juxtaposes them with their dramatic environments, allowing the sound track to provide the continuity for the fragmentation of the editing. *(New Yorker Films)*

created directly for the screen are *Singin' in the Rain* and *The Band Wagon*. Others are **loose adaptations** of stage musicals, like *My Fair Lady, Hair,* and *Little Shop of Horrors*.

The cinema is also an ideal operatic medium, as can be seen in Bergman's *The Magic Flute* and Joseph Losey's *Don Giovanni* (Mozart's two greatest operas). These movies are more flexible spatially than any stage productions could hope to be, without compromising the music. Only a handful of operatic films approach major stature, perhaps because only a handful of first-rate filmmakers have been attracted to the subgenre. One immense advantage is that movie subtitles are far more convenient than theatrical librettos for explaining the action. With subtitles, the spectator can concentrate on the immediacy of the musical moment, rather than having to place it within a larger narrative context. Each opera requires a unique approach, some "realistic" (5–20), others more stylized (5–21). One thing is certain: Pictures of singing heads may be accurate recordings of opera performances, but they aren't real movies.

Spoken Language

A common misconception, held even by otherwise sophisticated moviegoers, is that language in film cannot be as complex as it is in literature. The fact that Shakespeare has been successfully brought to the screen—with no significant impoverishment in either language or visual beauty—should stand as an obvious contradiction to this notion. In fact, a number of great films are not particularly literary. This is not to say that movies are incapable of literary distinction, but only that some filmmakers wish to emphasize other aspects of their art. Those who dismiss literary movies as uncinematic find themselves in the shaky position of condemning Welles, Bergman, Huston, Richardson, Losey, Wilder, Truffaut, and Woody Allen, to mention only a few directors with literary sensibilities.

In some respects, language in film can be more complex than in literature. In the first place, the words of a movie, like those of the live theater, are spoken, not written, and the human voice is capable of far more nuances than the cold printed page. The written word is a crude approximation of the connotative richness of spoken language. Thus, to take a simple example of no literary merit, the meaning of the words "I will see him tomorrow" seem obvious enough in written form. But an actor can emphasize one word over the others and thus change the meanings of the sentence completely. Here are a few possibilities:

I will *see* him tomorrow.	(Implying, but that's all I'll do.)
I will see him *tomorrow*.	(Implying, not today, or any other time.)
I will see him tomorrow.	(Implying, not you or anyone else.)
I *will* see him tomorrow.	(Implying, and I don't care if you approve.)
I will see *him* tomorrow.	(Implying, but not anyone else.)

Of course a novelist or poet could emphasize specific words by italicizing them. But unlike actors, writers don't generally underline words in every sentence. On

5–22. *The Spanish Earth* (Holland/U.S.A., 1937), *directed by Joris Ivens.*
Spoken language can provide abstract information to accompany the concrete visuals of a documentary. But language can also be used to produce an emotional effect. In this famous documentary, the great Dutch filmmaker Ivens, in collaboration with the American novelist Ernest Hemingway, exposed the mass killing of civilians during the Spanish Civil War of the late 1930s. With the materials of slaughter provided by his cronies Hitler and Mussolini, Franco wreaked devastation on thousands of innocent Spaniards, many of them women and children. Hemingway's commentary, spoken by the novelist himself, communicates the sense of helpless terror brought on by the bombings: "Before, death came when you were old and sick. But now it comes to all in this village. High in the sky and shining silver, it comes to all who have no place to run, no place to hide." *(Museum of Modern Art)*

the other hand, actors routinely go through their speeches to see which words to stress, which to "throw away," and the ways to best achieve these effects—in each and every sentence. To a gifted actor, the written speech is a mere blueprint, an outline, compared to the complexities of spoken speech. A performer with an excellent voice—an Alec Guinness or a James Earl Jones—could wrench ten or twelve meanings from this simple sentence, let alone a Shakespearean soliloquy.

Written punctuation is likewise a simplified approximation of speech rhythms. The pauses, hesitancies, and rapid slurs of speech can only be partially suggested by punctuation:

> I will . . . see him—tomorrow.
> I will see him—tomorrow!
> I . . . will . . . see him—tomorrow?

And so on. But how is one to capture all the meanings that have no punctuation equivalents? Even professional linguists, who have a vast array of diacritical marks to record speech, recognize that these symbols are primitive devices at best, capable of capturing only a fraction of the subtleties of the human voice. An actor like Laurence Olivier built much of his reputation on his genius in capturing little quirks of speech—an irrepressible giggle between words, for example, or a sudden vocal plummeting on one word, a gulp, or an hysterical upsurge in pitch. The gamut of sounds and rhythms in Olivier's delivery suggests the virtuosity of a musical instrument.

By definition, speech patterns deviating radically from the offical dialect are generally regarded as substandard—at least by those who take such pat distinctions seriously. Dialects can be a rich source of meaning in movies (and in life, too, for that matter). Since dialects are usually spoken by people outside the Establishment, they tend to convey a subversive ideology. For example, the comic art of Richard Pryor is steeped in the jivy idiom of America's black ghettos—best illustrated perhaps by his diabolically funny concert films (9–10). Similarly, such performers as Kris Kristofferson and Sissy Spacek have virtually specialized in "talkin' country." The earthiness of cockney and the robust dialects of Britain's midland industrial cities like Liverpool were popularized by

5–23. *Xala* (Senegal, 1974), *directed by Ousmane Sembene.*
Senegal, a former French colony, has a population of only four million, yet it has produced the most important movies of black Africa, most notably those of Sembene, the continent's best-known filmmaker. *Xala* (which roughly translates "the curse of impotence") is spoken in French and Wolof, the native language of Senegal. The movie is an exposé of the nation's servile ruling class, whose members have eagerly embraced the culture of their white colonial predecessors. (At this lavish wedding reception, for example, several Frenchified Beautiful People wonder what the English translation is for "le weekend.") The cultural commentator Hernandez Arregui has observed: "Culture becomes bilingual not due to the use of two languages but because of the conjuncture of two cultural patterns of thinking. One is national, that of the people, and the other is estranging, that of the classes subordinated to outside forces. The admiration that the upper classes express for the United States or Europe is the highest expression of their subjection." Like many Third World artists, Sembene advocates the creation of a truly indigenous culture, somewhat like Emerson's call in the nineteenth century for our own artists to stop producing tepid imitations of British models in favor of a truly American idiom. See *Film and Politics in the Third World,* edited by John D.H. Downing (New York: Praeger Publishers, 1988).   (*New Yorker Films*)

such working-class rock groups as the Rolling Stones and the Beatles. A number of Continental filmmakers have also exploited the expressive richness of dialects, most notably Lina Wertmüller (5–25).

Because language is spoken in movies and plays, these two mediums enjoy an advantage over printed language in that the words of a text can be juxtaposed with the ideas and emotions of a **subtext.** Briefly, a subtext refers to those implicit meanings *behind* the language of a film or play script. For example, the following lines of dialogue might be contained in a script:

> Woman: May I have a cigarette, please?
> Man: Yes, of course. (Lights her cigarette.)
> Woman: Thank you. You're very kind.
> Man: Don't mention it.

As written, these four not very exciting lines seem simple enough and rather neutral emotionally. But, depending on the dramatic context, they can be exploited to suggest other ideas, totally independent of the apparent meaning of the words. If the woman was flirting with the man, for example, she would

5–24. *Bull Durham* **(U.S.A., 1988),** *with Susan Sarandon and Kevin Costner, written and directed by Ron Shelton.*
Southern accents are among the most lyrical dialects of American speech. Perhaps this is why so many of America's finest writers are from the South. This movie, which is narrated by the Sarandon character (a North Carolinian and sometimes English instructor), is punctuated with lyrical flights of fancy that sometimes leave the menfolk speechless with wonder.   *(Orion Pictures)*

deliver the lines very differently than an efficient businesswoman. If they detested one another, the lines would take on another significance. If the man were flirting with a hostile female, the lines would be delivered in yet another way, suggesting other meanings. In short, the meaning of the passage is provided by the actors, not the language, which is merely camouflage. (For a more detailed discussion of the concept of a subtext, see Chapter 6.)

Any script meant to be spoken has a subtext, even one of great literary distinction. A good example from a classic text can be seen in Zeffirelli's *Romeo and Juliet,* in which Mercutio (John McEnery) is played not as the witty *bon vivant* who's intoxicated with his own talk, but as a neurotic young man with a shaky grasp of reality. This interpretation upset some traditionalists, but in the context of the movie, it reinforces the loving bond between Romeo and his best friend, and helps justify Romeo's impulsive (and self-destructive) act of revenge later in the film when Mercutio is killed by Tybalt.

Some contemporary filmmakers deliberately neutralize their language, claiming that the subtext is what they're really after. Harold Pinter, the dramatist and screenwriter, is perhaps the most famous example of a contemporary writer who stresses the significance of the subtext. In *The Homecoming,* a scene of extraordinary eroticism is conveyed through dialogue involving the request for a glass of water! Pinter claims that language is often a kind of "cross-talk," a way of concealing fears and anxieties. In some respects, this technique can be even more effective in film, where close-ups can convey the meanings behind words more subtly than an actor on a stage. Pinter's movie scripts are among the most

5–25. *All Screwed Up* **(Italy, 1973),** *directed by Lina Wertmüller.*
Wertmüller is acutely sensitive to the ideological implications of dialects. Much of her comedy is mined from the earthy idioms of her working-class southerners in contrast with the standard (Tuscan) dialect spoken in the north of Italy. Her characters frequently swear or express themselves in coarse language, which is often very funny. Needless to say, much of this comedy is lost in translation. The language is sometimes drained of its vitality, reduced to bland respectability. For example, "Piss off!" becomes "Go away," or worse yet, "Please leave me alone." (*New Line Cinema*)

suggestive subtexts of the contemporary cinema: *The Pumpkin Eater, The Servant, Accident, The Go-Between, The Caretaker, The Homecoming, The French Lieutenant's Woman,* and *Betrayal.*

But these are merely some of the advantages of language that film enjoys over literature—advantages shared, in large part, by the live theater. As an art of juxtapositions, movies can also extend the meanings of language by contrasting spoken words with images. The sentence "I will see him tomorrow" acquires still other meanings when the image shows the speaker smiling, for example, or frowning, or looking determined. All sorts of juxtapositions are possible. The sentence could be delivered with a determined emphasis, but an image of a frightened face (or eye, or a twitching mouth) can modify the verbal determination or even cancel it out. The juxtaposed image could be a **reaction shot**—thus emphasizing the effect of the statement on the listener. Or the camera could photograph an important object, implying a connection between the speaker, the words, and the object. If the speaker is photographed in long shot, his juxtaposition with his environment could also change the meanings of the words. The same line spoken in close-up would emphasize yet different meanings.

This advantage of simultaneity extends to other sounds. Music and sound effects can modify the meanings of words considerably. The same sentence spoken in an echo chamber will have different connotations from the sentence whispered intimately. If a clap of thunder coincided with the utterance of the sentence, the effect would be different from the chirping of birds or the whining of the wind. Since film is also a mechanical medium, the sentence could be modified by a deliberate distortion in the sound recording. In short, depending on the vocal emphasis, the visual emphasis, and the accompanying sound track,

5–26. *The Loneliness of the Long-Distance Runner* **(Great Britain, 1962),** *with Tom Courtenay, directed by Tony Richardson.*

Spoken language is steeped in ideology. It's an instant revealer of class, education, and cultural bias. In most countries of the world, regional dialects are regarded as substandard—at any rate by those speaking the "official" (i.e., ruling class) dialect. In Great Britain in particular, dialects correlate closely with the class system. People in power speak the same "Establishment" dialect that is taught in the exclusive private schools that still educate most ruling-class Britons. On the other hand, the working-class Nottingham dialect of the protagonist of this film (Courtenay) places him outside the spheres of power and prestige. He's an outsider, a lowly prole, déclassé. (*Audio-Brandon Films*) this simple sentence could have dozens of different meanings in film, some of them impossible to capture in written form.

There are two types of spoken language in movies—the monologue and dialogue. Monologues are often associated with documentaries, in which an off-screen narrator provides the audience with factual information accompanying the visuals. Most documentary theorists are agreed that the cardinal rule in the use of this technique is to avoid duplicating the information given in the image itself. The commentary should provide what is not apparent on the screen. The audience, in short, is provided with two types of information, one concrete (visuals), the other abstract (narration). Cinéma vérité documentarists have extended this technique to include interviews, a practice pioneered by the French filmmaker Jean Rouch. Thus, instead of an anonymous narrator, the sound track conveys the actual words of the subjects of the documentary—slum dwellers, perhaps, or students. The camera can focus on the speaker or can roam elsewhere, with the sound track providing the continuity.

Monologues have also been employed in fiction films. This technique is especially useful in condensing events and time. Narrative monologues can be

5–27. ***Sunset Boulevard*** (**U.S.A.,** **1950**), *with William Holden and Gloria Swanson, directed by Billy Wilder.*
Voice-over monologues are often used to produce ironic contrasts between the past and the present. Almost inevitably, such contrasts suggest a sense of destiny and fate. This film is narrated by a dead man (Holden), while the flashback images show us how he managed to get himself killed. *(Paramount Pictures)*

used omnisciently to provide an ironic contrast with the visuals. In Richardson's *Tom Jones,* John Osborne's script features an off-screen narrator who's nearly as witty and urbane as Fielding's, though necessarily less chatty. This narrator sets up the story, provides us with thumbnail sketches of the characters, connects many of the episodes with necessary transitions, and comments philosophically on the escapades of the incorrigible hero.

Off-screen narration tends to give a movie a sense of objectivity and often an air of predestination. Many of the works of Billy Wilder are structured in **flashbacks,** with ironic monologues emphasizing fatality: The main interest is not what happened, but how and why. In *Double Indemnity,* for example, the story is narrated by the fatally wounded hero, who admits his guilt at the opening of the film. As Wilder pointed out: "By identifying the criminals right off the bat—and identifying ourselves with them—we can concentrate on what follows: their efforts to escape, the net closing, closing."

The interior monologue is one of the most valuable tools of filmmakers, for with it they can convey what a character is thinking. The interior monologue is frequently used in adaptations of plays and novels. Before Olivier, most film soliloquies were delivered as they are on stage: That is, the camera and microphone record a character literally talking to himself. Olivier's *Hamlet* introduced a more cinematic soliloquy. In the "To be or not to be" speech, several of the lines are not spoken but "thought"—via a **voice-over** sound track. Suddenly, at a

5–28. *Blume in Love* (U.S.A., 1973), *with George Segal, Kris Kristofferson, and Susan Anspach, written and directed by Paul Mazursky.*
Interior monologues are especially effective in presenting us with a contrast between what's said socially and what's thought privately. In this movie, for example, Blume (Segal, right) narrates what he was really feeling when he attempted to ingratiate himself with his ex-wife and her lover. *(Warner Bros.)*

5–29. *Badlands* (**U.S.A., 1974**), *with Sissy Spacek, written and directed by Terrence Malick.*
Not all voice-over narratives are omniscient. This movie is narrated by a bored and dimwitted teenager (Spacek) who talks in *True Romance* clichés and hasn't a glimmer of insight into what wrecked her life. (*Warner Bros.*)

crucial line, Olivier spews out the words in exasperation. Through the use of the sound track, private ruminations and public speech can be combined in interesting ways, with new and often more subtle emphases.

A major difference between stage dialogue and screen dialogue is degree of density. One of the necessary conventions of the live theater is articulation: If something is bothering a character, we can usually assume that he or she will *talk* about the problem. The theater is a visual as well as aural medium, but in general the spoken word is dominant: We tend to hear before we see. If information is conveyed visually in the theater, it must be larger than life, for most of the audience is too far from the stage to perceive visual nuances. The convention of articulation is necessary, therefore, to compensate for this visual loss. Like most artistic conventions, stage dialogue is not usually realistic or natural, even in so-called realistic plays. In real life, people don't articulate their ideas and feelings with such precision. In movies, the convention of articulation can be relaxed. Since the close-up can show the most minute detail, verbal comment is often superfluous. This greater spatial flexibility means that film language doesn't have to carry the heavy burden of stage dialogue. In fact, since the image conveys most meanings, dialogue in film can be as spare and realistic as it is in everyday life, as in such starkly dialogued movies as Siegel's *Escape from Alcatraz* (5–30) and most of the works of Antonioni.

Movie dialogue doesn't have to conform to natural speech. If language is stylized, the director has several options for making it believable. Like Olivier, he or she can emphasize an intimate style of delivery—sometimes even whispering the lines. Welles's Shakespearean films are characterized by a visual flamboyance: The expressionistic stylization of the images in *Othello* complements the artificiality of the language. Generally speaking, if dialogue is nonrealistic, the images must be co-expressive: Sharp contrasts of style between language and visuals can produce jarring and often comic incongruities.

The advantages of language, then, make it indispensable to the film artist and not only to those of literary tastes. As René Clair foresaw many years ago, sound permits a director more visual freedom, not less. Because speech can reveal a person's class, region, occupation, prejudices, etc., the director doesn't need to waste time establishing these facts visually. A few lines of dialogue can convey all that's necessary, thus freeing the camera to go on to other matters. There are many instances where language is the most economical and precise way of conveying information in film.

Foreign language movies are shown either in dubbed versions or in their original language, with written subtitles. Both methods of translation have obvious limitations. Dubbed movies often have a hollow, tinny sound, and in most cases the dubbing is performed by less gifted actors than the originals. Sound and image are difficult to match in dubbed films, especially in the closer ranges where the movements of the actors' lips aren't synchronized with the sounds. Even bilingual actors who do their own dubbing are less nuanced when they're not speaking their native language. For example, Sophia Loren's performance in the English-language version of *Two Women* is very good, but it lacks the vocal expressiveness of her brilliant line-readings in the original Italian. In English, Loren's classy pear-shaped tones are somewhat at odds with her role as an earthy peasant. In a similar vein, actors with highly distinctive voices, like Mae West or

5–30. *Escape from Alcatraz* (U.S.A., 1979), *with Clint Eastwood, directed by Don Siegel.*
Effective dialogue is not always the result of literate scripts and richly expressive language, especially in realistic movies. Talk is usually kept to a stark minimum in Eastwood's films. He is at his best when we must infer what he is thinking: His face is far more expressive than the way he talks, for his words are few, delivered in a matter-of-fact monotone. In Eastwood's case, less is usually more.   (*Paramount Pictures*)

5–31. *Back to the Future* (U.S.A., 1985), *with Crispin Glover, Lea Thompson, and Michael J. Fox; written and directed by Robert Zemeckis.*
Language is always dated—especially colloquial language, which is filled with slang peculiar to a given generation. The hero of this film (Fox) is a 1985 teenager who returns to the past and meets up with his parents in the year 1955. Much of the humor in the movie revolves around the different connotations of language in each time period. *(Universal Studios)*

John Wayne, sound preposterous when dubbed in German or Japanese. On the other hand, dubbed movies permit the spectator to concentrate on the visuals rather than the subtitles, which are distracting and can absorb much of a viewer's energy. Nobody likes to "read" a movie.

Most experienced filmgoers still prefer subtitles, however, despite their cumbersomeness. In the first place, some spectators are sufficiently conversant in foreign languages to understand most of the dialogue (especially in Europe where virtually all educated people speak a second language, and in some cases three or four). An actor's tone of voice is often more important than the dialogue per se, and subtitled movies allow us to hear these vocal nuances. In short, subtitles permit us to hear what the original artists said, not what some disinterested technician—however clever—decided we would settle for.

5–32. *Good Morning, Vietnam* (U.S.A., 1987), *with Robin Williams, directed by Barry Levinson.*
Although the script to this movie is credited to Mitch Markowitz, many of the radio monologues (the best scenes in the film) were created by Williams, one of America's finest stand-up comedians and a brilliant improviser. *(Touchstone Pictures)*

FURTHER READING

CAMERON, EVAN WILLIAM et al., ed. *Sound and the Cinema: The Coming of Sound to American Film* (Pleasantville, N.Y.: Redgrave Publishing, 1980). A collection of useful articles.

EVANS, MARK, *Soundtrack: The Music of the Movies* (New York: Hopkinson and Blake, 1975). General history.

EVERSON, WILLIAM K., *American Silent Film* (New York: Oxford University Press, 1978). Historical study and aesthetic analysis.

HAGEN, EARL, *Scoring for Films* (New York: Wehman, 1972). Technical emphasis.

McCARTHY, CLIFFORD, *Film Composers in America* (New York: Da Capo, 1972). Survey of major figures.

MORDDEN, ETHAN, *The Hollywood Musical* (New York: St. Martin's Press, 1982). Eccentric, astute, well written.

PRENDERGAST, ROY M., *Film Music* (New York: Norton, 1977). Excellent analysis.

THOMAS, TONY, *Music for the Movies* (San Diego, Cal.: A. S. Barnes, 1973).

WALKER, ALEXANDER, *The Shattered Silents* (New York: William Morrow, 1979). A well-written history.

WEIS, ELISABETH, and JOHN BELTON, eds., *Film Sound: Theory and Practice* (New York: Columbia University Press, 1985). A collection of scholarly articles.

ACTING | 6

In the cinema the actor must think and let his thoughts work upon his face. The objective nature of the medium will do the rest. A theatrical performance requires magnification, a cinema performance requires an inner life.

—CHARLES DULLIN

Film acting is a complex and variable art which can be broken down into four categories:

1. *Extras*. These actors are used primarily to provide a sense of a crowd—as in "a cast of thousands." Players of this type are used as camera material, like a landscape or a set.

2. *Nonprofessional performers*. These are amateur players who are chosen not because of their acting ability, which can be negligible, but because of their authentic appearance—they *look* right for a given part.

3. *Trained professionals*. These stage and screen performers are capable of playing a variety of roles in a variety of styles. The majority of actors fall under this category.

4. *Stars*. These are famous performers who are widely recognized by the public. Their drawing power is one of the main attractions of a film or stage play. The **star system** was developed and has been dominated by the American cinema, though it's hardly unique to movies. Virtually all the performing arts—opera, dance, live theater, television, concert music—have exploited the box-office popularity of a charismatic performer.

However a film actor is classified, virtually all performers in this medium concede that their work is shaped by the person who literally and figuratively calls the shots. Even Charlie Chaplin, the most famous movie star of his era, admitted: "Film acting is unquestionably a director's medium." In short, the movie actor is ultimately a tool of the director—another "language system" through which the filmmaker communicates ideas and emotions.

Stage and Screen Acting

The differences between stage and screen acting are largely determined by the differences in space and time in each medium (see also Chapter 7, Drama). In general, the live theater seems to be a more satisfactory medium for the actor

6–1. *Valentino* **(U.S.A., 1977),** *with Rudolph Nureyev and Michelle Phillips, directed by Ken Russell.*
The beauty of the human form—both male and female—is one of the most persistent attractions of the cinema and can be traced back almost to its inception. Indeed, sexual allure has been a compelling aphrodisiac in most of the performing arts, dating back to ancient times. Even in painting and sculpture, eroticism is fundamental to an appreciation of the nude, as the art scholar Kenneth Clark has pointed out.   *(United Artists)*

because, once the curtain goes up, he or she tends to dominate the proceedings. In movies, this is not usually the case. Actress Kim Stanley expressed the differences well: "No matter what you do in film, it is, after all, bits and pieces for the director, and that's marvelous for the director but it doesn't allow the actor to learn to mold a part. In films, it's the director who is the artist. An actor has much more chance to create on stage."

Even the requirements are different in each medium. The essential requisites for the stage performer are to be seen and heard clearly. Thus, the ideal theatrical actor must have a flexible, trained voice. Most obviously, his or her voice must be powerful enough to be heard even in a theater containing thousands of seats. Since language is the major source of meaning in the theater, the nuances of the dialogue must be conveyed through vocal expressiveness. An actor's voice must be capable of much variety. It's necessary to know which words to stress and how to stress them, how to phrase properly for different types of lines, when to pause and for how long, and how fast or slow a line or speech ought to be delivered. Above all, the stage actor must be *believable,* even when reciting dialogue that's highly stylized and unnatural. Most of the credit for an exciting theatrical production is given to the performers, but much of the burden is also theirs, for when we're bored by a production of a play, we tend to assign the responsibility to the actors.

6–2. *The Trojan Women* **(Greece, 1971),** *with Vanessa Redgrave, directed by Michael Cacoyannis.*
Vanessa Redgrave is widely regarded as the greatest British actress of her generation. Descended from a famous theatrical family, she has distinguished herself in the live theater, movies, and television, winning awards in each medium. She has acted in the works of many classic authors, including Shakespeare, Chekhov, and (shown here) Euripides.   *(Cinerama Releasing)*

Physical requirements are less exacting in the theater than in movies. Most obviously, the stage actor must be seen—even from the back of the auditorium. Thus, it helps to be tall, for small actors tend to get lost on a large stage. It also helps to have large and regular features, although makeup can cover a multitude of deficiencies. For this reason, casting a forty-year-old actor as Romeo is not necessarily a disaster in the theater, for if the actor is in reasonably good physical shape, his age won't show beyond the first rows of seats. Because of the low visual saturation in the theater, actors can play roles twenty years beyond their actual age, provided their voices and bodies are flexible enough.

The stage actor's entire body is always in view, and for this reason he must be able to control it with some degree of precision. Some obvious activities as sitting, walking, and standing are performed differently on the stage than they are in real life. An actor must usually learn how to dance, how to fence, and how

6–3. *Raging Bull* (**U.S.A., 1980**), *with Robert De Niro, directed by Martin Scorsese.*
Acting is a demanding art, requiring dedication, discipline, and Spartan endurance. De Niro is famous for his rigorous preparations prior to production. This film is a biography of Jake LaMotta, the middle-weight boxing champion of the 1940s. De Niro trained for several months with the real La Motta (who served as technical advisor to the film) in order to capture the fighter's pugilistic style **(a)**. Amazed by De Niro's skill, La Motta claimed that the actor could be a professional boxer if he wanted. During a shooting hiatus, De Niro even put on fifty pounds so he wouldn't have to resort to padding in order to portray La Motta in later life, when his body was encased in fat **(b)**. De Niro prefers to bury himself in a role. He rarely exploits his personal charisma, insisting that life should take precedence over art. But De Niro's is an art that conceals art. "Some of the old movie stars were terrific," he explained, "but they romanticized. People chase illusions and these illusions are created by movies. I want to make things concrete and real and to break down the illusion. There's nothing more ironic or strange or contradictory than life itself. I don't want people years from now to say: 'Remember De Niro, he had real style'." *(United Artists)*

(a) **(b)**

to move naturally in period costumes. He must know what to do with his hands—when to let them hang and when to use them for expressive gestures. Furthermore, stage actors must know how to adjust their bodies to different characters: A seventeen-year-old girl moves differently than a woman of thirty; an aristocrat moves differently than a clerk of the same age. The body must communicate a wide variety of emotions in pantomime: A happy person even stands differently than one who is dejected, or fearful, or bored.

Theatrical acting preserves real time. The performer must build—scene by scene—toward the climactic scene near the end of the play. Usually the stage actor begins at a relatively low energy level, then increases with each progressive scene until, in the climax, the energy reaches its bursting point and finally tapers off in the resolution of the play. In short, the actor generates in psychic energy the play's own structure. Within this overall structure, the stage performer "builds" within each scene, although not every scene is automatically played at a greater intensity than its predecessor, for different plays build in different ways. What's essential for the stage actor is to sustain an energy level for the duration of a scene. Once the curtain rises, he's alone on the stage. Mistakes aren't easily corrected, nor can a scene be replayed or cut out.

In general, the film player can get along quite well with a minimum of stage technique. The essential requisite for a performer in the movies is what Antonioni calls "expressiveness." That is, he or she must *look* interesting. No amount of technique will compensate for an unphotogenic face (6–4). A number of stage performers have fared badly in the movies because of this deficiency. For example, Kim Stanley and Tallulah Bankhead were among the most admired stage stars in America, but their film work failed to excite much interest. Similarly, Ian Richardson is regarded as one of the most brilliant actors of the British stage—

6–4. *The Whisperers* (Great Britain, **1967**), *with Edith Evans, directed by Bryan Forbes.*

The cinematic close-up allows the film actor to concentrate totally on the truth of the moment—without the need to worry about projecting to the back rows. Gestures and facial expressions can be exquisitely nuanced. Stage actors generally must convey such nuances through words. The Hungarian theorist Béla Balázs believed that the movie close-up can isolate the human face from its surroundings and penetrate the soul: "What appears on the face and in facial expression is a spiritual experience," Balázs observed. This experience is impossible to achieve in the live theater, because the spectator is too distant from the performer. (*United Artists*)

(a)   (b)   (c)

(g)   (h)   (i)

(m)   (n)   (o)

(s)   (t)   (u)

6–5. Sequence from *Sabotage* **(Great Britain, 1936),** *with Sylvia Sidney and Oscar Homolka, directed by Alfred Hitchcock.*
Through the art of editing, a director can construct a highly emotional "performance" by juxtaposing shots of his actors with shots of objects. In scenes such as these, the actor's contribution tends to be minimal: The effect is achieved through the linking of two or more shots. This associational process is the basis of Pudovkin's theory of constructive editing.   (*Gaumont-British*)

(d)   (e)   (f)

(j)   (k)   (l)

(p)   (q)   (r)

(v)   (w)   (x)

where brilliant actors are commonplace—but his few film performances are lackluster. Some of the most famous stage actors in history—including Sarah Bernhardt—look preposterous on film: Her techniques are mannered and stagey to the point of caricature. In movies, then, too much technique can actually undercut a performance, can make it seem hammy and insincere.

Acting in the cinema is almost totally dependent upon the filmmaker's approach to the story materials. In general, the more **realistic** the director's techniques, the more necessary it is to rely on the abilities of the players. Such directors tend to favor **long shots,** which keep the performer's entire body within the **frame.** This is the camera distance that corresponds to the proscenium arch of the live theater. The realist also tends to favor **lengthy takes**—thus permitting the actors to sustain performances for relatively long periods without interruption. From the audience's point of view, it's easier to evaluate acting in a realistic movie because we are permitted to see sustained scenes without any apparent directorial interference. The camera remains essentially a recording device.

The more **formalistic** the director, the less likely he or she is to value the actor's contribution. Some of Hitchcock's most stunning cinematic effects were achieved by minimizing the contributions of actors. During the production of *Sabotage,* Hitchcock's leading lady, Sylvia Sidney, burst into tears on the set because she wasn't permitted to act a crucial scene. The episode involved a murder in which the sympathetic heroine kills her brutish husband in revenge for his murder of her young brother. On stage, of course, the heroine's feelings and thoughts would be communicated by the actress's exaggerated facial expressions. But in real life, Hitchcock observed, people's faces don't necessarily reveal what they think or feel. The director preferred to convey these ideas and emotions through **edited** juxtapositions (6–5).

The setting for the scene is a dinner table. The heroine looks at her husband who is eating as usual. Then a **close-up** shows a dish containing meat and vegetables with a knife and fork lying next to it; the wife's hands are seen behind the dish. Hitchcock then cuts to a **medium shot** of the wife thoughtfully slicing some meat. Next, a medium shot of the brother's empty chair. Close-up of the wife's hands with knife and fork. Close-up of a bird cage with canaries—a reminder to the heroine of her dead brother. Close-up of wife's thoughtful face. Close-up of the knife and plate. Suddenly a close-up of the husband's suspicious face: He notices the connection between the knife and her thoughtful expression, for the camera **pans,** rather than cuts, back to the knife. He gets up next to her. Hitchcock quickly cuts to a close-up of her hand reaching for the knife. Cut to an **extreme close-up** of the knife entering his body. Cut to a **two shot** of their faces, his convulsed with pain, hers in fear. Cut to a **deep-focus** long shot, in which his dead body drops out of frame. When Sylvia Sidney saw the finished product, she was delighted with the results. The entire scene, of course, required very little acting in the conventional sense of the term.

Antonioni has stated that he uses his actors only as part of the composition—"like a tree, a wall, or a cloud." Many of the major themes of his films are conveyed through long shots where the juxtaposition of people and their settings is used to suggest complex psychological and spiritual states. Perhaps more than any other director, Antonioni is sensitive to how meanings change, depending on the **mise en scène.** Similarly, the French director Robert

6–6. *Freaks* (U.S.A., 1932), *directed by Tod Browning.*
This bizarre and oddly poetic film about a traveling sideshow of freaks featured a supporting cast of real-life circus freaks. They were cast not for their acting ability, but for their authenticity. *(MGM)*

Bresson believes that a screen actor is not an interpretive artist but merely one of the "raw materials" of the mise en scène and the editing. He generally prefers to use nonprofessional actors in his movies because trained actors tend to want to convey emotions and ideas through performance, as in the live theater. For Bresson, films should be made cinematically rather than theatrically, by "bypassing the will of those who appear in them, using not what they do, but what they *are.*"

Generalizing about acting in movies is difficult because directors don't approach every film with the same attitudes. Elia Kazan and Ingmar Bergman, distinguished stage directors as well as filmmakers, varied their techniques considerably, depending on the dramatic needs of the film. Nor is there any "correct" approach to filming a scene. A director like Chaplin might convey a specific idea through acting, whereas Bresson might approach the same idea through editing or mise en scène. Each version could be effective: Whatever *works* is right.

But whether a director is a realist or **formalist,** the differences between film acting and stage acting remain fundamental. For example, a player in movies is not so restricted by vocal requirements since sound volume is controlled electronically. Marilyn Monroe's small breathy voice wouldn't have projected beyond the first few rows in the theater, but on film it was perfect for conveying that childlike vulnerability that gave her performances such poetic delicacy. Some film actors are popular precisely because of the offbeat charm of their voices. Since acting in movies is not so dependent upon vocal flexibility, many

223

6–7. *The Gold Rush* **(U.S.A., 1925),** *with Charles Chaplin and Mack Swain, directed by Chaplin.*

Actors in every medium (except radio) must be conscious of body language and what it reveals about character. Since silent actors were deprived of their voices, they externalized their feelings and thoughts through gesture, movement, facial expression, and body language—all of which had to be heightened to compensate for their lack of speech. In this shot, for example, Big Jim McKay is puzzled by the scary rumbling and quaking of their cabin. The hung-over Charlie explains—through pantomime—that his queasy stomach is the culprit.   (*rbc Films*)

performers have succeeded despite their wooden, inexpressive voices: Gary Cooper, John Wayne, Clint Eastwood.

Even the quality of a movie actor's voice can be controlled mechanically. Music and sound effects can totally change the meaning of a line of dialogue. Through electronic devices, a voice can be made to sound garbled, or booming, or hollow. Indeed, Antonioni claims that language in film is primarily pure sound and only secondarily meaningful as dialogue. Since much of the dialogue in a movie is **dubbed,** a director can re-record a line until it's perfect. Sometimes he'll select one or two words from one recorded take and blend them with the words of another, or even a third or fourth. This kind of synthesizing can be carried even further—by combining one actor's face with another actor's voice (6–8).

Similarly, the physical requirements for a film actor are different from those of a stage performer. The movie player doesn't have to be tall, even if he's a leading man type. Alan Ladd, for example, was quite short. His directors simply avoided showing his body in full unless there was no one else in frame to contrast with his height. He played love scenes standing on a box, his body cut off at the waist. **Low-angle** shots also tended to make him seem taller. A film actor's features don't have to be large, only expressive—particularly the eyes and mouth. Nor does he have to be handsome. For example, Humphrey Bogart was not a good-looking man, but the camera "liked him." That is, his face was uncannily photogenic, opening up to the camera in a way that often surprised his cinematographers. Sometimes this contrast between reality and its illusion can be intimidating. Complained Jean Arthur: "It's a strenuous job every day of your life to live up to the way you look on the screen."

An actor who moves clumsily is not necessarily at a disadvantage in film. The director can work around the problem by not using many long shots and by photographing the actor *after* he has moved. Complicated movements can be faked by using stuntmen or doubles. These shots are **intercut** with closer shots of the leading actor, and the edited juxtaposition leads the audience to assume that the main performer is involved in all the shots. Even in close-up, the film performer's physical appearance can be changed through the use of special **lenses, filters,** and lights.

6–8. *La Strada* (Italy, 1954), *with Richard Basehart and Giulietta Masina, directed by Federico Fellini.*
Virtually all Italian movies are dubbed after the footage has been photographed and sometimes even after it's been edited. Fellini selects his players according to their face, body type, or personality. Like many Italian filmmakers, he often uses foreign actors, even in major roles. The American Richard Basehart spoke his lines in English during this film's production. Once shooting was completed, Fellini hired an Italian actor with the same vocal quality to dub in the character's voice.   (*Audio-Brandon Films*)

Since the shot is the basic building unit in film, the actor doesn't have to sustain a performance for very long—even in realistic movies in which the **takes** can run to two or three minutes. In a highly fragmented film—in which shots can last for less than a second—one can scarcely refer to the performer's contribution as acting at all: He or she simply *is*.

The shooting schedule of a movie is determined by economic considerations. Thus, the shooting of various sequences isn't always artistically logical. An actor may be required to perform the climactic scene first and low-keyed exposition shots later. The screen actor, then, doesn't "build" emotionally as the stage actor must. The film player must be capable of an intense degree of concentration—turning emotions on and off for very short periods of time. Most of the time the player must seem totally natural, as if he or she weren't acting at all. "You do it just like in reality," Henry Fonda explained. Certainly the film player is almost always at the mercy of the director who later constructs the various shots into a coherent performance. Some directors have tricked actors into a performance, asking for one quality in order to get another.

Since acting in the cinema is confined to short segments of time and space, the film player doesn't need a long rehearsal period to establish a sense of ease with other actors, the set, or costumes. Many directors keep rehearsals to a minimum so as not to dissipate the spontaneity of the players, their sense of

6–9. *The Night of the Shooting Stars* **(Italy, 1982),** *directed by Paolo and Vittorio Taviani.* Realism in movies can be far more "real" than stage realism, for a theatrical actor's skill and discipline are always apparent to the audience. Film realism is often more convincing precisely because of the player's lack of technical skill. The nonprofessional players of this movie are artless and sincere, totally devoid of actorish mannerisms, and hence totally believable as ordinary peasants trying to survive during the harsh times of World War II.   *(United Artists)*

6–10. *Bringing Up Baby* (**U.S.A., 1938**), *with Cary Grant, Katharine Hepburn, and George Irving, directed by Howard Hawks.*

Hepburn always maintained that absolute concentration is one of the most important requisites of a performance. In movies especially, the camera is so close that an audience can detect any note of insincerity or wandering attention. The more artificial the situation, the more essential it is to play it seriously. This movie is almost like a Shakespearean comedy in its silliness—with its "enchanted forest," its whimsy, and its brazen artificiality. The booby country sheriff (Irving) might almost be the American cousin of Dogberry in *Much Ado About Nothing,* a title that suits Hawks's screwball comedy as much as Shakespeare's play. *(RKO)*

discovery and surprise. Unlike the stage player, the film actor doesn't have to create an intimate rapport with other performers: Sometimes they haven't even met until they arrive on the set or on location. Actors occasionally don't know their lines: This is remedied by having a prompter on the set, or by writing the lines on a blackboard off frame where the actor can read them.

A film actor is expected to play even the most intimate scenes with dozens of technicians on the set, working or observing. He must seem totally at ease, even though the lights are unbearably hot, and his running makeup must be corrected between shots. Since the camera distorts, actors are required to perform some scenes unnaturally. In an embrace, for example, lovers can't really look at each other in the eyes or they will appear cross-eyed on the screen. In **point-of-view shots,** actors must direct their lines at the camera rather than at another player. Much of the time the performer has no idea what he or she is doing, or where a shot might appear in the finished film, if indeed it appears at all, for many an actor's performance has been left on the cutting room floor. In short, the discontinuity of time and space in the cinema places the performer almost totally in the hands of the director.

The American Star System

The star system has been the backbone of the American film industry since the mid-1910s. Stars are the creation of the public, its reigning favorites. Their influence in the fields of fashion, values, and public behavior has been enormous. "The social history of a nation can be written in terms of its film stars," Raymond Durgnat has observed. Stars confer instant consequence to any film they appear in. Their fees have staggered the public. In the second decade of this century, Mary Pickford and Charles Chaplin were the two highest paid employees in the world. Contemporary stars like Barbra Streisand and Eddie Murphy command salaries of many millions per film, so popular are these box-office giants. Some have reigned five decades: Bette Davis and John Wayne, to name just two. Alexander Walker, among others, has pointed out that stars are the direct or indirect reflection of the needs, drives, and anxieties of American society: They are the food of dreams, allowing us to live out our deepest fanta-

6–11. Publicity photo of Rita Hayworth in *Gilda* **(U.S.A., 1946),** *directed by Charles Vidor.*

Good looks and sex appeal have always been the conspicuous traits of most film stars. Known in the 1940s as "The Love Goddess," Hayworth was never much of an actress, though her stunning beauty carried her through many a film. Shy and insecure, the much-married, much-divorced actress once remarked, sadly, that her lovers thought they were going to bed with Gilda, but woke up in the morning with Rita Hayworth. Disappointed. Again. *(Columbia Pictures)* sies and obsessions. Like the ancient gods and goddesses, stars have been adored, envied, and venerated as mythic and psychic icons.

Prior to 1910, actors' names were almost never included in movie credits because producers feared the players would then demand higher salaries. But the public named their favorites anyway. Mary Pickford, for example, was first known by her character's name, "Little Mary." From the beginning, the public often fused a star's artistic **persona** with his or her private personality (6–11). In Pickford's case, as with many others, the two were radically dissimilar. She specialized in playing waggish juveniles—the bouncy, high-spirited, and sentimental young heroines of such popular hits as *Rebecca of Sunnybrook Farm* (1917) and *Pollyanna* (1920), in which her blonde curls were her trademark. In actuality, Pickford was clever and sophisticated, and the most powerful woman in the American film industry of the silent era. "My career was planned," she insisted, "there was never anything accidental about it." By the time she was five, she was performing in the live theater. She began working with Griffith in 1909 and made seventy-five short films with him at Biograph before leaving the studio in 1912. Soon she was earning $40,000 per picture. By 1914 she was pulling in $150,000. She was neck-and-neck with Chaplin in the star salaries

6–12. MGM publicity photo of Oliver Hardy and Stan Laurel, circa 1932.
Especially in the silent era, audiences often confused actors with their artistic personas. Laurel and Hardy encouraged this identification by using their own names in their movies. Their personas had little to do with their actual personalities. Laurel was the creative force behind the team and invented most of the gag situations. Hardy rarely even attended story conferences, preferring to play golf. He modestly regarded himself as a straight man, rather than a great clown in his own right. The personas they developed were sunny, warm, and endearing. "We were dignified but dumb," Laurel said. "I haven't a lick of common sense, and Ollie is just as dumb, but he *thinks* he's smarter." Innocent and mischievous as children, they renew their harmless schemes against the grown-up world with hope undeterred. Usually they're affectionate with one another, but boys will be boys, and they do have their occasional spats. Ollie—fussy, dainty, self-important, the insufferable know-it-all—often gets impatient with the eternally vacuous Stan, who has infinite confidence—usually—in the superior wisdom of his best buddy in the world. (*MGM*)

sweepstakes, and collected from $300,000 to $500,000 per film between the years 1917 and 1919. In 1919 she helped form United Artists, with Chaplin, Griffith, and Douglas Fairbanks (her husband) as partners. As an independent producer, she grossed as much as $1.2 million per film. Reputedly she was the business brains behind United Artists. She also directed many of her own films, although never with official credit.

Unless the public is receptive to a given screen personality, audiences can be remarkably resistant to someone else's notion of a star. For example, producer Samuel Goldwyn ballyhooed his Russian import, Anna Sten, without stinting on costs. But audiences stayed away from her movies in droves. "God makes the stars," the chastened Goldwyn finally concluded. "It's up to the producers to find them."

Throughout the silent era, stars grew giddy with their wealth and power. Intoxicated by the opulence of Hollywood's royalty, the public was eager to learn more of its favorites. Fan (short for fanatic) magazines sprang up by the dozens, and the burgeoning studios churned out a steady stream of publicity—most of it imbecilic—to feed this insatiable curiosity. Paramount's rival queens, Gloria Swanson and Pola Negri, vied with each other in the extravagance of their lifestyles. Both of them married many times, and each managed to snare at least one petty nobleman among their stable of rapt admirers. "I have gone through a long apprenticeship," Swanson said. "I have gone through enough of being nobody. I have decided that when I am a star I will be every inch and every moment the star. Everyone from the studio gateman to the highest executive will know it." The mythology of stardom often incorporated this rags-to-riches motif. The humble origins of many stars encouraged the public to believe that anyone—even ordinary people—could be "discovered" and make it to Hollywood where all their dreams would come true.

The so-called golden age of the star system—roughly the 1930s and 1940s—coincided with the supremacy of the Hollywood studio system. Most of the stars during this period were under exclusive contract to the five major production companies: MGM, Warner Brothers, Paramount, Twentieth Century–Fox, and RKO—known in the trade as the Big Five, or the **majors.** Throughout this period, the majors produced approximately 90 percent of the fiction films in America. They also ruled the international market: Between the two world wars, American movies dominated 80 percent of the world's screens and were more popular with foreign audiences than all but a few natively produced movies.

After the talkie revolution, the majors turned to the live theater for its new stars. Such important newcomers as James Cagney, Bette Davis, Edward G. Robinson, Cary Grant, Mae West, and Katharine Hepburn became popular in part because of their distinctive manner of speaking—the "personality voices" as they were known in the trade. In their first years under studio contract, they were given maximum exposure. For example, Clark Gable appeared in fourteen movies in 1930, his first year at MGM. Each of his roles represented a different type, and the studio kept varying them until one clicked with the public. After a particularly popular performance, a star was usually locked into the same type of role—often under protest. Since the demand for stars was the most predictable economic variable in the business of filmmaking, the studios used their stars as a guarantee of box-office success. In short, stars provided some measure of stabil-

6–13. *One Flew Over the Cuckoo's Nest* **(U.S.A., 1975),** *with Jack Nicholson, directed by Milos Forman.*
American audiences have always idolized rebels, nonconformists, and mavericks. "I've never let anyone think they own me," Nicholson has stated. Independent and artistically adventurous, he has devoted his life to expanding his range as an artist, specializing in offbeat, unglamorous roles that subvert conventional morality.   *(United Artists)*

ity in a traditionally volatile industry. To this day, stars are referred to as "bankable" commodities—that is, insurance for large profits to investors.

The majors viewed their stars as valuable investments, and the build-up techniques developed by the studios involved much time, money, and energy. Promising neophytes served an apprenticeship as "starlets," a term reserved for females, although male newcomers were subjected to the same treatment. They were often assigned a new name, were taught how to talk, walk, and wear costumes. Frequently their social schedules were arranged by the studio's publicity department to insure maximum press exposure. Suitable "romances" were concocted to fuel the columns of the four hundred or more reporters and columnists who covered the Hollywood beat during the studio era. A few zealous souls even agreed to marry a studio-selected spouse if such an alliance would further their careers.

Though stars were often exploited by the studios, there were some compensations. As a player's box-office power increased, so did his or her demands. Top stars had their names above the title of the film, and they often had script approval stipulated in their contracts. Some of them also insisted on director, producer, and costar approval. Glamorous stars boasted their own cameramen,

6–14. *Two Women* **(Italy, 1961),** *with Sophia Loren, directed by Vittorio De Sica.*
The public's affection for its stars has often been based on personality rather than artistry, although the two aren't necessarily exclusive. Despite the fact that Loren has made very few good films, she remained a favorite with both critics and audiences for over twenty years. Her life story is in the classic rags-to-riches mold. She was born out of wedlock, and lived most of her first fourteen years in desperate poverty with her mother in a Naples slum. At the age of fourteen she won a beauty contest and became the protegée of film producer Carlo Ponti, who eventually became her husband. She appeared in a series of forgettable Italian movies before deciding to try her luck in America in 1957. In Hollywood, her mentors attempted to obliterate her individuality by embalming her in makeup and corseting her voluptuous figure to within an inch of its life. Her American films were mostly potboilers, but she usually emerged triumphant, thanks to her charm and compelling sensuality. The merriment and good humor she brought to her roles were products of her own personality rather than her scripts or directors. Unlike most sex queens, Loren was rarely self-conscious about her eroticism and often regarded it with ironic amusement. Eventually she returned to her native soil where she found a director more attuned to her talent, her fellow Neapolitan Vittorio De Sica. Her powerful performance as an earthy peasant in *Two Women* was a startling revelation, even to her admirers, and it won her the Best Actress Academy Award of 1961, the New York Film Critics' Award, and the top prize at the Cannes Film Festival. *(Embassy Pictures)*

who knew how to conceal physical defects and enhance virtues. Many of them demanded their own clothes designers, hair stylists, and lavish dressing rooms. The biggest stars had movies especially tailored for them, thus guaranteeing maximum camera exposure (6–15).

6–15. Publicity photos of Lucille Ball in *Mame* **(U.S.A., 1974),** *directed by Gene Saks.*
Mame, a $10-million production, was financed mostly with Lucille Ball's own money. Of
modest origins, she started her career at the age of fifteen as a showgirl, moved on to motion
pictures (mostly B-films), then found much greater fame and fortune in the 1950s with her
brilliant television series, *I Love Lucy.* She was the first woman president of a major Hollywood production company. Reputedly, Desilu Productions had an annual gross of $25
million. "I believe that a woman can only be as liberated as she thinks she is," Ball observed.
"Thanks to my mother's influence, I learned early to believe that women are equal to men in
every department, and I've never faltered in that thinking." *Mame* was a pet project. In
addition to starring and producing, Ball also closely supervised the technical aspects of the
picture. Theadora van Runkle designed seven hundred costumes, forty for Ball alone. Cost
of the star's costumes: $300,000. Although she was sixty-three at the time of production, she
looks twenty years younger, thanks to the stylized star makeup and the camera's indulgent
soft-focus photography.   (*Warner Bros.*)

And, of course, they were paid enormous sums of money. In 1938, for
example, there were over fifty stars who earned more than $100,000 a year. But
the studios got much more. Mae West rescued Paramount from bankruptcy in
the early 1930s. Later in the decade, Shirley Temple made over $20 million for
Twentieth Century–Fox. Furthermore, although there were a few important
exceptions, movies without stars generally failed at the box office. Serious stars
used money and power to further their art, not just to gratify their vanity. Bette
Davis was considered "difficult" during her stormy tenure at Warners because
she insisted on better scripts, more varied roles, more sensitive directors, and
stronger costars.

Top stars attracted the loyalty of both men and women, although as sociologist Leo Handel pointed out, 65 percent of the fans preferred stars of their own sex. The studios received up to 32 million fan letters per year, 85 percent of them from young females. Major stars received about three thousand letters per week, and the volume of their mail was regarded as an accurate barometer of their popularity. The studios spent as much as $2 million a year processing these letters, most of which asked for autographed photos. Box-office appeal was also gauged by the number of fan clubs devoted to a star. The stars with the greatest number of fan clubs were Gable, Jean Harlow, and Joan Crawford—all of them under contract to MGM, "The Home of the Stars." Gable alone had 70 clubs, which partly accounted for his supremacy as the top male star of the 1930s.

The mythology of stardom usually emphasizes the glamor of movie stars, lifting them above the mundane concerns of ordinary mortals. Critic Parker Tyler observed that stars fulfill an ancient need, almost religious in nature: "Somehow their wealth, fame, and beauty, their apparently unlimited field of worldly pleasure–these conditions tinge them with the supernatural, render them immune to the bitterness of ordinary frustrations." Of course, this mythology also involves the tragic victims of stardom, like Marilyn Monroe and James Dean. The fact that many stars have died young—at the height of their physical beauty—only enhances their romantic image of immutable perfection (6–17).

The realities behind the myths are considerably less romantic. For every actor who manages to scale the peaks of stardom, there are hundreds of thousands who fail, their hard work wasted, their sacrifices scoffed at, their dreams shattered. Maureen Stapleton has won important acting awards for her distinguished work in films, television, and the stage, but she has spoken eloquently of the hardships actors must endure in a world that often regards them as fortunate simpletons:

6–16. *East of Eden* **(U.S.A., 1955),** *with Julie Harris and James Dean, directed by Elia Kazan.*

This movie catapulted Dean to stardom. Millions of young people identified with his tortured sensitivity. He soon developed a reputation for being arrogant and self-destructive. He died in an auto crash at the age of 24, shortly after the release of this film. He was virtually deified by his cult followers, mostly young people, who idealized him as a symbol of misunderstood youth. Kazan was appalled by this cult. "He was the glorification of hatred and sickness," the director said. "When he got success he was victimized by it." *(Warner Bros.)*

I believe in the toughness of actors. I have a feeling of genuine pride in actors as my people. . . . We're called egomaniacs; we're thought of as children. Actors are supposed to be irresponsible, stupid, unaware, and a kind of joke. They're accused of having big egos. Well, the actor's ego is no different in size because he's an *actor.* A writer or a painter or a musician can go off into a corner and lick his wounds, but an actor stands out in front of the crowd and takes it. . . . Actors spend years and years being treated like dirt. They're constantly in a state of debasement, making the rounds of casting directors and having to look happy and great. I made the rounds for years, but I wasn't good at it. But then *nobody* is. You need a very strong stomach. You need a sense of the business as a whole, so that you don't get lacerated every time somebody tells you you're lousy. You need strength, and no matter how strong you get, you always need to get stronger. (Quoted in *The Player: A Profile of an Art*)

The tabloids in supermarket racks are filled with lurid stories of how film stars have screwed up their lives, or have made fools of themselves in public, or behaved like selfish brats. These types of stories sell newspapers, for they appeal to the public's envy and malice.

What is far less frequently written about is how stars are hounded out of their privacy by unscrupulous reporters and paparazzi. Nor do we often read about how stars like Bob Hope and Elizabeth Taylor have devoted thousands of hours to public service. Or about the patriotic activities of stars like John Wayne or Marlene Dietrich (6–19). Or the successful political careers of stars like Shirley Temple and Ronald Reagan. Or the political activism of hundreds of stars like Marlon Brando and Jane Fonda. Or the fantastic generosity of stars like Barbra Streisand and Paul Newman. Newman alone has donated over $16,000,000 to various charities.

Stars must pay a high price for their wealth and fame. They must get used to being treated like commodities with a price tag. Even at the beginning of the star system, they were reduced to simplified types: virgins, vamps, swashbucklers, flappers, and so on. Over the years, a vast repertory of types evolved: the Latin lover, the he-man, the heiress, the good–bad girl, the cynical reporter, the career girl, and many others. Of course, all great stars are unique even though they might fall under a well-known category. For example, the cheap blonde has long been one of America's favorite types, but such important stars as Mae West, Jean Harlow, and Marilyn Monroe are highly distinctive as individuals. A successful type was always imitated. In the mid-1920s, for example, the Swedish import Greta Garbo created a sophisticated and complex type, the *femme fatale.* Garbo inspired many imitations, including such important stars as Marlene Dietrich and Carole Lombard, who were first touted as "Garbo types," only with a sense of humor. In the 1950s, Sidney Poitier became the first black star to attract a wide following outside of his own race. In later years a number of other black performers attained stardom in part because Poitier had established the precedent. He was one of the great originals and hence worthy of imitation.

At about the turn of the last century, George Bernard Shaw wrote a famous essay comparing the two foremost stage stars of the day—Eleonora Duse and Sarah Bernhardt. Shaw's comparison is a useful springboard for a discussion

6–17. Publicity photo of Marilyn Monroe in *The Seven Year Itch* (U.S.A., 1955), *directed by Billy Wilder.*

Marilyn Monroe has become a symbol of the personal tragedy that can befall a star. She was born (illegitimate) to an emotionally unstable mother who spent most of her life in mental asylums. As a child, Norma Jean Baker was raised in a series of orphanages and foster homes. Even then—especially then—she dreamed of becoming a famous Hollywood star. She was raped at the age of eight, married to her first husband at sixteen. She used sex (like many before her) as a means to an end—stardom. In the late 1940s she had a few bit roles, mostly as sexy dumb blondes. Not until John Huston's *The Asphalt Jungle* (1950) did she create much of a stir. In that same year, Joseph Mankiewicz cast her in *All About Eve*, as "a graduate of the Copacabana School of Dramatic Art," as George Sanders drily deadpans in the film. (Sanders claimed he knew Marilyn would one day become a star "because she desperately needed to be one.") After Twentieth Century–Fox signed her to a contract, the studio didn't know what to do with her. She appeared in a series of third-rate studio projects, but despite their mediocrity, the public clamored for more Marilyn. She rightly blamed Fox for misman-aging her career: "Only the public can make a star. It's the studios who try to make a system of it," she bitterly complained. At the peak of her popularity, she left Hollywood in disgust, to study at the Actors Studio. When she returned, she demanded more money and better roles—and got both. Joshua Logan, who directed her in *Bus Stop* (1956), said she was "as near genius as any actress I ever knew." Supremely photogenic, she gave herself entirely to the camera, allowing it to probe her deepest vulnerabilities. Laurence Olivier, her costar and director in *The Prince and the Showgirl* (1957), marvelled at her cunning way of fusing guilelessness with carnality—the mind and soul of a little girl wrapped in the body of a whore. Throughout her years as a top star, her private life was a shambles. "She was an unfortunate doped-up woman most of the time," biographer Maurice Zolotow observed. Her failed marriages and love affairs were constantly in the headlines, and increasingly she turned to drugs and alcohol for solace. She was notorious for her irresponsibility, often not even bothering to show up on the set for days at a time, thus incurring enormous cost overruns. Because of her addiction to drugs and alcohol, even when she did show up she scarcely knew who—much less where—she was. She was found dead in 1962: an overdose of barbiturates and alcohol. *(Twentieth Century–Fox)*

6–18. *Uptown Saturday Night* **(U.S.A., 1974),** *with Bill Cosby and Sidney Poitier, directed by Poitier.*

Poitier was the first black actor to rise to the top ten not as a singer, dancer, or comedian but as a straight leading man. His wholesome good looks and all-American sense of decency were admired by white and black audiences alike. In the 1970s he turned to producing and directing films in addition to starring in them. Cosby is in the same all-American mold, though his achievements have been primarily in television rather than motion pictures. During the 1980s, his critically acclaimed *Cosby Show* was the most popular television series in America. See also Thomas Cripps, *Slow Fade to Black: The Negro in American Film* (New York: Oxford Unversity Press, 1977).   (*Warner Bros.*)

of the different kinds of film stars. Bernhardt, Shaw wrote, was a bravura personality, and she managed to tailor each different role to fit this personality. This is what her fans both expected and desired. Her personal charm was larger-than-life, yet undeniably captivating. Her performances were filled with brilliant effects that had come to be associated with her personality over the years. Duse, on the other hand, possessed a more quiet talent, less dazzling in its initial impact. She was totally different with each role, and her own personality never seemed to intrude on the playwright's character. Hers was an invisible art: Her impersonations were so totally believable that the viewer was likely to forget it *was* an impersonation. In effect, Shaw was pointing out the major distinctions between a *personality star* and an *actor star*.

Personality stars commonly refuse all parts that go against their type, especially if they're leading men or leading ladies. Performers like Barbra Streisand would never play cruel or psychopathic roles, for example, because such parts would conflict with her sympathetic image. If a star is locked into his or her type,

6–19. *The Blue Angel* **(Germany, 1930),** *with Marlene Dietrich, directed by Josef von Sternberg.*

Above all, Dietrich was a survivor. She began her career as a cabaret singer in her beloved Berlin in the 1920s. She gained fame with this movie, a huge international success. As a result, she came to America as von Sternberg's protégée. Together they made six exotic films at Paramount in the 1930s. A fierce anti-Nazi, she toured many U.S. military bases during World War II, entertaining the troops as a singer. She resumed her singing career in the postwar era, traveling all over the world and earning fabulous salaries. She managed to preserve her beauty (with the help of cosmetic surgery) and figure for three more decades, not retiring from show business until the late 1970s.   *(Janus Films)*

6–20. *The Outsiders* **(U.S.A., 1982),** *with Emilio Estevez, Rob Lowe, C. Thomas Howell, Matt Dillon, Ralph Macchio, Patrick Swayze, and Tom Cruise; directed by Francis Ford Coppola.*

A few rare individuals, like Francis Coppola, seem to have a knack for discovering star potential. His *Godfather* films created several of the most important stars of the 1970s, just as *The Outsiders* introduced some of the most promising young stars of the 1980s.   *(Pony Boy Inc.)*

any significant departure can result in box-office disaster. For example, when Pickford tried to abandon her little girl roles in the 1920s, her public stayed at home: They wanted to see Little Mary or nothing. She retired in disgust at the age of forty, just when most players are at the peak of their powers.

On the other hand, many stars prefer to remain in the same mold, playing variations on the same character type. John Wayne was the most popular star in film history. From 1949 to 1976 he was absent from the top ten only three times. "I play John Wayne in every part regardless of the character, and I've been doing okay, haven't I?" he once asked. In the public mind, he was the archetypal Westerner, a man of action—and violence—rather than words. His **iconography** is steeped in a distrust of sophistication and intellectuality. His name is virtually synonymous with masculinity—though his persona suggests more of the warrior than the lover. As he grew older, he also grew more human, developing his considerable talents as a comedian by mocking his own macho image. Wayne was fully aware of the enormous influence a star can wield in transmitting values, and in many of his films he embodied a right-wing ideology that made him a hero to conservative Americans. He was strongly promilitary in his sympathies and publicly applauded nationalism, guts, and self-sacrifice.

Film theorist Richard Dyer has pointed out that stars are signifying entities. Any sensitive analysis of a film with a star in its cast must take into account that star's iconographical significance. Stars like Jane Fonda embody complex political associations simply by demonstrating the lifestyle of her politics and displaying those political beliefs as an aspect of her personality/characterization. Like John Wayne—and most other stars—she conveys an ideology, implying ideal ways of behaving. As such, stars can have tremendous impact in transmitting values. Dyer also demonstrates how a star's iconography is always developing,

6–21. *Frances* **(U.S.A., 1982).** *with Jessica Lange, directed by Graeme Clifford.*
Many ambitious actors who first gained prominence through their good looks have deliberately sought unglamorous roles in order to demonstrate their acting abilities. Lange's first role was as King Kong's costar in the 1976 remake of that classic. In *Frances,* she plays Frances Farmer, a minor movie star of the 1930s, who was incarcerated in a brutal mental asylum for her erratic behavior.   *(Universal City Studios)*

incorporating elements from the star's actual life as well as previous roles. For example, Fonda's career can be divided into five phases:

1. *The Father.* Her entry into the film industry in 1960 was facilitated by Henry Fonda's prestige. Physically, she clearly resembled him, and he too was a well-known liberal, with an all-American iconography. Jane's roles during this period emphasized a rambunctious sexiness, with more of the tomboy than the siren. This phase culminated with *Cat Ballou* (1965).

2. *Sex.* This period is dominated by Fonda's French film director husband, Roger Vadim, who exploited her good looks and sensational figure in a series of erotic films, most notably *Barbarella* (France, 1968). Although the marriage ended in divorce, Fonda claimed that Vadim liberated her from her sexual hangups and all-American innocence.

3. *Acting.* She returned to America where she studied with Lee Strasberg at the Actors Studio in New York. Her depth and range as an artist expanded considerably during this period, and she was nominated for an Academy Award for her work in *They Shoot Horses, Don't They?* (1969). She won one for her performance as a prostitute in *Klute* (1971).

4. *Politics.* Fonda was radicalized by Vietnam and the women's movement.

6–22. *Tootsie (U.S.A., 1982), with Dustin Hoffman, directed by Sydney Pollack.* Hoffman is one of the most admired actor stars of his generation, changing radically from role to role. His range is exceptionally broad, encompassing such disparate roles as the klutzy college grad in *The Graduate* (1967); the sleazy urban vagrant Ratso Rizzo in *Midnight Cowboy* (1969); and the tragicomic frontiersman in *Little Big Man* (1970), in which Hoffman was required to age over a hundred years. In *Straw Dogs* (1972), Hoffman played a self-deluded, overintellectual mathematician; in *Papillon* (1973), a grizzled inmate of a penal colony. His performance as the persecuted and self-destructive comedian Lenny Bruce in *Lenny* (1974) is authentic to the point of mimicry. His performance as an autistic savant in *Rain Man* (1988) was lavishly praised. Even in leading man roles, like those in *All the President's Men* (1976) and *Kramer vs. Kramer* (1979), Hoffman rarely relies on his actual personality unless a given trait is appropriate to the character he's playing. One of his greatest performances is in the leading role of *Tootsie,* a triumph of irony and wit. (*Columbia Pictures*)

6–23. *From Here to Eternity* (U.S.A., 1953), *with Deborah Kerr and Burt Lancaster, directed by Fred Zinnemann.*
A star's image can be radically altered by one pivotal role. Prior to this movie, Kerr had been stereotyped as a young well-bred British matron, in parts she ironically referred to as her "tiara roles." Zinnemann cast her in this film because he thought her ladylike gentility would provide a provocative contrast to the character's sordid past. After receiving almost universal acclaim for her performance, Kerr's roles became far more diversified, garnering her six Best Actress Oscar nominations. (*Columbia Pictures*)

She spoke out frequently against the war, racism, and sexism. She also politicized her work, starring in movies that were frankly ideological, like *Tout va bien* (France, 1973), *A Doll's House* (Great Britain, 1974), and *Julia* (1977). Her left-wing political activities adversely affected her box-office popularity for a period, but she continued to speak out on important public issues, refusing to be intimidated.

5. *Independence.* *Coming Home* (1978) was produced by Fonda's own production company. She has enjoyed outstanding success as a producer. She has also written several books and has been a leader in the physical fitness movement. Today, Fonda is regarded as the most accomplished actress of her generation and is one of the most admired women in America.

The top box-office attractions tend to be personality stars. They stay on top by being themselves, by not trying to impersonate anyone. Gable insisted that all he did in front of the camera was to "act natural." Similarly, Marilyn Monroe was always at her best when she played roles that exploited her indecisiveness, her vulnerability, and her pathetic eagerness to please.

On the other hand, there have been many stars who refuse to be typecast and attempt the widest array of roles possible. Such actor stars as Davis, Hepburn, Brando, and De Niro have sometimes undertaken unpleasant character roles rather than conventional leads in order to expand their range, for variety and breadth have traditionally been the yardsticks by which great acting is measured (6–22). For example, just as Brando was being typed as the sexy young working-class stud (*A Streetcar Named Desire, On the Waterfront*), he completely reversed his image with a Shakespearean role (*Julius Caesar*) and a stint at musical comedy (*Guys and Dolls*). In *The Teahouse of the August Moon*, he played an Oriental houseboy, in *The Young Lions*, an effete German aristocrat. His Fletcher Christian in *Mutiny on the Bounty* was not the standard **star vehicle** that Clark Gable had made of the role in the earlier version of this film, but a performance that stressed the character's fastidious and rather effeminate snobbishness. In *The Godfather,* Brando astonished his public by playing an elderly Mafia don, and in *Last Tango in Paris,* a neurotic middle-aged romantic, totally obsessed with sexuality.

Many stars fall somewhere between the two extremes, veering toward personality in some films, toward impersonation in others. Such gifted performers as James Stewart, Cary Grant, and Audrey Hepburn played wider variations of certain types of roles. Nonetheless, we can't imagine a star like Miss Hepburn playing a woman of weak character or a coarse or stupid woman, so firmly entrenched is her image as an elegant and rather aristocratic female. Similarly, most people know what's meant by "the Clint Eastwood type."

The distinction between a professional actor and a star is not based on technical skill, but on mass popularity. By definition, a star must have enormous personal magnetism, a riveting quality that commands our attention. Few public personalities have inspired such deep and widespread affection as the great movie stars. Some are loved because they embody such traditional American values as plain speaking, integrity, and idealism: Gary Cooper and Jimmy Stew-

6–24. *Mr. Smith Goes to Washington* (U.S.A., 1939), *with James Stewart, directed by Frank Capra.*

Stewart had the ability to make acting appear so natural and sincere that for years the public hardly noticed how skillful he was as an actor—no tricks, no posturing, no big deal. In actuality, a great deal of skill went into Stewart's "artlessness." Almost everyone called him Jimmy. He was one of us. Audiences identified with his simple, decent values. They cared for him. If he suffered, they did too, because he represented what was best in themselves. *(Columbia Pictures)*

art are examples of this type. Others are identified with antiestablishment images, and include such celebrated loners as Bogie, Clint Eastwood, and Jack Nicholson. Players like Cary Grant and Carole Lombard are so captivating in their charm that they're fun to watch in almost anything. And of course many of them are spectacularly good-looking: Names like Garbo and Redford are virtually synonymous with godlike beauty.

Sophisticated filmmakers exploit the public's affection for its stars by creating ambiguous tensions between a role as written, as acted, and as directed. "Whenever the hero isn't portrayed by a star the whole picture suffers," Hitchcock observed. "Audiences are far less concerned about the predicament of a character who's played by someone they don't know." When a star rather than a conventional actor plays a role, much of the characterization is automatically fixed by the casting; but what the director and star then choose to add to the written role is what constitutes its *full* dramatic meaning. Some directors have capitalized on the star system with great artistic effectiveness, particularly studio-era filmmakers like Frank Capra (6–24).

Perhaps the ultimate glory for a star is to become an icon in American popular mythology. Like the gods and goddesses of ancient times, some stars are so universally known that one name alone is enough to evoke an entire complex of symbolic associations—"Marilyn," for example. Unlike the conventional actor (however gifted), the star automatically suggests ideas and emotions that are deeply embedded in his or her persona. These undertones are determined not only by the star's previous roles, but often by his or her actual personality as well. Naturally, over the course of many years, this symbolic information can begin to

6–25. MGM publicity photo of Elizabeth Taylor in 1951.

Elizabeth Taylor has been in the public eye ever since she was a child star in the 1940s. Indeed, she is virtually a creature of the public, its favorite, its pet celebrity. In addition to her spectacular beauty, she eventually became an accomplished actress. She is also famous for her many love affairs and marriages, which have been exhaustively chronicled in the international press. Her generosity is legendary: She has given millions to charity. For the past several years, she has been an indefatigable fundraiser to find a cure for AIDS, the deadly disease that killed her dear friend Rock Hudson. *(MGM)*

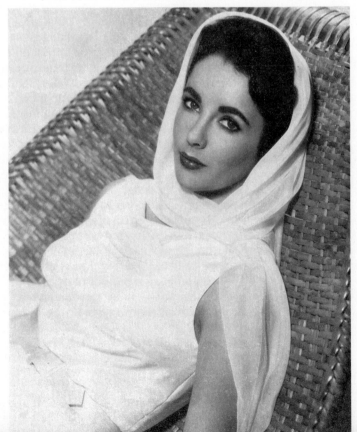

drain from public consciousness, but the iconography of a great star like Gary Cooper becomes part of a shared experience. As the French critic Edgar Morin has pointed out, when Cooper played a character, he automatically "gary-cooperized" it, infusing himself into the role and the role into himself. Since audiences felt a deep sense of identification with Coop and the values he symbolized, in a sense they were celebrating themselves—or at least their spiritual selves. The great originals are cultural **archetypes,** and their box-office popularity is an index of their success in synthesizing the aspirations of an era. As a number of cultural studies have shown, the iconography of a star can involve communal myths and symbols of considerable complexity and emotional richness.

Styles of Acting

Acting styles differ radically, depending on period, **genre,** tone, national origins, and directorial emphasis. Such considerations are the principal means by which acting styles are classified. Even within a given category, however, generalizations are, at best, a loose set of expectations, not Holy Writ. For example, the realist–formalist dialectic that has been used as a classification aid throughout this book can also be applied to the art of acting, but there are many variations and subdivisions. These terms are also subject to different interpretations from period to period. Lillian Gish was regarded as a great realistic actress in the silent era, but by today's standards, her performances look rather ethereal. In a parallel vein, the playing style of Klaus Kinski in such movies as *Aguirre, the Wrath of God* is stylized, but compared to an extreme form of **expressionistic** acting, such as that of Conrad Veidt in *The Cabinet of Dr. Caligari,* Kinski is relatively realistic (6–26). It's a matter of degree.

Classifying acting styles according to national origins is also likely to be misleading, at least for those countries that have evolved a wide spectrum of styles, like Japan, the United States, and Italy. For example, the Italians (and other Mediterranean peoples) are said to be theatrical by national temperament, acting out their feelings with animation, as opposed to the reserved deportment of the Swedes and other Northern Europeans. But within the Italian cinema alone, these generalizations are subject to considerable modification. Southern Italian characters tend to be acted in a manner that conforms to the volatile Latin stereotype, as can be seen in the movies of Lina Wertmüller (6–27). Northern Italians, on the other hand, are usually played with more restraint and far less spontaneity, as the works of Antonioni demonstrate.

Genre and directorial emphasis also influence acting styles significantly. For example, in stylized genres like the samurai film, Toshiro Mifune is bold, strutting, and larger-than-life, as in Kurosawa's *Yojimbo.* In a realistic contemporary story like *High and Low* (also directed by Kurosawa), Mifune's performance is all nuance and sobriety.

The *art* of silent acting encompasses a period of only some fifteen years or so, for though movies were being produced as early as 1895, most historians regard Griffith's *The Birth of a Nation* (1915) as the first indisputable masterpiece of the silent cinema. The changeover to sound was virtually universal by 1930. Within this brief span, however, a wide variety of playing styles evolved,

6–26. *Aguirre, the Wrath of God* (West Germany, 1973), *with Klaus Kinski, directed by Werner Herzog.*

Expressionistic acting is generally associated with the German cinema—a cinema of directors, rarely actors. Stripped of individualizing details, this style of acting stresses a symbolic concept rather than a believable three-dimensional character. It is presentational rather than representational, a style of extremes rather than norms. Psychological complexity is replaced by a stylized thematic essence. For example, Kinski's portrayal of a Spanish conquistador is conceived in terms of a treacherous serpent. His Dantean features a frozen mask of ferocity, Aguirre can suddenly twist and coil like a cobra poised for a strike. (*New Yorker Films*)

ranging from the detailed, underplayed realism of Gibson Gowland in *Greed,* to the grand, ponderous style of such tragedians as Emil Jannings in *The Last Command.* The great silent clowns like Chaplin, Keaton, Harold Lloyd, Harry Langdon, and Laurel and Hardy also developed highly personal styles that bear only a superficial resemblance to each other.

A popular misconception about the silent cinema is that all movies were photographed and projected at "silent speed"—16 frames per second (fps). In fact, silent speed was highly variable, subject to easy manipulation because cameras were hand cranked. Even within a single film, not every scene was necessarily photographed at the same speed. Generally speaking, comic scenes were undercranked to emphasize speed, while dramatic scenes were overcranked to slow down the action, usually at 20 or 22 fps. Since most present-day projectors feature only two speeds—16 silent and 24 sound—the original rhythms of the performances are violated. This is why players in silent dramas can appear jerky and slightly ludicrous. In comedies, this distortion can enhance the humor, which is why the performances of the silent clowns have retained much of their original charm. Outside the comic repertory, however, due allowances must be made for the distortions of technology.

The most popular and critically admired player of the silent cinema was Chaplin. The wide variety of comic skills he developed in his early years of vaudeville made him the most versatile of the clowns. In the area of pantomime, no one approached his inventiveness. Critics waxed eloquently on his balletic grace, and even the brilliant dancer Nijinsky proclaimed Chaplin his equal. His

6–27. *The Seduction of Mimi* (Italy, 1971), *with Giancarlo Giannini and Elena Fiore, directed by Lina Wertmüller.*
Farcical acting is one of the most difficult and misunderstood styles of performance. It requires an intense comic exaggeration, and can easily become tiresome and mechanical if the farceur is not able to preserve the humanity of the character. Here, Giannini plays a typical ethnic stereotype—a sleazy, heavy-lidded lothario who, in an act of sexual revenge, embarks on a campaign to seduce the unlovely wife of the man who has cuckolded him. Giannini is Wertmüller's favorite actor, and has appeared in many of her movies. Other famous actor–director teams include Dietrich and Sternberg, Wayne and Ford, Ullmann and Bergman, Bogart and Huston, Mifune and Kurosawa, Léaud and Truffaut, and many more. (*New Line Cinema*)

ability to blend comedy with pathos was unique. George Bernard Shaw, the greatest living playwright of this era, described Chaplin as "the only genius developed in motion pictures." After viewing Chaplin's powerful—and very funny—performance in *City Lights,* the fastidious critic Alexander Woolcott, who otherwise loathed movies, said: "I would be prepared to defend the proposition that this darling of the mob is the foremost living artist."

Greta Garbo perfected a romantic style of acting that had its roots in the silent cinema and held sway throughout the 1930s. Critics have sometimes referred to this mode of performance as star acting. "What, when drunk, one sees in other women, one sees in Garbo sober," said the British critic Kenneth Tynan. Almost invariably, MGM cast her as a woman with a mysterious past: mistress, courtesan, the "other woman"—the essence of the Eternal Female. Her face, in addition to being stunningly beautiful, could unite conflicting emotions, withholding and yielding simultaneously, like a succession of waves rippling across her features. Tall and slender, she moved gracefully, her collapsed shoulders suggesting the exhaustion of a wounded butterfly. She could also project a provocative bisexuality, as in *Queen Christina,* where her resolute strides and masculine attire provide a foil to her exquisite femininity.

The love goddess par excellence, Garbo was most famous for her love scenes, which epitomized her romantic style. She is often self-absorbed in these scenes, musing on a private irony that can even exclude the lover. Frequently she looks away from him, allowing the camera—and us—to savor the poignancy of her conflict. She rarely expresses her feelings in words, for her art thrives on silence, on the unspeakable. Her love scenes are sometimes played in literal solitude, with objects serving as erotic fetishes. The way she touches a bouquet of flowers, a bedpost, a telephone—these allude to the missing lover, recalling a

6–28. *Get Out Your Handkerchiefs* (**France, 1978**), *with (left to right) Gerard Depardieu, Carol Laure, and Patrick Dewaere; directed by Bertrand Blier.*
A film's tone dictates its acting style. Tone is determined primarily by genre, dialogue, and the director's attitude toward the dramatic materials. In this film, for example, Depardieu and Dewaere play characters who are both in love with the same woman, an impenetrable cipher who finds their exuberant charm eminently resistable. Like its American cousin, screwball comedy, Blier's movie is a *jeu d'esprit,* bubbling over with whimsical improbabilities, loony twists and turns in the plot, and spritely dialogue delivered in a throwaway style.   (*New Line Cinema*)

multitude of painful pleasures. She is often enraptured by her surroundings, "like Eve on the morning of creation," to use Tynan's memorable phrase. But she is also oppressed by the knowledge that such ecstasy cannot last; she arms herself against her fate with irony and stoicism. Garbo's performances are striking examples of how great acting can salvage bad scripts, and even bad direction. "Subtract Garbo from most of her movies and you are left with nothing," one critic noted.

The most important British film actors are also the most prominent in the live theater. The British repertory system is the envy of the civilized world. Virtually every medium-sized city has a resident drama company, where actors can learn their craft by playing a variety of roles from the classic repertory, especially the works of Shakespeare. As players improve, they rise through the ranks, attempting more complex roles. The best of them migrate to the larger cities, where the most prestigious theater companies are found. The discipline that most British actors have acquired in this repertory system has made them the most versatile of players. The finest of them are regularly employed in the theaters of London, which is also adjacent to the centers of film production of

6–29. *Ninotchka* (**U.S.A., 1939**), *with Greta Garbo, directed by Ernst Lubitsch.*
Ironically, the role that Garbo is best remembered for is her least typical, though it was one of her favorite parts. She plays a humorless Soviet commissar who has been sent to Paris to investigate the dubious doings of her comrades (pictured). They have proved all too suscepti-ble to the decadent blandishments of capitalism. Back in the U.S.S.R., Comrade Stalin was liquidating millions of people for far less. "How are things in Moscow?" they ask upon meeting. "Very good," she replies. "The last mass trials were a great success. There are going to be fewer but better Russians." *(MGM)*

Great Britain. This centralization allows them to move from the live theater to film to TV with a minimum of inconvenience.

British acting traditions tend to favor a mastery of externals, based on close observation. Virtually all players are trained in diction, movement, makeup, dialects, fencing, dancing, body control, and ensemble acting. For example, Laurence Olivier always built his characters from the outside in. He molded his features like a sculptor or painter. "I do not search the character for parts that are already in me," he explained, "but go out and find the personality I feel the author created." Like most British actors of his generation, Olivier had a keen memory for detail: "I hear remarks in the street or in a shop and I retain them. You must constantly observe: a walk, a limp, a run; how a head inclines to one side when listening; the twitch of an eyebrow; the hand that picks the nose when it thinks no one is looking; the mustache puller; the eyes that never look at you; the nose that sniffs long after the cold has gone."

Makeup for Olivier was magical. He loved hiding his real features behind beards, false complexions, fake noses, and wigs. "If you're wise," he warned, "you always take off the part with your makeup." He also prided himself on his ability to mimic dialects: "I always go to endless trouble to learn American accents, even for small television parts. If it's north Michigan, it's bloody well got to be north Michigan."

Olivier kept his body in peak condition. Even as an old man, he continued running and lifting weights. When illness curbed these forms of exercises, he

6–30a. *Best Seller* **(U.S.A., 1987),** *with James Woods, directed by Joe Flynn.*

Acting styles are determined in part by a player's energy level. High-voltage performers like Woods usually project out to the audience, commanding our attention with a nervous, edgy, bravura style. Much of our pleasure in a Woods performance is listening to how fast he can talk: Usually his tongue is racing after his thoughts. Other high-energy performers include Harold Lloyd, John Barrymore, James Cagney, Katharine Hepburn, Bette Davis, Gene Kelly, George C. Scott, and Barbra Streisand. *(Orion Pictures)*

(a)

6–30b. *The Last Metro* **(France, 1980),** *with Catherine Deneuve and Gerard Depardieu, directed by François Truffaut.*

Low-keyed performers like Deneuve are sometimes said to work "small" or "close to the lens." Rather than projecting out to the audience, these performers allow the camera to tune *in* on their behavior, which is seldom exaggerated for dramatic effect. Eyewitness accounts of Deneuve's acting usually stress how little she seems to be working. The subtleties are apparent only at very close ranges. Other players in this mode include Harry Langdon, Spencer Tracy, Henry Fonda, Marilyn Monroe, Montgomery Clift, Robert De-Niro, and Jack Nicholson. Of course dramatic context is all important in determining an actor's energy level. *(United Artists)*

(b)

took to swimming. At the age of 78, he was still swimming a half a mile almost every morning. "To be fit should be one of an actor's first priorities," he insisted. "To exercise daily is of utmost importance. The body is an instrument which must be finely tuned and played as often as possible. The actor should be able to control it from the tip of his head to his little toe" (quotes are from *Laurence Olivier on Acting*).

The post–World War II era tended to emphasize realistic styles of acting. In the early 1950s, a new interior style of acting, known as "the Method," or "the System," was introduced to American movie audiences. It was commonly associated with the former stage director Elia Kazan. Kazan's *On the Waterfront* was a huge success and a virtual showcase for this style of performance. It has since become the dominant style of acting in the American cinema as well as the live theater. The Method was an offshoot of a system of training actors and rehearsing that had been developed by Constantin Stanislavsky at the Moscow Art Theater. Stanislavsky's ideas were widely adopted in New York theater circles, especially by the Actors Studio in New York, which received much publicity during the 1950s because it had developed such well-known graduates as Marlon Brando, James Dean, Julie Harris, Paul Newman, and many others.

Kazan cofounded and taught at the Actors Studio until 1954, when he asked his former mentor, Lee Strasberg, to take over the organization. Within a short period, Strasberg became the most celebrated acting teacher in America, and his former students were—and still are—among the most famous performers in the world.

The central credo of Stanislavsky's system was: "You must live the part every moment you are playing it." He rejected the tradition of acting that emphasized externals. He believed that truth in acting can only be achieved by exploring a character's inner spirit which must be fused with the actor's own emotions. One of the most important techniques he developed is *emotional recall,* in which an actor delves into his or her own past to discover feelings which are analogous to those of the character. "In every part you do," Julie Harris explained, "there is some connection you can make with your own background or with some feeling you've had at one time or another." Stanislavsky's techniques were strongly psychoanalytical: By exploring their own subconscious, actors could trigger *real* emotions, which are recalled in every performance and transferred to the characters they are playing. He also devised techniques for helping actors focus their concentration on the "world" of the play—its concrete details and textures. In some form or another, these techniques are probably as old as the acting profession itself, but Stanislavsky was the first to systematize them with exercises and methods of analysis (hence the terms the System and the Method). Nor did he claim that inner truth and emotional sincerity are sufficient unto

6–32. *Tom Jones* **(Great Britain, 1963),** *with Albert Finney and Joan Greenwood, based on the novel by Henry Fielding, directed by Tony Richardson.*
Above all, British actors have perfected the art of reciting highly stylized dialogue—the language of Shakespeare, Shaw, Fielding, Wilde, and Pinter—without violating the believability of their characters. *(United Artists)*

themselves. He insisted that actors need to master the externals as well, particularly for classic plays, which require a somewhat stylized manner of speaking, moving, and wearing costumes.

Stanislavsky was famous for his lengthy rehearsal periods, in which players were encouraged to improvise with their roles in order to discover the resonances of the text—the **subtext,** which is analogous to Freud's concept of the subconscious. Kazan and other Method-oriented directors used this concept in directing movies: "The film director knows that beneath the surface of his screenplay there is a subtext, a calendar of intentions and feelings and inner events. What appears to be happening, he soon learns, is rarely what is happening. The subtext is one of the film director's most valuable tools. It is what he directs." Spoken dialogue is secondary for Method players. In order to capture a character's "inner events," actors sometimes throw away their lines, choke on them, or even mumble. Throughout the 1950s, Method actors like Brando and Dean were ridiculed by some critics for mumbling their lines.

Stanislavsky disapproved of the star system and individual virtuosity. In his own productions, he insisted on ensemble playing, with genuine interactions among the actor/characters. Players were encouraged to analyze all the specifics of a scene: What does the character really *want?* What has happened prior to the immediate moment? What time of day is it? And so on. When presented with a role utterly foreign to their experience, actors were urged to research the part so that it would be understood in their guts as well as their minds. Method actors are famous for their ability to bring out the emotional intensity of their characters. Method-oriented directors generally believe that a player must have a character's experience within him or her, and they go to considerable lengths to learn about the personal lives of their players in order to use such details for characterization.

6–33. *On the Waterfront* (**U.S.A., 1954**), *with Marlon Brando and Eva Marie Saint, directed by Elia Kazan.*
Kazan considers Brando as close to a genius as he has ever encountered among actors—a view that's widely shared by others, especially other actors. Many regard his performance in this movie as his best—emotionally powerful, tender, poetic. It won him his first Best Actor Academy Award, as well as the New York Film Critics' Award and the British Oscar as Best Foreign Actor—his third year in a row. Kazan was often surprised by his gifted protégé because he came up with ideas so fresh and arrived at in so underground a fashion that they seemed virtually discovered on the spot.   (*Columbia Pictures*)

In the 1960s, the French New Wave directors—especially Godard and Truffaut—popularized the technique of improvisation while their players were on camera. The resultant increase in realism was highly praised by critics. Of course there was nothing new in the technique itself. Actors often improvised in the silent cinema, and it was the foundation of silent comedy. For example, Chaplin, Keaton, and Laurel and Hardy needed to know only the premise of a given scene. The comic details were improvised and later refined in the editing stage. The cumbersome technology of sound put an end to most of these practices. Method-trained actors use improvisation primarily as an exploratory rehearsal technique, but their performances are usually set when the camera begins to roll.

Godard and Truffaut, in order to capture a greater sense of discovery and surprise, would occasionally instruct their players to make up their dialogue while a scene was actually being photographed. The flexible technology introduced by **cinéma vérité** allowed these directors to capture an unprecedented degree of spontaneity. In Truffaut's *The 400 Blows,* for example, the youthful protagonist (Jean-Pierre Léaud) is interviewed by a prison psychologist about

6–34. *The End of Summer* (**Japan, 1961**), *directed by Yasujiro Ozu.*
A master of psychological nuances, Ozu believed that in the art of acting, less is more. He detested melodramatic excesses and demanded the utmost realism from his players, who frequently chafed at his criticism that they were "acting" too much. He avoided using stars and often cast against type so that audiences would view the characters with no preconceptions. He usually chose his players according to their personality rather than their acting ability. Above all, Ozu explored the conflict between individual wishes and social necessity. His scenes are often staged in public settings, where politeness and social decorum require the stifling of personal disappointment. Ozu often instructed his players not to move, to express their feelings only with their eyes. Note how the two characters on the left are privately miles away, while still conforming superficially to the decorum of the occasion. *(New Yorker Films)*

his family life and sexual habits. Drawing heavily on his own experience, Léaud (who wasn't informed of the questions in advance) answers them with disarming frankness. Truffaut's camera is able to capture the boy's hesitations, his embarrassment, and his charming macho bravado. In one form or another, improvisation has become a valuable technique in the contemporary cinema. Such filmmakers as Robert Altman, Rainer Werner Fassbinder, and Martin Scorsese have employed it with brilliant results.

Casting

Casting a movie is almost an art in itself. It requires an acute sensitivity to a player's type, a **convention** inherited from the live theater. Most stage and screen performers are classified according to role categories: leading men, leading la-

6–35. *La Chinoise* **(France, 1967),** *with Juliet Berto, directed by Jean-Luc Godard.*
Though Godard was a pioneer in exploring the possibilities of realistic acting, after his
conversion to Marxism in the late 1960s he came to repudiate this style of performance,
dismissing it as "a bourgeois concept of representation." He was strongly influenced by the
German dramatist Bertolt Brecht. Like Brecht, Godard believed that performers should act
as *intermediaries* between the fictional characters they are playing and the spectators watching the movie. Instead of lulling the viewer with an illusion of reality that pretends to be
objective, the actor should confront the spectator directly, acknowledging his presence and
presenting him not with a vicarious emotional thrill but an analysis of how capitalist ideology works. In short, through the rejection of a realistic style of acting, the Marxist ideal of
demystification is embodied on an aesthetic level within the movie itself. Instead of pretend-
ing that his images and actors are a "reflection of reality," the filmmaker frankly demonstrates how they can be manipulated, thus allowing the viewer to accept or reject the ideas in
a more objective manner. See James Roy MacBean, *Film and Revolution* (Bloomington:
Indiana University Press, 1975).   *(Leacock Pennebaker, Inc.)*

dies, character actors, juveniles, villains, light comedians, tragedians, ingenues,
singing actors, dancing actors, and so on. Typing conventions are rarely violated.
For example, even though homely people obviously fall in love, romantic roles
are almost always performed by attractive players. Similarly, audiences are not
likely to be persuaded by a player with an all-American iconography (like Doris
Day) cast in European roles. Nor is one likely to accept a performer like Klaus
Kinski as the boy-next-door, unless one lives in a very weird neighborhood. Of
course a player's range is all-important in determining his or her type. Some, like
Gene Hackman, have extremely broad ranges, while others, like Woody Allen,
are confined to variations of the same type.

Typecasting was almost invariable in the silent cinema. In part, this was
because characters tended toward allegorical types rather than unique individu-

als, and often were even identified with a label: "The Man," "The Wife," "The Mother," "The Vamp," and so on. Blonde players were usually cast in parts emphasizing purity, earthy brunettes in erotic roles. Eisenstein insisted that players ought to be cast strictly to type and was inclined to favor non-professionals because of their greater authenticity. Why use an actor to impersonate a factory worker, he asked, when a filmmaker can use a *real* factory worker instead?

But trained actors tend to resent being typed and often attempt to broaden their range. Sometimes it works, sometimes it doesn't. Humphrey Bogart is a good example. For years he was stereotyped as a tough, cynical gangster, until he joined forces with director John Huston, who cast him as the hard-boiled detective Sam Spade in *The Maltese Falcon*. Huston weaned him even further from his type in *The Treasure of the Sierra Madre* in which Bogart played a crafty paranoid, the prospector Fred C. Dobbs. The actor totally reversed his image in

6–36. *The Bicycle Thief* **(Italy, 1948),** *with Lamberto Maggiorani and Enzo Staiola, directed by Vittorio De Sica.*

One of the most famous casting coups in film history is De Sica's selection of Maggiorani and Staiola as an impoverished laborer and his idolizing son. Both were nonprofessionals. Maggiorani actually was a laborer and had difficulty finding a factory job after this movie. When De Sica was trying to finance the film, one producer agreed to put up the money provided the leading role was played by Cary Grant! Needless to say, De Sica couldn't imagine an elegant and graceful actor like Grant in the role, and the director wisely went elsewhere for his financing.   *(Audio-Brandon Films)*

The African Queen in which he played Charlie Allnut, a lovable and funny drunk whose vulnerability endeared him to audiences and won Bogart a Best Actor Academy Award. But in *Beat the Devil,* Huston's celebrated casting instincts deserted him when he used Bogart in a role beyond his powers—as a sophisticated adventurer stranded with a shabby assortment of rogues and loons. The witty tongue-in-cheek dialogue fell flat in Bogart's self-conscious performance. A polished player like Cary Grant could have acted the part with much greater believability and grace.

"Casting is characterization," Hitchcock pointed out. Once a role has been cast, especially with a personality star, the essence of the fictional character is already established. In a sense, stars are more "real" than other characters, which

(a)

6–37a. *Romeo and Juliet* (U.S.A., 1936), *with Leslie Howard and Norma Shearer, directed by George Cukor.*
Cukor's version of Shakespeare's play is an example of the disasters that can befall a movie when a director casts against type. The lovers are a far cry from the youngsters called for in the original. Shearer was thirty-seven when she played the thirteen-year-old Juliet; Howard as Romeo was forty-four. At fifty-five, John Barrymore was preposterous as Mercutio, Romeo's firebrand friend. The spectacle of middle-aged adults behaving so childishly makes the whole dramatic action seem ludicrous. *(MGM)*

(b)

6–37b *Romeo and Juliet* (Great Britain/Italy, 1968), *with Leonard Whiting and Olivia Hussey, directed by Franco Zeffirelli.*
Zeffirelli's version of the play is much more successful because he cast to type and awarded the roles to two teenagers. To be sure, Cukor's actors speak the lines better, but Zeffirelli's *look* truer. The differences between the ages of an actor and character are far more important on screen than on stage, for the cinematic close shot can be merciless in revealing age. *(Paramount Pictures)*

is why many people refer to a character by the actor's name, rather than by the name of the person in the story. After working with Hitchcock on the script of *Strangers on a Train*, the novelist Raymond Chandler ridiculed the director's method of characterization: "His idea of character is rather primi.ive," Chandler complained: "Nice Young Man," "Society Girl," "Frightened Woman," and so on. Like many literary types, Chandler believed that characterization must be created through language. He was insensitive to the other options available to a filmmaker. For example, Hitchcock was a cunning exploiter of the star system—a technique that has nothing to do with language. For his leading ladies, for instance, he favored elegant blondes with an understated sexuality and rather aristocratic, ladylike manners—in short, the Society Girl type. But there are great individual differences between such heroines as Joan Fontaine, Ingrid Bergman, and Grace Kelly, to mention only three of Hitchcock's famous blondes.

Hitchcock's casting is often meant to deceive. His villains were usually actors of enormous personal charm—like James Mason in *North by Northwest*. Hitchcock counted on the audience's good will toward an established star, permitting his "heroes" to behave in ways that can only be described as morally

6–38. *The Gospel According to Saint Matthew* (Italy, 1964), *with Enrique Irazoqui, directed by Pier Paolo Pasolini.*
The casting of historical personages is always a ticklish matter, especially with revered figures like Jesus. One of the most successful portrayals is that of Irazoqui, a nonprofessional player whose quiet simplicity and Semitic appearance at least suggest a historical accuracy. In George Stevens's *The Greatest Story Ever Told* (1965), Jesus is played by Max Von Sydow, an actor of dignity and commanding presence. Other directors have been less fortunate. For example, in Nicholas Ray's *King of Kings* (1962), the part was essayed by Jeffrey Hunter, who specialized in heart-throb roles and good-hearted oafs. (One wag referred to the film as *I Was a Teenage Jesus*.) The most critically admired performance was by Willem Dafoe in Martin Scorsese's *The Last Temptation of Christ* (1988).   (*Continental*)

dubious. In *Rear Window,* for example, James Stewart is literally a voyeur, yet we can't bring ourselves to condemn such a wholesome type as Jimmy Stewart, the all-American boy. Audiences also assume that a star will remain in the movie until the final reel, at which point it's permissible—though seldom advisable—to kill him or her off. But in *Psycho,* the Janet Leigh character is brutally murdered in the first third of the film—a shocking violation of convention which jolts audiences out of their complacency. Sometimes Hitchcock cast awkward, self-conscious actors in roles requiring a note of evasive anxiety, like Farley Granger in *Rope* and *Strangers on a Train.* In cases such as these, bad acting is precisely what is called for—it's part of the characterization.

Many filmmakers believe that casting is so integral to character, they don't even begin work on a script until they know who's playing the major roles. Yasujiro Ozu confessed: "I could no more write, not knowing who the actor was going to be, than an artist could paint, not knowing what color he was using." Billy Wilder always tailored his dialogue to fit the personality of his players.

6–39. Publicity photo of Robert Redford and Mia Farrow in *The Great Gatsby* (U.S.A., 1974), *directed by Jack Clayton.*

Gatsby is a sad instance of how miscasting can throw off the entire meaning of a movie. The production had all the makings of a first-rate film, which is what everyone involved wanted to make. Technically, the leading roles were within the ranges of Redford and Farrow, who are both accomplished actors. But their iconography conflicted with their parts. What was needed in the role of Daisy Buchanan was a player who brought with her an air of glamor, mystery, and inaccessibility, a compelling radiance that would make Gatsby's extraordinary romanticism plausible. Perhaps a major star would have been more suitable than a straight actress like Farrow. With Redford, the problem was just the opposite. Jay Gatsby is a man of shady origins, awkward and somewhat vulgar, the kind of man few would notice if he weren't a millionaire. This is hardly a role suited to Redford, whose iconography is steeped in glamor. What was needed in the part was an "ordinary" actor, a mere mortal, not a WASP Adonis. Audiences might have been willing to believe that Farrow would pine for Redford for eight years, but few were inclined to accept the opposite. *(Paramount Pictures) iconography – study the portraits of a particular person.*

When Montgomery Clift backed out of playing the lead in *Sunset Boulevard*, Wilder rewrote the part to fit William Holden, who brought totally different character nuances to the role.

Like photography, mise en scène, movement, editing, and sound, acting is a kind of language system. The filmmaker uses actors as a medium for communicating ideas and emotions. Merely by casting a performer like Lamberto Maggiorani rather than Cary Grant, Vittorio De Sica radically altered the artistic impact of *Bicycle Thief.* Not that Maggiorani is a better actor than Grant. Quite the reverse is true, but their histrionic skills are not in question here. What is involved is the utter authenticity of Maggiorani as opposed to the complex iconography of Grant, an iconography rich in glamor, wit, and sophistication—and hence totally inappropriate for the role. As we have seen, strongly iconographic stars like Gary Cooper and Marilyn Monroe embody a complex network of emotional and ideological values, and these values are part of the filmmaker's artistic statement.

FURTHER READING

DMYTRYK, EDWARD, and JEAN PORTER, *On Screen Acting* (London: Focal Press, 1984). Practical emphasis.

DYER, RICHARD, *Stars* (London: British Film Institute, 1979). A systematic analysis, well-written.

HASKELL, MOLLY, *From Reverence to Rape* (Baltimore, Md: Penguin, 1974). Feminist study of images of women in American films.

MORIN, EDGAR, *The Stars* (New York: Grove Press, 1960). Theoretical emphasis.

MUNK, ERIKA, ed., *Stanislavsky in America* (New York: Hill and Wang, 1966). A collection of essays.

OLIVIER, LAURENCE, *Laurence Olivier on Acting* (New York: Simon & Schuster, 1986).

ROSS, LILLIAN, AND HELEN ROSS, *The Player: A Profile of an Art* (New York: Simon & Schuster, 1962). A collection of interviews with actors from stage, screen, and TV.

SCHICKEL, RICHARD, *The Stars* (New York: Dial Press, 1962). See also Richard Griffith, *The Movie Stars* (Garden City, N.Y.: Doubleday, 1970). Studies by two of America's best film critics.

SHIPMAN, DAVID, *The Great Movie Stars*, Vol. I, *The Golden Years* (New York: Bonanza Books, 1970); Vol. II, *The International Years* (New York: St. Martin's Press, 1972), Encyclopedic coverage, with sane, well-written evaluations.

WALKER, ALEXANDER, *Stardom, The Hollywood Phenomenon* (London: Penguin, 1974). Well-written history and analysis.

DRAMA |

The function of the cinema is to reveal, to bring to light certain details that the stage would have left untreated.

—ANDRÉ BAZIN

Many people cling to the naive belief that drama and film are two aspects of the same art, only drama is "live," while movies are "recorded." Certainly there are undeniable similarities between the two arts. Most obviously, both employ action as a principal means of communication: What people *do* is a major source of meaning. Live theater and movies are also collaborative enterprises, involving the coordination of writers, directors, actors, and technicians. Drama and film are both social arts, exhibited before groups of people, and experienced publicly as well as individually. But films are not mere recordings of plays. The language systems of each are fundamentally different. For the most part, movies have a far broader range of techniques at their disposal.

Time, Space, and Language

In the live theater, time is less flexible than in movies. The basic unit of construction in the theater is the scene, and the amount of dramatic time that elapses during a scene is roughly equal to the length of time it takes to perform. True, some plays traverse many years, but usually these years transpire "between curtains." We're informed that it is "seven years later" either by a stage direction or by the dialogue. The basic unit of construction in movies is the **shot.** Since the average shot lasts only ten or fifteen seconds (and can be as brief as a fraction of a second), the cinematic shot can lengthen or shorten time more subtly. Drama has to chop out huge blocks of time between the relatively few scenes and acts; films can expand or contract time between the many hundreds of shots. Theatrical time is usually continuous. It moves forward. Temporal dislocations like the **flashback** are rare in the live theater, but commonplace in movies.

Space in the live theater is also dependent on the basic unit of the scene. The action takes place in a unified area that has specific limits, usually defined by the proscenium arch. Drama, then, almost always deals with **closed forms:** We don't imagine that the action is being continued in the wings or the dressing rooms of the theater. The "proscenium arch" in film is the **frame**—a masking device that isolates objects and people only temporarily. Movies deal with a series of space fragments. Beyond the frame of a given shot, another aspect of the action waits to be photographed. A **close-up** of an object, for example, is generally a detail of a subsequent **long shot,** which will give us the context of the close-up. In the theater, it's more difficult to withhold information in this manner.

In the live theater, the viewer remains in a stationary position: The distance between the audience and the stage is constant. Of course an actor can move closer to an audience, but compared to the fluid space in the cinema, distance variation in the live theater is negligible. The film viewer, on the other hand, identifies with the camera's lens, which is not immobilized in a chair. This identification permits the viewer to "move" in any direction and from any distance. An **extreme close-up** allows us to count the lashes of an eyelid; the **extreme long shot** permits us to see miles in each direction. In short, the cinema allows the spectator to feel mobile.

These spatial differences don't necessarily favor one medium over the other. In the live theater, space is three-dimensional, is occupied by tangible

7–1. *Fantastic Voyage* **(U.S.A., 1966),** *art direction by Jack Martin Smith and Dale Hennesy, special effects by Art Cruickshank, directed by Richard Fleischer.*
Screen space can explore even microscopic areas: literally, through microcinematography, or figuratively, through special effects. The principal setting of this film—the interior of a human body—couldn't possibly be duplicated on stage. In order to perform a delicate brain operation, several scientists are reduced to the size of bacteria. They travel through the patient's bloodstream in a miniaturized submarine. This photo shows the crew's only survivors floating in the area of the optic nerve as they frantically search for the patient's eye in order to escape from his body before they return to normal size. *(Twentieth Century-Fox)*

people and objects, and is therefore more realistic. That is, our perception of space is essentially the same as in real life. The living presence of actors, with their subtle interactions—both with other actors and the audience—is impossible to duplicate in film. Movies provide us with a two-dimensional *image* of space and objects, and no interaction exists between the screen actors and the audience. For this reason, nudity is not so controversial an issue on the screen as in the live theater, for on stage the naked people are real, whereas in movies they're "only pictures" (7–3).

The stage player interacts with viewers, establishing a delicate rapport with each different audience. The screen player, on the other hand, is inexorably fixed on celluloid: He or she can't readjust to each audience, for the worlds of the screen and the viewer aren't connected and continuous as they are in the live theater. Movies often seem dated because acting styles can't be adjusted to newer audiences. Stage actors on the other hand can make even a two-thousand-year-old play seem fresh and relevant, for while the words remain the same, their interpretation and delivery can always be changed to conform with contemporary acting styles.

Because of the spatial differences, the viewer's participation is different in each medium. In the theater, the audience generally must be more active. Since all of the visual elements are provided within a given space, the viewer must sort out what's essential from what's incidental. Disregarding for the moment the importance of language in the theater, drama is a medium of low visual saturation. That is, the audience must fill in certain meanings in the absence of visual detail. A movie audience, on the other hand, is generally more passive. All the necessary details are provided by close-ups and by **edited** juxtapositions. Film, then, is a medium of high visual saturation—that is, the pictures are densely detailed with information, requiring little or no filling in.

Although both drama and film are eclectic arts, the theater is a narrower medium, one specializing in spoken language. Most of the meanings in the theater are found in words, which are densely saturated with information. For this reason, drama is generally considered a writer's medium. The primacy of the text makes it a kind of special branch of literature. In the live theater, we tend to hear before we see. The film director René Clair once noted that a blind man

7–2. *Gandhi* **(Great Britain, 1982),** *directed by Richard Attenborough.*
Epic stories can be treated on the stage, but they are always stylized. Theatrical space is too constricted for a realistic presentation. In movies, even a massacre involving thousands of people can be reconstructed in a realistic manner. *(Columbia Pictures)*

**7–3. *Dona Flor and Her Two Husbands*
(Brazil, 1977)**, *with José Wilker, Sonia
Braga, and Mauro Mendonca; directed by
Bruno Baretto.*

Nudity is common in movies, rare in the
live theater. A naked actor on stage usually triggers off a public outcry, but because movies are "only pictures" nudity
seldom provokes much controversy except in puritanical communities. As a result, cinema has been able to exploit nakedness as a symbolic comment, a way of
exploring universal impulses. For example, this "naughty" sex farce deals with a
woman who loves two men, one a ghost.
Her first husband (Wilker) was charming, exciting, and totally irresponsible.
He died during one of his many sexual
escapades, but his ghost—visible only to
us and his former wife—returns to enjoy
his conjugal prerogatives. Dona Flor's second husband is decent and reliable, a
good provider, a rock of stability. He's
also stupifyingly dull. In order to be totally happy, Dona Flor must satisfy both
needs—for a dynamo in the bedroom
and a pillar of society in the outside
world. She accordingly manages to arrange an amiable, if somewhat ghostly,
ménage à trois.   (*Carnaval/New Yorker Films*)

could still grasp the essentials of most stage plays. Movies, on the other hand, are
generally regarded as a visual art and a director's medium, for it is the director
who creates the images. Clair observed that a deaf man could still grasp most of
the essentials of a film. But these generalizations are relative, for some movies—
many of the works of Welles, for example—are densely saturated, both visually
and aurally.

Since plays stress the primacy of language, one of the major problems in
adapting them to the screen is determining how much of the language is necessary in a predominantly visual art like movies. George Cukor's version of Shakespeare's *Romeo and Juliet* (6–37) was a conservative film adaptation. Virtually
all the dialogue was retained, even the exposition and purely functional speeches
of no particular poetic merit. The result was a respectful but often tedious film in
which the visuals tended merely to illustrate the language. Often images and
dialogue contained the same information, producing an overblown, static quality
that actually contradicted the swift sense of action in the stage play.

Zeffirelli's film version of this play was much more successful. Verbal
exposition was cut almost completely and replaced (just as effectively) by visual

7-4. *Pickpocket* (France, 1959), *directed by Robert Bresson*.
In the live drama, if a small prop (like a wallet) is important, it must be highlighted conspicuously or the audience will fail to notice its existence, much less its importance. In the cinema, small articles can be isolated from their context. In this photo, Bresson captures a pickpocket's swift stroke as he lifts a wallet from a pedestrian on a busy walkway. This snapshot quality is difficult to produce on stage: The conventions of the medium are at odds with the essence of the subject matter. (*New Yorker Films*)

exposition. Single lines were pruned meticulously from some of the speeches where the same information could be conveyed by images. Most of the great poetry was preserved but often with **nonsynchronous** visuals to expand—not duplicate—the language. The essence of Shakespeare's play is found in the impulsive haste of its youthful protagonists, the dominolike swiftness of the chain of events, and the violence of much of the action. Zeffirelli heightened these characteristics by kineticizing many of the scenes. The fight sequences are often photographed with a hand-held camera that lurches and swirls with the combatants as they spill onto the streets of Verona. Zeffirelli's movie, though technically less faithful to the stage script, is actually more Shakespearean in spirit than the scrupulously literal version of Cukor.

Both theater and cinema are audiovisual mediums, then, but they differ in their stress of certain **conventions.** The two major sources of information in the live theater are action and dialogue. We observe what people do and what they say. Theatrical action is restricted primarily to objective long shots, to use a cinematic metaphor. Only fairly large actions are effective: the duel between Hamlet and Laertes, Amanda helping Laura to dress in *The Glass Menagerie,* and so on. Extreme long-shot ranges—to continue the cinematic metaphor— must be stylized in the live theater. The **epic** battles of Shakespeare's plays would look ridiculous if staged realistically. Likewise, close-up actions would be missed by all but those in the front rows unless the actions were exaggerated and stylized by the actors. Except for the most intimate theaters, close-up actions in the live drama have to be verbalized. That is, the most subtle actions and reactions of stage characters are usually conveyed by language rather than by visual means. We know of Hamlet's attitude toward Claudius primarily through Hamlet's soliloquies and dialogue. On the close-up level of action, then, what we see on stage is often not what people do, but what they *talk* about doing, or what's been done.

Because of these visual problems, most plays avoid actions requiring vast or minute spaces. Theatrical action is usually confined to the long- and **full-shot** range. If vast or minute spaces are required, the theater tends to resort to unrealistic conventions: to ballets and stylized tableaux for extreme long-shot actions, and to the convention of verbal articulation for close-up actions. Movies, on the other hand, can move easily among all these ranges. For this reason, the cinema often dramatizes the action that takes place on stage only "between the curtains." This is not to say that the cinema doesn't have its own set of conventions. The movable camera, **expressionistic** sound, and editing are just as artificial as the conventions of the live theater. In both cases, the audience accepts these conventions as the rules of the game.

The human being is central to the aesthetic of the theater: Words must be recited by people, conflicts must be embodied by actors. The cinema is not so dependent on humans. The aesthetic of film is based on photography, and anything that can be photographed can be the subject matter of a movie. For this reason, adapting a play to the screen, while difficult, is hardly impossible, for much of what can be done on the stage can be duplicated on the screen. To adapt most movies to the stage, however, would be much more difficult. Movies with

7–5. All About Eve (U.S.A., 1950), *with Bette Davis, Marilyn Monroe, and George Sanders, written and directed by Joseph L. Mankiewicz.*
All About Eve is about the New York live theater and its fascinatingly neurotic denizens. It's one of the few movies that could probably be converted into an effective stage play, for its action consists mostly of talk—glorious talk. Mankiewicz, who was fondly described by one critic as "Old Joe, the Talk Man," is above all a *verbal* stylist, a master of sophisticated dialogue and bitchy repartée.   *(Twentieth Century–Fox)*

7–6. Publicity photo for *Magnum Force* (U.S.A., 1973), *with Clint Eastwood and Adele Yoshioka, directed by Ted Post.* In the live theater, actors are selected not only on the basis of their looks and talent, but also on how well they match up with the other actors on stage. Theatrical directors must always conceive of their productions in terms of an ensemble effect. In the cinema, these considerations are secondary. In this movie, Eastwood, who stands 6' 4", is romantically paired with Adele Yoshioka, who is 5' 4". On stage, this height discrepancy would be a sight gag, but on the screen (or more accurately, off screen), the problem was easily resolved through the art of exclusion. *(Warner Bros.)*

exterior locations would be almost automatically ruled out, of course: How would one go about adapting John Ford's epic westerns like *Stagecoach*? But even films with interior locations would probably be impossible to translate into theatrical terms. True, the words would present no problem, and some actions would be transferable. But how would one deal with the time and space dislocations of Richard Lester's Beatles film, *A Hard Day's Night*? Theme and characterization in Joseph Losey's *The Servant* are communicated primarily through the use of camera angles—impossible to duplicate in the theater (10–9). The theme of Bergman's *The Silence* is conveyed primarily through images of empty corridors, doors, and windows. How could one transfer this technique to the stage?

One should not assume from this that the best method of adapting a play for the screen is to "open it up"—to substitute exterior locations for interiors.

7–7. *Stagecoach* (**U.S.A., 1939**), *directed by John Ford.*
The cinema is well suited to dealing with the relationship between people and nature—a rare theme in the live theater. Ford considered Monument Valley, Utah (pictured) as "the most complete, beautiful, and peaceful place on earth." He shot nine of his westerns here. *(United Artists)*

Cinema doesn't always mean extreme long shots, sweeping **pans,** and flashy editing. Hitchcock once observed that many filmed versions of plays fail precisely because the tight, compact structure of the original is lost when the film director "loosens it up" with inappropriate cinematic techniques. Particularly when a play emphasizes a sense of confinement, either physical or psychological—and a great many of them do—the best adaptors respect the spirit of the original by finding filmic equivalents (7–9).

The Director

In the mid-1950s, the French periodical *Cahiers du Cinéma* popularized the **auteur theory,** a view that stressed the dominance of the director in film art (see Chapter 10, Theory). According to this view, whoever controls the **mise en scène**—the medium of the story—is the true "author" of a movie. The other collaborators (writers, cinematographer, actors, editor, etc.) are merely the director's technical assistants. No doubt the auteur critics exaggerated the primacy of the director, particularly in America, where many film directors were at the mercy of the Hollywood studio system, which tended to emphasize group work

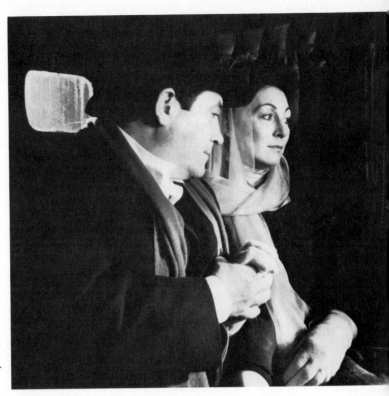

7–8. *The Dead* (U.S.A., 1987), *with Angelica Huston and Donal McCann, directed by John Huston.*
The cinema can be a medium of subtle nuances as well as epic events. This faithful adaptation of James Joyce's famous short story is comprised almost exclusively of "little things"—a touch of the hand, a wistful sidelong glance, a private moment of bitterness. On stage, such fragile materials would be considered hopelessly undramatic. But because the camera can move into the intimate ranges, such details can be woven into a poetic fabric of sheerest delicacy.   *(Vestron Pictures)*

rather than individual expression and publicized **stars** rather than directors. Nevertheless, the auteur critics were essentially correct about the most artistically significant films.

Even today, the most admired movies—from whatever country—tend to be director's films. To refer to a movie as "good except for its direction" is as contradictory as referring to a play as "good except for its script." Of course we can enjoy a poorly directed movie or a badly written play, but what we enjoy are usually the secondary aspects of the art—a touching performance, a striking set. Good acting and stylish camerawork have often redeemed rubbish material. Such enjoyable elements generally represent the individual triumph of a gifted interpretive artist (actor, set designer, cinematographer, etc.) over the mediocrity of the dominant artist—the director in film, the writer in the live theater.

On the stage, then, the director is essentially an interpretive artist. If we see a rotten production of *King Lear,* we don't dismiss Shakespeare's play, but only a specific interpretation of the play. True, the stage director creates certain patterns of movement, appropriate gestures for his actors, and spatial relationships, but all of these visual elements take second place to the language of the script, which is created by the playwright. The theatrical director's relation to the text is similar to the stage actor's relation to a role: He or she can add much to what's written down, but what is contributed is usually secondary to the text itself.

The stage director is a kind of go-between for the author and the production staff. That is, the director is responsible for the general interpretation of the script and usually defines the limits for the other interpretive artists: actors, designers, technicians. The director must see to it that all the production elements are harmonized and subordinated to an overall interpretation. His or her influence tends to be stronger during rehearsals than in the actual performance. Once the curtain opens before an audience, the director is powerless to control what then takes place.

On the other hand, screen directors have a good deal more control over the final product. They too dominate the preproduction activities, but unlike the stage director the filmmaker controls virtually every aspect of the finished work as well. The degree of precision a film director can achieve is impossible on the stage, for movie directors can rephotograph people and objects until they get exactly what they want. As we have seen, films communicate *primarily* through moving images, and it's the director who determines most of the visual elements:

7–9. *The Member of the Wedding* (U.S.A., 1953), *with Julie Harris and Ethel Waters, directed by Fred Zinnemann.*

Because of its spatial limitations, the live theatre is an ideal medium for dealing with the theme of confinement. One of the problems facing the film director who wishes to adapt a play is whether to "open it up"—that is, whether to dramatize off-stage actions on the screen. To do so would run the risk of releasing the spatial tensions of the original, which the dramatist exploits as part of the artistic form. Zinnemann's adaptation of Carson McCuller's play (itself based on her novel) confined most of the action to a single location. The theme of the novel, play, and movie is the same: the sense of entrapment of a girl (Harris) about to enter young womanhood. In the novel, her isolation is conveyed primarily by a limited-point-of-view narration. In the play, the theme is spatially symbolized by the narrow confines of a single set. In the film, this idea is communicated principally by the close, tightly framed shots, which seem to imprison both the young heroine and her closest friend, the family maid (Waters). Much of the language of the novel is sacrificed in the play, and even more is cut out of the movie version, which uses spatial equivalents for many of the verbal ideas.   (*Columbia Pictures*)

the choice of shots, angles, lighting effects, filters, optical effects, framing, composition, camera movements, and editing. Futhermore, the director usually authorizes the costume and set designs and the choice of locales.

The differences in control and precision can best be illustrated perhaps by examining their handling of the mise en scène. Stage directors are much more restricted: They must work within one stationary set per scene. All patterns of movement take place within this given area. Since this is a three-dimensional space, they have the advantage of depth as well as breadth to work with. Through the use of platforms, they can also exploit height on the stage. The theatrical director must use certain space conventions to assure maximum clarity. Thus, with a proscenium stage, the audience pretends it's peeping into a room where one wall has been removed. Naturally no furniture is placed against this "wall," nor do players turn their backs against it for very long periods or their dialogue wouldn't be audible. If a thrust stage is used, the audience surrounds the acting area on three sides, forcing the performers to rotate their movements and speeches so that no side is neglected. Again, this convention is necessary to assure maximum clarity.

In the cinema, the director converts three-dimensional space into a two-

7–10. *The Little Foxes* (U.S.A., 1941), *with Dan Duryea and Carl Benton Reid, directed by William Wyler.*

André Bazin believed that in adapting a play a filmmaker's greatest challenge is translating the artificial space of the theater into the realistic space of the cinema without losing the essence of the original. For example, in Lillian Hellman's stage play, this scene between a devious father and his creepy son takes place in the same living room set as most of the other scenes. Wyler's presentation is at once more effective and realistic. The two characters are shaving in the family bathroom while they haltingly probe the possibility of swindling a relative. Neither wants to reveal himself, neither looks at the other directly. Instead, they address each other by looking in their respective mirrors, their backs turned. "There is a hundred times more cinema, and of a better kind, in a shot in *The Little Foxes,*" Bazin claimed, "than in all the outdoor dolly shots, natural locations, exotic geography, and flipsides of sets with which the screen so far has tried to make up for stagey origins." *(RKO)*

7–11. *Fiddler on the Roof* (U.S.A., 1971), *with Topol, directed by Norman Jewison.*
Virtually all stage plays are social in emphasis. That is, they deal with the relationships
between people. The cinema can also deal with the relationship of people to things and
places. In transforming this stage musical to actual locations, Jewison enhanced the hero's
relationship to the land and his village—an important aspect of Sholem Aleichem's stories,
which are the original source of the story.   *(United Artists)*

dimensional image of space. Even with deep-focus photography, "depth" is not
literal (7–12). But the flat image has certain advantages. Since a camera can be
placed virtually anywhere, the film director is not confined to a stationary set
with a given number of "walls." The eye-level long shot more or less corresponds
to the theatrical proscenium arch. But in movies, the close-up also constitutes a
given space—in effect a cinematic "roomlet" with its own "walls" (the frame).
Each shot, then, represents a new given space with different (and temporary)
confines. Furthermore, the movable camera permits the director to rearrange
the "walls" many times for maximum expressiveness with no sacrifice of clarity.
Thus, in film, a character can enter the frame from below, from above, from any
side, and from any angle. By **dollying** or **craning,** a camera can also take us
"into" a set, permitting objects to pass by us.

Since the stage director's mise en scène is confined to the unit of the scene,
a certain amount of compromise is inevitable. He or she must combine a maximum of expressiveness with a maximum of clarity—not always an easy task,
especially in realistic productions. Film directors have to make fewer compromises of this sort, for they have a greater number of "scene-lets" at their disposal: Most movies average well over a thousand shots. The film director can
give us a half dozen shots of the same object—some emphasizing clarity, others
emphasizing expressiveness. Some shots can show a character with his back to

7–12. *Ikiru,* also known as *To Live* (Japan, 1952), *directed by Akira Kurosawa.*
On the stage, the size of objects is constant; in movies, it's relative. In this deep-focus shot, for example, the materials of three depth planes are precisely aligned to produce an ironic contrast. The protagonist (Takashi Shimura, whose picture adorns the Buddhist altar) was a lowly bureaucrat who did something really significant with his existence only in the final months of his life, when he realized he was dying of cancer. In the flashback portions of the movie, his battered hat is a symbol of his humility and dogged perseverance. His funeral wake (pictured) is a rigid, dismal affair, attended primarily by the deceased's fellow bureaucrats. The placement of the camera in this photo implicitly contrasts the unpretentious hat with the chagrined faces of the office workers with the formal photograph and altar. *(Brandon Films)*

the camera: The sound track guarantees the clarity of his speech. A character can be photographed through an obstruction of some kind—a pane of glass or the dense foliage of a forest. Eisenstein occasionally had one actor block out another by having the first stand before the camera. Such "impediments" are usually employed for symbolic reasons, but since the cinematic shot need not be lengthy, clarity can be suspended temporarily in favor of expressiveness.

These generalizations are postulated upon the assumption that the stage is essentially **realistic** in its handling of time and space, whereas the cinema is basically **formalistic.** But the differences are relative, of course. Indeed, an argument could be made that Strindberg's expressionistic plays—*The Dream Play,* for example—are more fragmented and subjective than a realistic movie like Keaton's *Steamboat Bill, Jr.,* which emphasizes the continuity of time and space.

In adapting a stage play, the filmmaker is confronted with thousands of choices, petty and monumental. These can alter the original in ways never

7–13. *Hedda* **(Great Britain, 1975),** *with Glenda Jackson (center), directed by Trevor Nunn.* This adaptation of Henrik Ibsen's *Hedda Gabler* acquires additional resonance when transferred to the screen, for the mise en scène is reconstituted for each shot. For example, in this shot, we can see how the title character (Jackson) literally comes between the other two characters, forcing them apart. Since each viewer in the live theater has a unique perspective of the stage, spatial techniques like this are rare. In the cinema they are common, for the camera determines one perspective for all.   *(Brut Productions)*

dreamed of by the original dramatist. Even with classic texts, a filmmaker can emphasize the psychological, the social, or the epic, since these are determined in large measure by the way space is used in movies. A filmmaker can stage the action on studio sets or in a natural setting, but the choice will significantly alter the meaning of the work.

Settings and Décor

In the best movies and stage productions, settings are not merely backdrops for the action, but symbolic extensions of the theme and characterization. Settings can convey an immense amount of information, especially in the cinema. Stage sets are generally less detailed than film sets, for the audience is too distant from the stage to perceive many small details. The director in this medium must generally work with fewer sets, usually one per act. Inevitably the stage director

7–14. *The Scarlet Empress* (U.S.A., 1934), *art direction by Hans Dreier, directed by Josef von Sternberg.*
Formalist filmmakers like von Sternberg are concerned with presenting a subjective, personal vision of reality that has no counterpart in the actual world. The goal is expressiveness, not authenticity. This movie deals with the life of Catherine the Great, but the costumes, décor, and even the statuary (all closely supervised by von Sternberg) owe little to what literally existed in eighteenth-century Russia. When asked why he preferred to work with studio sets rather than actual historical locations, von Sternberg replied, "Because I am a poet." *(Paramount Pictures)*

must settle for less precision and variety than screen directors, who have virtually no limits of this kind, especially when shooting on location.

Spatial considerations force the stage director to make constant compromises with his sets. If he uses too much of the upstage (rear) area, the audience won't be able to see or hear well. If he uses high platforms to give an actor dominance, the director then has the problem of getting the actor back on the main level quickly and plausibly. The stage director must also use a constant-sized space: Settings are usually confined to "long shots." If he wants to suggest a vast field, for example, he must resort to certain conventions. He can stage an action in such a way as to suggest that the playing area is only a small corner of the field. Or he can stylize his set with the aid of a cyclorama, which gives the illusion of a vast sky in the background. If he wants to suggest a confined area, he can do so only for short periods, for an audience grows restless when actors are restricted to a small playing area for long periods. Stage directors can use vertical, horizontal, and oblique lines in a set to suggest psychological states; but these lines (or colors or objects) cannot be cut out from scenes where they are inappropriate, as they could be in a film.

The film director has far more freedom in the use of settings. Most important, of course, the cinema permits a director to shoot out-of-doors—an enormous advantage. The major works of a number of great directors would have been impossible without this freedom: Griffith, Eisenstein, Keaton, Kurosawa, Antonioni, Ford, De Sica, Renoir. Epic films would be virtually impossible without the extreme long shots of vast expanses of land. Other **genres,** particularly those requiring a degree of stylization or deliberate unreality, have been associated with the studio: musicals, horror films, and many period films. Such genres often stress a kind of magical, sealed-off universe, and images taken from real life tend to clash with these essentially claustrophobic qualities.

However, these are merely generalizations. There are some westerns that have been shot mostly indoors, and some musicals that have been photographed in actual locations. If a location is extravagantly beautiful, there's no reason why a romantic musical can't exploit such a setting. The Paris locations of Minnelli's *Gigi* are a good example of how actual locations can enhance a stylized genre. In short, it all depends on how it's done. As the French historian Georges Sadoul pointed out: "The dichotomy between the studio and the street, the antithesis between Lumière and Méliès, are false oppositions when one attempts to find in them the solution to the problems of realism and art. Films completely outside time have been shot out of doors; completely realistic films have been shot in the studio."

In set design, as in other aspects of movies, the terms realism and formalism are simply convenient critical labels. Most sets *tend* toward one style or the other, but few are pure examples. For instance, in *The Birth of a Nation,* Griffith proudly proclaims that a number of his scenes are historical facsimiles of real places and events—like Ford's Theater where Lincoln was assassinated, or the signing of the Emancipation Proclamation. These scenes were modeled on actual photographs of the period. Yet Griffith's facsimiles were created in a studio. On the other hand, real locations can be exploited to create a somewhat artificial—formalistic—effect. For example, in shooting *Ten Days That Shook the World,* Eisenstein had the Winter Palace at his disposal for several months. Yet the images in the movie are baroque: richly textured and formally complex. Although Eisenstein chose actual locations for their authenticity, they are never just picturesque backgrounds to the action. Each shot is carefully designed. Each exploits the inherent *form* of the setting, contributing significantly to the emotional impact of the sequence (10–8). Realistic or formalistic?

Realism is never a simple term. In movies it's used to describe a variety of styles. Some critics employ modifiers like "poetic realism," "documentary realism," and "studio realism" to make finer distinctions. The nature of beauty in realism is also a complex issue. Beauty of form is an important component of poetic realism. The early works of Fellini, such as *The Nights of Cabiria,* are handsomely mounted and slightly aestheticized to appeal to our visual sense. Similarly, John Ford shot nine of his westerns in Monument Valley (7–7) because of its spectacular beauty. Among other things, Ford was a great landscape artist. Many realistic films shot in the studio are also slightly stylized to exploit this "incidental" visual beauty.

In other realistic films, beauty—in this conventional sense—plays a lesser role. A major criterion of aesthetic value in a movie like Pontecorvo's *Battle of Algiers* is its deliberate roughness. The story deals with the struggle for liberation of the Algerian people from their French colonial masters. It was shot entirely in the streets and houses of Algiers. The setting is rarely exploited for its aesthetic

(a)

7–15. Production photo of _The Sands of Iwo Jima_ (U.S.A., 1949), _with John Wayne (front and center), directed by Allan Dwan._

Because a studio allows a director more control and precision than an actual location, some filmmakers use the so-called **process shot** in scenes requiring exterior locations. What this technique involves is the rear projection of a moving image on a translucent screen. Live actors and a portion of a set are placed in front of this screen, and the entire action and background are then photographed by a camera that is synchronized with the rear projector. The finished product **(b)** looks reasonably authentic, although backgrounds tend to look suspiciously washed out and flat in comparison to foreground elements. _(Republic Pictures)_

(b)

7–16. *The Cabinet of Dr. Caligari* **(Germany, 1919),** *with Conrad Veidt and Werner Krauss (wearing hat); production design by Hermann Warm, Walter Röhrig, and Walter Reimann; directed by Robert Wiene.*

The German Expressionist movement of the post–World War I era emphasized visual design above all. The movement's main contributions were in the live theater, the graphic arts, and the cinema. The great stage director Max Reinhardt was a seminal influence. In his theory of design, Reinhardt advocated an ideal of "landscapes imbued with soul." The declared aim of most German Expressionists was to eliminate nature for a state of absolute abstraction. It is a style steeped in anxiety and terror. The sets are deliberately artificial: flat, obviously painted, with no attempt to preserve the conventions of perspective and scale. They are meant to represent a state of mind, not a place. The lighting and set designs are carefully coordinated, with one shading off into the other. A tortured hallucinatory atmosphere is evoked by the twisted shapes that violate the surface of the image. Horizontal and vertical lines are avoided in favor of diagonals which produce a sense of instability and visual anguish. The jerky, machinelike acting is meant to convey the essence of depersonalization. In the cinema, the German Expressionist movement lasted only from 1919 to 1923, but its influence has been enormous, especially in the United States. *(Museum of Modern Art)*

beauty. In fact, Pontecorvo's lack of formal organization, his refusal to yield an inch in matters of "style," is his principal virtue as an artist. The moral power of the materials takes precedence over formal considerations. The setting's beauty is in its truth. In films such as these, style (that is, distortion) is regarded as prettification, a form of insincerity, and therefore ugly. Even outright ugliness can be a criterion of aesthetic beauty. The gaudy sets and décor in *Touch of Evil* are organic to the nature of the materials (7–17).

7–17. *Touch of Evil* **(U.S.A., 1958),** *art direction by Alexander Golitzen and Robert Clatworthy, directed by Orson Welles.*
Like a filmmaker's other collaborators, art directors gear their style to suit the spirit of the story. The sleazy bordertown setting of this movie required the utmost vulgarity in the art design. But Welles was able to transcend this deliberate bad taste by aestheticizing it—through his masterful control of the camera, the lighting, and the editing. Paradoxically, *Touch of Evil* is a bravura masterpiece of style, yet its materials consist almost exclusively of ugliness.   (*Universal-International*)

To the unsympathetic, the cult of realism verges on madness. But there's a method to it. For example, John Huston shot *The African Queen* in the tropics because he knew he wouldn't have to worry about a thousand little details, such as how to get the actors to sweat a lot, or how to get their clothes to stick to their bodies. Perhaps the most famous, if not infamous, example of this passion for authenticity is Erich von Stroheim, who detested studio sets. In *Greed,* he insisted that his actors actually live in a seedy boarding house to get the "feel" of the film's low-life setting. He forced them to wear shabby clothing and deprived them of all the amenities that their characters would lack in actuality. Perhaps because of the severe hardships his cast and crew suffered, the movie's authenticity is incontestable.

Spectacle films usually require the most elaborate sets. Historical reconstructions of ancient Rome or Egypt are enormously expensive to build, and they can make or break a film in this genre because spectacle is the major attraction. Perhaps the most famous sets of this type are found in the Babylonian story of Griffith's *Intolerance.* The unprecedented monumentality of these sets is what skyrocketed Griffith's budget to an all-time high of $1.9 million—an astronomical figure by 1916 standards, hefty even by today's. The banquet scene for Belshazzar's feast alone cost a reputed $250,000 and employed over four thousand extras. The story required the construction of a walled city so vast that for years it remained a standing monument—called "Griffith's Folly" by cynics in the trade. The set extended nearly three-quarters of a mile in length. The court was flanked by enormous colonnades supporting pillars fifty feet high, each one supporting a huge statue of an erect elephant-god. Behind the court were towers and ramparts, their tops planted with cascading flowers and exotic trees representing Belshazzar's famous hanging gardens. The outer walls of the city were 200 feet high, yet were wide enough so that two chariots were able to roar past each other on the road that perched on top. Astonishingly, this and other sets in the film were built without architectural plans. As Griffith kept making addi-

7–18. Miniature set for Letter From an Unknown Woman (U.S.A., 1948), *directed by Max Ophüls.*
Period films often benefit from the slight sense of unreality of studio sets. If a set is needed only for establishing purposes, miniatures are often constructed. These scaled-down sets can be as tall as six or eight feet, depending on the amount of detail and realism needed. Note the two studio floodlights behind the houses of this miniature and the flat, two-dimensional apartment dwellings on the horizon in the upper right. *(Universal Pictures)*

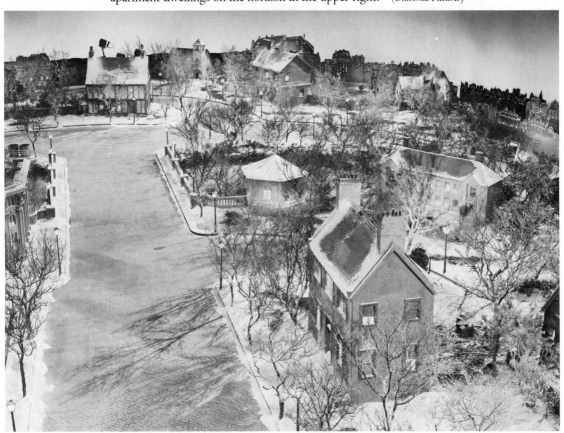

tional suggestions, his art director, Frank "Huck" Wortman, and his crew kept expanding the set from day to day.

Expressionistic sets are usually created in the studio where the contaminations of reality cannot penetrate. Magic, not realism, is the aim. Méliès is the prototypical example. He was called "the Jules Verne of films" because his feats of prestidigitation astonished the public. The first in a long line of special effects wizards, Méliès usually painted his sets, often with *trompe-l'oeil* perspectives to suggest depth. He combined live actors with fanciful settings to produce a dream-like atmosphere. He used **animation, miniatures,** and a wide range of optical tricks, charming his audiences with vistas of imaginary realms (4–3).

Expressionistic sets appeal to our sense of the marvellous. The work of Danilo Donati, Italy's best-known designer, is a good example. The extravagant artificiality of the sets and costumes in such movies as Fellini's *Satyricon, Amarcord,* and *Casanova* are pure products of the imagination—Fellini's as well as Donati's. The director often provides his designer with preliminary sketches, and the two artists work closely in determining the visual design of each film. Their conjurations can be moving, as well as witty and beautiful. For example, *Amarcord* is a stylized reminiscence of Fellini's youth in his home town of Rimini. (The title, from the Romagnan dialect, means "I remember.") But Fellini shot the movie in a studio, not on location. He wanted to capture feelings, not facts. Throughout the film, the townspeople feel stifled by the provincial isolation of their community. They are filled with loneliness, and long for something extraordinary to transform their lives. When they hear that a mammoth luxury liner, the Rex, will pass through the ocean waters a few miles beyond the town's shore, many of these wistful souls decide to row out to sea to greet the ship. Hundreds of them crowd into every available boat and stream away from the beach like fervent pilgrims on a quest. Then they wait. Evening settles,

7–19. *Grand Hotel* (**U.S.A., 1932**), *with Greta Garbo, art direction by Cedric Gibbons, gowns by Adrian, directed by Edmund Goulding.*
MGM, "the Tiffany of studios," prided itself on its opulent and glossy production values. It was the most prosperous studio in Hollywood in the 1930s, boasting 23 sound stages and 117 acres of standing backlots, which included a small lake, a harbor, a park, a jungle, and many streets of houses in different periods and styles. The "Metro look" was largely determined by Gibbons, who was the studio's art director from 1924 to 1956. (*MGM*)

bringing with it a thick fog. Still they wait. In one boat, Gradisca, the charming town sexpot, confides to some sympathetic friends of her dissatisfaction with her life. At thirty she is still single, childless, and unfulfilled. Her "heart overflows with love," yet she has never found a "truly dedicated man." In the dark silence, she weeps softly over the prospect of a barren future. Midnight passes, and still the townspeople wait faithfully. Then, when most of the characters are sleeping in their fragile boats, they're awakened by a boy's shout: "It's here!" Like a graceful apparition, the light-bedecked Rex glides past in all its regal grandeur (7–20). Nino Rota's rapturous music swells to a crescendo as the townspeople wave and shout joyously. Gradisca's eyes stream with tears of exhiliration and yearning while a blind accordionist asks excitedly, "Tell me what it looks like!"

7–20. *Amarcord* (Italy, 1973), *art direction and costumes by Danilo Donati, cinematography by Giuseppe Rotunno, directed by Federico Fellini.*
For Fellini, who began his career as a realist, the studio has become a place to create magic—along with his fellow magicians Donati and Rotunno. "To me and other directors like me," Fellini has said, "the cinema is a way of interpreting and remaking reality through fantasy and imagination. The use of the studio is an indispensable part of what we are doing." Donati is perhaps the foremost expressionist designer of the contemporary cinema. His style is so intimately associated with Fellini that it's difficult to know where one sensibility leaves off and the other begins. Rotunno is also a major contributor to this unique vision, which combines elements from comic strips, adolescent sexual fantasies, the circus, old 1930s movies, and a Catholic High Mass. *(New World Pictures)*

7–21. *Little Caesar* **(U.S.A., 1930),** *with Edward G. Robinson (standing), art direction by Anton Grot, directed by Mervyn LeRoy.*
Grot was art director at Warners from 1927 to 1948. Unlike his counterparts Gibbons, Dreier, and Polglase, however, Grot often took an active hand in designing the studio's major films. His earliest work is somewhat in the German Expressionist tradition, but he soon became one of the most versatile of artists. He designed films like the gritty and realistic *Little Caesar,* as well as the Busby Berkeley musical *Gold Diggers of 1933,* with its **surrealistic,** dreamlike sets. (*Warner Bros.*)

Then, as mysteriously as it appeared, the phantom ship is swallowed by the fog and slips silently off into the night.

During the golden age of the Hollywood studio system, each of the **majors** had a characteristic visual style, determined in large part by the designers at each studio. Some were called production designers, others art directors, a few simply set designers. Their job was to determine the "look" of each film, and they worked closely with producers and directors to assure that the sets, décor, costumes, and photographic style were coordinated to produce a unified effect. For example, MGM specialized in glamour, luxury, and opulent production values, and their art director Cedric Gibbons virtually stamped each film with "the Metro look" (7–19). Since all of the studios attempted to diversify their products as much as possible, however, their art directors had to be versatile. For instance, RKO's Van Nest Polglase supervised the design of such diverse movies as *King Kong, Top Hat, The Informer,* and *Citizen Kane.* Paramount's Hans Dreier began his career at Germany's famous UFA studio. He was usually at his best creating a sense of mystery and romantic fantasy, as in the films of Josef von Sternberg (7–14). Dreier also designed the superb Art Deco sets for Lubitsch's *Trouble in Paradise,* as well as the deliberately gaudy Hollywood "villa" in Wilder's *Sunset Boulevard.* Warner Brothers's art director, Anton Grot, was a specialist in grubby, realistic locales (7–21). The studio claimed that its films were "Torn from Today's Headlines!" to quote from its publicity blurbs. Warners favored topical genres with an emphasis on working-class life: gangster films, urban melodramas, and proletarian musicals. Like his counterparts at other studios, however, Grot could work in a variety of styles and genres. For example, he designed the enchanting sets for *A Midsummer Night's Dream.* Unfortunately, there's not much else in this movie that's enchanting.

7–22. *How Green Was My Valley* (U.S.A., 1941), *art direction by Nathan Juran and Richard Day, directed by John Ford.*

The art directors at Twentieth Century–Fox specialized in realistic sets, like this turn-of-the-century Welsh mining village, which covered eighty-six acres and was built in a California valley. Elaborate sets like these were not dismantled after production, for with suitable alterations they could be converted into other locations. For example, two years after Ford's film, this set was transformed into a Nazi-occupied Norwegian village for *The Moon Is Down.* (Twentieth Century–Fox)

Certain types of locales were in such constant demand that the studios constructed permanent **backlot sets,** which were used in film after film: a turn-of-the-century street, a European square, an urban slum, and so on. Of course these were suitably altered with new furnishings to make them look different each time they were used. The studio with the largest number of backlots was MGM, although Warners, Paramount, and Twentieth Century–Fox also boasted a considerable number of them. Not all standing sets were located close to the studio. It was cheaper to construct some outside the environs of Los Angeles where real estate values weren't at a premium. If a movie called for a huge realistic set—like the Welsh mining village for *How Green Was My Valley*—it was often built miles away from the studio (7–22). Similarly, most of the studios owned western frontier towns, ranches, and midwestern type farms which were located outside the Los Angeles area.

What matters most in a setting is how it embodies the essence of the story materials and the artistic vision of the filmmaker. As the British designer Robert Mallet-Stevens noted: "A film set, in order to be a good set, must act. Whether realistic or expressionistic, modern or ancient, it must play its part. The set must present the character before he has even appeared. It must indicate his social position, his tastes, his habits, his lifestyle, his personality. The sets must be intimately linked with the action."

Settings can also be used to suggest a sense of progression in the characters. For example, in Fellini's *La Strada,* one of his most realistic movies, the protagonist and his simple-minded assistant are shown as reasonably happy, traveling together from town to town with their tacky theatrical act. After he abandons her, he heads for the mountains. Gradually, the landscape changes: Trees are stripped of their foliage, snow and dirty slush cover the ground, the sky is a murky gray. The changing setting is a gauge of the protagonist's spiritual condition: Nature itself seems to grieve after the helpless assistant is left alone to die.

On the stage, a setting is generally admired with the opening of the curtain, then forgotten as the actors take over the center of interest. In the movies, a director can keep cutting back to the setting to remind the audience of its significance. A film can fragment a set into a series of shots, now emphasizing one aspect of a room, later another, depending on the needs of the director in finding appropriate visual analogues for thematic and psychological ideas. In Losey's *The Servant,* a stairway is used as a major thematic symbol. The film deals with a servant's gradual control over his master. Losey uses the stairway as a kind of psychological battlefield where the relative positions of the two men on the stairs give the audience a sense of who's winning the battle. Losey also uses

7–23. *Dodes'ka-den* (Japan, 1970), *art direction by Yoshiro and Shinobu Muraki, directed by Akira Kurosawa.*
As critic Donald Richie has noted, American filmmakers are supreme storytellers, the Europeans excel in the treatment of theme and character, and the Japanese are unsurpassed in the creation of atmosphere. Most of the action of this movie takes place in a junkyard, an appropriate analogue for the human refuse and outcasts who inhabit it. The junkyard is sometimes matter-of-factly realistic, as in this scene. At other times, depending on which character Kurosawa focuses on, the same setting can be sinister and terrifying, or strikingly beautiful, like an enchanted landscape. (*Janus Films*)

the rails on the stairway to suggest prison bars: The master of the house is often photographed from behind these bars.

Even the furniture of a room can be exploited for psychological and thematic reasons. In one of his classes, Eisenstein once discussed at length the significance of a table for a set. The class exercise centered on an adaptation of Balzac's novel *Père Goriot*. The scene is set at a dinner table that Balzac described as circular. But Eisenstein convincingly argued that a round table is wrong cinematically, for it implies equality, with each person linked in a circle. To convey the stratified class structure of the boarding house, Eisenstein suggested the use of a long rectangular table, with the haughty mistress of the house at the head, the favored tenants close to her sides, and the lowly Goriot alone, near the base of the table.

Such attention to detail often distinguishes a master of film from a mere technician who settles for only a general effect. The setting of a movie—far more than any play—can even take over as the central interest (7–24). In Kubrick's *2001*, the director spends most of his time lovingly photographing the instruments of a spaceship, various space stations, and the enormous expanses of outer space itself. The few people in the movie seem almost incidental and certainly far less interesting than the real center of concern—the setting. It would be impossible to produce *2001* on stage: The materials of the film are not theatrically

7–24. Blade Runner (U.S.A., 1982), *with Harrison Ford, directed by Ridley Scott.*
A hybrid of science-fiction, *film noir,* detective thriller, bounty-hunter western, and love story, *Blade Runner* is also eclectic in its visual style, a collaborative effort that includes the contributions of art director David Snyder, production designer Lawrence G. Paul, special visual effects designer Douglas Trumbull, and cinematographer Jordan Cronenweth. The story is set in Los Angeles in the year 2019. Nature has gone berserk, deluging the teeming city with an almost constant downpour. Smoke, fog, and steam add to the fumigated congestion. It is a city of dreadful night, punctuated by neon signs in day-glo colors, cheap Orientalized billboards, and a profusion of advertising come-ons. Hunks of long-discarded machinery litter the landscape. The sound track throbs with eerie sounds, echoes, pounding pistons, and the noises of flying vehicles shuttling through the poisonous atmosphere. It is a city choking on its own technology.   *(Warner Bros.)*

convertible. Kubrick's movie is a vivid illustration of Bazin's observation that the function of the cinema is "to bring to light certain details that the stage would have left untreated."

A systematic analysis of a set involves a consideration of the following characteristics:

1. *Exterior* or *interior*. If the set is an exterior, how does nature function as a symbolic analogue to the mood, theme, or characterization?
2. *Style*. Is the set realistic and lifelike, or is it stylized and deliberately distorted? Is it in a particular style, such as colonial American, art deco, sleek contemporary, etc.?
3. *Studio* or *location*. If the set is an actual location, why was it chosen? What does it say about the characters?
4. *Period*. What era does the set represent?
5. *Class*. What is the apparent income level of the owners?
6. *Size*. How large is the set? Rich people tend to take up more space than the poor, who are usually crowded in their living area.

7–25. *The Leopard* (Italy, 1963), *with Rina Morelli (center), art direction by Mario Garbuglia, costumes by Piero Tosi, directed by Luchino Visconti.*
Visconti had the unusual distinction of being both a Marxist and an aristocrat (he was the Duke of Modrone). A master of the period film, he was exceptionally sensitive to the symbolic significance of costumes and décor. They are part of Visconti's political statement. For example, the clutter, texture, and florid patterns of the Victorian furnishings in this movie suggest a stifling, hothouse artificiality, sealed off from nature. The costumes, impeccably accurate to period, are elegant, constricting, and totally without utility. They were meant to be. Idle people of independent income—that is, income derived from the labor of others—rarely concern themselves with utility in clothing. *(Twentieth Century–Fox)*

7-26. *Tucker: The Man and His Dream* **(U.S.A., 1988),** *with Jeff Bridges, art direction by Dean Tavoularis, cinematography by Vittorio Storaro, directed by Francis Ford Coppola.*
A movie's production values refer to the box-office appeal of its physical mounting—its sets, costumes, and cinematography. In this masterful re-creation of the 1940s, Tavoularis and Storaro were able to capture the faded sepia Moderne style of the period without overwhelming the human materials of the story.   *(Paramount Pictures)*

7. *Decoration.* How is the set furnished? Are there any status symbols, oddities of taste, etc.?

8. *Symbolic function.* What kind of overall image does the set and its furnishings project?

Costumes and Makeup

In the most sensitive films and plays, costumes and makeup aren't merely frills added to enhance an illusion, but aspects of character and theme. Their style can reveal class, self-image, even psychological states. Depending on their cut, texture, and bulk, certain costumes can suggest agitation, fastidiousness, delicacy, dignity, and so on. A costume, then, is a medium, especially in the cinema, where a close-up of a fabric can suggest information that's independent even of the wearer. One of the directors most sensitive to the meanings of costumes was Sergei Eisenstein. In his *Alexander Nevsky*, the invading German hordes are made terrifying primarily through their costumes. The soldiers' helmets, for example, don't reveal the eyes: Two sinister slits are cut into the fronts of the

7–27. **Publicity photo of Kay Francis in** *Trouble in Paradise* **(U.S.A., 1932),** *gowns by Travis Banton, directed by Ernst Lubitsch.*
During the Hollywood big studio era, costume designers like MGM's Adrian and Paramount's Travis Banton exerted an enormous influence on the fashion industry. Audiences were so eager to dress in the style of their favorite stars that fashion trends were created by popular movies. This fur-trimmed velvet gown is so elegant that it could be worn today and still elicit admiration.   (*Paramount Pictures*)

metal helmets. Their inhumanity is further emphasized by the animal claws and horns the officers have at the top of their helmets as insignia. The highly ornate armor they wear suggests their decadence and machinelike impersonality. An evil churchman is costumed in a black monk's habit: The sinister hood throws most of his hawklike features into darkness. In contrast, Nevsky and the Russian peasants are costumed in loose, flowing garments. Even their war armor reflects a warm, humane quality. Their helmets are shaped like Russian church onion domes and permit most of the features of the face to be seen. Their chain mail reminds the viewer of the fishing nets of the earlier portions of the movie, where the peasants are shown happiest at their work repairing their fishing nets.

Color symbolism is used by Zeffirelli in *Romeo and Juliet*. Juliet's family, the Capulets, are characterized as aggressive parvenues: Their colors are appropriately "hot" reds, yellows, and oranges. Romeo's family, on the other hand, is older and perhaps more established, but in obvious decline. They are costumed in blues, deep greens, and purples. These two color schemes are echoed in the liveries of the servants of each house, which helps the audience identify the combatants in the brawling scenes. The color of the costumes can also be used to suggest change and transition. The first view of Juliet, for example, shows her in a vibrant red dress. After she marries Romeo, her colors are in the cool blue spectrum. Line as well as color can be used to suggest psychological qualities. Verticals, for example, tend to emphasize stateliness and dignity (Lady Montague); horizontal lines tend to emphasize earthiness and comicality (Juliet's nurse).

7-28. *Greystoke: The Legend of Tarzan, Lord of the Apes* (**Great Britain, 1984**), *directed by Hugh Hudson.*
Viewers are astonished by the extraordinary expressiveness of the apes in this movie, so uncanny in their ability to mimic human emotions that they almost seem human. Even more astonishing is the fact that the ape characters *are* human—they were played by actors wearing the brilliant makeup and costumes designed by Rick Baker and Paul Engelsen.   (*Warner Bros.*)

Perhaps the most famous costume in film history is Chaplin's Charlie the tramp outfit. The costume is an indication of both class and character, conveying the complex mixture of vanity and dash that makes Charlie so appealing. The moustache, derby hat, and cane all suggest the fastidious dandy. The cane is used to give the impression of self-importance as Charlie swaggers confidently before a hostile world. But the baggy trousers several sizes too large, the oversized shoes, the too-tight coat—all these suggest Charlie's insignificance and poverty. Chaplin's view of humanity is symbolized by that costume: vain, absurd, and—finally—poignantly vulnerable.

In most cases, especially period films, costumes are designed for the performers who will be wearing them. The costumer must always be conscious of the actor's body type—whether he or she is thin, overweight, tall, short, etc.—in order to compensate for any deficiency. If a performer is famous for a given trait—Dietrich's legs, Marilyn's bosom, Schwarzenegger's chest—the costumer will often design the actor's clothes to highlight these attractions. Even in period films, the costumer has a wide array of styles to chose from, and his or her choice will often be determined by what the actor looks best in within the parameters defined by the milieu of the story.

During the Hollywood studio era, powerful stars often insisted on costumes

7–29. *Scarface, Shame of a Nation* (U.S.A., 1932), *with Paul Muni (center), directed by Howard Hawks.*

In stylized genres, costumes can have iconographical significance. For example, in gangster films the flashy clothing that the gangster wears is a symbol of his success, a way of parading his newly acquired status. The gangster prefers an ostentatious style of dress—ritzy, tailored, usually a bit gaudy. In the 1930s, the wide-brimmed fedora hat (often worn indoors as well as out) was almost obligatory. Gangsters enjoy strutting in evening clothes, especially in low-class dives, where they can lord it over the working stiffs. (*United Artists*)

and makeup that heightened their natural endowments, regardless of period accuracy. This was a practice that was encouraged by the studio bosses, who wanted their stars to look as glamorous as possible by suggesting a "contemporary look." The results are usually jarring and incongruous. Even prestigious directors like John Ford gave in to this tradition of vanity. In Ford's otherwise superb western, *My Darling Clementine* (1946), which is set in a rough frontier community, actress Linda Darnell, one of Twentieth Century–Fox's biggest stars, was allowed to wear glamorous star makeup and a 1940s-style hairdo, even though the character she was playing was a cheap Mexican "saloon girl"—a coy period euphemism for a prostitute. She looks as though she just stepped out of a Max Factor salon after receiving the Deluxe Treatment.

In realistic contemporary stories, costumes are often bought off the rack rather than individually designed. This is especially true in stories dealing with ordinary people, people who buy their clothes in department stores. When the characters are lower class or poor, costumers often purchase used clothing. For example, in *On the Waterfront,* which deals with dock workers and other working-class characters, the costumes are frayed and torn. Costumer Anna Hill Johnstone bought them in used clothing stores in the neighborhood adjoining the waterfront area.

Costumes, then, represent another language system in movies, a symbolic form of communication that can be as complex and revealing as the other language systems filmmakers employ. A systematic analysis of a costume includes a consideration of the following characteristics:

1. *Period.* What era does the costume fall into? Is it an accurate reconstruction? If not, why?
2. *Class.* What is the apparent income level of the person wearing the costume?

7–30. Publicity photo of Hairspray (U.S.A., 1988), *with (l. to r.) Jerry Stiller, Ricki Lake, Divine, Colleen Fitzpatrick, Debbie Harry, and Sonny Bono, directed by John Waters.*
This campy spoof of the early 1960s ridicules not only the fashions and hairstyles of that era, but also its shallow, materialistic values. It does so, however, with great affection, and even a touch of nostalgia.   *(New Line Cinema)*

3. *Sex.* Does a women's costume emphasize her femininity, or is it neutral or masculine? Does a man's costume emphasize his virility, or is it fussy or effeminate?

4. *Age.* Is the costume appropriate to the character's age, or is it deliberately too youthful, dowdy, or old-fashioned?

5. *Fabric.* Is the material coarse, sturdy and plain, or sheer and delicate?

6. *Accessories.* Does the costume include jewelry, hats, canes, and other accessories? What kind of shoes?

7. *Color.* What are the symbolic implications of the colors? Are they "hot" or "cool"? Subdued or bright? Solids or patterns?

8. *Body Exposure.* How much of the body is revealed or concealed? The more body revealed, the more erotic the costume. Is it form-fitting or shapeless?

9. *Function.* Is the costume meant for leisure or for work? Is it meant to impress by its beauty and splendor, or is it merely utilitarian?

7-31. *Frankenstein* (U.S.A., 1931), *with Boris Karloff and Dwight Frye, makeup by Jack Pierce, directed by James Whale.*
The horror film was one of Universal Pictures' specialties. During the silent era, Lon Chaney popularized Grand Guignol roles that required elaborate makeup, which was uncomfortable and painful to wear. Chaney designed and applied his own makeup. Pierce's monster makeup for Karloff was similarly complex, involving many hours of careful preparation. (Note the distortion of the set and lights in this shot: The horror film has its stylistic roots in German Expressionism.) (*Universal Pictures*)

10. *Image.* What is the overall impression that the costume creates—sexy, constricting, boring, gaudy, conventional, eccentric, prim, cheap-looking, elegant?

Makeup in the cinema is generally more subtle than on stage. The theatrical actor uses makeup primarily to enlarge his features so that they'll be visible from long distances. On the screen, makeup tends to be more understated, although Chaplin used stage makeup for the tramp character since he was generally photographed in long shot. Even the most delicate changes in makeup can

7–32. Publicity photo of Marlene Diet-rich in *The Devil Is a Woman* **(U.S.A., 1935),** *directed by Josef von Sternberg.*
Star makeup stylizes the features of a per-former (usually female) into a mask of immutable perfection. Dietrich's exqui-site bone structure is augmented by the artificially arched eyebrows, the sunken cheeks, the lipstick-enlarged mouth, and the artfully arranged curl that adorns her forehead.　(*Paramount Pictures*)

be perceived in the cinema. Mia Farrow's pale green face in *Rosemary's Baby,* for example, was used to suggest the progressive corruption of her body while she is pregnant with the devil's child. Similarly, the ghoulish makeup of the actors in Fellini's *Satyricon* suggests the degeneracy and death-in-life aspect of the Roman population of the period. In *The Graduate,* Anne Bancroft is almost chalk white in the scene where she is betrayed by her lover.

In *Tom Jones,* Richardson used elaborate, artificial makeup on the city characters like Lady Bellaston to suggest their deceitfulness and decadence. (In the eighteenth-century comedy of manners, cosmetics are a favorite source of imagery to suggest falseness and hypocrisy.) The country characters, on the other hand, especially Sophy Weston, are made up more naturally, with no wigs, powder, and patches.

Cinematic makeup is closely associated with the type of performer wearing it. In general, stars prefer makeup that tends to glamorize them. Monroe, Garbo, and Harlow usually had an ethereal quality. Marlene Dietrich probably knew more about makeup than any star of her generation—glamour makeup that is (7–32). Straight actors and actor stars are less concerned with glamour unless the characters they're playing are in fact glamorous. In an effort to submerge their own personalities, such performers often use makeup to disfigure the familiarity of their features. Brando and Olivier were particularly likely to wear false noses, wigs, and distorting cosmetics. Because Orson Welles was known primarily for playing strong domineering roles, he resorted to such tricks in makeup to maximize the differences between his roles. Nonprofessional players probably wear the least amount of makeup, since they're chosen precisely because of their interesting and authentic physical appearance.

FURTHER READING

BARSACQ, LEON, *Caligari's Cabinets and Other Grand Illusions: A History of Film Design* (New York: New American Library, 1978). Copiously illustrated, written by a distinguished French designer.

CHIERICHETTI, DAVID, *Hollywood Costume Design* (New York: Harmony Books, 1976). Copiously illustrated.

ECKERT, CHARLES, *Focus on Shakespearean Films* (Englewood Cliffs, N.J.: Prentice-Hall, 1972). An anthology of scholarly articles.

EISNER, LOTTE, *The Haunted Screen: Expressionism in the German Cinema and the Influence of Max Reinhardt* (Berkeley: University of California Press, 1973). A copiously illustrated critical study.

HURT, JAMES, ed., *Focus on Film and Theatre* (Englewood Cliffs, N.J.: Prentice-Hall, 1975). A collection of articles.

LEESE, ELIZABETH, *Costume Design in the Movies* (New York: Ungar, 1978). Well illustrated.

McCONATHY, DALE, and DIANA VREELAND, *Hollywood Costume* (Englewood Cliffs, N.J.: Prentice-Hall, 1977). Lavishly illustrated, authoritative.

MORDDEN, ETHAN, *The Hollywood Studios* (New York: Alfred A. Knopf, 1988). A well-written account of the "house style" of the major studios of the golden age—the 1930s and 1940s.

NICOLL, ALLARDYCE, *Film and Theatre* (New York: Thomas Y. Crowell, 1936). An early standard work.

ROACH, MARY ELLEN, and JOANNE BUBOLZ EICHER, *Dress, Adornment, and the Social Order* (New York: John Wiley, 1965). A collection of useful articles.

STORY | 8

*Narratives are composed in order to reward, modify, frustrate, or
defeat the perceiver's search for coherence.*

—DAVID BORDWELL

Since ancient times, people have been intrigued by the seductive powers of storytelling. In *The Poetics*, Aristotle distinguished between two types of fictional narratives: *mimesis* (showing) and *diegesis* (telling). *Mimesis* is the province of the live theater, where the events "tell themselves." *Diegesis,* the province of the literary epic and the novel, is a story told by a narrator who is sometimes reliable, sometimes not. Cinema combines both forms of storytelling and hence is a more complex medium, with a wider range of narrative techniques at its disposal.

Narratology

Scholars in modern times have also studied narrative forms, with most of the focus devoted to literature, film, and drama. Narratology, as this new interdisciplinary field was called in the 1980s, is a study of how stories work, how we make sense of the raw materials of a narrative, how we fit them together to form a coherent whole. It is also the study of different narrative structures, storytelling strategies, aesthetic conventions, types of stories (**genres**), and their symbolic implications.

8–1. *Platoon* **(U.S.A., 1986),** *with Charlie Sheen (upper left) and Willem Dafoe (center), directed by Oliver Stone.*
A movie's plot doesn't have to be complicated to be effective. The narrative structure of *Platoon* is as stark as a medieval morality play. An impressionable youth (Sheen) is like an Everyman figure, influenced by an Angel of Mercy (Dafoe) and a Satanic figure of Evil (Tom Berenger), both army sergeants. Symbolically, these two forces are warring aspects within the youth, fighting for control of his soul.   *(Orion Pictures)*

In traditional terms, narratologists are interested in the "rhetoric" of story-telling; that is, the *forms* that "message senders" employ to communicate with "message receivers." In cinema, a problem with this triadic communications model is determining who the sender is. The implied author is the filmmaker. However, many stories are not created by a single storyteller. Multiple author-ship of scripts is common, especially in the United States, where the story is often pieced together by producers, directors, writers, and **stars**—a truly joint enterprise. Even prestigious filmmakers like Fellini, Kurosawa, and Truffaut preferred collaborating with others in creating the events of a story.

The problem of the elusive film author is complicated when a movie has a **voice-over** narration. Usually this off-screen narrator is also a character in the story and hence has a vested interest in "helping" us interpret the events. A film's narrator is not necessarily neutral. Nor is he or she necessarily the film-maker's mouthpiece. Sometimes the narrator—as in the **first-person** novel—is the main character of a movie, as in *Annie Hall* (8–2). (For a fuller discussion of these ideas, see the "Spoken Language" section of Chapter 5, Sound, and "Point of View" in Chapter 9, Literature.)

Narration also differs according to a movie's style. In **realistic** films, the implied author is virtually invisible. The events "speak for themselves," as they do in most stage plays. The story seems to unfold automatically, usually in chronological sequence.

In **classical** narrative structures, we are generally more aware of a shaping hand in the storyline. Boring gaps in the narrative are edited out by a discreet storyteller who keeps a low profile yet still keeps the action on-track, moving toward a specific destination—the resolution of the story's central conflict.

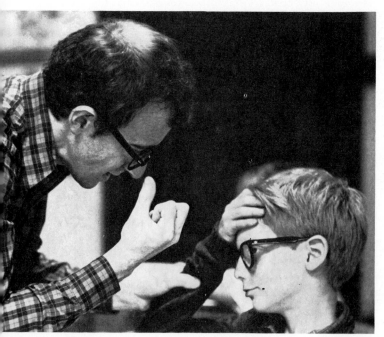

8–2. *Annie Hall* **(U.S.A., 1977),** *with Woody Allen and Jonathan Munk, directed by Allen.*
This romantic comedy is narrated by a fictionalized character, Alvie Singer, who is played by Allen. Alvie's life is remark-ably similar to Woody Allen's, yet the story's narrator is not the same as the film's author. Still, ambiguous complexi-ties can be fun. In this scene, for example, Alvie drifts through some scenes from his childhood and encounters himself as a nine-year-old neurotic, deeply immersed in gloom. *(United Artists)*

In **formalistic** narratives, the author is overtly manipulative, sometimes scrambling the chronology of the story, or heightening or restructuring events to maximize a thematic idea. The story is told from a subjective perspective.

Narratology is often arcane, and occasionally incomprehensible, because of its abstract language and jargon. Exotic terms are often used to describe traditional concepts. For example, the differences between a story and its plot structure (that is, between a narrative's content and its form) can be expressed in

8–3. *Masculine–Feminine* (France, 1966), *with Jean-Pierre Léaud and Chantal Goya, directed by Jean-Luc Godard.*
"I consider myself an essayist," Godard said, "producing essays in novel form or novels in essay form: only instead of writing, I film them." Godard's cinematic essays are a frontal attack on the dominance of classical cinema. "The Americans are good at storytelling," he noted, "the French are not. Flaubert and Proust can't tell stories. They do something else. So does the cinema. I prefer to use a kind of tapestry, a background on which I can embroider on my own ideas." Instead of scripts, Godard set up dramatic situations, then asked his actors to improvise their dialogue, as in this interview scene—a technique he derived from the documentary movement called *cinéma vérité*. He intersperses these scenes with digressions, opinions, and jokes. Above all, he wanted to capture the spontaneity of the moment, which he believed was more authentic when he and his actors had to fend for themselves, without the security of a script. "If you know in advance everything you are going to do, it isn't worth doing," Godard insisted. "If a show is all written down, what is the point of filming it? What use is cinema if it trails after literature?" See also Louis D. Giannetti, "Godard's *Masculine–Feminine:* The Cinematic Essay," in *Godard and Others: Essays in Film Form* (Cranbury, N.J.: Fairleigh Dickinson University Press, 1975). *(Columbia Pictures)*

8–4. _Barfly_ (U.S.A., 1987), _with Mickey Rourke and Faye Dunaway, written by Charles Bukowski, directed by Barbet Schroeder._
Action is dependent on character. Unlike most American movies, _Barfly_ does not feature goal-oriented characters. The fanciful protagonist (Rourke) is a talented writer as well as a dedicated drunk, but he would rather sit and booze than pursue a purposeful literary career. Hence, the plot meanders unpredictably, for it's propelled by outside forces, not the passive main character. _(Cannon Films)_

a bewildering assortment of terms. "Story" versus "discourse" are favored by many American scholars. Others prefer _histoire_ versus _discours, mythos_ versus _logos,_ or _fabula_ versus _syuzhet._

What are the differences between story and plot? The story can be defined as the general subject matter, the raw materials of a dramatic action in chronological sequence. The plot, on the other hand, involves the storyteller's method of superimposing a structural pattern over the story.

The implied author motivates the characters and provides a cause–effect logic to the sequence of events. Peter Brooks defines plot as "the design and intention of narrative, what shapes a story and gives it a certain direction or intention of meaning." In short, plot involves the implied author's point of view as well as the structuring of the scenes into an aesthetic pattern.

The Spectator

It's impossible to understand a movie without being actively engaged in a dynamic interplay with its narrative logic. Most of us have been watching movies and television for so long that we're hardly aware of our instantaneous adjustments to an unfolding plot. We absorb auditory and visual stimuli at an incredibly rapid rate. Like a complex computer, our brain click-clicks away in many language systems simultaneously: photographic, spatial, kinetic, vocal, histrionic, musical, sartorial, etc.

But in the American cinema especially, the story reigns supreme. All the other language systems are subordinated to the plot, the structural spine of virtually all American fiction films, and most foreign movies as well.

David Bordwell and others have explored how the spectator is constantly interacting with a movie's narrative. We attempt to superimpose our sense of order and coherence on the film's world. In most cases, we bring a set of expectations to a movie even before we've seen it. Our knowledge of a given era or genre leads us to expect a predictable set of variables. For example, most westerns take place in the late nineteenth century and are set in the American western frontier. From books, TV, and other westerns, we have a rough knowledge of how frontier people were supposed to dress and behave.

When narratives fail to act according to tradition, **convention,** or our sense of history, as in Mel Brooks's *Blazing Saddles* (8–5), we are forced to reassess our cognitive methods and our attitude toward the narrative. Either we adjust to

8–5. *Blazing Saddles* **(U.S.A., 1974),** *directed by Mel Brooks.*
Like most of Brooks's works, *Blazing Saddles* is a parody of a popular genre, in this case, the western. Throughout the movie, he constantly undermines the narrative by introducing elements that are out of period, like Madeline Kahn's deadpan performance as Lili von Schtupp, the Teutonic Titwillow, a delicious parody of Marlene Dietrich. At the end of the film, Brooks deliberately sabotages his narrative's shakey credibility by having a cowboy chase spill over into a totally different genre—a sophisticated 1930s type dance number *à la* Busby Berkeley.   *(Warner Bros.)*

the author's presentation, or we reject the offending innovation as inappropriate, crude, or self-indulgent.

Narrational strategies are often determined by genre. For example, in those types of movies that thrive on suspense (thrillers, police stories, mysteries), the narrative will deliberately withhold information, forcing us to guess, to fill in the gaps. In romantic comedies, on the other hand, we generally know the outcome in advance. The emphasis is on *how* boy wins girl (or vice versa), not if he or she wins.

Our prior knowledge of a film's star also defines its narrative parameters. We wouldn't expect to see Clint Eastwood in a Shakespearean adaptation, or even in a conventional love story. Eastwood's expertise is in action genres, especially westerns and contemporary urban crime stories. With personality stars especially, we can guess the essential nature of a film's narrative in advance. With actor stars like Meryl Streep, however, we are less certain about what to expect, for Streep's range is extraordinarily broad.

Audiences also judge a film in advance by the connotations of its title. A movie with a moronic title like *Attack of the Killer Bimbos* is not likely to be shown at the prestigious New York Film Festival. On the other hand, *Lady Windermere's Fan* would probably not play at the local mall theater because of its somewhat effete, aristocratic-sounding title. Of course there are always exceptions. *Sammy and Rosie Get Laid* sounds like a porno film, but it's actually a respected (and sexy) British social comedy. Its title is deliberately aggressive, a bit crude. It's meant to be.

Once a movie begins, we begin to define its narrative limits. The style of the credits and the accompanying score help us to determine the tone of the picture. In the early exposition scenes, the filmmaker sets up the story variables and mood, establishing the premise that will drive the narrative forward. The

8–6. *The Decline of the American Empire* (Canada, 1986), *with Yves Jacques and Dorothee Berryman, directed by Denys Arcand.*

Many movies are structured around the Grand Hotel formula, so-called after the 1932 movie that features an assortment of characters who are temporarily thrown together in a single location. This anthology formula is ideal for exploring multiple narratives, with no single storyline predominating. This movie is a witty exploration of sexual license and the decline of moral responsibility among a group of French-Canadian academics.   *(Cineplex Odeon Films)* beginning scenes imply how the narrative will be developed, and where it's likely to end up.

The opening expository scenes also establish the internal "world" of the story—what's possible, what's probable, what's not very likely, and so on. In retrospect, there should be no loose threads in a story if the implied author has done a careful job of foreshadowing. In *E.T.: The Extra-Terrestrial*, for example, Spielberg prepares us for the supernatural events that occur in the middle and later portions of the movie because the opening scene (showing us how E.T. got left behind by his spaceship) establishes supernaturalism as a narrative variable.

When a critic asked the radical innovator Jean-Luc Godard if he believed that a movie should have a beginning, middle, and end, the iconoclastic filmmaker replied: "Yes—but not necessarily in that order." The opening exposition scenes of most movies establish the time frame of the story—whether it will unfold in **flashbacks,** in the present, or in some combination. The exposition also establishes the ground rules about fantasy scenes, dreams, and the stylistic variables associated with these levels of the story (8–7).

An elaborate game is played out between a cinematic narrative and the spectator. While watching a movie, we must sort out irrelevant details, hypothesize, test our hypotheses, retreat if necessary, adapt, formulate explanations, and so on. The spectator is constantly subjecting the narrative to questions. Why does the heroine do that? Why does her boyfriend respond that way? What will the mother do now? And so on.

The more complex the plot, the more cunning we must be—sorting, sifting, weighing new evidence, inferring motives and explanations, ever suspicious of being taken off guard. We constantly monitor the narrative for unexpected reversals, especially in deceptive genres, like thrillers, detective movies, and police films.

8–7. *8½* **(Italy, 1963),** *with Sandra Milo, directed by Federico Fellini.*
Although it is one of the most admired movies in the history of the cinema, Fellini's masterpiece features a plot that's diabolically baroque. Most viewers are unable to comprehend it all on first viewing because it's constantly shifting levels of consciousness without warning. Fantasies spill over onto reality, which splashes over memories, which fuse with dreams, which turn into nightmares which . . . *(Embassy Pictures)*

8–8. *My Life as a Dog* (Sweden, 1987), *with Anton Glanzelius (center), directed by Lasse Hallstrom.*
Some movies are so unusual that it's virtually impossible to predict where the plot will lead. In this film, for example, the young hero is separated from his parents and moves in with an eccentric uncle and aunt in a remote village. His escapades in the country are bizarre, funny, and totally unpredictable. *(Skouras Pictures)*

In short, we are never really passive in the face of a film's plot. Even when the story is boring, mechanical, and utterly derivative, we still can get sucked into its plot machinations. We want to know where the action is leading: We can find out only if we go along.

The Classical Paradigm

The classical paradigm is a term invented by scholars to describe a certain kind of narrative structure that has dominated fiction film production ever since the 1910s. It's by far the most popular type of story organization, especially in the United States, where it reigns virtually unchallenged. The model is called "classical" because it's a norm of actual practice, not necessarily because of a high degree of artistic excellence. In other words, bad movies as well as good ones use this narrative formula.

Derived from the live theater, the classical paradigm is a set of conventions, not rules. This narrative model is based on a conflict between a protagonist, who initiates the action, and an antagonist, who resists it. Most films in this form begin with an implied dramatic question. We want to know how the protagonist will get what he or she wants in the face of considerable opposition. The following scenes intensify this conflict in a rising pattern of action. This escalation is treated in terms of cause–effect, with each scene implying a link to the next.

The conflict builds to its maximum tension in the climax. Here, the protagonist and antagonist clash overtly. One wins, the other loses. After their confrontation, the dramatic intensity subsides in the resolution. The story ends with some kind of formal closure—traditionally a wedding or a dance in comedies, a death in tragedies, a reunion or return to normal in dramas. The final **shot**—because of its privileged position—is often meant to be a philosophical overview of some kind, a summing up of the significance of the previous material.

The classical paradigm emphasizes dramatic unity, plausible motivations, and coherence of its constituent parts. Each shot is seamlessly elided to the next in an effort to produce a smooth flow of action, and often a sense of inevitability. To add urgency to the conflict, filmmakers sometimes include some kind of deadline, thus intensifying the emotion. During the Hollywood studio era especially, classical structures often featured double plot lines, in which a romantic

8–9. The Classical Paradigm.

Aristotle implicitly suggested the structure of classical drama in *The Poetics,* but it was not until the nineteenth century that the inverted V structure was diagrammed by the German scholar, Gustav Freytag. This type of narrative structure begins with an overt conflict, which is increasingly intensified with the rising action of the following scenes. Details that don't relate to this conflict are eliminated or kept incidental. The battle between the main character and his or her antagonists reaches its highest pitch in the climax. In the resolution, the strands of the story are tied up and life returns to normal with a closing off of the action.

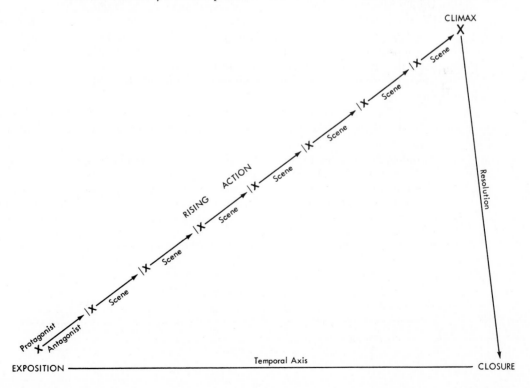

love story was developed to parallel the main line of action. In love stories, a comic second couple often paralleled the main lovers.

Classical plot structures are linear, and often take the form of a journey, a chase, or a search. Even characters are defined primarily in terms of what they do. "Action is character" insists Syd Field, the author of several handbooks on screenwriting. "What a person does is what he is, not what he says." Field and other advocates of the classical paradigm are not very interested in passive characters—people to whom things are done. (These types of characters are more typical in foreign films.) Classicists favor characters who are goal-oriented so that we can take a rooting interest in their plans of action.

Field's conceptual model is expressed in traditional theatrical terms (8–10). A screenplay is composed of three acts. Act I, "The Setup," occupies the first quarter of the script. It establishes the dramatic premise: What is the main character's goal and what obstacles are likely to get in the way of its attainment? Act II, "The Confrontation," consists of the middle two quarters of the story, with a major reversal of fortune at the midpoint. This portion of the screenplay complicates the conflict with plot twists and an increasing sense of urgency, showing the main character fighting against obstacles. Act III, "The Resolution," constitutes the final quarter of the story. This section dramatizes what happens as a result of the climactic confrontation.

One of the greatest plots in the history of cinema is found in Buster Keaton's *The General,* a textbook example of the classical paradigm. It fits Freytag's inverted V structure as well as Field's three-act play approach. As Daniel Moews has pointed out, all of Keaton's feature-length comedies employ the same basic comic formula. Buster begins as a sincere but clumsy greenhorn who bungles every attempt to ingratiate himself with a person he holds in awe— usually a pretty girl. At the conclusion of the day, he falls asleep, lonely, depressed, and dispirited. When he awakens, he's a new man. He goes on to succeed, usually at the same or parallel activities of the earlier portions of the movie.

A Civil War comedy loosely based on an actual event, *The General* is laid out with the narrative elegance of a play by Congreve. The first act establishes

8–10.

According to Syd Field, the narrative structure of a movie can be broken down into three acts. The story should contain about 10 to 20 "plot points," major twists or key events in the action. At the midpoint of the second act, there is usually a big reversal of expectations, sending the action spinning in a new direction. Although this diagram might not be helpful in analyzing most realistic or formalistic narratives, it is surprisingly apt in movies employing a classical structure.

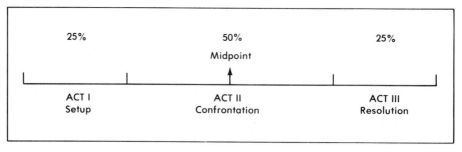

the two loves in the hero's life: his train, "The General," and Annabelle Lee, his somewhat flaky girlfriend. His only friends, apparently, are two prepubescent boys. (Among other things, the movie is a coming-of-age story.) When war is declared, our hero, Johnnie Gray, trying to impress his girl, attempts to enlist. But he's rejected by the authorities: He's more valuable to the South as an engineer. Through a misunderstanding, Annabelle thinks Johnnie is a coward. "I don't want you to speak to me again until you are in uniform," she haughtily informs him. End of Act I.

A full year is edited out of the story as we begin Act II. (The rest of the movie covers only about twenty-four hours.) We see the plans of the Union officers to hijack a Confederate train, thereby cutting off the supply lines of the Southern army. The Yankee leader's map shows the major stops and rivers along the railroad route. In fact, this map is a geographical outline of Act II.

On the day that the hijacking is to take place, Annabelle Lee boards Johnnie's train in order to visit her wounded father. She snubs her former suiter. The hijacking of the train sets off the rising action. The second quarter of the movie is a chase sequence: Johnnie pursues the stolen General (with Annabelle on board) as it flees northward. There are a series of gag clusters, each involving different props, such as telegraph wires, switched tracks, a water tower, a cannon (8–12), and so on. Johnnie is usually the butt of the jokes.

8–11. An outline of the plot structure of *The General*.
The plot moves forward with such smoothness and poise that we're hardly aware of its dazzling symmetry until the second chase, when most of the earlier gag clusters are triumphantly reprised.

8–12. *The General* **(U.S.A., 1926),** *with Buster Keaton, directed by Keaton and Clyde Bruckman.*
Silent film comedians were masters of improvisation, capable of spinning off a profusion of gags with a single prop. For example, the gag cluster involving this cannon is a miniature drama, complete with exposition, variations on a theme that constitutes the rising action, and a thrilling climax that serves as a topper to the sequence. Even more extraordinary, Keaton and his regular crew never used written scripts or shooting schedules. They knew only the premise of the film and its conclusion. The rest was improvised. They shot for about eight weeks, making due allowances for baseball games between scenes. Later Keaton viewed all the footage, edited out the dull stuff, and created the narrative structure.   *(United Artists)*

At the midpoint of the film, our hero sneaks into the enemy's camp, alone and exhausted. Nonetheless, he manages to rescue Annabelle. They fall asleep in the woods in a downpour, discouraged, almost wiped out.

The next day, a second chase begins, reversing the pattern of the previous day, and taking up the third quarter of the plot. Now the jokes are inflicted on the pursuing Yankees as Johnnie and Annabelle speed southward in the recaptured General. The gag clusters are also reversed. Most of them are parallels to those of the first chase: telegraph wires, logs on the tracks, a water tower, a burning bridge, and so on. Just in time, Johnnie and Annabelle arrive at the Confederate camp and warn the troops of an impending Union attack.

Act III is a battle sequence between the two great armies. Johnnie shows himself to be a doggedly perseverant soldier, though not always a successful one. He is rewarded for his heroism with a commission in the army. He also wins back the love of his girl. All ends happily.

Keaton's narrative structure follows an elaborately counterbalanced pattern, in which the earlier humiliations are triumphantly canceled out on the

8–13. *Chinatown* (U.S.A., 1974), *with Jack Nicholson and Faye Dunaway, directed by Roman Polanski.*
In genres that depend on mystery and suspense for their effects, the narrative often withholds information, forcing us to fill in the gaps, teasing and tantalizing us with possible solutions to mysteries that aren't totally resolved until the end of the movie. *(Paramount Pictures)*

second day. Described thus schematically, Keaton's plots sound rather mechanical. But as his French admirers have pointed out, his architectural rigor can be likened to the works of the great neoclassical artists of the eighteenth century, with their intricately worked out parallels and neatly balanced symmetries.

Ordinarily, one would consider such an artificial plot structure as an example of a formalist narrative. However, the execution of each section is rigorously realistic. Keaton performed all his own gags (many of them dangerous), usually on the first **take.** He also insisted on absolute accuracy in the costuming, the sets, and even the trains, which are historically true to the period. This combination of realistic execution with a formally patterned narrative is typical of classical cinema. Classicism is an intermediate style that blends conventions from both stylistic extremes.

Realistic Narratives

Traditionally, critics have linked realism to "life," formalism with "pattern." Realism is defined as an absence of style, whereas style is a preeminent concern among formalists. Realists reject artifice in order to portray the material world "transparently," without distortion or even mediation. Conversely, formalists are concerned with fantasy materials or throwaway subject matter in order to emphasize the world of the imagination or beauty for its own sake.

Today, these views are considered naive, at least so far as realism is concerned. Contemporary critics and scholars regard realism as a *style,* with an elaborate set of conventions that are less obvious perhaps, but just as artificial as those employed by expressionists.

Both realistic and formalistic narratives are patterned and manipulated, but the realistic storyteller attempts to submerge the pattern, to bury it beneath

8–14. *I Vitelloni* **(Italy, 1953),** *with Alberto Sordi (right center), directed by Federico Fellini.* Like many realistic movies, this film features multiple plot lines arranged in "random" order to suggest a series of comic and poignant fragments from the lives of aging dreamers and loafers. The movie might almost be called *Scenes from Provincial Life.*   *(Contemporary Films)*

the surface "clutter" and apparent randomness of the dramatic events. In other words, the pretense that a realistic narrative is "unmanipulated" or "like life" is precisely that—a pretense, an aesthetic deception.

Realists prefer loose, discursive plots, with no clearly defined beginning, middle, or end. We dip into the story at an arbitrary point. Usually we aren't presented with a clear-cut conflict, as in classical narratives. Rather, the conflict emerges unobtrusively from the unforced events of the exposition. The story itself is presented as a "slice of life," that is, as a poetic fragment, not a neatly structured tale. Rarely is reality neatly structured; realistic art must follow suit. Life goes on, even after the final reel.

Realists often borrow their structures from the cycles of nature. For example, many of the movies of Ozu are given seasonal titles that symbolize an appropriate human counterpart—*Early Summer, Late Autumn, Early Spring, The End of Summer, Late Spring* (8–15). Other realistic films are structured around a limited period of time, like summer vacation or a school semester. Such movies sometimes center on rites of passage, like birth, puberty, first love, first job, marriage, painful separations, death.

Often we can't guess the principle of narrative coherence until the end of the movie, especially if it has a circular or cyclical structure, as many realistic

8–15. *Late Spring* (Japan, 1959), *with Chishu Ryu (seated) and Setsuko Hara (center), directed by Yasujiro Ozu.*

One of the most common genres in Japan is the home drama. It was the only genre Ozu worked in, and he was one of its most popular practitioners. This type of film deals with the day-to-day routines of domestic life. Although Ozu is a profoundly philosophical artist, his movies consist almost entirely of "little things"—the bitter pills of self-denial that ultimately render life disappointing. Many of Ozu's films have seasonal titles that symbolically evoke appropriate human analogues. *Late Spring*, for example, deals with the attempts of a decent widower (Ryu) to marry off his only daughter (Hara) before she wilts into spinsterhood. *(New Yorker Films)*

films do. For example, Robert Altman's *M*A*S*H* opens with the fresh arrival of two soldier-surgeons, Hawkeye Pierce and Duke Forrest. The movie ends when their tour of duty is over. Yet the M*A*S*H unit will continue saving lives, even after these two excellent surgeons have left. (This same structural principle is used in a later military comedy, Barry Levinson's *Good Morning, Vietnam*.)

The episodic structure of *M*A*S*H* is what appealed to those who adapted it as a television series. Realistic film narratives frequently seem episodic, the sequence of events almost interchangeable. The plot doesn't "build" inexorably, but seems to drift into surprising scenes that don't necessarily propel the story forward. These are offered for their own sake, as examples of "real-life" oddities.

Spectators who like fast-moving stories are often impatient with realistic films, which frequently move slowly. This is especially true in the earlier scenes, while we wait for the main narrative strand to emerge. "Digressions" often turn

8–16. *Sid and Nancy* **(U.S.A., 1986),** *with Gary Oldman, directed by Alex Cox.* Ever since the later nineteenth century, when it became a dominant international style in the arts, realism has provoked controversy for its "sordid" or "shocking" subject matter, its preoccupation with details that the conventional majority finds repulsive/fascinating. This is the sad love story of punk rocker Sid Vicious (Oldman) and his groupie girlfriend, Nancy Sprungen. The film frankly depicts scenes of drunkenness, brawls, heroin addiction, filthy hotel rooms, and, ultimately, violent death.   *(Samuel Goldwyn)*

out to be parallels to the central plotline. But this parallelism must be inferred; it's rarely pointed out explicitly. Other traits of realistic narratives include:

1. A nonintrusive implied author who "reports" objectively and avoids making judgments.
2. A rejection of clichés, stale conventions, stock situations and characters in favor of the unique, the concrete, the specific.
3. A fondness for exposé, with "shocking" or "low" subject matter which is often criticized for its grittiness and "bad taste."
4. An antisentimental point of view that rejects glib happy endings, wishful thinking, miraculous cures, and other forms of phony optimism.
5. An avoidance of melodrama and exaggeration in favor of understatement and dedramatization.
6. A scientific view of causality and motivation, with a corresponding rejection of romantic concepts like Destiny and Fate.
7. An avoidance of the **lyrical** impulse in favor of a plain, straightforward presentation.

8–17. *Lacombe, Lucien* **(France, 1974),** *with Pierre Blaise (holding machinegun), directed by Louis Malle.*

The Nazi era has become mythologized in the twentieth century as a period of unspeakable horrors and depravities, complete with a Mephistophelian evil mastermind, Hitler. (How else can we understand the enormity that has come to be called the Holocaust, with its millions of innocent people murdered in cold blood?) This movie attempts to demythologize the Nazi experience, to render it understandable in ordinary, everyday terms. Melodrama and exaggeration are banished in favor of a scrupulously dedramatized account of how an alienated, oafish loner (Blaise) in a remote French village became a Nazi collaborator.   *(Twentieth Century–Fox)*

Formalistic Narratives

Formalistic narratives revel in their artificiality. Time is often scrambled and rearranged to hammer home a thematic point more forcefully. The design of the plot is not concealed but heightened. It's part of the show. Formalistic plots come in a wide assortment, but usually they are structured according to the filmmaker's theme. For example, Alfred Hitchcock was obsessed by themes dealing with "doubles" and "the wrong man"—a technically innocent man who is accused of a crime committed by an undetected counterpart.

Hitchcock's *The Wrong Man* is his most explicit treatment of these narrative motifs (8–18). The entire plot is doubled, structured in twos. There are two imprisonments, two handwriting tests, two conversations in the kitchen, two legal hearings, two visits to a clinic, two visits to the lawyer. The hero is arrested twice by two policemen. He is identified (wrongly) by two witnesses at two different shops. There are two transfers of guilt: The main character (Henry Fonda) is accused of a crime he didn't commit, and midway through the movie, his emotionally disturbed wife (Vera Miles) takes on the guilt, requiring her to be committed to an asylum. "People say that Hitchcock lets the wires show too often," Jean-Luc Godard noted. "But because he shows them, they are no longer wires. They are the pillars of a marvelous architectural design made to withstand our scrutiny."

Many formalistic narratives are intruded upon by the author, whose personality is part of the show. For example, it's virtually impossible to ignore the personality of Buñuel in his films. He slyly interjects his sardonic black humor into his narratives. He loves to undermine his characters—their pomposity, their self-deception, their mean little souls (8–19). Godard's personality is also highly intrusive, especially in his nontraditional narratives, which he called "cinematic essays."

Formalistic narratives are often interrupted by lyrical interludes, exercises in pure style—like the enchanting dance numbers in the Fred Astaire–Ginger Rogers RKO musicals of the 1930s. In fact, stylized genre films like musicals, science fiction, and fantasies offer the richest potential for displays of stylistic rapture and bravura effects. These lyrical interludes interrupt the forward momentum of the plot, which is often a mere pretext anyway.

8–18. *The Wrong Man* (U.S.A., 1956), *with Henry Fonda, directed by Alfred Hitchcock.*
Most of the scenes in this movie are structured in pairs, corresponding to the innocent main character (Fonda) and his guilty counterpart. Despite the plot's artificiality, the treatment of the story is extremely realistic, almost documentarylike. The film is based on a true story. It was shot on location, with nonprofessional actors in minor roles. The leading players are deglamorized and ordinary almost to the point of drabness. This combination of realistic treatment and artificial plot structure is typical of American classic cinema.   *(Warner Bros.)*

An excellent example of a formalistic narrative is *Mon Oncle d'Amerique* (My Uncle in America), directed by Alain Resnais, with a script by Resnais and Jean Grualt. The film's structure is indebted to Godard's essay form, which can combine elements from the documentary with fiction. The ideas in the movie are the stuff of Psychology 101. Resnais frames and intersperses his fictional episodes with footage of an actual medical doctor and behavioral scientist, Dr. Henri Laborit, who indulges in the French mania for dissection, analysis, and classification. He wittily discusses the relationship of human behavior to the makeup of the brain, the conscious and subconscious environment, social conditioning, the nervous system, zoology, and biology. He alludes to the behavior-modification theories of B.F. Skinner and other theories of human development.

The fictional episodes in the movie are concrete demonstrations of these theories. The characters are autonomous, not mechanized zombies. Nonetheless, they are victims of forces they hardly understand. Resnais focuses on three appealing characters. Each is the product of a unique biological makeup and cultural environment. Their paths intersect by chance. "These people have everything to make them happy," Resnais observed, "yet they're not happy at all. Why?"

8–19. *The Discreet Charm of the Bourgeoisie* **(France, 1972),** *directed by Luis Buñuel.*
Most of Buñuel's movies feature bizarre scenes that are left unexplained, as though they were the most normal thing in the world. He delighted in satirizing middle-class hypocrisies, treating them with a kind of affectionate bemusement mingled with contempt. In this film, he presents us with a series of loosely connected episodes dealing with the inane rituals of a group of well-heeled semizombies. Interspersing these episodes are shots of the main characters walking on an empty road (pictured). No one questions why they are there. No one seems to know where they are going. Buñuel doesn't say.   *(Twentieth Century–Fox)*

8–20. *Mon Oncle d'Amerique* (France, 1980), *with Gerard Depardieu, directed by Alain Resnais.*
Depardieu portrays a hard-working idealist whose conservative values and faith in God are severely tested. The significance of the title? It's taken from European pop mythology—the proverbial adventurous uncle who left for America, made a fortune, and will someday return loaded with money to solve all their problems. Resnais was also thinking of Samuel Beckett's bitter comedy, *Waiting for Godot,* which revolves around an obscure figure (God?) who's constantly waited for, but never shows up.   *(New World Pictures)*

Resnais then shows us why through his dazzling editing and multiple narratives. In a kaleidoscope of shifting perspectives, Resnais juxtaposes snippets of the characters's lives, dreams, and memories with Dr. Laborit's abstract formulations, statistics, and wry observations. The three main characters are movie freaks, and at various points during the story, Resnais intercuts brief clips from the films of their childhood idols—Jean Marais, Danielle Darrieux, and Jean Gabin. Some of these movie clips bear a not-so-coincidental resemblance to the dramatic situations of the characters. Resnais is also paying homage to three great stars of the French cinema.

Nonfictional Narratives

There are three broad classifications of motion pictures: fiction, documentary, and **avant-garde.** Documentaries and avant-garde films usually don't tell stories, at least not in the conventional (that is, fictional) sense. Of course, documentaries and avant-garde movies are structured, but neither utilizes a plot. Rather, the story—if any—is structured according to a theme or an argument, especially

8–21. *Pumping Iron* (U.S.A., 1977), *with Arnold Schwarzenegger, directed by George Butler and Robert Fiore.*
Even documentaries can be structured according to the classical paradigm, though not very often. In this playful exploration of the world of bodybuilding, however, the filmmakers are able to generate a considerable amount of suspense as we see various contestants vying for the Mr. Olympia title. In the movie's climax, the title goes to Schwarzenegger (who was not well known at the time), thanks to his charm and confidence. *(Public Broadcasting System)*

in documentaries. In the avant-garde cinema, the structure is often a matter of the filmmaker's subjective instincts.

First, documentaries. Unlike most fiction films, documentaries deal with facts—real people, places, and events rather than invented ones. Documentarists believe that they're not creating a world so much as reporting on the one that already exists. They are not just recorders of external reality, however, for like fiction filmmakers, they shape their raw materials through their selection of details. These details are organized into a coherent artistic pattern. Many documentaries deliberately keep the structure of their films simple and unobtrusive. They want their version of the facts to suggest the same apparent randomness of life itself.

Sound familiar? In fact, the concepts of realism and formalism are almost as useful in discussing documentaries as fiction films. However, the overwhelming majority of documentarists would insist that their main interest is with subject matter rather than style.

The realistic documentary is best illustrated by the **cinéma vérité** or "direct cinema" movement of the 1960s. Because of the need to be able to capture news stories quickly, efficiently, and with a minimal crew, television journalism was responsible for the development of a new technology, which in turn eventually led to a new philosophy of truth in documentary cinema. The technology included:

1. A lightweight 16 mm hand-held camera, allowing the cinematographer to roam virtually anywhere with ease.
2. Flexible **zoom lenses,** allowing the cinematographer to go from 12 mm **wide-angle** positions to 120 mm **telephoto** positions in one adjusting bar.

8–22. *Law and Order* (**U.S.A., 1969**), *directed by Frederick Wiseman.*
Cinéma vérité, or direct cinema, prided itself on its objectivity and straightforward presentation. Of course, these documentarists realized that total neutrality is an impossible goal to
achieve. Even Wiseman, among the most objective of documentarists, insists that his movies
are a subjective *interpretation* of actual events, people, and places. He tries to be as "fair" as
possible in presenting his materials. For example, he refuses to use off-frame narrators. The
subjects of the film are allowed to speak for themselves, and the burden of interpretation is
placed on the spectators, who must analyze the significance of the material on their
own.   *(Zipporah Films)*

3. New **fast film stocks,** permitting scenes to be photographed without the
    necessity of setting up lights. So sensitive were these stocks to available
    lighting that even nighttime scenes with minimal illumination could be
    recorded with acceptable clarity.
4. A portable tape recorder, allowing a technician to record sound directly in
    automatic **synchronization** with the visuals. This equipment was so easy to
    use that only two people—one at the camera, the other with the sound
    system—were required to bring in a news story.

The flexibility of this hardware permitted documentarists to redefine the
concept of authenticity. This new aesthetic amounted to a rejection of pre-
planning and carefully detailed scripts. A script involves preconceptions about
reality and tends to cancel out any sense of spontaneity or ambiguity. Direct
cinema rejected such preconceptions as fictional: Reality is not being observed,
but is being arranged to conform to what the script says it is. The documentarist
is superimposing a *plot* over the materials. Re-creations of any kind were no

8–23. *Harlan County, U.S.A.* **(U.S.A., 1977),** *directed by Barbara Kopple.*
Direct cinema is most effective with materials that are intrinsically dramatic, like crisis
situations in which a conflict is about to reach its climax. For example, during the production
of this documentary, which deals with a bitter coalminers's strike for decent working conditions, Kopple and her crew were repeatedly plunged in the middle of violence. In one
sequence, they are actually fired upon by a trigger-happy yahoo. The camera recorded it all.
Implicit in the concept of documentary is the verb *to document*—to verify, to provide an
irrefutable record of an event. In a nonfiction film, these privileged moments of truth
generally take precedence over considerations of narrative.   *(Museum of Modern Art)*

longer necessary because, if the crew members are present while an event is
actually taking place, they can capture it while it's happening.

The concept of minimal interference with reality became the dominating
preoccupation of the American and Canadian schools of cinéma vérité. The
filmmaker must not control events in any way. Re-creations—even with the
people and places actually involved—were unacceptable. Editing was kept to a
minimum, for otherwise it could lead to a false impression of the sequence of
events. Actual time and space were preserved whenever possible by using
lengthy takes.

Cinéma vérité also uses sound minimally. These filmmakers were—and
still are—hostile to the "voice of God" commentaries that accompanied traditional documentaries. Off-screen narration tends to interpret images for the
spectator, thus relieving us of the necessity of analyzing for ourselves. Some
direct cinema advocates dispense with voice-over narration entirely (8–22).

The tradition of the formalistic or subjective documentary can be traced
back to the Soviet filmmaker Dziga-Vertov. Like most Soviet artists of the
1920s, Vertov was a propagandist. He believed that the cinema should be a tool

8–24. ***Padre, Padrone*** **(Italy, 1977),** *with Omero Antonutti, directed by Paolo and Vittorio Taviani.*
An eclectic art that defies neat categories, the cinema abounds in hybrid genres. The distinctions between fiction and documentary are difficult to make in movies like *Padre, Padrone* (My Father, My Master), which deals in part with the everyday lives of a group of peasants on the primitive island of Sardinia. The people in the movie are played by nonprofessional actors. The story is narrated by a distinguished scholar on whose life the film is based. But there are also many fictional and fantasy elements in the movie. We are allowed to hear the imagined thoughts of many of the secondary characters, and even the complaints of a goat!   *(Cinema 5)*

of the Revolution, a way of instructing workers about how to view events from an ideological perspective. "Art," he once wrote, "is not a *mirror* which reflects the historical struggle, but a *weapon* of that struggle."

Like most formalists, Vertov believed that filmmakers shouldn't merely record external reality; rather, they should analyze it. They must see beneath the surface chaos of the external world to reveal its infrastructure—its underlying connections with the institutions of power. The revolutionary documentarist teaches ideological lessons, explaining social and economic relationships that aren't always apparent, especially in capitalistic societies, where the interests of the ruling class are served by keeping the working class in ignorance about how the economic system works.

Documentarists in this formalistic tradition tend to build their movies thematically, arranging and structuring the story materials to demonstrate a thesis, like the news stories on television's prestigious *60 Minutes*. In many cases, the sequence of shots and even entire scenes can be switched around with relatively little loss of sense or logic. The structure of the film is not based on chronology or narrative coherence, but on the documentarist's argument (8–25).

8–25. *Point of Order!* (U.S.A., 1964), *directed by Emile De Antonio.*
Materials that might seem politically neutral can acquire ideological significance when the footage is reedited expressively. Many documentaries in the Vertov mold—like this exposé of the political immorality of Senator Joe McCarthy—were originally photographed by relatively impartial newsreel cameramen. The ideology is conveyed by the way in which this neutral material is restructured on the editing bench, a striking instance of how "plot" (or narrative structure) can radically alter "story." All montage films making use of newsreels descend from Vertov's theories. See also Jay Leyda, *Films Beget Films* (New York: Hill & Wang, 1964).   *(Continental Distributing)*

Avant-garde films are so variable that it's hard to generalize about their narrative structures. Most of these movies don't even try to tell a story. Autobiographical elements are common. Many avant-garde artists are primarily concerned with conveying their "inner impulses," their personal and subjective involvements with people, ideas, and experiences. For this reason, avant-garde movies are sometimes obscure and even incomprehensible. Many of these filmmakers create their own personal language and symbology (8–26).

With few exceptions, avant-garde films are not written out in advance. In part this is because the same artist usually shoots and edits the footage, and is therefore able to control the material at these stages of the filmmaking process. They also value chance and spontaneity in their movies, and in order to exploit these elements, they avoid the inflexibility of a script.

Maya Deren, an American avant-garde filmmaker of the 1940s, differentiated her kind of movie (which she called "personal" or "poetic") from mainstream commercial films primarily in terms of structure. Like a lyric poem, personal films are "vertical" investigations of a theme or situation. The film-

8–26. *Frank Film* (U.S.A., 1973), *directed by Frank Mouris.*
Avant-garde movies are often autobiographical and self-reflexive—they call attention to themselves, their aesthetic workings, and their creators. Mouris's film consists of magazine cutouts that he animated to illustrate the main influences of his youth. The sound track features two voices (both Mouris's), one listing a series of words beginning with the letter F, the other wittily recounting his life story to date.   *(Pyramid Films)*

maker is not concerned so much with what's happening as with what a situation feels like or what it means. The film artist is concerned with probing the depths and layers of meaning of a given moment.

Fiction movies, on the other hand, are like novels and plays, according to Deren. They're essentially "horizontal" in their development. Narrative filmmakers employ linear structures that must progress from situation to situation, from feeling to feeling. Fiction directors don't have much time to explore the implications of a given idea or emotion, for they must keep the plot "moving along."

Other avant-garde filmmakers disdain any kind of recognizable subject matter. Hans Richter and other early avant-garde artists in Europe totally rejected narrative. Richter was a champion of the "absolute film," which consists solely of abstract shapes and designs (see 4–6). Insisting that movies should have nothing to do with acting, stories, or literary themes, Richter believed that film—like music and abstract painting—should be concerned with pure nonrepresentational forms. Many contemporary avant-garde filmmakers share these biases (8–27).

Genre and Myth

A genre film is a specific type of movie—a war picture, a gangster film, science fiction, and so on. There are literally hundreds of them, especially in the United States and Japan, where virtually all fiction movies can be classified according to genre. Genres are distinguished by a characteristic set of conventions in style, subject matter, and values. Genre is also a convenient way of focusing and organizing the story materials.

8–27. *Razor Blades* (U.S.A., 1968), *directed by Paul Sharits*.

Structuralism is an avant-garde movement that rejects narrative in favor of an abstract structure that owes nothing to subject matter. In the structuralist cinema, the codes of cognition are totally self-defined. They are structured according to the principles of recurrence, dialectical polarities, time and space increments, and so on. The process of deciphering these cognitive codes and their interrelationships is analogous to the film's working itself out, fulfilling its structural destiny. In Sharit's flicker film, two images (requiring separate screens and projectors) are simultaneously juxtaposed. Each filmstrip consists of irregularly recurring images—two or three frames in duration, interspersed by blank or color frames—or purely abstract designs, like colored stripes or circular shapes. The rapid flickering of images creates a mesmerizing stroboscopic effect, testing the audience's psychological and physiological tolerance. The content of the film is its structural form rather than the subject matter of the images as images.- *(Anthology Film Archives)*

Many genre films are directed at a specific audience. Coming-of-age films are generally aimed at teenagers. Action-adventure genres tend to focus on all-male activities. Women are usually relegated to an incidental function, or they provide "romantic interest." The American woman's picture and Japanese mother films focus on domestic life. In these female-oriented genres, men are conventionalized in a similar manner—usually as breadwinners, sexual objects, or "the other man."

André Bazin once referred to the western as "a form in search of a content." The same could be said of all genre films. A genre is a loose set of expectations, then, not a divine injunction. That is, each example of a given story type is related to its predecessors, but not in ironclad bondage. Some genre films are good; others are terrible. It's not the genre that determines artistic excellence, but how well the artist exploits the conventions of its form.

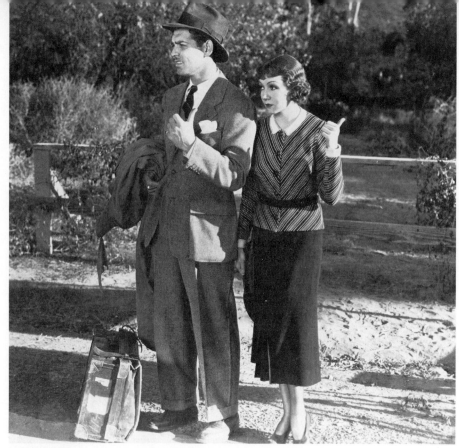

8–28. *It Happened One Night* **(U.S.A., 1934),** *with Clark Gable and Claudette Colbert, written by Robert Riskin, directed by Frank Capra.*

Genres can be classified according to subject matter, style, period, national origin, and a variety of other criteria. In the 1930s, a new American genre was born: screwball comedy. Its heyday was roughly 1934–1945. Essentially love stories, these films featured zany but glamourous lovers, often from different social classes. More realistic than the slapstick of the silent era, screwball comedy is also more collaborative, requiring the sophisticated blending of talents of writers, actors, and directors. The snappy dialogue crackles with wit and speed. Sappy, sentimental speeches are often meant to deceive. The narrative premises are absurdly improbable, and the plots, which are intricate and filled with preposterous twists and turns, tend to snowball out of control. The movies center on a comic/romantic couple rather than a solitary protagonist. Often they are initially hostile, with one trying to outwit or out-maneuver the other. Much of the comedy results from the utter seriousness of the characters, who are usually unaware that they're funny, even though they engage in the most loony masquerades and deceptions. Sometimes one of them is engaged to a sexless prude or a humorless bore: This lends an urgency to the attraction between the coprotagonists, who are clearly made for each other. The genre usually includes a menagerie of secondary characters who are as wacky as the lovers. *(Columbia Pictures)*

The major shortcoming of genre pictures of course is that they're easy to imitate and have been debased by stale mechanical repetition. Genre conventions are mere clichés unless they're united with significant innovations in style or subject matter. But this is true of all the arts, not just in movies. As Aristotle noted in *The Poetics*, genres are qualitatively neutral: The conventions of classical tragedy are basically the same whether they're employed by a genius or a forgotten hack. Certain genres enjoy more cultural prestige because they have attracted the most gifted artists. Genres that haven't are widely regarded as innately inartistic, but in many cases their déclassé status is due to neglect rather than intrinsic hopelessness. For example, the earliest film critics considered slapstick comedy an infantile genre—until such important comic artists as Chaplin and Keaton entered the field. Today, no critic would malign the genre, for it boasts a considerable number of masterpieces.

The most critically admired genre films strike a balance between the form's preestablished conventions and the artist's unique contributions. The artists of ancient Greece drew upon a common body of mythology, and no one thought it strange when dramatists and poets returned to these tales again and again. Incompetent artists merely repeat. Serious artists reinterpret. By exploiting the broad outlines of a well-known tale or story type, the storyteller can play off its main features, creating provocative tensions between the genre's conventions and the artist's inventions, between the familiar and the original, the general and the particular. Myths embody the common ideals and aspirations of a civiliza-

8–29. *The Godfather* **(U.S.A., 1972),** *with Marlon Brando and Robert Duvall (rear left), directed by Francis Ford Coppola.*
Genre films are generally profuse in archetypal elements. In this, the most famous gangster film in history, the very title resonates with larger-than-life forebodings. In Italian-American culture, a godfather is a respected authority figure, a revered parental surrogate. In the subculture of the Mafia, "Godfather" is what criminal chieftains are often called. The Brando figure is also a benevolent patriarch to the members of his immediate family, a legendary hero, a God-Father.   *(Paramount Pictures)*

8–30. *Rocky* **(U.S.A., 1976),** *with Sylvester Stallone, directed by John Avildsen.*
One of the most popular story patterns in America is the Horatio Alger myth—the inspiring tale of a social nobody who, through hard work and perseverance, and against all odds, manages to pull himself up by his bootstraps and achieve extraordinary success. *(United Artists)*

tion, and by returning to these communal tales, the artist becomes, in a sense, a psychic explorer, bridging the chasm between the known and the unknown. The stylized conventions and **archetypal** story patterns of genres encourage viewers to participate ritualistically in the basic beliefs, fears, and anxieties of their age.

Filmmakers are attracted to genres because they automatically synthesize a vast amount of cultural information, freeing them to explore more personal concerns. A nongeneric movie must be more self-contained. The artist is forced to communicate virtually all the major ideas and emotions within the work itself—a task that preempts much of his screen time. On the other hand, the genre artist never starts from scratch. He can build upon the accomplishments of his predecessors, enriching their ideas or calling them into question, depending on his inclinations.

The most enduring genres tend to adapt to changing social conditions. Most of them begin as naive allegories of Good versus Evil. Over the years they become more complex in both form and thematic range. Finally they veer into an ironic mode, mocking many of the genre's original values and conventions. Some critics claim that this evolution is inevitable and doesn't necessarily represent an aesthetic improvement.

Film critics and scholars classify genre movies into four main cycles:

1. *Primitive.* This phase is usually naive, though powerful in its emotional impact, in part because of the novelty of the form. Many of the conventions of the genre are established in this phase.

2. *Classical.* This intermediate stage embodies such classical ideals as balance, richness, and poise. The genre's values are assured and widely shared by the audience.

3. *Revisionist.* The genre is generally more symbolic, ambiguous, less certain in its values. This phase tends to be stylistically complex, appealing more to the intellect than to the emotions. Often the genre's preestablished conventions are exploited as ironic foils to question or undermine popular beliefs.

4. *Parodic.* This phase of a genre's development is an outright mockery of its conventions, reducing them to howling clichés and presenting them in a comic manner.

For example, the western's primitive phase is exemplified by Edwin S. Porter's *The Great Train Robbery* (1903), the first western ever made, and an enormously popular movie with the public. It was imitated and embellished upon for decades. The western's classical phase could be typified by many of the works of John Ford, especially *Stagecoach* (1939), one of the few westerns of that era to

8–31. *Risky Business* (U.S.A., 1983), with Tom Cruise and Rebecca De Mornay, written and directed by Paul Brickman.

Because 75 percent of the contemporary American film audience is composed of young people, rite-of-passage comedies—also known as coming-of-age films—appeal directly to this adolescent following. The worst of them pander shamelessly to this audience's sentimental and narcissistic view of itself, but a few—like *Risky Business*—are slyly revisionist. The protagonist's transition from childhood innocence to adult experience is subtly undermined by the film's increasingly low-key lighting style, and its bittersweet tone of cynicism. Cruise's character begins as a straight, hard-working high school student, naive but likable. In his impatience for worldly success and status, he betrays his parents's trust by using their home as a bordello while they are away on a short trip. With the help of an enterprising hooker (De Mornay), he pimps for his friends, supplying them with the services of several ladies of the evening, who share his entrepreneurial spirit. They reap a profit of $8000 in a single night. By the end of the movie, he is a bona fide member in good standing of the world of adults, savoring the sweet smell of success. *(Warner Bros.)*

win wide critical approval as well as box-office success. *High Noon* (1952) was one of the first revisionist westerns, ironically questioning many of the populist values of the genre's classical phase. Throughout the following two decades, most westerns remained in this skeptical mode, including such major works as *The Wild Bunch* (1969) and *McCabe and Mrs. Miller* (1971). Some critics pointed to Mel Brooks's parodic *Blazing Saddles* (1974) as the genre's death-blow, for many of its conventions are mercilessly lampooned. However, genres have a way of springing back to life after being allowed to rest for a few years. For example, Clint Eastwood's popular *Pale Rider* (1985) is unbashedly classical. Many cultural theorists insist that questions of individual value in a genre's evolution are largely matters of taste and fashion, not the intrinsic merit of the phase per se.

Some of the most suggestive critical studies have explored the relationship of a genre to the society that nurtured it. This sociopsychic approach was pioneered by the French literary critic Hippolyte Taine in the nineteenth century. Taine claimed that the social and intellectual anxieties of a given era and nation will find expression in its art. The implicit function of an artist is to harmonize and reconcile cultural clashes of value. He believed that art must be analyzed for

8–32. *On the Town* **(U.S.A., 1949),** *with (clockwise, from one o'clock) Gene Kelly, Vera-Ellen, Ann Miller, Betty Garrett, Frank Sinatra, and Jules Munshin, directed by Kelly and Stanley Donen.*
Musicals were among the most popular genres throughout the big studio era, appealing to men as well as women, to young audiences as well as adults. Most musicals heighten the artificiality of their narrative structures. For example, in this movie, everything comes in threes—three dashing sailor heroes and three spirited working-girl heroines. *(MGM)*

both its overt and its covert meaning, that beneath its explicit content there exists a vast reservoir of latent social and psychic information (8–33).

    This approach tends to work best with popular genres, which reflect the shared values and fears of a large audience. Such genres might be regarded as contemporary myths, lending philosophical meaning to the facts of everyday life. As social conditions change, genres often change with them, challenging some traditional customs and beliefs, reaffirming others. Gangster films, for example, are often covert critiques of American capitalism. They are often vehicles for exploring rebellion myths and are especially popular during periods of social breakdown. The protagonists—usually played by small men—are likened to ruthless businessmen, their climb to power a sardonic parody of the Horatio Alger myth. During the Jazz Age, gangster films like *Underworld* (1927) dealt

8–33. *Invasion of the Body Snatchers* **(U.S.A., 1956),** *directed by Don Siegel.*
Genre films often appeal to subconscious anxieties in the audience. For example, many Japanese science-fiction films of the 1950s dealt with hideous mutations that resulted from atomic radiation. A number of cultural commentators have remarked on the "paranoid style" of most American sci-fi movies of the 1950s, when the "Red Scare" intensified the Cold War atmosphere between the United States and the Soviet Union. Siegel's low-budget classic deals with how some alien pod-people insidiously invade human bodies, reducing their owners to anonymous zombies, incapable of feelings. The movie was produced during an era when many Americans were seriously discussing the possibility of building bomb shelters to "protect" themselves from an expected nuclear attack by the U.S.S.R.   *(Allied Artists)*

with the violence and glamour of the Prohibition era in an essentially apolitical manner. During the harshest years of the Depression in the early 1930s, the genre became subversively ideological. Movies like *Little Caesar* (1930) reflected the country's shaken confidence in authority and traditional social institutions. In the final years of the Depression, gangster films like *Dead End* (1937) were pleas for liberal reform, arguing that crime is the result of broken homes, lack of opportunity, and slum living. Gangsters of all periods tend to suffer from an inability to relate to women, but during the 1940s, movies like *White Heat* (1949) featured protagonists who were outright sexual neurotics. In the 1950s, partly as a result of the highly publicized Kefauver Senate Crime Investigations, gangster movies like *The Phenix City Story* (1955) took the form of confidential exposés of syndicate crime. Francis Ford Coppola's *The Godfather* (1972) and *The Godfather, Part II* (1974) are a virtual recapitulation of the history of the genre,

8–34. *E.T.: The Extra-Terrestrial* **(U.S.A., 1982),** *with Henry Thomas and E.T., directed by Steven Spielberg.*

All narratives can be interpreted on a symbolic level. There is a principle of universality that can be inferred no matter how unique or strange a given story may be. In this scene from Spielberg's masterpiece, E.T. and his friend Eliot must say goodbye. But E.T. will live forever inside Eliot's mind. Symbolically, the boy will soon outgrow his childhood world of imaginary best friends, scary-looking creatures, and the vast Unknown. But he will never forget the beauty and innocence of that world. Nor will we. "A film is a ribbon of dreams," Orson Welles once stated. "The camera is much more than a recording apparatus; it is a medium via which messages reach us from another world that is not ours and that brings us to the heart of a great secret. Here magic begins." *(Universal Studios)*

spanning three generations of characters and reflecting the weary cynicism of a nation still numbed by the hearts-and-minds hoax of Vietnam and the Watergate conspiracy. As Sergio Leone's fablelike title suggests, *Once Upon a Time in America* (1984) is frankly mythic, treating the traditional rise-and-fall structure of the genre in an almost ritualistic manner.

The ideas of Sigmund Freud and Carl Jung have also influenced many genre theorists. Like Taine, both psychiatrists believed that art is a reflection of underlying structures of meaning, that it satisfies certain subconscious needs in both the artist and audience. For Freud, art was a form of daydreaming and wish fulfillment, vicariously resolving urgent impulses and desires that can't be satisfied in reality. Pornographic films are perhaps the most obvious example of how anxieties can be assuaged in this surrogate manner, and in fact Freud believed that most neuroses were sexually based. He thought that art was a by-product of neurosis, although essentially a socially beneficial one. Like neurosis, art is characterized by a repetition compulsion, the need to go over the same stories

8–35. ***Sweet Hours*** **(Spain, 1982),** *with Inaki Airra and Assumpta Serna, directed by Carlos Saura.*

Almost all civilizations have myths dealing with the rebellion of son against father, resulting in son and mother reunited in exclusive love. Sigmund Freud, the father of psychoanalysis, identified one such variant as the Oedipus complex (named for the Greek mythical hero), which he believed was the paradigm of prepubescent human sexuality. Its feminine form is known as the Electra complex, a name also derived from Greek myth. In most cases, this narrative motif is submerged beneath the surface details of a story, or sufficiently disguised so as to appeal primarily to the subconscious. Saura's *Sweet Hours* plays with this motif in an overt manner. The movie deals with the love affair between a filmmaker (Aierra) and an actress (Serna) who is playing his mother in an autobiographical film he is making about his childhood.   *(New York Films)*

and rituals in order to reinact and temporarily resolve certain psychic conflicts (8–35).

Jung began his career as a disciple of Freud, but eventually broke away, believing that Freud's theories lacked a communal dimension. Jung was fascinated by myths, fairy tales, and folklore, which he believed contained symbols and story patterns that were universal to all individuals in all cultures and periods. According to Jung, unconscious complexes consist of archetypal symbols that are as deeply rooted and as inexplicable as instincts. He called this submerged reservoir of symbols the *collective unconscious,* which he thought had a primordial foundation, traceable to primitive times. Many of these archetypal patterns are bipolar and embody the basic concepts of religion, art, and society: god–devil, light–dark, active–passive, male–female, static–dynamic, and so on. Jung believed that the artist consciously or unconsciously draws on these archetypes as raw material, which must then be rendered into the generic forms favored by a given culture. For Jung, every work of art (and especially generic

8–36. *Pinocchio* (U.S.A., 1940), *by Walt Disney.*
The French cultural anthropologist Claude Lévi-Strauss noted that myths have no author, no origin, no core axis—they allow "free play" in a variety of artistic forms. Disney's work draws heavily from fairy tales, myths, and folklore, which are profuse in archetypal elements. *Pinocchio* is a good example of how these elements can be emphasized rather than submerged beneath a surface realism. Early in the film, the boy/puppet Pinocchio is told that in order to be a "real boy," he must show that he is "brave, truthful, and unselfish." The three principal episodes of the movie represent ritualistic trials, testing the youth's moral fortitude. He dismally fails the first two, but redeems himself in the concluding whale episode, where he does indeed demonstrate courage, honesty, and unselfishness (pictured). Other archetypal elements include a monster (Monstro, the whale), magical transformations, a father's search for his lost son, supernatural creatures like a talking cricket (Jiminy Cricket, Pinocchio's "conscience"), a son's search for his imprisoned father, an anthropomorphized portrayal of nature, and a fairy godmother who rescues the improvident young hero when he fails to act responsibly. Like most of Disney's works, the values in *Pinocchio* are traditional and conservative, an affirmation of the sanctity of the family unit, the importance of a Higher Power in guiding our destinies, and the need to play by society's rules.   (© *Walt Disney Productions*)

art) is an infinitesimal exploration of a universal experience—an instinctive groping toward an ancient wisdom. He also believed that popular culture offers the most unobstructed view of archetypes and myths, while elite culture tends to submerge them beneath a complex surface detail.

A story can be many things. To a producer it's a property that has a box-office value. To a writer it's a screenplay. To a film star it's a vehicle. To a director it's an artistic medium. To a genre critic it's a classifiable narrative form. To a sociologist it's an index of public sentiment. To a psychiatrist it's an instinctive exploration of hidden fears or communal ideals. To a moviegoer it can be all of these, and more.

FURTHER READING

BORDWELL, DAVID, *Narration in the Fiction Film* (Madison: University of Wisconsin Press, 1985). The fullest discussion of the role of the spectator.

BROWNE, NICK, *The Rhetoric of Filmic Narration* (Ann Arbor, Mich.: UMI Research Press, 1982). A survey of rhetorical strategies.

CHATMAN, SEYMOUR, *Story and Discourse* (Ithaca, N.Y.: Cornell University Press, 1978). Well written, clear, and useful, covering literature as well as film.

FELL, JOHN L., *Film and the Narrative Tradition* (Berkeley: University of California Press, 1974). Historical influences on early film narrative, covering stage melodramas, comic strips, dime novels, and other forms of pop culture.

FIELD, SYD, *The Screenwriter's Workbook* (New York: Dell, 1984). A practical handbook, emphasizing the classical paradigm.

LEITCH, THOMAS M., *What Stories Are: Narrative Theory and Interpretation.* (University Park and London: Pennsylvania State University Press, 1986). Theoretical emphasis, covering literature and drama as well as film.

MARTIN, WALLACE, *Recent Theories of Narrative* (Ithaca, N.Y.: Cornell University Press, 1986). Lucid and helpful, primarily about literature.

MITCHELL, W.J.T., ed., *On Narrative* (Chicago and London: University of Chicago Press, 1981). Collection of scholarly articles, mostly on literature.

MOEWS, DANIEL, *Keaton: The Silent Features Close Up* (Berkeley: University of California Press, 1977). An excellent critical study, especially strong on Keaton's plots.

SCHOLES, ROBERT, and ROBERT KELLOG, *The Nature of Narrative* (New York: Oxford University Press, 1966). Theoretical emphasis, covering literature as well as film.

LITERATURE | 9

The filmmaker/author writes with his camera as a writer writes
with his pen.

—ALEXANDRE ASTRUC

9–1. *Broadcast News* **(U.S.A., 1987),** *with (r. to l.) William Hurt, Holly Hunter, and Albert Brooks, written and directed by James L. Brooks.*
Many American filmmakers began their careers as television writers. James L. Brooks wrote for several high-quality sitcoms, most notably the critically acclaimed *Mary Tyler Moore Show.* His first movie, *Terms of Endearment* (1983), was an adaptation of a Larry McMurtry novel. The film won Academy Awards for best picture, best director, and best screenplay. *Broadcast News,* which was highly praised for its literate screenplay, was written directly for the screen.   *(Twentieth Century-Fox)*

This chapter investigates the role of the written word in movies. The screenwriter and the screenplay are perhaps the most obvious literary aspects of cinema. Figurative comparisons—motifs, symbols, metaphors, allusions—are found in both literature and film, and not necessarily just in "literary" films. Point of view is also a central concern of both fiction writers and filmmakers. Point of view involves how a story can be slanted in a given direction by the person telling the story. It's been variously estimated that from one fifth to one fourth of all feature films have been literary adaptations. Nor has the relationship between movies and literature been one way. Many commentators have noted the cinematic qualities of much twentieth-century fiction and poetry, including Joyce's *Ulysses* and Eliot's "The Love Song of J. Alfred Prufrock."

The Screenwriter

Perhaps more than any of the director's other collaborators, the screenwriter has been brought forward from time to time as the main "author" of a film. After all, writers are generally responsible for the dialogue. They outline most of the action (sometimes in detail). And they often set forth the main theme of a movie. But generalizing about the writer's contribution in the movie-making process is an exercise in futility because the writer's role varies immensely from film to film, and from director to director. In the first place, some filmmakers have hardly bothered with scripts. Especially in the silent era, improvisation was the rule rather than the exception. Others used only the barest outlines. Even in more recent times, filmmakers like Jean-Luc Godard have rarely used scripts. Most of his movies were begun with only a few ideas jotted down on a scrap of paper.

Many of the greatest directors have written their own scripts: Cocteau, Eisenstein, Bergman, and Herzog, to name only a few. In the American cinema, there are also many writer–directors: Griffith, Chaplin, Stroheim, Huston, Welles, Mankiewicz, Wilder, Sturges, Woody Allen, and Coppola are among the most famous. The majority of important directors have taken a major hand in writing their scripts, but they bring in other writers to expand on their ideas. Fellini, Truffaut, and Kurosawa all worked in this manner. Surprisingly few major directors depend totally on others for their scripts (9–2).

The American studio system tended to encourage multiple authorship of scripts. Often writers had a certain specialty such as dialogue, comedy, construc-

9–2. *Umberto D* (Italy, 1951), *with Carlo Battisti (right), written by Cesare Zavattini, directed by Vittorio De Sica.*
Zavattini is the most famous scenarist of the Italian cinema, and one of its most important theorists. (See the section on neorealism in Chapter 10). His best work was done in collaboration with De Sica, including such important works as *Shoeshine, The Bicycle Thief, Miracle in Milan, Umberto D, Two Women, The Garden of the Finzi-Continis,* and *A Brief Vacation.* De Sica worked in close collaboration with his scenarists. For example, the protagonist of this film, a retired government employee (Battisti), is a veiled portrait of the director's father, Umberto De Sica, to whom the film is dedicated. *(Audio-Brandon Films)*

tion, atmosphere, and so on. Some writers were best at doctoring weak scripts. Others were good idea people but lacked the skill to execute their ideas. In such collaborative enterprises, the screen credits are not always an accurate reflection of who contributed what to a movie. Futhermore, although many directors such as Hitchcock, Capra, and Lubitsch contributed a great deal to the final shape of their scripts, they rarely included their names in the credits, allowing the official writer to take it all.

For many years, American critics were inclined to believe that art must be solemn—if not actually dull—to be respectable. Indeed, even in the heyday of the Hollywood studio system, such intellectual writers as Dalton Trumbo, Carl Foreman, and Dore Schary enjoyed tremendous prestige because their scripts were filled with fine speeches dealing with Justice, Brotherhood, and Democracy. Today these purple patches of dialogue seem clumsy, schoolmarmish, and ultimately dishonest, for often even rough, unlettered characters burst forth with eloquent speeches that are totally out of character.

Not that these values aren't important. But to be effective artistically, ideas must be dramatized with tact and honesty, not parcelled out to the characters like high-sounding speeches on a patriotic holiday. For example, in the novel *The Grapes of Wrath*, John Steinbeck frequently praises the toughness of the Joad family. They have been thrown off their farm during the Great Depression and are forced to seek a new life in California, where conditions are even worse for them.

In John Ford's movie version, there is no narrator, so the characters must speak for themselves. Nunnally Johnson's screenplay is not devoid of ideas, but the ideas are expressed in the words of the *characters*. A good example is Ma Joad's comments to her husband in the final scene of the movie. They are in their

9–3. *Twentieth Century* (U.S.A., 1934), *with John Barrymore and Carole Lombard, written by Ben Hecht and Charles MacArthur, based on their play, directed by Howard Hawks.*

The legendary wit and ex-newspaperman Ben Hecht was perhaps the most admired Hollywood screenwriter of the big studio era. His specialty was comedy—the more outrageous, the better. He delighted in satirizing American hick values. Conventional morality is shown to be as hypocritical as it is dull. Since the censorship code of his era insisted that heroes and heroines had to be upright and moral, he resolved to avoid writing about such paragons of respectability: "The thing to do was to skip the heroes and heroines," Hecht concluded, "to write a movie containing only villains and bawds. I would not have to tell any lies then." *(Columbia Pictures)* shabby truck, driving to a new job—20 days as fruit pickers. Pa Joad (Russell Simpson) admits to his wife (Jane Darwell) that for a while he thought the family was finished. She answers: "I know. That's what makes us tough. Rich fellas come up an' they die, an' their kids ain't no good, an' they die out. But we keep a-comin'. We're the people that live. They can't wipe us out. They can't lick us. We'll go on forever Pa, 'cause we're the people." (Quoted from Johnson's script in *Twenty Best Film Plays,* Vol. I, eds. John Gassner and Dudley Nichols; New York: Garland Publishing, 1977)

The final image of the film follows: a thrilling extreme long shot, in which the fragile Joad vehicle merges imperceptibly with a procession of other dilapidated trucks and autos, forming an unbroken river of traffic—Ford's visual tribute to the courage and resilience of the human spirit.

Generally speaking, students, artists, and intellectuals are the individuals most likely to discuss ideas and abstractions without a sense of self-consciousness. To be convincing, eloquent language must be dramatically probable. We must believe that the words aren't just the writer's preachments dressed up as dialogue.

9–4. *The Return of the Secaucus Seven* (U.S.A., 1980), *with Maggie Renzi, Bruce Mac-Donald, and Jean Passanante; written and directed by John Sayles.*
Working outside the mainstream industry as an independent novelist and filmmaker, John Sayles is above all a *writer*-director. His characters in this movie are bright and articulate, with a strong sense of irony. Their dialogue is often funny and wryly self-deprecating. Though somewhat crude technically, the movie succeeds largely because of its fresh, sparkling dialogue, and the understated throwaway style of the acting.   *(Libra/Specialty Release)*

Indeed, some filmmakers are at their best with talky scripts—provided it's scintillating talk, as in the best movies of Wertmüller, Bergman, and Woody Allen (9–5). The French, Swedish, and British cinemas are also exceptionally literate. Among the important writers who have written for the screen in Great Britain are George Bernard Shaw, Graham Greene, Alan Sillitoe, John Osborne, Harold Pinter, David Storey, and Hanif Kureishi.

Despite the enormous importance that the script can play in a sound film, some directors scoff at the notion that a writer could be the dominant artist in the cinema. Antonioni once remarked that Dostoyevsky's *Crime and Punishment* was a rather ordinary crime thriller—the genius of the novel lies in *how* it's told, not in the subject matter per se. Certainly the large number of excellent movies based on routine or even mediocre books seems to bear out such a view.

Movie scripts seldom make for interesting reading, precisely because they are like blueprints of the finished product. Unlike a play, which usually can be read with pleasure, too much is missing in a screenplay. Even highly detailed scripts seldom offer us a sense of a film's **mise en scène,** one of the principal

9–5. *The Purple Rose of Cairo* (U.S.A., 1985), *with Jeff Daniels and Danny Aiello, written and directed by Woody Allen.*
Woody Allen is widely regarded as the most gifted writer–director of his generation, combining wit with romantic whimsy, poignancy with thought. Almost all of his movies are comedies, of virtually every type—satires, parodies, romantic comedies, fantasies, comedies of manners, and farces. He averages about one film per year. He has also written a number of stage plays and several volumes of humorous essays. Most of his essays originally appeared in the prestigious *New Yorker,* which has published the writings of the finest authors in America. The fertility of his invention is nowhere better illustrated than in this movie, a humorous and insightful treatment of the relation of life to art.   *(Orion Pictures)*

methods of expression at the director's disposal. With characteristic wit, Andrew Sarris has pointed out how the director's choice of shot—or the way in which the action is photographed—is the crucial element in most films:

> The choice between a close-up and a long-shot, for example, may quite often transcend the plot. If the story of Little Red Riding Hood is told with the Wolf in close-up and Little Red Riding Hood in long-shot, the director is concerned primarily with the emotional problems of a wolf with a compulsion to eat little girls. If Little Red Riding Hood is in close-up and the Wolf in long-shot, the emphasis is shifted to the emotional problems of vestigial virginity in a wicked world. Thus, two different stories are being told with the same basic anecdotal material. What is at stake in the two versions of Little Red Riding Hood are two contrasting directorial attitudes toward life. One director identifies more with the Wolf—the male, the compulsive, the corrupted, even evil itself. The second director identifies with the little girl—the innocence, the illusion, the ideal and hope of the race. Needless to say, few critics bother to make any distinction, proving perhaps that direction as creation is still only dimly understood. (Quoted from "The Fall and Rise of the Film Director," in *Interviews with Film Directors*; New York: Avon Books, 1967)

9–6. *Salvador* **(U.S.A., 1985),** *with Elpedia Carillo, James Woods, and James Belushi; written and directed by Oliver Stone.*
Compared to European and Third World filmmakers, American movie artists tend to avoid overtly political films because they're rarely successful at the box office. Stone is an exception. All of his works thus far are unabashedly ideological, exploring political subjects from an aggressively left-wing perspective.   *(Hemdale Releasing Corporation)*

The Screenplay

A film script is rarely an autonomous literary product, otherwise they would be published with greater frequency. The screenplays of a few prestigious filmmakers, like Woody Allen, Ingmar Bergman, and Federico Fellini, have reached print. But even these are merely linguistic approximations of the films themselves. Perhaps the worst kind of literary by-products of movies are "novelizations"—commissioned novel versions of popular films which are usually written by hired hacks to cash in on a movie's box-office popularity.

Screenplays are often modified by the actors who play the characters. This is especially true in scripts written for personality **stars.** Naturally their roles will usually include the qualities that make the star popular. For example, screenwriters who wrote for Gary Cooper knew that he was at his best when he said the least. In our own time, Clint Eastwood is famous for his terse one-liners: "Go

9–7. *My Beautiful Launderette* **(Great Britain, 1986),** *with Gordon Warnecke and Daniel Day Lewis, written by Hanif Kureishi, directed by Stephen Frears.*
One of Britain's most outspoken young writers (plays and fiction as well as screenplays), Hanif Kureishi enjoys shocking the staid literary establishment. His themes characteristically revolve around conflicts between cultures, races, classes, and sexes. Most of his characters are funny as well as bright. Despite being from different classes and ethnic backgrounds, the two leading characters in this film (pictured) are business partners and lovers. They're totally unapologetic about their sexuality, which is not treated as a big deal. Kureishi, who is half English and half Pakistani, is especially interested in minorities, people outside the English mainstream, which is male, white, and heterosexual. "Gay men and black men have been excluded from history," Kureishi has said. "They're trying to understand themselves. Like women, black people and gay people have been marginalized in society, lacking in power, ridiculed." *(Orion Classics)*

ahead—make my day." Eastwood's characters, like Cooper's, are usually suspicious of people who are smooth talkers, like snake-oil salesmen.

On the other hand, a good talker is a joy to hear. Joseph L. Mankiewicz was one of the most admired writer–directors of the Hollywood big studio era. His finest work, *All About Eve* (7–5), features several brilliantly written roles. One of the best is the acid-tongued theater critic, Addison Dewitt, played with bitchy *sang-froid* by George Sanders. Late in the movie, Eve Harrington (Anne Baxter), a young actress who has lied, cheated, and slept her way to the top, tries to brush off Dewitt, her current companion, because he's no longer useful to her. Dewitt sees right through her and has no intention of playing her fool. She huffily walks to the door and opens it. "You're too short for that gesture," he dryly observes. "Besides, it went out with Mrs. Fisk." He then proceeds to destroy her pretentions by exposing all of her lies. "Your name is not Eve Harrington. It is Gertrude Slescynski," he begins. "It is true that your parents were poor. They still are. And they would like to know how you are—and where. They haven't heard from you for three years."

Eve finally collapses as he finishes his withering diatribe: "That I should want you at all suddenly strikes me as the height of improbability. That, in itself, is probably the reason. You're an improbable person, Eve, and so am I. We have that in common. Also a contempt for humanity, an inability to love or be loved, insatiable ambition—and talent. We deserve each other." (Quoted from *More About All About Eve;* New York: Bantam, 1974; which contains Mankiewicz's script and a lengthy interview)

Most of the characters in *All About Eve* are well educated and literate. Those in *On the Waterfront,* which was written by Budd Schulberg, are working-class longshoremen. Such characters usually attempt to conceal their emotions

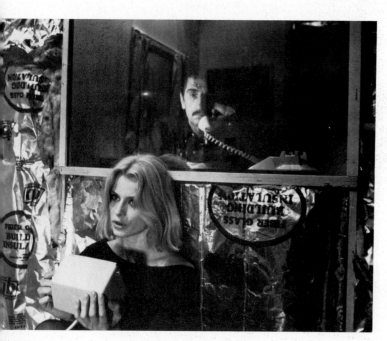

9–8. Paris, Texas (West Germany, 1984), *with Nastassja Kinski and Harry Dean Stanton, written by Sam Shepard, directed by Wim Wenders.*
The mysterious, metaphorical richness of Sam Shepard's screenplay is typical of his literary style. In addition to being a respected stage and screen actor, Shepard is also one of America's finest contemporary playwrights. *(Twentieth Century–Fox)*

behind a macho façade. But in scenes of intense emotions, the words, though simple, are powerful. The famous taxi scene between the Malloy brothers, Charley (Rod Steiger) and Terry (Marlon Brando), is a good example. Charley, the older and shrewder of the two, once convinced his brother to throw an important boxing match. Terry is no longer a boxer, but a stooge for the same union racketeer that Charley works for, Johnny Friendly. Charley tries to blame Terry's manager for what happened. Angry, Terry answers:

> It wasn't him! It was you, Charley. You and Johnny. Like the night the two of youse come in the dressing room and says, 'Kid, this ain't your night— we're going for the price on Wilson.' *It ain't my night.* I'd of taken Wilson apart that night! I was ready—remember the early rounds throwing them combinations. So what happens—This bum Wilson he gets the title shot— outdoors in the ball park!—and what do I get—a couple of bucks and a one-way ticket to Palookaville. It was you, Charley. You was my brother. You should of looked out for me. Instead of making me take them dives for the short-end money. . . . I could've been a contender. I could've had class and been somebody. Real class. Instead of a bum, let's face it, which is what I am. It was you, Charley. (Quoted from *On the Waterfront: A Screenplay;* Carbondale: Southern Illinois University Press, 1980)

Good dialogue is often the result of having a good ear—for catching the correct rhythms of speech, the right choice of words, the length of people's sentences, the jargon, slang, or swears people use. The foulmouthed characters in Martin Scorsese's *Mean Streets* (3–25) speak in torrents of four-letter words, the linguistic equivalents of the violence of their lives. In contexts such as these, polite or laundered prose would constitute bad writing.

One of the pleasures of Nicholas Meyer's screenplay (adapted from his own novel) of *The Seven Per-Cent Solution* is the way he captures the elegantly

9–9. *Moonstruck* (**U.S.A., 1987**), *with Cher and Nicolas Cage, written by John Patrick Shanley, directed by Norman Jewison.* Shanley's Oscar-winning screenplay is filled with funny one-liners, screwball characters, and dialogue that sometimes soars with romantic lyricism, like a Puccini aria. All this enchanting silliness is justified by one of the oldest gimmicks in literature—a magical full moon. *(MGM)*

literary nineteenth-century prose style of his protagonist, Sherlock Holmes. Here's Holmes when he's first tricked into meeting a foreign doctor at the physician's home in Vienna:

> Beyond the fact that you are a brilliant Jewish physician who was born in Hungary and studied for a time in Paris, and that some radical theories of yours have alienated the respectable medical community so that you have severed your connections with various hospitals and branches of the medical fraternity—beyond this, I can deduce little. You are married, with a child of five; you enjoy Shakespeare and possess a sense of honor. (Quoted from *Film Scenes for Actors,* ed. Joshua Karton; New York: Bantam Books, 1983)

The doctor turns out to be none other than Sigmund Freud. Naturally, he's astonished that Holmes can deduce so much upon merely entering a room.

Most screenplays are businesslike and practical. Since they are not meant for publication, the action sequences are usually described simply, with no literary flourishes. There are a few exceptions to this rule, however. One of them is John Osborne's polished screenplay of *Tom Jones,* based on the eighteenth-century English novel by Henry Fielding. The fox hunt scene in the movie is magnificently effective, thanks to Tony Richardson's skillful direction. But Richardson obviously got his inspiration from Osborne's screenplay:

> The hunt is no pretty Christmas calendar affair but a thumping dangerous vicious business, in which everyone takes part so wholeheartedly that it seems to express all in the raw, wild vitality that is so near to the surface of their lives. It is passionate and violent. Squire Western howls dementedly

9–10. *Richard Pryor—Live in Concert* **(U.S.A., 1979),** *written by and starring Richard Pryor.*
Pryor's concert films are so brilliantly performed that many people forget that the standup comedy was *written* first. As usual, Pryor ranges over a wide variety of topics—race, sex, macho men, death. His literary style is indebted to the idiom of America's inner-city ghettos—raunchy, cocky, foulmouthed, and very funny. *(Bill Sargent)*

9–11. *Some Like It Hot* (U.S.A., 1959), *with Jack Lemmon and Tony Curtis, screenplay by Billy Wilder and I.A.L. Diamond, directed by Wilder.*
Billy Wilder was one of the most respected writer–directors of the post-World War II era. He was regarded as a master of the well-made scenario: Each detail has a precise interlocking function. "In a good script, *everything* is necessary or it ain't good," he insisted. "And if you take out one piece, you better replace it with a different piece, or you got trouble." He was able to mine comedy from the unlikeliest sources, like transvestism. Forced to disguise themselves as women while on the lam from the mob, the musician heroes of this film join an all-girl band to escape detection. Most of the gags revolve around the incongruity of two virile men trying to cope with the agony of womanhood. Lemmon, for example, keeps losing one of his chests.
(United Artists)

as he flogs his horse over the muddy earth. The curate kicks his beefy heels in the air, bellowing with blood and pleasure. Big, ugly, unlovable dogs tear at the earth. Tom reels and roars on his horse, his face ruddy and damp, almost insensible with the lust and the cry and the gallop, with the hot quarry of flesh in the crisp air, the blood and flesh of men, the blood and fur of animals. Everyone is caught up in the bloody fever. (Quoted from *Tom Jones, A Film Script,* by John Osborne; New York: Grove Press, 1964)

North by Northwest: Reading Version

Ernest Lehman's screenplay for Hitchcock's *North by Northwest* has considerable fluidity as a piece of writing. Its excellence consists not of its literary distinction so much as its clearly defined actions, providing the director with the raw materials for the shots of the movie. The following is a lengthy excerpt from the screenplay. How Hitchcock translated this literary description into the individual sequence of shots in the movie can be seen in Chapter 4, Editing.

Like many of Hitchcock's movies, *North by Northwest* revolves around the wrong-man theme. The protagonist is an innocent man accused of and persecuted for a crime he didn't commit. In this film, Roger Thornhill (Cary Grant), a glib but charming advertising executive, is accidentally mistaken for a government agent named Kaplan. Thornhill is abducted by enemy agents, almost murdered by them, then fatefully implicated in the murder of a U.N. diplomat. Pursued by both the police and the enemy agents, he flees to Chicago in desperation, hoping to discover the real Kaplan, who presumably will establish Thornhill's innocence. When he arrives in Chicago, he is told that Kaplan will meet him alone at a designated location. The following excerpt relates what then takes place.

Helicopter Shot—Exterior, Highway 41—Afternoon

We START CLOSE on a Greyhound bus, SHOOTING DOWN on it and TRAVELING ALONG with it as it speeds in an easterly direction at seventy m.p.h. Gradually, CAMERA DRAWS AWAY from the bus, going higher but never losing sight of the vehicle, which recedes into the distance below and becomes a toylike object on an endless ribbon of deserted highway that stretches across miles of flat prairie. Now the bus is slowing down. It is nearing a junction where a small dirt road coming from nowhere crosses the highway and continues on to nowhere. The bus stops. A man gets out. It is THORNHILL. But to us he is only a tiny figure. The bus starts away, moves on out of sight. And now THORNHILL stands alone beside the road—a tiny figure in the middle of nowhere.

On the Ground—with Thornhill—(Master Scene)

He glances about, studying his surroundings. The terrain is flat and treeless, even more desolate from this vantage point than it seemed from the air. Here and there patches of low-growing farm crops add some contour to the land. A hot sun beats down. UTTER SILENCE hangs heavily in the air. THORNHILL glances at his wristwatch. It is three twenty-five.

In the distance, the FAINT HUM of a MOTOR VEHICLE IS HEARD. THORNHILL looks off to the west. The HUM GROWS LOUDER as the car draws nearer. THORNHILL steps closer to the edge of the highway. A black sedan looms up, traveling at high speed. For a moment we are not sure it is not hurtling right at THORNHILL. And then it zooms past him, recedes into the distance, becoming a FAINT HUM, a tiny speck, and then SILENCE again.

THORNHILL takes out a handkerchief, mops his face. He is beginning to sweat now. It could be from nervousness, as well as the heat. Another FAINT HUM, coming from the east, GROWING LOUDER as he glances off and sees another distant speck becoming a speeding car, this one a closed convertible. Again, anticipation on THORNHILL's face. Again, the vague uneasiness of indefinable danger approaching at high speed. And again, ZOOM—a cloud of dust—a car receding into the distance—a FAINT HUM—and SILENCE.

His lips tighten. He glances at his watch again. He steps out into the middle of the highway, looks first in one direction, then the other. Nothing in sight. He loosens his tie, opens his shirt collar, looks up at the sun. Behind him, in the distance, another vehicle is HEARD approaching. He turns, looks off to the west. This one is a huge transcontinental moving van,

ROARING TOWARD HIM at high speed. With quick apprehension he moves off the highway to the dusty side of the road as the van thunders past and disappears. Its FADING SOUND is replaced with a NEW SOUND, the CHUGGING of an OLD FLIVVER.

THORNHILL looks off in the direction of the approaching SOUND, sees a flivver nearing the highway from the intersecting dirt road. When the car reaches the highway, it comes to a stop. A middle-aged woman is behind the wheel. Her passenger is a nondescript MAN of about fifty. He could certainly be a farmer. He gets out of the car. It makes a U-turn and drives off in the direction from which it came. THORNHILL watches the MAN and takes up a position across the highway from him. The MAN glances at THORNHILL without visible interest, then looks off up the highway toward the east as though waiting for something to come along.

THORNHILL stares at the MAN, wondering if this is George Kaplan.

The MAN looks idly across the highway at THORNHILL, his face expressionless.

THORNHILL wipes his face with his handkerchief, never taking his eyes off the MAN across the highway. The FAINT SOUND of an APPROACHING PLANE has gradually come up over the scene. As the SOUND GROWS LOUDER, THORNHILL looks up to his left and sees a low-flying biplane approach from the northwest. He watches it with mounting interest as it heads straight for the spot where he and the stranger face each other across the highway. Suddenly it is upon them, only a hundred feet above the ground, and then, like a giant bird, as THORNHILL turns with the plane's passage, it flies over them, and continues on. THORNHILL stares after the plane, his back to the highway. When the plane has gone several hundred yards beyond the highway, it loses altitude, levels off only a few feet above the ground and begins to fly back and forth in straight lines parallel to the highway, letting loose a trail of powdered dust from beneath its fuselage as it goes. Any farmer would recognize the operation as simple crop-dusting.

THORNHILL looks across the highway, sees that the stranger is watching the plane with idle interest. THORNHILL's lips set with determination. He crosses over and goes up to the MAN.

THORNHILL: Hot day.

MAN: Seen worse.

THORNHILL: Are you . . . uh . . . by any chance supposed to be meeting someone here?

MAN (still watching the plane): Waitin' for the bus. Due any minute.

THORNHILL: Oh . . .

MAN (idly): Some of them crop-duster pilots get rich, if they live long enough . . .

THORNHILL: Then your name isn't . . . Kaplan.

MAN (glances at him): Can't say it is, 'cause it ain't. (He looks off up the highway) Well—here she comes, right on time.

THORNHILL looks off to the east, sees a Greyhound bus approaching. The MAN peers off at the plane again, and frowns.

MAN: That's funny.

THORNHILL: What?

MAN: That plane's dustin' crops where there ain't no crops.

THORNHILL looks across at the droning plane with growing suspicion as the stranger steps out onto the highway and flags the bus to a stop. THORNHILL turns toward the stranger as though to say something to him. But it is too late. The man has boarded the bus, its doors are closing, and it is pulling away. THORNHILL is alone again.

Almost immediately, he HEARS the PLANE ENGINE BEING GUNNED TO A HIGHER SPEED. He glances off sharply, sees the plane veering off its parallel course and heading toward him. He stands there wide-eyed, rooted to the spot. The plane roars on, a few feet off the ground. There are two men in the twin cockpits, goggled, unrecognizable, menacing. He yells out to them, but his voice is lost in the NOISE of the PLANE. In a moment it will be upon him and decapitate him. Desperately he drops to the ground and presses himself flat as the plane zooms over him with a great noise, almost combing his hair with a landing wheel.

THORNHILL scrambles to his feet, sees the plane banking and turning. He looks about wildly, sees a telephone pole and dashes for it as the plane comes at him again. He ducks behind the pole. The plane heads straight for him, veers to the right at the last moment. We HEAR two sharp CRACKS of GUNFIRE mixed with the SOUND of the ENGINE, as two bullets slam into the pole just above THORNHILL's head.

THORNHILL reacts to this new peril, sees the plane banking for another run at him. A car is speeding along the highway from the west. THORNHILL dashes out onto the road, tries to flag the car down but the driver ignores him. He dives into a ditch and rolls away as another series of SHOTS are HEARD and bullets rake the ground that he has just occupied.

He gets to his feet, looks about, sees a cornfield about fifty yards from the highway, glances up at the plane making its turn, and decides to make a dash for the cover of the tall-growing corn.

SHOOTING DOWN FROM A HELICOPTER about one hundred feet above the ground, we SEE THORNHILL running toward the cornfield and the plane in pursuit.

SHOOTING FROM WITHIN THE CORNFIELD, WE SEE THORNHILL come crashing in, scuttling to the right and lying flat and motionless as we HEAR THE PLANE ZOOM OVER HIM WITH A BURST OF GUNFIRE and bullets rip into the corn, but at a safe distance from THORNHILL. He raises his head cautiously, gasping for breath, as he HEARS THE PLANE MOVE OFF AND INTO ITS TURN.

SHOOTING DOWN FROM THE HELICOPTER, we see the plane leveling off and starting a run over the cornfield, which betrays no sign of the hidden THORNHILL. Skimming over the top of the cornstalks, the plane gives forth no burst of gunfire now. Instead, it lets loose thick clouds of poisonous dust which settle down into the corn.

9–12. *North by Northwest* **(U.S.A., 1959),** *with Cary Grant, screenplay by Ernest Lehman, directed by Alfred Hitchcock.* Much of the success of this movie is due to Grant's engaging performance as Roger O. Thornhill (the "O" stands for nothing), who's a little too slick for his own good. Only an actor of Grant's great skill could handle the comedy of his role without sacrificing credibility as a person who is being put through a living hell. *(MGM)*

WITHIN THE CORNFIELD, THORNHILL, still lying flat, begins to gasp and choke as the poisonous dust envelops him. Tears stream from his eyes but he does not dare move as he HEARS THE PLANE COMING OVER THE FIELD AGAIN. When the plane zooms by and another cloud of dust hits him, he jumps to his feet and crashes out into the open, half blinded and gasping for breath. Far off down the highway to the right, he SEES a huge Diesel gasoline-tanker approaching. He starts running toward the highway to intercept it.

SHOOTING FROM THE HELICOPTER, WE SEE THORNHILL dashing for the highway, the plane leveling off for another run at him, and the Diesel tanker speeding closer.

SHOOTING ACROSS THE HIGHWAY, WE SEE THORNHILL running and stumbling TOWARD CAMERA, the plane closing in between him, and the Diesel tanker approaching from the left. He dashes out into the middle of the highway and waves his arms wildly.

The Diesel tanker THUNDERS down the highway toward THORNHILL, KLAXON BLASTING impatiently.

The plane speeds relentlessly toward THORNHILL from the field bordering the highway.

THORNHILL stands alone and helpless in the middle of the highway, waving his arms. The plane draws closer. The tanker is almost upon him. It isn't going to stop. He can HEAR THE KLAXON BLASTING him out of the way. There is nothing he can do. The plane has caught up with him. The tanker won't stop. It's GOT to stop. He hurls himself to the pavement directly in its path. There is A SCREAM OF BRAKES and SKIDDING TIRES, THE ROAR OF THE PLANE ENGINE and then a tremendous BOOM as the Diesel truck grinds to a stop inches from Thornhill's body just as the plane, hopelessly committed and caught unprepared by the sudden stop, slams into the traveling gasoline tanker and plane and gasoline explode into a great sheet of flame.

In the next few moments, all is confusion. THORNHILL, unhurt, rolls out from under the wheels of the Diesel truck. The drivers clamber out of the front seat and drop to the highway. Black clouds of smoke billow up from the funeral pyre of the plane and its cremated occupants. We recognize the flaming body of one of the men in the plane. It is LIGHT, one of THORNHILL's original abductors. An elderly open pick-up truck with a second-hand refrigerator standing in it, which has been approaching from the east, pulls up at the side of the road. Its driver, a FARMER, jumps out and hurries toward the wreckage.

FARMER: What happened? What happened?

The Diesel truck drivers are too dazed to answer. Flames and smoke drive them all back. THORNHILL, unnoticed, heads toward the unoccupied pick-up truck. Another car comes up from the west, stops, and its driver runs toward the other men. They stare, transfixed, at the holocaust. Suddenly, from behind them, they HEAR the PICKUP TRUCK's motor starting. The FARMER who owns the truck turns, and is startled to see his truck being driven away by an utter stranger.

FARMER: Hey!

He runs after the truck. But the stranger—who is THORNHILL—steps harder on the accelerator and speeds off in the direction of Chicago.

Figurative Comparisons

In his essay "La Caméra-Stylo," Alexandre Astruc observed that one of the traditional problems of film has been its difficulty in expressing thought and ideas. The invention of sound, of course, was an enormous advantage to filmmakers, for with spoken language they could express virtually any kind of abstract thought. But film directors also wanted to explore the possibilities of the image as a conveyor of abstract ideas. Even before the sound era, filmmakers had devised a number of nonverbal figurative techniques.

A figurative technique can be defined as an artistic device that suggests abstract ideas through comparison, either implied or overt. There are a number of these techniques in both literature and cinema. The most common are **motifs,** **symbols,** and **metaphors.** In actual practice, there's a considerable amount of overlapping between these terms. All of them are "symbolic" in the sense that an object or event means something beyond its literal significance. Perhaps the

9-13. *Day for Night* **(France, 1973),** *with François Truffaut (leather jacket), directed by Truffaut.*

Film titles are chosen with great deliberation because they are meant to embody the central concept behind a movie. Film titles, in short, are symbolic. The original-language title of this film is *La Nuit Américaine,* "The American Night." It reflects Truffaut's great love for American culture, especially its cinema, and deals with the making of an "old-fashioned" kind of movie—the kind they made in Hollywood in the 1940s. (Truffaut even includes a tender homage to *Citizen Kane.*) "La nuit américaine" is also what the French call the day-for-night filter, which converts sunlit scenes into nighttime scenes. The filter transforms reality—makes it magical. For Truffaut, cinema is magic.   *(Warner Bros.)*

most pragmatic method of differentiating these techniques is their degree of obtrusiveness. Instead of locking each of these terms into an airtight compartment, however, we ought to view them as general demarcations, with motifs representing the least obtrusive extreme, metaphors representing the most conspicuous, and each category overlapping somewhat with its neighbor.

Motifs are so totally integrated within the realistic texture of a film that we can almost refer to them as submerged or invisible symbols. A motif can be a technique, an object, or anything that's systematically repeated in a movie yet doesn't call attention to itself. Even after repeated viewings, a motif is not always apparent, for its symbolic significance is never permitted to emerge or detach itself from its context (9-14).

Symbols can also be palpable things, but they imply additional meanings that are relatively apparent to the sensitive observer. Futhermore, the symbolic meanings of these things can shift with the dramatic context. A good example of the shifting implications of a symbol can be seen in the uncut version of Kurosawa's *The Seven Samurai* (9-15). In this movie, a young samurai and a

(a) (b)

9–14a & b. *Cries and Whispers* (Sweden, 1972), *with Liv Ullmann (a) and Kari Sylwan (b), written and directed by Ingmar Bergman.*
A recurrent motif in this movie is the human face split in two, suggesting self-division, the hidden self, the public versus the private self.   *(New World Pictures)*

peasant girl are attracted to each other, but their class differences present insur-mountable barriers. In a scene that takes place late at night, the two accidentally meet. Kurosawa emphasizes their separation by keeping them in separate **frames,** a raging outdoor fire acting as a kind of barrier (a and b). But their attraction is too strong, and they then appear in the same shot, the fire between them now suggesting the only obstacle, yet paradoxically, also suggesting the sexual passion they both feel (c). They draw toward each other, and the fire is now to one side, its sexual symbolism dominating (d). They go inside a hut, and the light from the fire outside emphasizes the eroticism of the scene (e). As they begin to make love in a dark corner of the hut, the shadows cast by the fire's light on the reeds of the hut seem to streak across their bodies (f). Suddenly, the girl's father discovers the lovers, and the billowing flames of the fire suggest his moral outrage (g). He is so incensed that he must be restrained by the samurai chief, both of them almost washed out visually by the intensity of the fire's light (h). It begins to rain, and the sorrowing young samurai walks away despondently (i). At the end of the sequence Kurosawa offers a close-up of the fire as the rain extinguishes its flames (j).

A *metaphor* is usually defined as a comparison of some kind that cannot be literally true. Two terms not ordinarily associated are yoked together, producing a sense of literal incongruity. "Poisonous time," "torn with grief," "devoured by love" are all verbal metaphors involving symbolic rather than literal descriptions. Editing is a frequent source of metaphors in film, for two shots can be linked together to produce a third, and symbolic, idea. This is the basis of Eisenstein's theory of montage. In *October,* for example, he satirized the fears and anxieties of an antirevolutionary politician by **intercutting** shots of a "heavenly choir" of harpists with shots of the politician delivering his cowardly speech. The row of pretty blonde harp players is brought in "from nowhere"; that is, they are certainly not found in the locale (a meeting hall), but are introduced solely for metaphoric purposes. Special-effects cinematography is also used to create metaphoric ideas. For example, through the use of the **optical printer,** two or more objects can be yoked together in the same frame to create ideas that have no literal existence in reality (9–16). Cinematic metaphors are always somewhat obtrusive; unlike motifs and most symbols, metaphors are less integrated contextually, less "realistic" in terms of our ordinary perceptions.

There are two other kinds of figurative techniques in film and literature: **allegory** and **allusions.** The first is seldom employed in movies since it tends toward simplemindedness. What's usually involved in this technique is a total avoidance of realism and probability. A one-to-one correspondence exists between a character or situation and a specific symbolic idea (9–17). One of the

9–15. *The Seven Samurai* **(Japan, 1954),** *directed by Akira Kurosawa.*
Realistic films tend to employ symbols less densely than formalist movies, and the symbolism is almost always contextually probable. For example, in addition to being a symbol, the fire in this scene is also a fire.   *(Toho International)*

(a)

(b)

(c)

(d)

(e)

(f)

(g)

(h)

(i)

(j)

most famous examples of allegory is the character of Death in Bergman's *The Seventh Seal*. Needless to say, there's not much ambiguity involved in what the character is supposed to symbolize. Allegorical narratives are especially popular in the German cinema. For example, virtually all the works of Werner Herzog deal with the idea of life in general, the nature of the human condition in broadly symbolic terms.

An *allusion* is a common type of literary analogy. It's an implied reference, usually to a well-known event, person, or work of art. The protagonist of Hawks's *Scarface* was modeled on the gangster Al Capone (who had a well-

9–16. *Psycho* **(U.S.A., 1960)**, *directed by Alfred Hitchcock.*
Cinematic metaphors can be created through the use of special effects, as in this dissolve which yields the final shot of the film—the dredging up of a car from a swamp. Three images are dissolved: (1) a shot of a catatonic youth (Anthony Perkins) looking directly at us; (2) a duplicate shot of his mother's skeleton, whose skull flickers briefly beneath her son's features and whose personality he has now assumed; and (3) a heavy chain which seems anchored to his/her heart, hauling up the murder victim's car which contains her corpse.   *(Paramount Pictures)*

9–17. *The Grand Highway* **(France, 1987)**, *with Vanessa Guedj and Antoine Hubert, directed by Jean-Loup Hubert.*
As its allegorical title suggests, this movie deals with the idea of life as a road. The story is told from the point of view of a young boy and his mischievous female friend (pictured), who view the world of adults as a pathetic but funny spectacle.

(Miramax Films)

(a)

9–18a. *A Hard Day's Night* (Great Britain, 1964), *with The Beatles, directed by Richard Lester.* *(Universal City Studios)*

9–18b. *Love, Loot and Crash* (U.S.A., 1915), *with the Keystone Kops, directed by Mack Sennett.* *(Museum of Modern Art)*

The police chase scene in the Beatles classic is an allusion—and an affectionate homage—to Mack Sennett's anarchistic Keystone Kops chases, which were usually shot in fast motion.

(b)

publicized scar in the shape of a cross on his cheek), an allusion that wasn't lost on audiences of the time. Filmmakers often draw on religious mythology for their allusions. For example, the Judeo-Christian myth of the Garden of Eden is used in such disparate works as *The Garden of the Finzi-Continis, Days of Heaven, How Green Was My Valley,* and *The Tree of the Wooden Clogs.*

In the cinema, an overt reference or allusion to another movie, director, or memorable shot is sometimes called a *homage.* The cinematic homage is a kind of quote, the director's graceful tribute to a colleague or established master. Homages were popularized by Godard and Truffaut, whose movies are profuse in such tributes. In Godard's *A Woman Is a Woman,* for example, two decidedly nonmusical characters burst out in spontaneous song and dance while expressing their desire to appear in an MGM musical by Gene Kelly, choreographed by Bob Fosse. Fosse's *All That Jazz* contains many homages to his idol Fellini, and especially to 8½. Steven Spielberg often pays tribute to his two idols, Walt Disney and Alfred Hitchcock.

Point of View

Point of view in fiction generally concerns the narrator, through whose eyes the events of a story are viewed. The ideas and incidents are sifted through the consciousness and language of the storyteller. He or she may or may not be a participant in the action, and may or may not be a reliable guide for the reader to follow. There are four basic types of point of view in literary fiction: (1) the first person, (2) the omniscient, (3) the third person, and (4) the objective. In movies, point of view tends to be less rigorous than in novels, for while there are cinematic equivalents of the four basic types of narration, fiction films tend to fall naturally into the omniscient form.

The **first-person narrator** tells his own story. In some cases, he is an objective observer who can be relied upon to relate the events accurately. Nick Carraway in Fitzgerald's *The Great Gatsby* is a good example of this kind of narrator. Other first-person narrators are subjectively involved in the main action and can't be totally relied upon. In *Huckleberry Finn,* the immature Huck relates all the events as he experienced them. Huck obviously can't supply his readers with all the necessary information when he himself does not possess it. In employing this type of first-person narrator, the novelist must somehow permit the reader to see the truth without violating the plausibility of the narrator. Generally, a novelist solves this problem by providing the reader with clues that permit him to see more clearly than the narrator himself. For example, when Huck enthusiastically recounts the glamor of a circus and the "amazing feats" of its performers, the more sophisticated reader sees beyond Huck's words and infers that the performers are in fact a rather shabby crew and their theatrical acts merely cheap deceptions.

Many films employ first-person narrative techniques, but only sporadically. The cinematic equivalent to the "voice" of the literary narrator is the "eye" of the camera, and this difference is an important one. In literature, the distinction between the narrator and the reader is clear: It's as if the reader were listening to a friend tell a story. In film, however, the viewer identifies with the lens, and

9—19. *Nashville* **(U.S.A., 1975),** *with Lily Tomlin and Robert Doqui, directed by Robert Altman.*

Throughout the 1970s, Altman revolutionized filmmaking with his improvisational techniques. Though the screenplay to *Nashville* is credited to Joan Tewkesbury, in fact she never wrote a conventional script. As she explained: "What you have to do for a director like Bob is to provide an environment in which he can work." For example, *Nashville* is structured mosaically, tracing the activities of twenty-four eccentric characters over a five-day period in the city of Nashville, the heart of the country-music industry. One wag referred to the film as "twenty-four characters in search of a movie." Tewkesbury created many of the characters in sketch form, then mapped out what each major character would be doing at any given time. Most of the dialogue and details for the actions were created by the actors. They even composed their own songs. "It's like jazz," Altman explained. "You're not planning any of this that you film. You're capturing." *(Paramount Pictures)*

thus tends to fuse with the narrator. To produce first-person narration in film, the camera would have to record all the action through the eyes of the character, which, in effect, would also make the viewer the protagonist.

In *The Lady of the Lake,* Robert Montgomery attempted to use the first-person camera throughout the film. It was an interesting experiment, but a failure, for several reasons. In the first place, the director was forced into a number of absurdities. Having the characters address the camera was not too much of a problem, for **point-of-view shots** are common in most movies. However, there were several actions where the device simply broke down. When a woman walked up to the hero and kissed him, for example, she had to slink toward the camera and begin to embrace it while her face came closer to the lens. Similarly, when the hero was involved in a fist fight, the antagonist literally had to attack the camera, which jarred appropriately whenever the "narrator" was dealt a blow. The problem with the exclusive use of the first-person camera, then, is its literalness. Futhermore, it tends to create a sense of frustration in the viewer, who wants to *see* the hero. In fiction, we get to know the person through his words, through his judgments and values, which are reflected in his language. But in movies, we get to know a character by seeing how he reacts to people and events. Unless the director breaks the first-person camera convention, we can never see the hero, we can only see what he sees.

The **omniscient point of view** is often associated with the nineteenth-century novel. Generally, such narrators are not participants in a story, but are all-knowing observers who supply the reader with all the facts he or she needs to know in order to appreciate the story. Such narrators can span many locations and time periods, and can enter the consciousness of a number of different characters, telling us what they think and feel. Omniscient narrators can be relatively detached from the story, as in *War and Peace,* or they can take on a distinct personality of their own, as in *Tom Jones* where the amiable storyteller amuses us with his wry observations and judgments.

Omniscient narration is almost inevitable in film. Each time the director moves the camera—either within a shot or between shots—we are offered a new point-of-view from which to evaluate the scene. The filmmaker can cut easily from a subjective point-of-view shot (first person) to a variety of objective shots. He can concentrate on a single reaction (close-up) or the simultaneous reactions of several characters **(long shot).** Within a matter of seconds, the film director can show us a cause and an effect, an action and a reaction. He can connect various time periods and locations almost instantaneously (parallel editing), or literally superimpose different times periods (dissolve or **multiple exposure**). The omniscient camera can be a dispassionate observer, as it is in many of Chaplin's films, or it can be a witty commentator—an evaluater of events— as it often is in Hitchcock's films or those of Lubitsch.

9–20. *Ragtime* (U.S.A., 1981), *with James Cagney, directed by Milos Forman.* Much is usually eliminated from a novel as complex as E. L. Doctorow's *Ragtime,* but much is also added. The novelist can focus only on a few details at a time in a linear sequence. Movies can bombard us with hundreds of details simultaneously, as Leo Braudy has pointed out: "The muted emphasis on gesture, makeup, intonation, and bodily movement possible in film can enrich a character with details that would intrude blatantly if they were separately verbalized in a novel." *(Paramount Pictures)*

9–21. *Lolita* **(U.S.A./Great Britain, 1962),** *with Peter Sellers and James Mason, based on the novel by Vladimir Nabokov, directed by Stanley Kubrick.*
Novelists and dramatists are not always dismayed when filmmakers drastically alter an original property. Nabokov wrote the first draft of this screenplay, but it was much too long. Kubrick and his producer James B. Harris rewrote it extensively, preserving about 20 percent of the original. Nonetheless, Nabokov considered it a first-rate film with magnificent actors, and he called Kubrick "a great director." See Vladimir Nabokov, *Lolita: A Screenplay* (New York: McGraw-Hill, 1974), which includes many scenes that were cut from the film version. *(MGM)*

In the third person, a nonparticipating narrator tells a story from the consciousness of a single character. In some novels, this narrator completely penetrates the mind of a character; in others, there is virtually no penetration. In Jane Austen's *Pride and Prejudice,* for example, we learn what Elizabeth Bennett thinks and feels about events, but we're never permitted to enter the consciousness of the other characters. We can only guess what they feel through Elizabeth's interpretations—which are often inaccurate. Her interpretations are not offered directly to the reader as in the first person, but through the intermediacy of the narrator, who tells us her responses.

In movies, there is a rough equivalent to the third person, but it's not so rigorous as in literature. Usually, third-person narration is found in documentaries where an anonymous commentator tells us about the background of a central character. In Sidney Meyer's *The Quiet One,* for example, the visuals dramatize certain traumatic events in the life of an impoverished youngster, Donald. On the sound track, James Agee's commentary tells us some of the reasons why Donald behaves as he does, how he feels about his parents, his peers, and his teachers.

The *objective point of view* is also a variation of the omniscient. Objective

9–22. *The Unbearable Lightness of Being* (U.S.A., 1988), *with Daniel Day Lewis and Lena Olin, directed by Philip Kaufman.*

This movie is an adaptation of the celebrated novel of ideas by the Czechoslovakian intellectual-in-exile, Milan Kundera. The screenplay was written by Kaufman and Jean-Claude Carriere. Something was lost in translation. The novel is told from the point of view of an ironic and witty third-person narrator. He is really the most important "character" in the book. There is no equivalent for him in the movie, which has no voice-over narration. Kundera is a bitter foe of the Communist regime that controls his country with an iron fist: "Anyone who thinks that the Communist regimes of Central Europe are exclusively the work of criminals is overlooking a basic truth: the criminal regimes were made not by criminals but by enthusiasts convinced they had discovered the only road to paradise. They defended that road so valiantly that they were forced to execute many people." Much of this bitter wit is lost in the movie. On the other hand, the film is superior to the book in some respects. The sexual scenes in the movie are a lot sexier and specific than those in the novel, where sex is treated as an abstract idea, as a symbol. *(The Saul Zaentz Company)*

narration is the most detached of all: It doesn't enter the consciousness of any character, but merely reports events from the outside. Indeed, this voice has been likened to a camera in that it records events impartially. It presents facts and allows readers to interpret for themselves. The objective voice is more congenial to film than to literature, for movies literally do use a camera. The cinematic objective point of view is generally used by realistic directors who keep their camera at long shot and avoid all distortions or "commentary" such as **angles,** lenses, and **filters.**

Literary Adaptations

A great many movies are adaptations of literary sources. In some respects, adapting a novel or play requires more skill and originality than working with an original screenplay. Futhermore, the better the literary work, the more difficult the adaptation. For this reason, many film adaptations are based on mediocre sources, for few people will get upset at the modifications required in film if the source itself isn't of the highest caliber. There are many adaptations that are superior to their originals: *The Birth of a Nation,* for instance, was based on Thomas Dixon's trashy novel *The Klansman,* which is more blatantly racist than the film. Some commentators believe that if a work of art has reached its fullest artistic expression in one form, an adaptation will inevitably be inferior. According to this argument, no film adaptation of *Pride and Prejudice* could equal the original, nor could any novel hope to capture the richness of *Persona,* or even *Citizen Kane* which is a rather literary movie. There's a good deal of sense in this view, for we've seen how literature and film tend to solve problems differently, how the true content of each medium is organically governed by its forms.

The real problem of the adapter is not how to reproduce the *content* of a literary work (an impossibility), but how close he or she should remain to the raw data of the *subject matter,* in the sense that these terms have been used throughout this book. This degree of fidelity is what determines the three types of adaptations: the **loose,** the **faithful,** and the **literal.** Of course these classifications are for convenience only, for in actual practice most movies fall somewhere in between.

The *loose adaptation* is barely that. Generally, only an idea, a situation, or a character is taken from a literary source, then developed independently. Loose film adaptations can be likened to Shakespeare's treatment of a story from Plutarch or Bandello, or to the plays of ancient Greek dramatists, who often drew upon a common mythology. A film that falls into this class is Kurosawa's *Ran,* which transforms Shakespeare's *King Lear* into a quite different tale set in medieval Japan, though the filmmaker retains several plot elements from Shakespeare's original (see also 9–24).

Faithful adaptations, as the phrase implies, attempt to re-create the literary

9–23. *Cabaret* **(U.S.A., 1972),** *with Liza Minnelli, choreographed and directed by Bob Fosse.*

Some stories have been adapted in so many mediums the artistic permutations seem almost incestuous. Christopher Isherwood first created the main characters and corrupt milieu of the early Nazi period in his collection of short stories, *Goodbye to Berlin.* Some of the materials of these stories were adapted by John Van Druten in a play *I Am a Camera* which itself was adapted into a nonmusical film of the same title. Some years later, these materials were adapted into a stage musical entitled *Cabaret.* Fosse's musical film, adapted by Jay Allen and Hugh Wheeler, used much of the stage music, but also incorporated a good deal of the original Isherwood material. *(Allied Artists)*

9–24. *Throne of Blood* (**Japan, 1957**), *based on Shakespeare's* **Macbeth,** *directed by Akira Kurosawa.*

The loose adaptation takes a few general ideas from an original source, then develops them independently. Many commentators consider Kurosawa's film the greatest of all Shakespearean adaptations precisely because the filmmaker doesn't attempt to compete with *Macbeth*. Kurosawa's samurai movie is a *cinematic* masterpiece, these commentators claim, owing relatively little to language for its power. Its similarities to Shakespeare's literary masterpiece are superficial, just as the play's similarities to Holingshed's *Chronicles* (Shakespeare's primary source) are of no great artistic significance.   *(Audio-Brandon Films)*

source in filmic terms, keeping as close to the spirit of the original as possible (9–25). André Bazin likened the faithful adapter to a translator who tries to find equivalents to the original. Of course, Bazin realized that fundamental differences exist between the two mediums: The translator's problem in converting the word "road" to "*strada*" or "*strasse*" is not so acute as a filmmaker's problem in transforming the word into a picture. An example of a faithful adaptation is Richardson's *Tom Jones*. John Osborne's screenplay preserves much of the novel's plot structure, its major events, and most of the important characters. Even the witty omniscient narrator is retained. But the film is not merely an illustration of the novel. In the first place, Fielding's book is too packed with incidents for a film adaptation. The many inn scenes, for example, are reduced to a central episode: the Upton Inn sequence. Two minor aspects of the novel are enlarged in the movie: the famous eating scene between Tom and Mrs. Waters and the fox-hunting episode. These sequences are included because two of Fielding's favorite sources of metaphors throughout the novel are drawn from eating and hunting. In effect, Osborne uses these scattered metaphors as raw material, or filmic "equivalents," in Bazin's sense.

Literal adaptations are pretty much restricted to plays. As we have seen,

9–25. ***The Man Who Would Be King*** (U.S.A., 1976), *with (right to left) Sean Connery and Michael Caine, written by John Huston and Gladys Hill, based on a story by Rudyard Kipling, directed by Huston.*

Virtually all of Huston's works are based on novels, plays, and short stories. James Agee noted that the better the original material, the better Huston functions as an artist. His adaptations have encompassed such disparate authors as Dashiell Hammett, B. Traven, Stephen Crane, Herman Melville, Arthur Miller, Tennessee Williams, Carson McCullers, Flannery O'Connor, James Joyce, and the writers of the Book of Genesis. "I don't seek to interpret, to put my own stamp on the material," Huston pointed out. "I try to be as faithful to the original material as I can." *(Allied Artists)*

the two basic modes of drama—action and dialogue—are also found in films. The major problem with stage adaptations is in the handling of space and time rather than language. If the film adapter were to leave the camera at long shot and restrict the editing to scene shifts only, the result would be similar to the original. But we've seen that few filmmakers would be willing merely to record a play, nor indeed should they, for in doing so they would lose much of the excitement of the original and contribute none of the advantages of the adapting medium, particularly its greater freedom in treating space and time.

Movies can add many dimensions to a play, especially through the use of close-ups and edited juxtapositions. Since these techniques aren't found in the theater, even "literal" adaptations are not strictly literal; they're simply more subtle in their modifications. Stage dialogue is often retained in film adaptations, but its effect is different on the audience. In the live theater, the meaning of the

9–26. *The Glass Menagerie* (**U.S.A.,** **1987**)*, with Joanne Woodward and John Malkovich, based on the play by Tennessee Williams, directed by Paul Newman.*
Virtually all literary adaptations were originally stage plays, for the language and actions of the live theater are cinematically convertible. The most significant changes in a literal adaptation of a play are more likely to involve differences in space rather than language. *(Cineplex Odeon Films)*

language is determined by the fact that the characters are on the same stage at the same time, reacting to the same words (9-26). In a movie, time and space are fragmented by the individual shots. Futhermore, since even a literary film is primarily visual and only secondarily verbal, nearly all the dialogue is modified by the images. The differences between loose, faithful, and literal adaptations, then, are essentially matters of degree. In each case, the cinematic form inevitably alters the content of the literary original.

FURTHER READING

BEJA, MORRIS, *Film and Literature* (New York: Longman, Inc., 1979). Theoretical emphasis.

BLUESTONE, GEORGE, *Novels into Film* (Baltimore, Md.: John Hopkins University Press, 1957). Classic study, with a valuable introductory essay.

BOYUM, JOY GOULD, *Double Exposure: Fiction into Film* (New York: New American Library, 1985). Analyses of eighteen literary adaptations by an intelligent critic.

BRANNIGAN, EDWARD R., *Point of View in the Cinema* (Amsterdam: Mouton Publishers, 1984). A theory of narration and subjectivity in classical cinema.

CORLISS, RICHARD, *The Hollywood Screenwriters* (New York: Avon Books, 1972). Encyclopedic coverage of many of the best screenwriters of the Hollywood studio era.

GOLDMAN, WILLIAM, *Adventures in the Screen Trade* (New York: Warner Books, 1983). Personal account by a respected Hollywood screenwriter.

GRANT, BARRY KEITH, ED., *Film Genre Reader* (Austin: University of Texas Press, 1986). A collection of scholarly essays.

LUHR, WILLIAM, and PETER LEHMAN, *Authorship and Narrative in the Cinema* (New York: Oxford University Press, 1977). Scholarly study.

McCONNELL, FRANK, *Storytelling and Mythmaking* (New York: Oxford University Press, 1979). Theoretical emphasis.

WILSON, GEORGE M., *Narration in Light: Studies in Cinematic Point of View* (Baltimore, Md., and London: Johns Hopkins University Press, 1986). Theoretical emphasis.

THEORY | 10

Surely there are no hard and fast rules: It all depends on how it's done.

—PAULINE KAEL

Most theories of film are concerned with the wider context of the medium—its social, political, and philosophical implications. Theorists have also explored the essential nature of cinema—what differentiates it from other art forms, what its basic properties are. For the most part, film theory has been dominated by Europeans, especially the French. The tradition of criticism in the United States has been less theoretical and more pragmatic in its thrust. In recent times, however, American movie critics have shown a greater interest in the theoretical implications of the medium, though the bias in favor of practical criticism remains strong. A theory is an intellectual grid, a set of aesthetic generalizations, not eternal verities. Some theories are more useful than others in understanding specific movies. No single theory can explain them all. For this reason, recent

10–1. *The Maltese Falcon* (**U.S.A., 1941**), *with Humphrey Bogart, Peter Lorre, Mary Astor, and Sydney Greenstreet; directed by John Huston.*
Theory is the handmaiden of art, not vice versa. Movies can be explored from a variety of theoretical perspectives, each with its own set of values and parameters of inquiry. One's theoretical orientation will depend in large part on what one is looking for. For example, *The Maltese Falcon* can be placed in at least seven theoretical contexts: (1) An auteur critic would regard it as a typical Huston film. (2) It could also be analyzed as a Bogart vehicle, exploiting and expanding the star's iconography. (3) An industry historian would place the picture within its commercial context—as a superior example of the Warner Brothers product of this era. (4) A genre theorist would be interested in it as a classic example of the detective thriller, and one of the first of the so-called deadly female pictures that were so popular in the United States during World War II. (5) A theorist interested in the relationship of movies to literature might focus on Huston's script, based on Dashiell Hammet's celebrated novel of the same title. (6) A stylistic critic would analyze the picture within the context of film noir, an important style in the American cinema of the 1940s. (7) A Marxist might interpret the movie as a parable on greed, an implicit condemnation of the vices of capitalism. Each theoretical grid charts a different cinematic topography.   (*Warner Bros.*)

developments in the field have stressed an eclectic approach, synthesizing a variety of theoretical strategies (10–1).

Traditionally, theorists have focused their attention on three areas of inquiry: (**1**) the work of art, (**2**) the artist, and (**3**) the audience. Those who have stressed the work of art have explored the inner dynamics of movies—how they communicate, the language systems they employ. Film theorists can be divided into **realists** and **formalists**, just as filmmakers tend to favor one style or the other. The most important artist-oriented approach is the **auteur theory**, the belief that a movie is best understood by focusing on its artistic creator, the director. **Marxist** theories are prominent in Europe, the Third World, and of course the communist bloc countries. Marxists can also be divided into realists and formalists, although both are strongly oriented toward issues of ideology. Marxist theorists have been in the forefront in exploring how social context and the means of production can affect meaning in cinema. Structuralism and semiology were the dominant theories after 1970, and both tend to emphasize a synthetic approach, combining such concerns as **genre**, authorship, style, **iconography**, social context, and ideology. In the area of historiography—the theoretical assumptions underlying film history—recent trends have also emphasized an integrated approach.

Theories of Realism

Most theories of realism emphasize the documentary aspects of film art. Movies are evaluated primarily in terms of how accurately they reflect external reality. The camera is regarded as essentially a recording mechanism rather than an expressive medium in its own right. The subject matter is paramount in the cinema of realism, technique its discreetly transparent handmaiden. As we have seen in the case of André Bazin (Chapter 4), most theories of realism have a moral and ethical bias and are often rooted in the values of Christian and Marxist humanism.

Realist theorists like Cesare Zavattini and Siegfried Kracauer believe that cinema is essentially an extension of photography and shares with it a pronounced affinity for recording the visible world around us. Unlike other art forms, photography and cinema tend to leave the raw materials of reality more or less intact. There is a minimum of interference and manipulation on the artist's part, for film is not an art of invention so much as an art of "being there."

Roberto Rossellini's *Open City* (10–3) inaugurated the Italian neorealist movement, one of the triumphs of the cinema of realism. The movie deals with the collaboration of Catholics and Communists in fighting the Nazi occupation of Rome shortly before the American army liberated the city. Technically, the film is rather crude. Since good quality film stock was impossible to obtain, Rossellini had to use inferior newsreel stock. Nevertheless, the technical flaws and the resultant grainy images convey a sense of journalistic immediacy and authenticity. (Many neorealists began their careers as journalists, and Rossellini himself began as a documentarist.) Virtually all the movie was shot at actual locations, and there are many exterior shots in which no additional lights were used. With

10–2. *Reds* **(U.S.A., 1981),** *cinematography by Giuseppe Rotunno, directed by Warren Beatty.*

Realism is generally characterized by a plain style that doesn't call attention to itself. However, this stylistic austerity is by no means universal. For example, Beatty's movie contains many outbursts of visual lyricism to emphasize the intense emotions of the characters and their involvement in the 1917 Russian Revolution. This poetic, backlit shot produces a radiant sunburst effect, throwing the foreground materials into silhouette. *(Paramount Pictures)*

the exception of the principal players, the actors were nonprofessionals. The structure of the movie is episodic—a series of vignettes showing the reactions of Roman citizens to the German occupation.

Open City is saturated with a sense of unrelenting honesty. "This is the way things are," Rossellini is said to have declared after the film premiered. The statement became the motto of the neorealist movement. The film provided a rallying point for an entire generation of Italian filmmakers whose creative talents had been stifled by the repressive Fascist regime of the prewar era. Within the next few years, there followed an astonishing series of movies that catapulted the Italians into the front ranks of the international cinema. The major filmmakers of the movement were Rossellini, Luchino Visconti, and Vittorio De Sica and his frequent scriptwriter Cesare Zavattini.

There are considerable differences between these men and even between their early and later works. Furthermore, neorealism implied a style as well as an ideology. Rossellini emphasized the ethical dimension: "For me, Neorealism is above all a moral position from which to look at the world. It then became an aesthetic position, but at the beginning it was moral." De Sica, Zavattini, and Visconti also stressed morality as the touchstone of neorealism.

The main ideological characteristics of the movement can be summarized as follows: **(1)** a new democratic spirit, with emphasis on the value of ordinary people like laborers, peasants, and factory workers; **(2)** a compassionate point of view and a refusal to make facile moral judgments; **(3)** a preoccupation with Italy's Fascist past and its aftermath of wartime devastation, poverty, unemployment, prostitution, and the black market; **(4)** a blending of Christian and Marxist humanism; and **(5)** an emphasis on emotions rather than abstract ideas.

The stylistic features of neorealism include: **(1)** an avoidance of neatly plotted stories in favor of loose, episodic structures that evolve organically from the situations of the characters; **(2)** a documentary visual style; **(3)** the use of actual locations—usually exteriors—rather than studio sets; **(4)** the use of nonprofessional actors, sometimes even for principal roles; **(5)** an avoidance of literary dialogue in favor of conversational speech, including dialects; and **(6)** an avoidance of artifice in the **editing**, camerawork, and lighting in favor of a simple "styleless" style.

10–3. *Open City* **(Italy, 1945),** *with Marcello Pagliero, directed by Roberto Rossellini.*
The torture scenes of this famous Resistance film were so realistic that they were cut out of
some prints. In this episode, a Nazi S.S. officer applies a blowtorch to the body of a
communist partisan in an effort to force him to reveal the names of his comrades in the
underground. The crucifixion allusion is deliberate, even though the character is a nonbeliever. It parallels the death of another partisan, a Catholic priest, who is executed by a
military firing squad. The French critic André Bazin was a champion of Italian neorealism,
applauding its moral fervor even more than its technical restraint. "Is not neorealism primarily a kind of humanism, and only secondarily a style of filmmaking?" he asked.   (*Pathé
Contemporary Films*)

Realists have shown a persistent hostility toward plot and neatly structured
stories. For example, Cesare Zavattini more than any single individual defined the
ordinary and the everyday as the main business of the cinema. Spectacular events
and extraordinary characters should be avoided at all costs, he believed. He
claimed that his ideal movie would consist of ninety consecutive minutes from a
person's actual life. There should be no barriers between reality and the spectator,
no directorial virtuosity to "deform" the integrity of life as it is. The artistry should
be invisible, the materials "found" rather than shaped or manipulated.

Suspicious of conventional plot structures, Zavattini dismissed them as
dead formulas. He insisted on the dramatic superiority of life as it is experienced
by ordinary people. Filmmakers should be concerned with the "excavation" of
reality. Instead of plots, they should emphasize facts and all their "echoes and
reverberations." According to Zavattini, filmmaking is not a matter of "inventing fables" that are superimposed over the factual materials of life, but of search-

10–4. *The Tree of the Wooden Clogs* (Italy, 1978), *directed by Ermanno Olmi.*
As a movement, Italian neorealism was pretty much over by the mid-1950s, but as a style
and an attitude toward reality, its influence spread to many other countries. A number of
present-day Italian filmmakers have continued in the tradition of neorealism. For example,
Olmi's movies are steeped in the values of Christian humanism. In this film, which was shot
on authentic locations with nonprofessional players, he celebrates the everyday lives of
several peasant families around 1900. For them, God is a living presence—a source of
guidance, hope, and solace. Their faith is childlike, trusting, like that of St. Francis of Assisi.
In a series of documentarylike vignettes, Olmi unfolds their gentle drama, extolling their
patience, their tough stoicism, their dignity. Above all, he exalts the sacredness of the human
spirit. For Olmi, they are the salt of the earth.   (*New Yorker Films*)

ing unrelentingly to uncover the dramatic implications of these facts. The purpose of the cinema is to explore the "dailiness" of events, to reveal certain details
that had always been there but had never been noticed.

In his book *Theory of Film: The Redemption of Physical Reality,* the
German-trained theorist Siegfried Kracauer also attacks plot as a natural enemy
of realism. According to Kracauer, the cinema is characterized by a number of
natural affinities. First of all, it tends to favor "unstaged reality"—that is, the
most appropriate subject matter gives the illusion of having been found rather
than arranged. Second, film tends to stress the random, the fortuitous. Kracauer
is fond of the phrase "nature caught in the act," meaning that film is best suited
to recording events and objects that might be overlooked in life. The realistic
cinema is a cinema of "found moments" and poignant revelations of humanity. A
third affinity that Kracauer notes is indeterminacy. The best movies suggest
endlessness. They imply a slice-of-life, a fragment of a larger reality rather than a
self-contained whole. By refusing to tie up all the loose ends at the conclusion of
the movie, the filmmaker can suggest the limitlessness of reality.

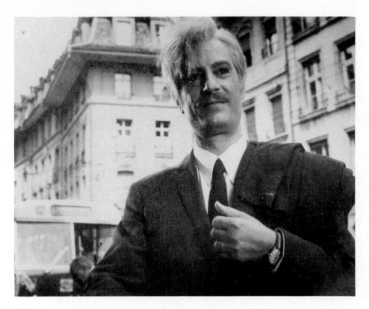

10–5. ***Bread and Chocolate*** **(Italy, 1978),** *with Nino Manfredi, directed by Franco Brusati.*
The Italian cinema has remained profoundly political. Indeed, probably no other country has produced a Marxist cinema of such commanding international prestige. In addition to Brusati, the Italian left (which encompasses over a half dozen parties) boasts such contemporary filmmakers as Bertolucci, Antonioni, Gillo Pontecorvo, Mario Monicelli, Elio Petri, Marco Bellocchio, Lina Wertmüller, Francesco Rosi, and Vittorio and Paolo Taviani.   (*World Northal Release*)

Kracauer is hostile toward movies that demonstrate a "formative tendency." Historical films and fantasies he regards as tending to move away from the basic concerns of the medium. He also dismisses most literary and dramatic adaptations because he believes that literature is ultimately concerned with "interior realities," what people are thinking and feeling, whereas movies explore surfaces, exterior reality. He regards all stylistic self-consciousness as "uncinematic," because instead of emphasizing the subject matter, the filmmaker calls attention to *how* it is presented.

Theories of film realism are not very helpful in understanding the complexities of formalist movies—the works of an Eisenstein or a Steven Spielberg. On the other hand, they do help to explain the raw emotional power of such masterpieces of realism as *Bicycle Thief,* which was directed by Vittorio De Sica and scripted primarily by Zavattini.

Bicycle Thief was acted entirely by nonprofessionals and consists of simple events in the life of a laborer (played by Lamberto Maggiorani, who was an actual factory worker). In 1948, when the film was released, nearly a quarter of the work force in Italy was unemployed. At the opening of the movie, we are introduced to the protagonist, a family man with a wife and two children to support. He has been out of work for two years. Finally, a billboard-posting job opens up, but in order to accept it, he must have a bicycle. To get his bike out of hock, he and his wife pawn their sheets and bedding. On his first day on the job, the bicycle is stolen. The rest of the movie deals with his attempts to recover the bike. The man's search grows increasingly more frantic as he crisscrosses the city with his idolizing son, Bruno. After a series of false leads, the two finally track down one of the thieves, but the protagonist is outwitted by him and humiliated in front of his boy.

10–6. *Ugetsu* **(Japan, 1953),** *with Masayuki Mori and Machiko Kyo, directed by Kenji Mizoguchi.*

Realistic critics and theorists tend to underestimate the flexibility of an audience's response to nonrealistic movies. To be sure, it's easier for a filmmaker to create the illusion of reality if the story deals with everyday events, for the world of the movie and the actual world are essentially the same. On the other hand, a gifted artist can make even fantasy materials "realistic." A movie like *Ugetsu*, which is set in the remote past and features spirits and demons, presents us with a self-contained magical universe which we are able to enter by temporarily forgetting the outside world of reality. In short, audiences are highly sophisticated in their responses to nonrealistic films. We can almost totally suspend our disbelief, partially suspend it, or alternate between extremes according to the aesthetic demands of the world of the movie. *(Janus Films)*

Realizing that he will lose his livelihood without a bike, the desperate man—after sending his son away—sneaks off and attempts to steal one himself. But the boy observes from a distance as his father peddles frantically to escape a pursuing mob. He is caught and again humiliated in front of a crowd—which includes his incredulous son. With the bitterness of betrayed innocence, the youngster suddenly realizes that his dad is not the heroic figure he had formerly thought, but an ordinary man who in desperation yielded to a degrading temptation. Like most neorealist films, *Bicycle Thief* doesn't offer a slick solution. There are no miraculous interventions in the final reel. The concluding scene shows the boy walking alongside his father in an anonymous crowd, both of them choking with shame and weeping silently. Almost imperceptibly, the boy's hand gropes for his father's as they walk homeward, their only comfort a mutual compassion.

10–7. *M*A*S*H* (U.S.A., 1969), *directed by Robert Altman.*

When art grows decadent, George Bernard Shaw observed, realism usually provides the cure. *M*A*S*H* is a military comedy, traditionally a stylized genre in which battle scenes, if any, are treated humorously. This movie contains no battle scenes, but we're always kept aware of the larger human stakes behind the comic chaos. For example, the surgical episodes are filled with blood, blasted limbs, and discarded corpses. Though ostensibly about the Korean War of the early 1950s, the film was photographed in a TV documentary style that reminded viewers of the Vietnam carnage unreeling each night on the evening news. (*Twentieth Century–Fox*)

Formalist Film Theories

Formalist film theorists believe that the art of cinema is possible precisely because a movie is unlike everyday reality. The filmmaker exploits the limitations of the medium—its two-dimensionality, its confining **frame**, its fragmented time–space continuum—to produce a world that resembles the real world only in a superficial sense. The real world is merely a repository of raw material that needs to be shaped and heightened in order to be effective as art. Film art doesn't consist of a reproduction of reality, but a translation of observed characteristics into the *forms* of the medium.

Rudolf Arnheim, a gestalt psychologist, put forth an important theory of cinematic formalism in his book *Film as Art,* which was originally published in German in 1933. Arnheim's book is primarily concerned with the perception of experience. His theory is based on the different modes of perception of the camera on the one hand, and the human eye on the other. Anticipating some of

10–8. *October* **(USSR, 1928),** *directed by Sergei Eisenstein.*
October, also known as *Ten Days That Shook the World,* was shot on location, yet the movie is also a triumph of formalism, particularly in its editing and mise en scène. Implicit in the concept of formalism is the supremacy of pattern over life. That is, even in films that attempt to preserve a surface realism, the volumes, weights, lines, textures, and lights are subtly coordinated within the frame to maximize their aesthetic appeal.   (*Museum of Modern Art*)

the theories of the communications specialist Marshall McLuhan, Arnheim insists that the camera's image of a bowl of fruit, for instance, is fundamentally different from our perception of the fruit bowl in actual life. Or, in McLuhan's terms, the information we receive in each instance is determined by the form of its content. Formalist theorists celebrate these differences, believing that what makes photography fall short of perfect reproduction is also what makes cinema an art, not just a species of xerography.

Formalists have pointed out many instances where divergences exist between the camera's image of reality and what the human eye sees. For example, film directors must choose which viewpoint to photograph a scene from. They don't necessarily choose the clearest view, for often this does not emphasize the major characteristics of the scene, its expressive essence. In life, we perceive objects in depth and can penetrate the space that surrounds most things. In movies, space is an illusion, for the screen has only two dimensions, permitting the director to manipulate objects and perspectives in the **mise en scène.** For example, important objects can be placed where they are most likely to be noticed first. Unimportant objects can be relegated to inferior positions, at the edges or rear of the image.

In real life, space and time are experienced as continuous phenomena.

10—9. *The Servant* (Great Britain, 1964), *with Dirk Bogarde (forward), directed by Joseph Losey.*

A scene can be photographed in literally hundreds of different ways, but the formalist selects the camera setup that best captures its symbolic or psychological implications. In this shot, for example, a young woman (Wendy Craig) suddenly realizes the enormous power a valet (Bogarde) wields over her weak fiancé (James Fox). She is isolated on the left, half-plunged in darkness. A curtained doorway separates her from her lover, who is so stupified with drugs he scarcely knows where he is, much less what's really going on. The servant cooly turns his back on them, the camera's low angle further emphasizing his effortless control over his "master." *(Landau Distributing)*

10—10. *Scarlet Street* (U.S.A., 1945), *with Edward G. Robinson, directed by Fritz Lang.*
Formalism is a concept that can be applied to a film's plot. Lang was a master of that much-maligned genre, the crime melodrama. He preferred this form because it allows a high degree of abstraction in the story, without having to make too many concessions in the name of realism. Like most of Lang's movies in this genre, *Scarlet Street* is divided into two sections, the second half paralleling the first. The tight, symmetrical story equation allows for no digressions, no spontaneous lyrical interludes. There are no accidents or extraneous details in this machinelike universe. Everything is relevant, especially apparent irrelevancies. The narrative structure is as inexorable as a mathematical proof. *(Universal Pictures)*

10–11. *Splash* (U.S.A., 1985), *with Tom Hanks and Daryl Hannah, directed by Ron Howard.*
A common misconception about formalistic films is that they are merely light entertainment, far removed from serious concerns. For example, this movie deals with a young man who falls in love with a strange young woman, who turns out to be a mermaid. The film is a symbolic fantasy, and it's certainly entertaining, but it also explores fundamental values—about loyalty, family, work, and commitment.
(Buena Vista)

Through editing, filmmakers can chop up space and time and rearrange them in a more meaningful manner. Like other artists, the film director selects certain expressive details from the chaotic plenitude of physical reality. By juxtaposing these space and time fragments, the filmmaker creates a continuity that doesn't exist in raw nature. This of course, was the basic position of the Soviet montage theorists (Chapter 4).

Formalists are always concerned with patterns, methods of restructuring reality into aesthetically appealing designs. Patterns can be expressed visually, through the photography and mise en scène; or aurally, in stylized dialogue, symbolic sound effects, and musical **motifs.** Camera movements are often kinetic patterns superimposed on the visual materials, commenting on them in some heightened manner.

The problems with most formalist theories are the same as with realists: There are too many exceptions. They are certainly useful in an appreciation of Hitchcock's works, for example, or Keaton's. But how helpful is the theory in explaining the films of Renoir or De Sica? We respond to their movies because of their similarities with physical reality, not their divergences from it. Ultimately, of course, these are matters of emphasis, for films are too pluralistic to be pigeonholed into one tidy theory.

The Auteur Theory

In the mid-1950s, the French journal *Cahiers du Cinéma* revolutionized film criticism with its concept of *la politique des auteurs.* This committed policy of authors was put forth by the pugnacious young critic François Truffaut. The

auteur theory became the focal point of a critical controversy that eventually spread to England and America. Before long, the theory became a militant rallying cry, particularly among younger critics, dominating such lively journals as *Movie* in Great Britain, *Film Culture* in America, and both French and English language editions of *Cahiers du Cinéma*. While there were a number of writers who rejected the theory as simplistic, auteurism dominated film criticism throughout the 1960s. The movement began as a defiant gesture of contempt toward the film establishment of the time.

Actually, the main lines of the theory aren't particularly outrageous, at least not in retrospect. Truffaut, Godard, and their critical colleagues proposed that the greatest movies are dominated by the personal vision of the director. A filmmaker's "signature" can be perceived through an examination of his or her total output, which is characterized by a unity of theme and style. The writer's contribution is less important than the director's, because subject matter is artistically neutral. It can be treated with brilliance or bare competence. Movies ought to be judged on the basis of *how*, not *what*. Like other formalists, the auteur critics claimed that what makes a good film is not the subject matter as such, but its stylistic treatment. The director dominates the treatment, provided he or she is a strong director, an *auteur*.

Drawing primarily from the cinematic traditions of the United States, the *Cahiers* critics also developed a sophisticated theory of film genre. Indeed, André Bazin, the editor of the journal, believed that the genius of the American cinema was its repository of ready-made forms: westerns, thrillers, musicals, action films, comedies, and so on. "The tradition of genres is a base of operations for creative freedom," Bazin pointed out. Genre is an enriching, not a constricting tradition. The auteurists argued that the best movies are **dialectical**, in which the conventions of a genre are held in aesthetic tension with the personality of the artist.

The American auteurs that these critics praised had worked within the studio system, which had broken the artistic pretensions of many lesser filmmakers. What the auteurists especially admired was how gifted directors could circumvent studio interference and even hackneyed scripts through their technical expertise. The subject matter of Hitchcock's thrillers or Ford's westerns was not significantly different from others working in these genres. Yet both auteurs managed to create great films, precisely because the real content was conveyed through the mise en scène, the editing, and all the other formal devices at the director's disposal.

The sheer breadth of their knowledge of film history permitted these critics to reevaluate the major works of a wide variety of directors. In many instances, they completely reversed previous critical judgments. Before long, personality cults developed around the most popular directors. On the whole, these were filmmakers who had been virtually ignored by the critical establishment of the previous generation: Hitchcock, Ford, Hawks, Lang, and many others. The auteur critics were often dogmatic in their dislikes as well as their likes. Bazin expressed alarm at their negativism. To praise a bad movie, he felt, was unfortunate; but to condemn a good one was a serious failing. He especially disliked their tendency to hero worship, which led to superficial a priori judgments. Movies by cult directors were indiscriminately praised while those by directors

10–12. Photo montage of Jean-Pierre Léaud as Antoine Doinel in (left to right) *Love on the Run* (1979), *Stolen Kisses* (1968), "Antoine et Colette" (an episode in the anthology film, *Love at Twenty,* 1962), and the drawing from *The 400 Blows* (1959). **Missing from the Doinel series is** *Bed and Board* **(1970).**
Above all, the auteurists emphasized the personality of the artist as the main criterion of value. François Truffaut, who originally formulated *la politique des auteurs,* went on to create some of the most distinctively personal movies of the New Wave. His Doinel series is one of the crowning achievements of the *nouvelle vague.* These semiautobiographical movies trace the adventures (mostly amorous) of its likable but slightly neurotic hero, Antoine Doinel. Truffaut's protégé Léaud was the best-known actor of the French New Wave.   (*New World Pictures*)

out of fashion were automatically comdemned. Auteurists were fond of ranking directors, and their listings could be bizarre. Perfectly routine commercial directors like Nicholas Ray were elevated above such important masters as John Huston and Billy Wilder.

The principal spokesman for the auteur theory in the United States was Andrew Sarris, the influential critic of the *Village Voice.* More knowledgeable about the complexities of the **star** and studio system than his French counterparts, Sarris nonetheless defended their basic argument, especially the principle of tension between an artist's personal vision and the genre assignments that these directors were given by their Hollywood bosses.

Quite correctly, these critics insisted that total artistic freedom isn't always a virtue. After all, Michelangelo, Dickens, and Shakespeare, among others, accepted commissioned subjects. Though this principle of dialectical tension is a sound one—in the other arts as well as cinema—some auteurists carried it to ridiculous extremes. In the first place, there is the problem of degree. It's doubtful that even a genius like Bergman or Kubrick could do much with the script and stars of *Abbott and Costello Meet the Mummy.* In other words, a director's got to

10–13. *Weekend* **(France, 1967),** *directed by Jean-Luc Godard.*
The New Wave filmmakers were extraordinarily eclectic, combining contradictory styles with casual nonchalance. This apocalyptic vision of contemporary life is strewn with violence, pessimism, and black comedy. Its technical virtuosity is breathtaking. Documentary scenes are juxtaposed with stylized tableaux, lengthy takes with shots that splatter the screen with machine-gun rapidity. Godard also includes interview scenes, enigmatic private obsessions, speeches directed at the camera, puns, wordplay, jokes, audacious traveling shots, abrupt jump-cuts, allegorical characters, and frequent reminders that the movie is a movie—and a weird one at that. *(Grove Press)*

have a fighting chance with the material. When the subject matter sinks beneath a certain potential, the result is not tension but artistic annihilation.

The most gifted American directors of the studio era were **producer–directors** who worked independently within the major studios. These tended to be the same artists the auteur critics admired most. But the lion's share of American fiction movies produced during this era were studio films. That is, the director functioned as a member of a team and usually had little to say about the scripting, casting, or editing. Many of these directors were skillful technicians, but they were essentially craftsmen rather than artists.

Michael Curtiz is a good example. For most of his career he was a contract director at Warner Brothers. Known for his speed and efficiency, Curtiz directed dozens of movies in a variety of styles and genres. He often took on several projects at the same time. Curtiz had no "personal vision" in the sense that the auteur theory defines it; he was just getting a job done. He often did it very well. Even so, movies like *Yankee Doodle Dandy* and *Casablanca* can be discussed more profitably as Warner Brothers movies rather than Michael Curtiz movies. The same principle applies to most of the other Hollywood studios. In our day, it applies to films that are controlled by producers and financiers.

Other films have been dominated by stars. Few people would think of referring to a Mae West movie as anything else, and the same holds true for the W.C. Fields comedies or the works of Laurel and Hardy. The ultimate in the star as auteur is the so-called star vehicle, a film specifically tailored to showcase the talents of a personality—but in front of the camera, not behind it (10–15).

The auteur theory suffers from a number of other weaknesses. There are some excellent films that have been made by directors who are otherwise mediocre. For example, Joseph H. Lewis's *Gun Crazy* is a superb movie, but it's atypical of his output. Conversely, great directors sometimes produce bombs.

10-14. *Entre Nous* **(France, 1983),** *with Isabelle Huppert and Miou Miou, directed by Diane Kurys.*

The legacy of the New Wave has allowed younger filmmakers like Diane Kurys to explore highly personal subjects. For example, this movie is based on an intimate friendship between her mother and best friend, a friendship that eventually destroyed her mother's shaky marriage.   *(United Artists)*

10-15. *Coming to America* **(U.S.A., 1988),** *with Eddie Murphy and Arsenio Hall, directed by John Landis.*

Murphy skyrocketed to stardom in television's seminal *Saturday Night Live* series. He repeated his spectacular success in movies. Like his other films, *Coming to America* was a huge popular success. It is a star vehicle, specifically tailored to showcase Murphy's comic talents. He is rarely off camera, and the plot is merely a pretext to allow him maximum creative freedom. The movie is competently directed, but the dominant artistic personality is clearly Murphy's.   *(Paramount Pictures)*

The works of such major filmmakers as Ford, Godard, Renoir, and Buñuel are radically inconsistent in terms of quality, and some of their movies are outright awful. The auteur theory emphasizes history and a director's total output, which tends to favor older directors at the expense of newcomers. Some artists have explored a variety of themes in many different styles and genres: Carol Reed, Sidney Lumet, and John Frankenheimer (10–16) are good examples. There are also some great filmmakers who are crude directorial technicians. For example, Chaplin and Herzog in no way approach the stylistic fluency of Michael Curtiz, or a dozen other contract directors of his era, yet there are very few artists who have created such distinctively personal movies as Chaplin and Herzog.

Despite its shortcomings and excesses, the auteur theory had a liberating effect on film criticism, establishing the director as the key figure at least in the art of cinema, if not always the industry. By the 1970s, the major battle had been won. Virtually all serious discussions of movies were at least partly couched in terms of the director's personal vision. To this day, the concept of directorial dominance remains firmly established, at least with films of high artistic merit.

10–16. *The Manchurian Candidate* **(U.S.A., 1962),** *with Angela Lansbury and Laurence Harvey, screenplay by George Alexrod, based on the novel by Richard Condon, directed by John Frankenheimer.* A weakness of the auteur theory is its tendency to gloss over the collaborative nature of the filmmaking enterprise. True, the director coordinates the contributions of others, modulating them into a unified whole. But some of these contributions are of major significance. For example, without slighting the brilliance of Frankenheimer's direction in this movie, much of its effect derives from the story and dialogue, not to speak of the fine cast. Frankenheimer has always insisted that cinema is a collaborative art. Furthermore, he has explored a variety of styles, genres, and themes. In short, he has no consistent "artistic signature"—a major concern of auteur critics. Frankenheimer has not been one of their favorites. (*United Artists*)

Marxist Film Theories

Most of the writings of Karl Marx concentrate on the evils of capitalism in nineteenth-century western Europe. He devoted surprisingly little space to the virtues of socialism, except to prophesy that it would produce a better, more humane society. When the leaders of the 1917 Russian revolution toppled the czarist regime, they had virtually no guidelines in the practical administration of

10–17. *Pixote* (Brazil, 1981), *with Fernando Ramos da Silva and Marilla Pera, directed by Hector Babenco.*

In the Third World, Marxism often fuses with nationalism. The ten-year-old protagonist of this movie is an orphaned vagabond. He is typical of millions of abandoned street urchins in a country where 50 percent of the population is under twenty-one years old, and 125 million people live in abject poverty. The Marxist strain in the Third World cinema can be summarized by the following characteristics: (1) The use of art as a tool for social change. (2) The belief that all art is at least implicitly ideological, affirming or challenging the status quo. (3) The assumption that capitalism and neocolonialism exploit the working class to further the interests of a small ruling class. (4) A demystification of power, demonstrating how it's actually wielded and whom it benefits. (5) An identification with oppressed groups such as women, children, outcasts, and racial minorities. (6) The belief that environment largely determines human behavior. (7) A rejection of religion and the supernatural in favor of a strict scientific materialism. (8) The need for a united front in combatting oppression, and the futility of individual rebellion. (9) A belief in the equal worth and potential of all human beings. (10) A dialectical view of history and knowledge, in which progress is the result of a conflict and ultimate synthesis of opposites. *(Unifilm/Embrafilme)*

a revolutionary government. Hence, they experimented. In the arts, there was a startling proliferation of activity, fervently revolutionary, innovative, and radical in style as well as substance. In movies, such filmmakers as Pudovkin, Eisenstein, and Vertov reaped a rich harvest in this permissive cultural climate.

In the early 1930s, however, all experimentation came to a halt and was replaced by Stalin's propagandistic theory of Socialist Realism, which became the official artistic style of the Soviet Union and later of the communist countries of eastern Europe. After Stalin's death in 1953, artists were gradually allowed more creative freedom, particularly in matters of style. In matters of ideology, they adhered closely to Marx's basic dictum: "The history of all human society, past and present, has been the history of class struggle."

Today, Marxism is by no means a monolithic theory. For example, Third-World Marxism differs considerably from the so-called armchair Marxism of the western European intelligentsia, which tends to be theoretical and oriented more toward analysis than action. It also differs from Soviet-style communism in that

10–18. *The Godfather, Part II* **(U.S.A., 1974),** *with Robert De Niro, directed by Francis Ford Coppola.*

A Marxist reading of a movie doesn't necessarily exclude other interpretations. Critic John Hess has argued that Coppola comes closer to a Marxist analysis of American society than any other Hollywood filmmaker: "The film's all-pervasive theme is the warmth, strength, and beauty of family ties which, in bourgeois society, alone appear to meet the desperate need we all feel for human community. The counter theme and the real strength of the film is its demonstration that the benefits of the family structure and the hope for community have been destroyed by capitalism." *(Paramount Pictures)*

the USSR and its client states are relatively prosperous societies with advanced technologies, and are ruled by entrenched bureaucracies that are controlled by a political elite. Third-World Marxism is more pragmatic and flexible. It is concerned less with ideological abstractions than with urgent social realities—poverty, ignorance, injustice. Their filmmakers strongly identify with the oppressed masses—which isn't just an empty phrase in the Third World. All Marxists believe that a given country's wealth and resources should be equitably shared, but they differ radically in how this ideal should be implemented.

Marxist film theories can be understood only within the wider context of the Marxist *Weltanschauung,* or world view. Marxism is a political, social, and philosophical system of ideas that forms the foundation of such widely differing societies as the Soviet Union, the People's Republic of China, the disparate nations of eastern Europe, and such isolated countries as Cuba and Nicaragua. Marxism has also exerted a cultural influence in western Europe and the underdeveloped countries of the Third World (10–17).

In the United States, its influence was strong during the 1930s, then faded after World War II, only to be revived in the late 1960s by the so-called New Left. With only a few exceptions, the influence of Marxism in the American cinema had been relatively weak—until this period of political unrest. A number of contemporary American filmmakers have strong leftist leanings, and Marxism also dominates such American film journals as *Jump Cut* and *Cinéaste.* Marxism is also prominent in many American university film programs.

In short, Marxism is a dynamic philosophy, altering significantly from year to year and from country to country. Thousands of volumes have been written on the varying interpretations of the basic ideas of Marx, Engels, and Lenin, not to speak of the modifications of such later figures as Stalin, Mao Tse-tung, and Gorbachev. Needless to say, only the barest outline of the Marxist Weltanschauung can be offered here.

Marxists believe that the fundamental basis of all human societies is economic. Those who control and consume the largest share of the material wealth form the ruling class. Marxists condemn capitalist and neocapitalist societies because the bulk of the material wealth is controlled by a small elite, insuring its ever-increasing wealth and power by its control—either direct or indirect—over the basic means of production. The actual producers of this wealth—the workers—must be content with a disproportionately small percentage of the economic pie. This leads to a diminished sense of power and self-determination.

In capitalist societies, workers are "alienated" from their work, their peers, and their society because they are forced to compete economically against each other rather than cooperating in a joint effort to build a better society for all citizens. "Private property is theft," Shaw claimed, and most of his fellow Marxists would agree. This is why virtually all the means of production in socialist nations are publicly owned and operated—in theory if not always in practice—in the public's best interests.

Marxists view history **dialectically**, and in objective materialist terms. Social structures and institutions are not mysteriously sanctioned by some cosmic outside force. They are built by *people,* who have selfish economic interests to preserve. Employing scientific and rational methods, the Marxist attempts to demystify ruling-class subterfuges, such as the concept of divine right, tradition,

10–19. ***Danton*** **(France/Poland), 1982),** *with Wojciech Pszoniak (standing, in velvet robes), directed by Andrzej Wajda.*

Most Marxist critics and theorists agree that one of the artist's main goals is the demystification of power. Who has the power and why? How does the ruling class maintain its control? What images do they use to portray themselves to the people being ruled? Wajda's movie deals with the French Revolution and the betrayal of its original egalitarian ideals during the Reign of Terror in 1793. The conflict between the democratic Danton, "the People's Friend," and the cold, authoritarian Robespierre (Pszoniak) was more than coincidentally analogous to the situation in Poland and the conflict between Solidarity leader Lech Walesa and the military regime that then ruled Poland autocratically. In order to dignify his power, Robespierre poses in classical Roman garb for Jacques-Louis David, formerly court painter to Louis XVI, presently engaged in painting a "revolutionary" canvas, which became one of the most famous depictions of the French Revolution. David's style emphasized larger-than-life heroic figures and superbly athletic bodies (such as that of the bored nude model waiting for instructions). It was a style for the gods—or those posing as gods.   *(Columbia Pictures)*

or social and religious fealty. Every human community has a structure of power, however much its rulers attempt to conceal it. Mysticism, religion, and all forms of philosophical idealism are dismissed as ploys to encourage workers to think in otherworldly terms rather than of their material needs in the here and now. Marxists believe an examination of history reveals that the interests of a ruling class are always challenged by a usurping class, producing a dialectical redistribution of wealth and power. Indeed, the optimism underlying Marxist theory is posited on the belief that history is evolving toward a classless society, in which wealth (and hence power) will be equally distributed.

10–20. *Yol* **(Turkey, 1981),** *with Tarik Akan (standing) and Şerif Sezer, directed by Yilmaz Güney and Şerif Goren.*
Güney directed this movie by proxy while he was serving an eighteen-year prison sentence for his revolutionary beliefs. Among the many forms of oppression he exposes in *Yol* (The Way) is the victimization of women: "The women I show in my films belong to the oppressed social classes," he pointed out. "But they suffer a second oppression since they belong to the oppressed sex. And through women we can show the contradictions, the ambiguity of men . . . in a multi-dimensional way—men who can be courageous, heroic, who can rebel, yet at the same time can be very reactionary towards their women." *(Columbia Pictures)*

Marxists analyze all human activity from this ideological perspective. Even those areas of life that aren't generally regarded as particularly political, like the arts, are evaluated in terms of material commodities, class, and power. Art is not politically neutral. It's produced by individuals for specific consumers. Implicit in all art, whether Marxist or not, is an acceptance or rejection of the social structure in which the art was produced. Marxist cultural critics never examine a work of art outside its ideological context, for the value and degree of truth (as they see it) of any artistic product will be determined by who produced it and for whom. Even "art for art's sake," or the denial of all but purely formal and aesthetic meanings in a work of art, is viewed as a political act—that is, as an implicit acceptance of the status quo.

Marxist critics are sensitive to the ideological implications of apparently neutral phenomena. Most of them are agreed that any dominant ideology in any society presents itself as the ideology of that society as a whole. This is especially true of classical cinema, as critic Daniel Dayan has pointed out: "Classical cin-

10–21. *Fox and His Friends* **(West Germany, 1975),** *with Rainer Werner Fassbinder (left) and Peter Chatel, directed by Fassbinder.*
Like his fellow Marxists, Godard, Bertolucci, and Wertmüller, Fassbinder often combined the themes of sex and politics. In this movie, Fassbinder—who was a militant homosexual—explored class conflicts within the gay subculture. It too has a ruling-class elite, and an underclass that's exploited sexually as well as economically. "It's incidental that the story happens among gays," Fassbinder pointed out. "It could have worked just as well in another milieu." *(New Yorker Films)*

ema is the ventriloquist of ideology," Dayan insists. "Who is ordering these images and for what purpose?" are questions classical filmmakers wish to avoid, for they want the representation to "speak for itself." Viewers absorb the ideological values without being aware of it. Marxists have also pointed out that the casting of a movie can be profoundly ideological. Players such as the right-wing John Wayne or the left-wing Jane Fonda embody political values that are intrinsic to a film's meaning. Language can be ideological (5–23), as can dialects (5–25). Sets, costumes, and furnishings can convey political ideas (7–25).

Even within the Marxist fold, filmmakers can be classified as formalists or realists. Formalists like Pudovkin, Eisenstein, and Vertov dominated the Soviet cinema in its golden age, the 1920s. In our own time, such Marxists as Godard and Bertolucci have pursued a formalist course in the capitalist democracies of the West. The essential argument of Marxist formalism is: A revolutionary society must have a revolutionary art—in *style* as well as subject matter.

After the despot Stalin solidified his position within the Soviet Communist

10–22. *The Organizer* (**Italy, 1963**), *with Marcello Mastroianni (wearing glasses), directed by Mario Monicelli.*

This movie embodies many of the ideals of the Marxist cinema of realism, including the concept of historicity: portraying historical events with scrupulous accuracy, in order to show present-day audiences how basic rights were once regarded as outrageous demands by the ruling class of a given era. The film also dramatizes the dangers of individual action, and the need for a united front. Mastroianni plays a bumbling but shrewd professor who advises a group of naive textile workers on strike strategies. Their awesome enterprise is a communal effort, not the work of a single individual. The original title, *I Compagni,* means The Comrades. When the movie was shown in America, its title was changed to *The Organizer,* suggesting a more individualistic, less democratic emphasis. *(Continental Distributing)*

Party, he put an end to many of these notions. Eisenstein and his more daring colleagues were accused of formalism, an effete preoccupation with technique at the expense of subject matter. Many artists were condemned for elitism, producing art accessible only to intellectuals and other artists, not to ordinary citizens. Such filmmakers were chastised for their excessive individualism, which was officially viewed as a bourgeois trait, out of keeping with the revolutionary ideals of collective action and collaboration between equals (10–22).

Realism is the dominant style in the communist bloc countries, but it is by no means universal. Furthermore, the best realist filmmakers are not crudely propagandistic. Indeed, most of the best Soviet films are rather neutral politically. In Poland and Hungary, a few movies even have been critical of the government for its lack of responsiveness and its corruptibility.

George Lukács, the Hungarian aesthetician, was one of the most persuasive—and enduring—apologists for the theory of realism. Although he was concerned primarily with the novel, his observations could also be applied to the cinema. Lukács expressed serious misgivings about socialist art, especially its psychological crudities. Unlike the hardline Stalinists, Lukács rejected outright the simple-minded notion that evil could be explained away by a character's ignorance of or refusal to accept Marxist ideology. Reality is far more complex, he argued, and realistic art should likewise be more complex.

If a conflict arises over ideological correctness and objective reality, the artist's first allegiance is to reality, for otherwise how are ideological errors of judgment and fact to be corrected for future generations? Like most realists, Lukács disliked any form of extremism as an end in itself, especially stylistic eccentricities. He believed that realism was the most comprehensive artistic style, the one closest to the copiousness of the observable physical world, and hence to the scientific materialist approach of Marxism. All great fiction is essentially realistic, he claimed, even the "progressive bourgeois realism" of the nineteenth century, which included Balzac, Tolstoy, and Chekhov. Lukács particularly admired how these artists portrayed their characters in a concrete social existence (10–25). "It is a condition of great realism that the artist must honestly

10–23. *Los Olvidados* **(Mexico, 1951),** *directed by Luis Buñuel.*
Buñuel's movies aren't admired by orthodox liberals, primarily because he refuses to sentimentalize the effects of poverty. The youthful protagonists of this film (which is also known as *The Young and the Damned*) are economically oppressed, trapped in an urban jungle where decency is a liability. Hence, they are vicious, cruel, and violent. That's what poverty does to people, Buñuel matter-of-factly points out. To remedy the situation, we need a revolution, not hypocritical clichés about the sanctity of the human spirit.   *(Audio-Brandon Films)*

record, without fear or favor, everything he sees around him." To accomplish this goal, the artist must be objective and self-effacing, those same characteristics that were praised by such cinematic realists as Bazin, Kracauer, and Zavattini.

The shortcomings of Marxist theories might be viewed as the vices of their virtues. Their intellectual rigor, their systematic methods of inquiry, and their seriousness of purpose are all admirable. But these virtues are not enough, and sometimes can actually obstruct the aesthetic impact of movies. The scientific jargon of Marxist criticism can be somewhat hard to take. Labels are sometimes substituted for honest analysis. Their "objective" formats of presentation are often turgid, impersonal, devoid of color and spontaneity. They can be pedantic to the point of scholasticism. Because of their materialist emphasis, Marxists scorn such "mystifications" as creativity, genius, and mystery, which they regard as "outmoded concepts." Even very gifted Marxists, like Walter Benjamin, dismissed these terms as "fascist"—which is arrant nonsense. Such critics confuse *taste*—whether personal or official—with absolute value. Marxists are also contemptuous of such seductive qualities as glamor and eroticism. They are notoriously insensitive to comedy, despite the fact that some of the best Marxist filmmakers—especially in Italy—are also comic artists.

10–24. *Siberiade* **(USSR, 1979),** *directed by Andre Konchalovsky.*
Konchalovsky has made movies in America as well as the Soviet Union and he believes that the artist's problems are similar in both countries: "It's the same in Russia and America. You pitch the story and try to sell it. In Hollywood you have to convince them it's commercial. In Russia you have to convince them it's ideological . . . . The system never has a face. It's faceless. It's stupid to be upset with a system. You just have to understand how it operates, what you are willing to give up in order to get something. You decide what you can sacrifice in order to get what you want. It's a very pragmatic thing. You're either in or out, and it's better to be in." *(IFEX Films)*

10–25. *The Grapes of Wrath* (U.S.A., 1940), *with Henry Fonda, Jane Darwell, and Dorris Bowdon; directed by John Ford.* Because it lacks revolutionary consciousness and scientific rigor, Ford's masterpiece would probably be regarded as "progressive bourgeois realism" by most Marxist critics. They value such works because the characters are placed in a concrete social (and by implication, political) milieu that is objectively and comprehensively portrayed.   (*Twentieth Century–Fox*)

A theory is only as good as its practitioner is sensitive. Applied mechanically, Marxism, like any other theory, can seem soulless. Marxist theory is weak in dealing with such matters as tone—that most elusive of aesthetic terms. For example, a crudely mechanistic Marxist analysis of Howard Hawks's *Bringing Up Baby* (6–10) would yield quite different conclusions than a common-sense approach. The movie deals with the desperate schemes of an idle society woman (Katharine Hepburn) in luring a dedicated scientist (Cary Grant) away from his work—to join her in amorous frolic. This is scarcely a goal that would be applauded by doctrinaire Marxists, who take a grim view of social irresponsibility. Furthermore, the apolitical Hawks was born rich, attended elite schools, and was conservative in his values. He also died richer than he was born. Armed with such knowledge, a plodding Marxist might logically conclude that *Bringing Up Baby* is a perfect example of the decadence of capitalist art. Such a conclusion would not win many converts, for it totally misses the film's tone, its antic air of silliness and fun. The charm of Hawks's screwball comedy is found precisely in its liberating spirit of irresponsibility. In short, Marxism—like any other theory—must be relevant to the *experience* of a movie. Otherwise, it's just another collection of mechanistic formulations and dogmatic pronouncements.

Eclectic and Synthetic Theories

Eclecticism isn't really a theory so much as a method of practical criticism. This is the favored approach of many film critics in the United States, such as *The New Yorker's* Pauline Kael, who once wrote: "I believe that we respond most and best to work in any art form (and to other experience as well) if we are pluralistic, flexible, relative in our judgments, if we are eclectic." Such critics place a movie in whatever context seems most appropriate, drawing from diverse sources, systems, and styles. Actually, almost all critics are eclectic to some degree. For example, while Andrew Sarris has been identified with the auteur theory, he is equally at home approaching a movie in terms of its star, its period, its national origin, or its ideological context.

Eclecticism is sometimes called the tradition of sensibility because a high value is placed on the aesthetic discriminations of a person of taste and discernment. Such critics are often urbane, well educated, and conversant in the other arts. The cultural cross-references in the writings of such critics as Roger Ebert and Stanley Kauffmann range over a wide spectrum, including literature, drama, politics, and the visual arts. They frequently allude to the ideas of such seminal thinkers as Freud, Marx, Darwin, and Jung. Sometimes critics combine an ideological perspective—such as feminism—with practical criticism, sociology, and history, as in the criticism of Molly Haskell and Julia Lesage (10–26). The best eclectic critics are gifted writers, including such distinguished prose stylists as James Agee and Pauline Kael. Polished writing is valued *as* writing, in addition to the ideas it conveys.

Eclectic critics reject the notion that a single theory can explain all movies. They regard this as a cookie-cutter approach to criticism. Most of them insist that an individual's reaction to a film is deeply personal. For this reason, the best a critic can do is explain his or her personal responses as forcefully as possible. But it's just an opinion, however well founded or gracefully argued. The best criticism of this type is informative even if we disagree with its conclusions. Because personal taste is the main determinant of value in eclectic criticism, these commentators often admit to their blind spots—and *all* critics have blind spots.

10–26. *Working Girls* (**U.S.A., 1988**), *with Louise Smith, directed by Lizzie Borden.*

Eclectic critics often combine movie criticism with social movements such as feminism, exploring not only the sexual values within a film, but the ideological context of its production. Traditionally, women have been excluded from positions of power within the American film industry. (The situation is even worse in most other countries.) Some, like Lizzie Borden, have circumvented this legacy of discrimination by producing their films independently. Most of the powerful women in the industry (Jane Fonda, Streisand, Goldie Hawn) reached the top by way of the star system, where sexism is economically unfeasible. *(Miramax Films)*

Everyone has had the experience of being left totally cold by a movie that's widely hailed as a masterpiece. We can't help the way we *feel,* however much our feelings go against popular sentiment. The eclectic critic almost always begins with his or her feelings about a movie, then works outward, trying to objectify these instincts with concrete arguments. To guard against personal eccentricity, they implicitly place a film within the context of a great tradition of masterpieces—that is, those works that have stood the test of time and are still considered milestones in the evolution of the cinema. This great tradition is constantly under reevaluation. It's a loose critical consensus rather than an iron-clad body of privileged works.

Eclecticism has been faulted on a number of counts. Because of its extreme subjectivity, this approach has been criticized as mere impressionism by more rigorously systematic theorists, who insist that aesthetic evaluations ought to be governed by a body of theoretical principles rather than a critic's unique sensibility, however refined. Eclectic critics are rarely in agreement because each of them is reacting to a movie according to his or her own tastes rather than a larger theoretical framework, with its built-in system of checks and balances. For all their vaunted expertise and cultural prestige, eclectic critics have track records that don't always bear close scrutiny. For example, when Fellini's *8½* was released in 1963, many serious critics in America and Europe dismissed the movie as self-indulgent, formless, and even incoherent. Yet in a 1972 survey of international critics, *8½* placed fourth in their list of the ten greatest films of all time. Conversely, even good critics have pronounced a film an instant masterpiece—only to regret their impetuosity in the cool distance of time, after the movie has been long forgotten.

Eclectic critics tend to be stoical about these matters, accepting them as perils of the trade. Perhaps Pauline Kael has expressed their attitude best:

> The role of the critic is to help people see what is in the work, what is in it that shouldn't be, what is not in it that could be. He is a good critic if he helps people understand more about the work than they could see for themselves; he is a great critic, if by his understanding and feeling for the work, by his passion, he can excite people so that they want to experience more of the art that is there, waiting to be seized. He is not necessarily a bad critic if he makes errors in judgment. (Infallible taste is inconceivable; what could it be measured against?) He is a bad critic if he does not awaken the curiosity, enlarge the interests and understanding of his audience. The art of the critic is to transmit his knowledge of and enthusiasm for art to others. (Quoted from *I Lost It at the Movies;* New York: Bantam, 1966)

Structuralism and Semiology

Kael and her fellow eclectics celebrate the subjective, individual element in film criticism. Others have lamented it. In the early 1970s, two interrelated cinematic theories developed, partly in response to the inadequacies of the criticism of personal sensibility. *Structuralism* and *semiology* were attempts to introduce a new scientific rigor to film criticism, to allow for more systematic and detailed

10–27. *Blonde Venus* **(U.S.A., 1932),** *with Marlene Dietrich, directed by Josef von Sternberg.* Semiologists believe that the shot—the traditional unit of construction in film—is too general and inclusive to be of much use in a systematic analysis of a movie. The symbolic sign, they argue, is a more precise unit of signification. Every cinematic shot consists of dozens of signifying codes that are hierarchically structured. Employing what they call the "principle of pertinence," semiologists decode cinematic discourse by first establishing what the dominant signs are, then analyzing the subsidiary codes. This methodology is similar to a detailed analysis of mise en scène, only in addition to spatial, textural, and photographic codes, semiologists would also explore other relevant signs—kinetic, linguistic, musical, rhythmic, etc. In this shot, a semiologist would explore the symbolic significance of such major signs as Dietrich's white suit. Why a masculine suit? Why white? What does the papier-mâché dragon signify? The distorted perspective lines of the set? The "shady ladies" behind the archways? The symbolism of stage and audience? The tight framing and closed form of the image? The protagonist's worldly song? Within the dramatic context, semiologists would also explore the rhythms of the editing and camera movements, the symbolism of the kinetic motions of the performer, and so on. Traditionally, critics likened the cinematic shot to a word, and a series of edited shots to a sequence of words in a sentence. A semiologist would dismiss such analogies as patently simple-minded. Perhaps an individual *sign* might be likened to a word, but the equivalent to a shot—even a banal one— would require many paragraphs if not pages of words. A complex shot can contain a hundred separate signs, each with its own precise symbolic significance. *(Paramount Pictures)*

(a)

10–28a. *McQ* **(U.S.A., 1974),** *with John Wayne and Diana Muldaur, directed by John Sturges.* (*Warner Bros.*)

10–28b. *The Bank* **(U.S.A., 1915),** *with Charles Chaplin, directed by Chaplin.* (*Museum of Modern Art*)

Semiology can help critics to isolate and identify signs in a movie, but not to show how skillfully they function within a work of art. Since the theory stresses quantification, it tends to be more effective in analyzing formalist films, which contain more classifiable signs. But different types of signs or codes are not compatible, and hence, qualitative judgments are difficult to make on strictly quantitative data. For example, the shot from *McQ* contains many different signs, which are structured into an image of great visual complexity. Chaplin's shot, on the other hand, is relatively simple, and contains few classifiable signs other than the expression on the tramp's face. Sturges is a director of considerable skill, but he's certainly not in Chaplin's class. Yet a semiological analysis of these two works might lead to the conclusion that Sturges is the better artist, because he uses more signs in his films.

(b)

analyses of movies. Borrowing their methodology from such diverse disciplines as linguistics, anthropology, psychology, and philosophy, these two theories concentrated on the development of a more precise analytical terminology.

Structuralism and semiology have also focused intently on the American cinema as the principal area of inquiry, for a number of reasons. In the first place, these theories have been dominated by the British and French, traditionally the most enthusiastic foreign admirers of the cinema of the United States. American movies also provided these critics with a stylistic norm—the **classical paradigm**. Marxists among this group have explored the implications of the capitalistic mode of production of American films. Cultural commentators have concentrated on characteristically American myths and genres.

Semiology (or *semiotics,* as it's also called) is a study of *how* movies signify. The manner in which information is signified is indissolubly linked with *what's* being signified. The French theorist Christian Metz was in the forefront in developing semiotics as a technique of film analysis. Using many of the concepts and much of the terminology of structural linguistics, Metz and others developed a theory of cinematic communication founded on the concept of signs or codes. The language of cinema, like all types of discourse, verbal and nonverbal, is primarily symbolic: It consists of a complex network of signs we instinctively decipher while experiencing a movie (10–27).

In most discussions of film, the **shot** was generally accepted as the basic unit of construction. Semiotic theorists rejected this unit as too vague and inclusive. They insisted on a more precise concept. Accordingly, they suggested that the sign be adopted as the minimal unit of signification. A single shot from a movie generally contains dozens of signs, forming an intricate hierarchy of counterpoised meanings. In a sense, this book, and especially the earlier chapters, can be viewed as a classification of signs, although necessarily more limited in scope than the type of identification and classification envisioned by Metz and other semiologists.

For example, each of these chapters is concerned with a kind of master code, which can be broken down into code subdivisions, which themselves can be reduced to even more minimal signs. Thus, Chapter 1 might be called a photography master code. This master could be broken down into subdivisions: shots, **angles**, lighting keys, colors, lenses, filters, optical effects, and so on. Each of these, in turn, could be subdivided again. The shots, for example, could be broken down to **extreme long, long, medium, close-up, extreme close-up, deep-focus.** This same principle could be applied to other master codes: spatial codes (mise en scène), kinetic codes (movement), and so on. Codes of language would be as complex as the entire discipline of linguistics; acting codes would involve a precise breakdown of the various techniques of signification used by players.

Semiotic techniques can be valuable in aiding film critics and scholars to analyze movies with more precision. But the theory suffers some defects. For one thing, these are descriptive classifications only, not normative. In other words, semiotics will permit a critic to discern a sign, but it's still up to the critic to evaluate how effective artistically any given sign is within an aesthetic context. Formalist movies seem to lend themselves to easier classification than realistic movies. For example, it's much simpler to describe the complex mise en scène of *McQ* than to explicate the meanings of Chaplin's expression in *The Bank* (10–

28).These signs aren't really comparable. They exist on incompatible levels, like different language systems of a computer. Since formalist signs are easier to quantify, some critics tend to value films with a greater number of signs (or at least a greater number of classifiable signs) as more complex than, and hence aesthetically superior to, a film with a lower density of signs.

Another serious problem with this theory is its awful jargon, which sometimes verges on self-parody. All specialized disciplines—including cinema—have a certain number of necessary technical terms, but semiotics often chokes on its own "scientific" wordiness. Even within the field, one commentator pointed out that referring to a perfectly ordinary phenomenon as "signifier" or "signified," "syntagm," or "paradigm" doesn't in itself advance social knowledge to any particular degree.

As Metz pointed out, semiology is concerned with the systematic classification of types of codes used in the cinema; structuralism is the study of how various codes function within a single structure, within one movie. Structuralism is strongly eclectic and often combines the techniques of semiotics with other theoretical perspectives, such as auteurism, genre studies, stylistic analyses, and so on. For example, Colin MacArthur's *Underworld USA* is a structuralist analysis of gangster and crime films and the style known as **film noir.** MacArthur uses

10–29. *Tender Mercies* **(U.S.A., 1983),** *with Robert Duvall and Allan Hubbard, directed by Bruce Beresford.*

A crucial shortcoming of semiotic methodology is its failure to deal with nonmaterialist *values* in cinema. For example, this movie explores how a drunken country music star (Duvall) finds spiritual redemption in the born-again Christian faith of the woman he loves. A strictly semiotic analysis of the film would prove inadequate in exploring these spiritual values.   *(Universal Pictures)*

semiotic classifications in exploring the iconography of the genre films of such artists as Billy Wilder (1–12) and others.

Structuralists and semiologists have been fascinated by the concept of a *deep structure*—an underlying network of symbolic meaning that is related to a movie's surface structure, but is also somewhat independent of it. This deep structure can be analyzed from a number of perspectives, including Freudian psychoanalysis, Marxist economics, Jungian concepts of the collective unconscious, and the theory of structural anthropology popularized by the Frenchman Claude Lévi-Strauss.

The methods of Lévi-Strauss are based on an examination of regional myths, which he believed express certain underlying structures of thought in codified form. These myths exist in variant forms and usually contain the same or similar binary structures—pairs of opposites. By collapsing the surface (narrative) structure of myths, their symbolic motifs can be analyzed in a more systematic and meaningful manner. These polarities are usually found in dialectical conflict: Depending on the culture analyzed, they can be agricultural (for example, water vs. drought), sexual (male vs. female), generational (youth vs. age), and so on. Because these myths are expressed in symbolic codes, often their full meanings are hidden even from their creators. Lévi-Strauss believed that once the full implications of a myth are understood, it's discarded as a cliché.

These structural techniques can be used to analyze a national cinema, a genre, or a specific movie. For example, the conflict between "traditional" and "modern" values can be seen in virtually all Japanese movies, and in Japanese society in general (10–30). The roots of this conflict extend back to the later nineteenth century, when Japan transformed itself from a feudal country to a modern technological society patterned after the Western industrial states, especially Great Britain and the United States. The Japanese are simultaneously repelled and attracted by both sets of polarities:

Traditional	Modern
Japanese	Western
Feudal	Democratic
Past	Future
Society	Individual
Hierarchy	Equality
Nature	Technology
Duty	Inclination
Self-sacrifice	Self-expression
Consensus	Diversity
Age	Youth
Authority	Autonomy
Conservative	Liberal
Fatalism	Optimism
Obedience	Independence
Form	Substance
Security	Anxiety

10–30. *An Autumn Afternoon* (**Japan, 1962),** *with Chishu Ryu (right), directed by Yasujiro Ozu.*

The films of Ozu were not widely seen in the West until the 1970s. Prior to this time, his movies were regarded as "too Japanese" to be appreciated by foreign audiences, because he was a champion of traditional values, particularly that quintessential Japanese institution, the family. If Kurosawa is the artistic spokesman for modern values and the anguished individual, then Ozu speaks for the conservative majority, especially parents. But his movies are not mindless endorsements of family life, for Ozu was also an ironist, well aware of the gap between reality and the ideal—the principal source of his irony. In this film, for example, the protagonist (Ryu) is a gentle, aging widower who lives with his unmarried daughter in mutual devotion. His loneliness is assuaged by a few drinking buddies who spend much of their free time at the local bar. After hearing of the marriage of a friend's daughter, the widower decides that it's time for his daughter to move on as well. He arranges a marriage with a decent young man recommended by his friends. The movie ends on a bittersweet note of irony as the father muses contentedly on the success of his arrangements. He also realizes that he's getting on in years. And that he is alone.   (*New Yorker Films*)

A number of structuralists have explored genre films in a similar manner. For example, Jim Kitses, Peter Wollen, and others have pointed out how westerns are often vehicles for exploring clashes of value between East and West in American culture. By clustering the thematic motifs around a "master antimony" (a controlling or dominant code), a western can be analyzed according to its deep structure rather than its plot, which is often conventionalized (and less meaningful) in genre films. Such critics have demonstrated how each cultural polarity symbolizes a complex of positive and negative traits:

West	East
Wilderness	Civilization
Individualism	Community
Self-interest	Social welfare
Freedom	Restriction
Anarchy	Law and order
Savagery	Refinement
Private honor	Institutional justice
Paganism	Christianity
Nature	Culture
Masculine	Feminine
Pragmatism	Idealism
Agrarian	Industrial
Purity	Corruption
Dynamic	Static
Future	Past
Experience	Knowledge
American	European

Semiotics and structuralism have expanded the parameters of film theory considerably. Their pluralistic approach allows for much more flexibility, complexity, and depth in the critical enterprise. But these theories are merely tools of analysis. By themselves, they can tell us nothing of the *value* of signs and codes within a film. Like every other theory, then, these are only as good as their practitioners. The writer's intelligence, taste, passion, knowledge, and sensitivity are what produce good criticism, not necessarily the theoretical methodology employed.

Historiography

Historiography deals with the theory of history—the assumptions, principles, and methodologies of historical study. Film history is a relatively recent area of inquiry—barely a hundred years is not a very lengthy period of study compared to that of the traditional arts. As in other areas of film theory, much of the best work in the field of film historiography has taken place during the past two decades.

Film historians scoff at the naive notion that there is *a* film history. Rather, they insist that there are many film histories, and each is defined by the historian's particular interests, biases, and prejudices. Theorists have chartered four different types of film history, each with its own set of philosophical assumptions, methods, and sources of evidence. These four are: (**1**) aesthetic film histories—film as art; (**2**) technological film histories—motion pictures as inventions and machines; **(3)** economic histories—film as industry; and **(4)** social histories—movies as a reflection of the audience's values, desires, and fears.

Most film historians regard cinema as too sprawling and complex to be covered by any single history. They view the field as a vast, infinite mass of data that needs to be sifted through and organized in order to be made coherent. Each historian concentrates on a given type of evidence, highlighting its significance while deemphasizing or ignoring "irrelevant" data. Critics sometimes refer to this process of selection and emphasis as **foregrounding**—isolating fragments of evidence for the purpose of closer study—which is always an implicit value judgment. Each type of film historian necessarily wrenches these fragments from their ecological context, thus presenting us with a somewhat skewed view of the whole. Each type of historian will also choose to focus on different movies, personalities, and events.

Aesthetic film historians concern themselves with a tradition of masterpieces and great filmmakers. Constantly subject to reevaluation, this tradition encompasses a broad consensus of critics, historians, and scholars. This is an elite form of history, ignoring the vast majority of motion pictures in order to concentrate on a relative handful of important works of art that have endured the test of time—that is, movies that are still great despite our viewing them in a

10–31. *Gone With the Wind* (U.S.A., 1939), *with Clark Gable and Vivien Leigh, directed by Victor Fleming.*
Aesthetic film histories tend to gloss over this film, which is not a great favorite among critics and scholars, though it is respected as popular entertainment. Economic and social film histories devote much more space in their discussions, for it is one of the most popular and commercially successful movies ever made, and as such, it commands their attention. Several books have been written about *Gone With the Wind,* but they focus on the film as a commercial product and as popular mythology rather than as a work of art. *(MGM)*

totally different context. Aesthetic historians value a work primarily for its artistic richness, irrespective of whether the film was commercially successful. Thus, in most aesthetic histories, a huge popular success like *Gone With the Wind* receives less discussion than *Citizen Kane,* which failed at the box office.

Most college textbook histories—such as Gerald Mast's *A Short History of the Movies,* David A. Cook's *A History of Narrative Film,* and *Flashback,* by Louis Giannetti and Scott Eyman—attempt to integrate as much as possible from technological, economic, and social film histories, but their main emphasis is on film as art. Opponents of this type of history have scoffed at its "Great Man" assumptions—that is, film history is largely the study of a few gifted individuals, not the dynamic matrix of social, industrial, and technological influences that inevitably affect all filmmakers, gifted or not.

The American scholar Raymond Fielding has put forth the philosophy of technological historians succinctly: "The history of motion pictures—as an art

10–32. *Medium Cool* **(U.S.A., 1969),** *with Robert Forster (at camera) and Peter Bonerz (sound), directed by Haskell Wexler.*
Technological film histories stress the importance of mechanical innovations in the evolution of the cinema. New technologies create new aesthetics. For example, in the late 1950s, television journalists needed simple, lightweight equipment in order to capture news stories quickly, while they were actually happening. The development of the so-called hand-held camera (actually, usually mounted on a shoulder harness or tripod), portable sound equipment, **zoom lenses,** and more light-sensitive **fast film stocks** was in response to this need. In the 1960s, this new technology was appropriated by fiction filmmakers, allowing them to shoot movies more spontaneously and in actual locations, and thus to create a more authentic style of realism.   (*Paramount Pictures*)

form, as a medium of communication, and as an industry— has been determined principally by technological innovations." Historians of this type are also concerned with "Great Men," such as W. K. L. Dickson, Thomas Edison, George Eastman, and Lee Deforest—inventors and scientists rather than artists or industry moguls. Technological historians are concerned with the implications—artistic, commercial, and ideological—of such innovations as portable cameras, **synchronous sound**, color, improved film stocks, 3-D, stereophonic sound, steadycams, and so on (10–32).

Cinema is the most expensive artistic medium in history, and its development has been largely determined by its financial sponsors—this is the thesis of most economic film histories, such as Benjamin B. Hampton's *History of the American Film Industry from Its Beginnings to 1931,* and Thomas H. Guback's *The International Film Industry: Western Europe and America Since 1945.* In most European countries the cinema in its early stages of development fell into the hands of artists who shared most of the values and tastes of the educated elite. In the Soviet Union and other communist countries, film production has been carefully regulated by the government, and the movies produced in these countries reflect most of the values of the political elite.

In America, the film industry developed within a capitalistic system of production. The Hollywood studio system was an attempt on the part of a handful of large corporations—MGM, Paramount, Warner Brothers, etc.—to monopolize the production of fiction films, and hence maximize their profits. For about three decades—roughly from 1925 to 1955—the major studios succeeded, producing about 90 percent of the fiction films in America, largely because the companies were **vertically integrated**. That is, they controlled all three phases of the industry: **(1)** production—the Hollywood studios; **(2)** distribution—financial headquarters in New York; and **(3)** exhibition—the large chains of big-city first-run theaters owned by the company.

During the era of studio dominance, virtually every filmmaker had to come to grips with this economic reality. The studio system was the only ballgame in town, and the **majors** were in business to make profits, the bigger the better. In short, the profit motive has been the main driving force in the evolution of the American film industry, and movies tend to reaffirm the ideological values of their sponsors. However, even economic historians would concede that other motives have also figured in the production of American movies—the desire for prestige, artistic integrity, and so on. Likewise, movies made in communist countries are occasionally critical of the social system that produced them. History—of any kind—is filled with contradictions.

Social histories are mainly concerned with the audience. They emphasize film as a collective experience, as a reflection of mass sentiments during any given era. These sentiments can be overtly articulated, or subliminally insinuated by appealing to our subconscious desires. Social historians often turn to statistics and sociological data for supporting evidence. Books like Robert Sklar's *Movie-Made America* and Garth Jowett's *Film: The Democratic Art* are filled with revealing statistics about audience likes and dislikes.

Social historians have also devoted a great deal of attention to the American star system, arguing that popular stars are usually a reflection of audience values and anxieties. Unfortunately, these concerns do not lend themselves to

10–33. *Broadway Danny Rose* (U.S.A., 1984), *with Woody Allen and Mia Farrow, written and directed by Allen.*
Economic film histories concentrate on who pays the bills, who sponsors the making of a movie and why. Like many prestigious European filmmakers, Allen is able to finance his movies without any strings attached. He enjoys total artistic control. His goal is not the amassing of huge profits, but creative independence. Most of his movies have been made on small budgets, with the same loyal crew of actors and technicians. This communal spirit has allowed them to produce about one movie a year. Though few of Allen's movies have been huge hits, they were sufficiently profitable to maintain a constant cash flow. *(Orion Pictures)*

quantitative analysis, and social historians are sometimes criticized for their intuitive leaps in logic. Historians of this sort are also interested in social stereotypes—how a movie portrays blacks, women, authority figures, and so on.

In *Film History: Theory and Practice*, Robert C. Allen and Douglas Gomery set forth the principal advantages and shortcomings of the various types of film history, arguing that a more integrated approach would minimize the dangers of distortion. Indeed, as in other areas of film theory, film history is increasingly being viewed as a monolithic ecological system that must be studied from various perspectives in order to be comprehensively understood.

FURTHER READING

ALLEN, ROBERT C., and DOUGLAS GOMERY, *Film History: Theory and Practice* (New York: Alfred A. Knopf, 1985). A provocative study of the problems of writing film history.

ANDREW, DUDLEY, *Concepts in Film Theory* (New York: Oxford University Press, 1984). A lucid exploration of the major areas of debate within the field.

———, *The Major Film Theories* (New York: Oxford University Press, 1976). A helpful and clearly written exposition of the theories of such figures as Arnheim, Eisenstein, Kracauer, Bazin, Metz, and others.

MACBEAN, JAMES ROY, *Film and Revolution* (Bloomington: Indiana University Press, 1975). Marxist approach, with major emphasis on Jean-Luc Godard.

MACCANN, RICHARD DYER, ed., *Film: A Montage of Theories* (New York: Dutton, 1966). A wide variety of theoretical documents.

MAST, GERALD, and MARSHALL COHEN, eds., *Film Theory and Criticism,* 3rd ed. (New York: Oxford University Press, 1985). An excellent collection of articles, from a variety of perspectives.

NICHOLS, BILL, *Ideology and the Image* (Bloomington: Indiana University Press, 1981). Social representation in the cinema and other media—a demystification.

OVERBEY, DAVID, ed., *Springtime in Italy: A Reader on Neorealism* (New York: Archon, 1979). Includes pieces by Moravia, Visconti, De Sica, Rossellini, and others.

SARRIS, ANDREW, *The American Cinema* (New York: Dutton, 1968). A basic document of the auteur theory.

TUDOR, ANDREW, *Theories of Film* (New York: Viking, 1974). Includes essays on Eisenstein, Grierson, Bazin, Kracauer, auteurism, and genre theory.

SYNTHESIS: Citizen Kane | 11

*The motion-picture medium has an extraordinary range of
expression. It has in common with the plastic arts the fact that it is
a visual composition projected on a two-dimensional surface;
with dance, that it can deal in the arrangement of movement;
with theatre, that it can create a dramatic intensity of events; with
music, that it can compose in the rhythms and phrases of time and
can be attended by song and instrument; with poetry, that it can
juxtapose images; with literature generally, that it can encompass
in its sound track the abstractions available only to language.*

—MAYA DEREN

As Maya Deren's observation suggests, analyzing a movie is no easy task. The previous chapters of this book isolate the various language systems of movies, exploring each system's range of expression. Film is a more complex medium than the traditional arts because movies synthesize many language systems simultaneously, bombarding the spectator with literally hundreds of symbolic ideas and emotions at the same time, some of them overt, others subliminal. Of course, filmmakers rarely employ each language system at full tilt. In every scene—indeed, in every shot—there is a principle of hierarchical subordination. The combinations are constantly in flux, like the couplings, divergencies, and recouplings of a group of dancers.

The French critic André Bazin described *Citizen Kane* as "a discourse on method" because of its encyclopedic technical range. The film, directed by Orson Welles (1915–1985), is an ideal choice to demonstrate how these various language systems interact dynamically within a single text. The following pages can only touch on the high points of this famous movie, but the analysis can serve as a guide for a systematic explication of any film.

Citizen Kane is the life story of a powerful newspaper magnate, Charles Foster Kane, who is as contradictory as he is controversial. The film is a fictionalized biography of the ruthless publishing baron William Randolph Hearst (1863–1951). Actually, the characters in the movie are composites, drawn from the lives of several famous American tycoons, but Hearst was the most obvious. Herman Mankiewicz, the coauthor of the screenplay, knew Hearst personally, and was a friend of the old yellow journalist's mistress, screen **star** Marion Davies. Davies was among the best-liked personalities in the film industry, and except for her fondness for alcohol and jigsaw puzzles, was quite unlike the Susan Alexander character in *Citizen Kane*.

The movie recounts the major events of the protagonist's lengthy life. Born in comparative obscurity, the eight-year-old Charles is sent away to boarding school after his mother inherits a huge fortune through a fluke. Kane's guardian throughout his youth is the banker Walter P. Thatcher, a pompous blowhard and political reactionary. After living a life of frivolous self-indulgence, Kane decides in his mid-twenties to become a newspaper publisher. Along with his close associates, the doggedly loyal Bernstein and the suave Jed Leland, he dedicates himself to championing the cause of the underprivileged and attacking corrupt institutions of power. At the height of his career, Kane marries the refined Emily Norton, niece of the President of the United States. But the marriage eventually turns stale, then rancid. In middle age, Kane consoles himself by secretly taking a mistress, Susan Alexander, a pretty but rather empty-headed shopgirl with vague aspirations of becoming a singer.

Buoyed by his fame and popularity, Kane runs for governor of New York. His opponent, Boss Jim Gettys, attempts to blackmail him into withdrawing from the race by threatening to go public with the hypocrisy of Kane's marriage and to expose his cozy arrangement with Susan. Outraged, Kane refuses to capitulate, even though he knows that the scandal will publicly humiliate his wife, his son, and Susan. Kane loses the election, and the respect of his best friend, Jed Leland. Emily divorces Kane, taking their young son with her.

Kane redirects his energies toward the career of a proxy, his new young wife, Susan Alexander Kane. He is determined to make her into a great opera star, despite the inconvenient fact that she has no discernible talent. Ignoring her objections, indifferent to her public mortification, Kane pushes the talentless Susan to the brink of suicide. Thwarted again, he finally agrees to give up on his scheme to make her an opera star. Instead, he builds an enormous isolated palace, Xanadu, where he and Susan retire into semiseclusion. After years of being bullied into submission by Kane, Susan rebels and walks out on him. Finally, alone and embittered, the old man dies amidst the empty opulence of Xanadu.

Photography

Cinematographer Gregg Toland considered *Citizen Kane* the high point of his career. The veteran cinematographer thought he might be able to learn something from the "boy genius," whose accomplishments were mostly in radio and the Broadway theater. Welles, used to setting up his own lights in the live theater, thought that movie directors were also responsible for the lighting.

11–1. Publicity photo of Orson Welles and cinematographer Gregg Toland during the production of *Citizen Kane* (U.S.A., 1941).
Toland, the most admired cinematographer of his generation, asked Welles if he could photograph the young director's first feature film. He was fascinated by Welles's bold theatricality, and often suggested more effective ways of shooting scenes. They discussed each shot in the movie, which is eclectic in its visual style, integrating a variety of influences. Welles was strongly drawn to the lighting theories of such theatrical designers as Gordon Craig and Adolphe Appia, and to many of the techniques of the German Expressionist movement. Welles was also influenced by the moody low-key photography of John Ford's *Stagecoach*. Welles was so grateful for the help of the veteran cinematographer that he gave Toland a conspicuous credit title—unusual in this era. *(RKO)*

Intrigued, Toland let him go ahead, allowing Welles to determine the design of most of the lights, but quietly instructing the camera crew to make the necessary technical adjustments.

Everyone saw at once that *Citizen Kane* didn't look like most American movies of its era. There is not an indifferently photographed image in the film. Even the exposition scenes—normally dispatched with efficient **medium two shots**—are startlingly photographed (11–2). Not that the techniques were new. **Deep-focus, low-key lighting,** rich textures, audacious compositions, dynamic contrasts between foregrounds and backgrounds, back lighting, sets with ceilings, side lighting, steep **angles, epic long shots** juxtaposed with **extreme close-ups,** dizzying **crane shots,** special effects galore—none of these was new. But no one had previously used them in such a "seven layer-cake profusion," to quote critic James Naremore.

Photographically, *Kane* ushered in a revolution, implicitly challenging the **classical** ideal of a transparent style that doesn't call attention to itself. In *Citizen Kane,* the stylistic virtuosity is part of the show. The lighting in the movie is generally in moderate **high key** in those scenes depicting Kane's youth and those dealing with his years as a crusading young publisher. As he grows older and

11–2. *Citizen Kane.*

Kane ushered in an era of flamboyant visual effects in the American cinema, and as such represented an assault on the classical ideal of an invisible style. Lights are often from below or other unexpected sources, creating startling clashes and abstract patterns, and infusing the photographed materials with a sense of visual exuberance. There's nothing invisible about the lighting of this shot, for example. As written, the scene is merely exposition, setting up the movie's narrative premise. Some reporters are talking in a screening room, and while they talk, the light from the projection booth splashes into the darkened auditorium, flooding the silhouetted figures in a sea of undulating luminescence. *(RKO)*

more cynical, the lighting grows darker, more harshly contrasting. Kane's home, the palatial Xanadu, seems steeped in perpetual night. Only spotlight patches of light penetrate the oppressive gloom, revealing the contours of a chair, a sofa, yet another piece of heroic sculpture. But the pervasive atmosphere is dank, impenetrable. The darkness shrouds an unspeakable evil.

Spotlights are also used in closer shots for symbolic effects. The mixture of decency and corruption in Kane is suggested by the contrasting lights: Sometimes his face seems split in half, with one side brightly illuminated, the other hidden in darkness. What is concealed is often more important than what's revealed. In an early scene between the idealistic Kane and his two associates, for example, the protagonist tells Bernstein and Leland of his intention to publish a "Declaration of Principles" on the front page of his newspaper, promising his readers that he will be an honest and tireless champion of their rights as citizens and human beings. When Kane bends down to sign the document,

11–3. *Citizen Kane,* with Orson Welles, Joseph Cotten, and Everett Sloane (at far end of table). Welles's deep-focus photography is meant to be admired for its virtuosity as well as its functionalism. André Bazin, an enthusiastic champion of deep-focus techniques, believed that it reduces the importance of editing and preserves the cohesiveness of real space and time. Many spatial planes can be captured simultaneously in a single **take,** maintaining the objectivity of a scene. Bazin felt that audiences were thus encouraged to be more creative— less passive—in understanding the relationships between people and things. In this photo, for example, we are free to look at the faces of over two dozen characters. "The public may choose, with its eyes, what it wants to see of a shot," Welles said. "I don't like to force it." (*RKO*)

however, his face is suddenly plunged in darkness—an ominous foreshadowing of Kane's later character.

Gregg Toland had often experimented with deep-focus photography during the 1930s, mostly while working with director William Wyler. But the deep focus in *Kane* is more flamboyant than Wyler's use of this technique (11–3). Deep-focus photography involves the use of **wide-angle lenses,** which tend to exaggerate the distances between people—an appropriate symbolic analogue for a story dealing with separation, alienation, and loneliness.

Deep focus also tends to encourage the audience to actively mine a shot for its information. In a scene involving Susan Alexander's suicide attempt, for example, a cause–effect relationship is suggested in the opening shot. Susan has taken a lethal dose of medication and lies comatose on her bed in a semidarkened room. At the bottom of the screen, in **close-up** range, stands an empty glass and a bottle of medication; in the middle of the screen, in medium

11–4. *Citizen Kane, with Ray Collins.*
RKO's highly respected special effects department consisted of thirty-five people, most of whom worked on *Kane.* Vernon L. Walker was in charge. Over 80 percent of the movie required some kind of special effects work, such as miniatures, matte shots, **double** and **multiple exposures.** Many scenes required reprinting—that is, combining two or more separate images onto one through the use of the **optical printer.** For example, this shot combines three separately photographed images—Boss Jim Gettys (Collins) standing on a balcony overlooking Madison Square Garden, with Kane down below delivering a campaign speech to a huge audience. The frame of the balcony masks the dividing line between the two areas. The auditorium area combines live action (stage) with a matte painting (audience); the balcony set consists of two walls. Welles was thus able to give the movie an epic scope, while keeping production costs relatively low. Total cost of the picture: just under $700,000—not lavish by the standards of 1941. *(RKO)*

range, lies Susan, wheezing softly; in the upper portion of the screen, in long-shot range, Kane bangs outside the door, then forces it open and enters the room. The layering of the **mise en scène** is a visual accusation: **(1)** the lethal dose was taken by **(2)** Susan Alexander Kane because of **(3)** Kane's inhumanity.

Special effects are used throughout the movie for a variety of reasons. In some settings—such as the exterior shots of Xanadu—the special effects lend the locale a slightly phantasmagorical quality. In other scenes, such as the political rally, special effects provide a realistic facsimile of large crowds and a huge auditorium (11–4).

The American cinema of the 1940s was to grow progressively darker, both thematically and photographically, thanks in part to the enormous influence of *Citizen Kane.* The most important style of the decade was **film noir**—literally, "black cinema." It was a style suited to the times. Welles's style continued in a noir vein, especially in such movies as *The Lady from Shanghai* and *Touch of Evil.* Toland's death in 1948 at the age of forty-four was an irreparable loss to the American cinema.

Mise en Scène

Coming from the world of live theater, Welles was an expert at staging action dynamically. Long shots are a more effective—and more theatrical—medium for the art of mise en scène, and hence, there are relatively few close shots in the movie. Most of the images are tightly framed and in **closed form.** Most of them are also composed in depth, with important information in the foreground, midground, and background. The **proxemic ranges** between the characters are choreographed balletically, to suggest their shifting power relationships. For example, an early scene in the movie shows Kane, Bernstein, and Leland taking over the staid offices of *The Inquirer,* the conservative newspaper young Kane has just bought because he thinks it might be fun to run a newspaper. While workmen and assistants stream in and out of the frame, carrying equipment, furniture, and personal belongings, Kane carries on a whimsical conversation with the stuffy, soon-to-be ex-editor, Mr. Carter, a Dickensian study in spluttering comic exasperation.

Perhaps the best way of understanding the complexity of Welles's mise en scène is to analyze a single shot. The dramatic context of Figure 11–6 is offered in the caption.

1. *Shot and camera proxemics.* This is a deep-focus shot, extending from a medium range in the foreground to an extreme long-shot range in the background. The camera is at a personal distance from Thatcher and Mrs. Kane, a social distance from Kane senior, and a public distance from Charles. The boy is playing happily, shouting disconnected phrases like "The Union forever!" Kane senior is stubbornly resisting their plans, while Thatcher and Mrs. Kane, more frigid than the outside weather, listen wearily.

2. *Angle.* The camera is at a slightly high angle, since more of the floor can be seen than the ceiling. The angle suggests a slight air of fatality.

11–5. *Citizen Kane, with Dorothy Comingore (at lower left base of fireplace) and Orson Welles.* In scenes depicting Kane as an old man, the camera is often far away, making him seem remote, inaccessible. Even when he is closer to the lens, as in this shot, the deep-focus photography keeps the rest of the world at a distance, with vast empty spaces between him and other people. We are often forced to search the mise en scène in order to locate the characters. In this photo, for example, Susan is dwarfed into insignificance by the enormous fireplace and the heroic sculpture behind her. She is a mere **subsidiary contrast,** not even so important as the statuary, and much less important than the **dominant,** Kane. These static shots are so totally drained of intimacy and spontaneity that they're almost funny, if they weren't so sad. *(RKO)*

3. *Lenses and filters.* Though it is difficult to discern in this photo, a wide-angle lens is used in order to capture its depth of field. The lens exaggerates the distances between the characters. No apparent filters.

4. *Lighting style.* The interior is photographed in moderate high key; the exterior—consisting mostly of blinding white snow—is in extreme high key.

5. *Dominant contrast.* Because of his central position within the **frame** and the high contrast between his dark clothes and the glaring snow, Charles tends to attract our eye first—he is also the subject of controversy in the foreground.

6. *Subsidiary contrasts.* Our eye then travels from Kane senior to Thatcher, Mrs. Kane, and the spotlighted document they are preparing to sign.

7. *Composition.* The image is split vertically in half, a tug of war, with two figures on the left, two on the right. The foreground table balances off the background table and rear wall. The composition segments and isolates the characters.

8. *Form.* The image is in closed form, its carefully coordinated components suggesting the self-containment of a stage setting enclosed by a proscenium arch.

11–6. *Citizen Kane,* *with Harry Shannon, Buddy Swan (in window), George Coulouris, and Agnes Moorehead.*
Almost all of the compositions in *Kane* are intricate and richly textured, at times baroquely ornate. But the visual complexity is not mere rhetorical ornamentation. The images are designed to reveal a maximum of information, often in an ironic manner. In this scene, for example, eight-year-old Charles plays with his sled outside in the snow while his future is being determined indoors by his mother and Thatcher. The boy's father watches impotently, sputtering a few feeble protests. The mise en scène is compartmentalized into twos, with the wall serving as the vertical dividing line. Kane senior and young Charles are grouped to the left in the upper portion of the frame; Thatcher and the severe Mrs. Kane dominate the right lower half, their pens poised to sign the contract that will soon separate Charles from his parents. Ironically, Mrs. Kane is motivated by love and self-sacrifice. She is sending Charles away in order to protect him from his father, a swaggering lout whose treatment of his son veers from forced jocularity to unpredictable outbursts of anger.   (*RKO*)

9. *Framing*. The shot is tightly framed, with little latitude for movement. Each character seems confined to his or her own space cubicle. The excluded Charles is imprisoned within the frame of the window—an enclosure within an enclosure. His freedom is illusionary.

10. *Depth*. The image is photographed in four depth planes: **(a)** the foreground table and its occupants; **(b)** Kane senior; **(c)** the rear portions of the parlor; and **(d)** Charles playing outside in the distance.

11. *Staging positions*. Kane senior is in the quarter turn position, relatively intimate vis-à-vis the spectator. Thatcher is at full front, but his eyes are lowered, avoiding our gaze. Mrs. Kane is in the profile position, preoccupied with her spouse.

12. *Character proxemics*. Thatcher and Mrs. Kane are in intimate proximity. They are at an aloof social distance from Kane senior, and a remote public distance from Charles.

Movement

From the very beginning of his film career, Welles was a master of the mobile camera. In *Citizen Kane*, camera movements are generally equated with the vitality and energy of youth. A static camera, on the other hand, tends to be associated with illness, old age, and death. These same **kinetic** principles apply to Kane's movements. As a young man, he is a whirlwind of energy, playfully gliding through life with scarcely enough breath to finish his sentences before his attention is distracted and he sweeps to another location. As an old man, how-

11–7. *Citizen Kane.*
In many respects, *Kane* is structured like a mystery story, a search to penetrate a great enigma. Welles is able to suggest this idea in the very opening sequence, through a series of dissolves and traveling shots. The movie begins with a sign: NO TRESPASSING. Ignoring it, the camera cranes up over the sign and over a wire fence. We dissolve from an ornate grillwork to an iron gate showing the letter "K." Xanadu is in the background, suffocating in mist, a solitary window light its only sign of habitation. Here lies the mystery. Here the search begins. *(RKO)*.

ever, he almost groans with each calculated step. Often he is photographed in stationary positions, or sitting down. He seems bored and exhausted, especially in the Xanadu scenes with Susan (see 11–5).

No one has used crane shots so spectacularly as Welles. But once again, the virtuosity is rarely indulged in for its own sake. The bravura crane shots embody important symbolic ideas. For example, after learning of Kane's death, a reporter attempts to interview Susan Alexander. The sequence begins in a torrential rainstorm. We see a poster and picture of Susan, advertising her engagement as a singer in a nightclub. As the sound track shudders with a rumble of thunder, the camera cranes up, up through the rain, up to the roof of the building, then plunges through a garish neon sign, "El Rancho," descends to the skylight where a blinding flash of lightning masks the camera's passage through the window itself, sweeps down to the deserted nightclub, where Susan is hunched at a table in a drunken stupor, prostrate with grief. (She is the only character in the film who is devastated by the news of Kane's death.) Both the camera and the reporter encounter numerous obstacles—the rain, the sign, the very walls of the building must be penetrated before we can even see Susan, much less hear her speak. The crane shot embodies a brutal invasion of privacy, a disregard for the barriers Susan has placed around her in her misery.

In Susan's opera debut, a traveling shot is used for comic effect, its payoff a virtual punchline. As she begins her first aria, the camera begins to rise, as if to ascend to the heavens. While she continues singing, her thin, watery voice grows progressively more feeble as the camera continues its upward journey, past sandbags, ropes, and platforms, until it finally comes to rest on two stagehands

11–8. *Citizen Kane, with Everett Sloane, Orson Welles, and Joseph Cotten.*
As a young man, Kane is a dynamo of energy, and his youthful high spirits are often conveyed kinetically—with brisk traveling shots that parallel the protagonist's movements. In this scene, for example, he nervously lurches forward and backwards, then forward again, the camera retreating and lunging back with him. *(RKO)*

on the catwalk, looking down at the performance. They listen for a moment longer, then turn to face each other. One stagehand waggishly puts his finger to his nose, as if to say, "She really stinks."

Like all movies—like every human enterprise—*Citizen Kane* is flawed. A number of scenes in the film are merely adequate, nothing more. One such scene, singled out by several critics, appears late in the movie, when Susan finally walks out on Kane forever. Enraged, the old man tears up Susan's bedroom, scattering its contents and demolishing its furnishings. Welles obviously wanted to convey Kane's fury through the sheer kinetic energy of the old man destroying the room. But the shots tend to be too lengthy and the camera too distant from the action. The violence of Kane's rage would be more effectively communicated if Welles had kept the camera closer in, so that the movements would dominate more. He also should have **edited** more, to convey the idea of fragmentation and confusion. As played, the scene works well enough, but for many viewers it seems somewhat anticlimactic. Kinetic energy must parallel its subject matter or the motion can seem too much—or too little.

11–9. *Citizen Kane, with George Coulouris, Orson Welles, and Everett Sloane.*
Welles frequently uses lengthy takes in his staging, choreographing the movements of the camera and the characters rather than cutting to a series of separate shots. Even in relatively static scenes such as this, these lengthy takes provide the mise en scène with a sense of fluidity and dynamic change, while still entrapping the three characters within the same space. The setting is a large office in 1929. The Great Depression has dealt Kane a severe setback, forcing him to relinquish control over his publishing empire. The sequence begins with a close shot of a legal document, while Bernstein recites its contents. He lowers the document, thus revealing Thatcher, now an old man, presiding over the dissolution. The camera adjusts slightly, and we then see Kane, listening grimly.   *(RKO)*

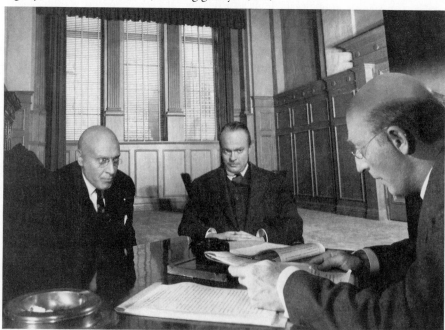

Editing

The editing in *Citizen Kane* is a calculated display of bravura, leaping over days, months, even years, with casual nonchalance. It's difficult to isolate the editing in this film because it often works in concert with the sound techniques, not to speak of the fragmentation of the story.

Often Welles uses editing to condense a great deal of time, using the sound as a continuity device. For example, to demonstrate Kane's gradual estrangement from his first wife, Emily, Welles features a series of breakfast scenes, employing only a few lines of dialogue with each brief episode. Beginning with some honeymoon sweet-talk, the mood quickly shifts to slight irritation, then strained annoyance, bitter resentment, and finally, silence and alienation. The sequence begins with the lovers sharing the intimacy of the same medium shot. As the marriage deteriorates, Welles cross-cuts to separate shots of each, even though they are sitting at the same table. The one-minute sequence ends with a long shot of the two at opposite ends of a lengthy table, each reading a different newspaper (11–10).

Welles uses a similar technique in showing how Susan Alexander eventually becomes Kane's mistress. The first time he meets her, he is splashed with mud on the street. She offers him some hot water, if he wants to come up to her small apartment for it. While there, they become friends. She admits that she sings a little and he asks her to perform for him. While she begins to sing her song at an old piano, the image **dissolves** to a parallel shot, only now she is in a large, handsomely decorated apartment, where she finishes the song at a grander piano, dressed in an elegant gown. We don't need to be shown what happened "between" these two shots. We can infer what happened by Susan's much improved circumstances.

11–10. *Citizen Kane, with Orson Welles and Ruth Warrick.*
Welles often combines editing with another technique, which he uses as a payoff. In the famous breakfast montage sequence portraying the disintegration of Kane's marriage to Emily, for example, he concludes with this final shot. The distance between the two says it all: They have nothing to say to each other.   *(RKO)*

11–11. *Citizen Kane, with Orson Welles.*
Budgetary considerations often determined the cunning editing strategies of the film, which was edited by Robert Wise. In the political campaign sequence, for example, Welles cuts from long shots of Kane delivering his speech to closer shots of his family and associates listening in the audience. These isolated fragments are intercut with **reestablishing shots** of the entire auditorium (see 11–4). The huge hall and its thousands of inhabitants weren't real: The cutting makes them *seem* real—by association. *(RKO)*

Sound

Coming from the world of live radio drama, Welles was often credited with inventing many film sound techniques when in fact he was primarily a consolidator, synthesizing and expanding the piecemeal accomplishments of his predecessors. In radio, sounds have to evoke images. An actor speaking through an echo chamber suggests a visual context—a huge auditorium, for example. A distant train whistle suggests a panoramic landscape, and so on. Welles applied this aural principle to his movie sound track. With the help of his sound technician, James G. Stewart, Welles discovered that almost every visual technique has its sound equivalent. Each of the shots, for example, has an appropriate sound quality involving volume, degree of definition, and texture. Long and extreme long shot sounds are fuzzy and remote; close-up sounds are crisp, clear, and generally loud. High-angle shots are often accompanied by high-pitched music

11-12. Publicity photo of Orson Welles and composer—conductor Bernard Herrmann during a recording session for *Citizen Kane.*

Herrmann was the composer for Welles's Mercury Theatre of the Air, and when Welles went to Hollywood, he took Herrmann with him. *Citizen Kane* was his first movie score. The two worked closely together, Welles often cutting his film to accommodate the musical numbers, rather than vice versa, which was usually the case in Hollywood. Herrmann was present throughout the production, taking twelve weeks to compose the score, an unusually lengthy period of time. Difficult, intensely egotistical, an uncompromising perfectionist, Herrmann did most of his best work for Welles and Alfred Hitchcock, including the scores for *The Magnificent Ambersons, Vertigo, North by Northwest, Psycho,* and many others.

(RKO)

and sound effects; low-angle shots by brooding and low-pitched sounds. Sounds can be dissolved and overlapped like a **montage** sequence.

Welles frequently leaps from one time period or location to another with a shocking sound transition. For example, the film's opening prologue concludes with Kane's death, which is accompanied by the gradual snuffing out of the sound. Suddenly, we are almost assaulted with a Voice-of-God narrator booming out "News on the March!"—the beginning of the newsreel sequence. In another sequence, Jed Leland is delivering a campaign speech, in which he describes Kane as "the fighting liberal, the friend of the workingman, the next governor of this state, who entered upon this campaign . . ." Cut to Kane in Madison Square Garden, continuing ". . . with one purpose only . . ."

Welles frequently overlaps his dialogue, especially in the comical sequences where several people are trying to speak at the same time. In Xanadu, the rooms are so huge that Kane and Susan must shout at each other in order to be heard, producing an incongruous effect that's both sad and funny (11–5). The Madison Square Garden facsimile is convincing in part because we *hear* the shouts and cheers of the enormous crowds, and hence imagine that we see them as well.

Bernard Herrmann's musical score is similarly sophisticated. Musical motifs are assigned to several of the major characters and events. Many of these motifs are introduced in the newsreel sequence, then picked up later in the film, often in a minor key, or played at a different tempo, depending on the mood of the scene. For example, the poignant Rosebud motif is introduced in the opening sequence, and when Rosebud is brought up during the course of the investigation, a variation of the musical motif often underlines the dialogue. When Welles finally reveals to us—but not to the characters—the mystery of Rosebud, the

11–13. *Citizen Kane,* with Dorothy Comingore.

Kane demonstrates that virtually every kind of visual has its aural counterpart. This montage sequence is reinforced by an aural montage of Susan Alexander's shrieking arias, orchestral music, popping flashbulbs, and the sounds of newspaper presses rolling. The pounding sounds are machinelike and inexorable, battering its sacrificial victim until she is stupefied by terror and exhaustion.   *(RKO)*

musical motif swells powerfully into prominence, producing one of the most thrilling revelations in all of cinema.

Herrmann's score often parallels Welles's visuals. For instance, in the montage of breakfast scenes between Kane and his first wife, the disintegration of the marriage is paralleled by the variations in the music. The sequence opens with a soft romantic waltz, tenderly underscoring the fascination each feels for the other. This is followed by a slight comical musical variation. As the relationship becomes more strained, the orchestration becomes harsher, more dissonant. In the final scene, neither one bothers to speak anymore. Their silence is accompanied by a brooding, neurotic variation on the opening musical theme.

In many scenes Welles employs sound for symbolic purposes. For example, he uses a dissolve and montage sequence to show Susan on her disastrous operatic tour (11–13). On the sound track, her aria can be heard, distorted into a screeching, dismal wail. The sequence ends with the gradual dimming of the light, to symbolize Susan's increasing despair. On the accompanying sound track, we hear her voice winding down to a wounded moan, as though someone pulled the plug on a record player in the middle of a song.

Acting

Welles had his own stable of writers, assistants, and actors, who worked with him in both radio and the New York live theater. When he went to Hollywood, he took many of them with him, including fifteen actors. Except for Welles, none of these players was well known, and even Welles was known primarily as a radio performer. (He captured the imagination of the mass audience when his notorious *War of the Worlds* broadcast of 1938 panicked thousands of Americans who believed that we were actually being invaded by creatures from Mars. Welles was delighted of course. As a result of this cause célèbre, he got his picture on the cover of *Time* when he was only twenty-two years old.)

Citizen Kane boasts a first-rate cast. There are a few so-so performances, but none that is weak, and several that are outstanding, most notably those of Welles, Dorothy Comingore, Joseph Cotten, Everett Sloane, and Agnes Moorehead. Like most performers who are used to acting repertory-style, members of the cast work as an ensemble; the total effect is one of dramatic scenes that mesh seamlessly. The Mercury players look like seasoned film performers, not the young neophytes they actually were. For most of them, this was their first movie, yet they are always natural, sincere, and believable.

Even some of the cameo roles are performed with distinction. Since these parts are limited to only a few lines of dialogue, the actors must be able to convey the complexity of their characters—who are often contradictory—without appearing inconsistent. For example, Ray Collins performs Boss Jim Gettys as a cunning survivor. Streetwise and cynical, he is a man who has seen it all. Or at least he thought he had seen it all until he came up against Kane. Gettys seems quietly shocked that Kane, a supposedly high-class opponent, would be so low-

11–14. *Citizen Kane, with Orson Welles and Joseph Cotten.*
Jed Leland (Cotten) represents the moral conscience of the film, Kane's idealistic alter ego. Roles like this are difficult to play well, since they can easily degenerate into sentimental clichés of piety. Cotten toughens up the role by refusing to make Leland too likable. Although sensitive and intelligent, Leland is also a bit of a prig, "a New England schoolmarm," to use his own phrase. Like Bernstein, he loves Kane and is loyal to him when they are all young and committed to social reform. But when he finally recognizes Kane's ego for the destructive force it is, Jed pulls back, disillusioned. *(RKO)*

class as to publish a doctored photo of Gettys "in a convict suit with stripes, so his children could see the picture in the paper, or his mother." We can't help but sympathize with Gettys's outrage, notwithstanding the fact that otherwise he is a creep.

Although she appears in only one scene, Agnes Moorehead as Kane's mother leaves an indelible impression. (Moorehead was to go on to an even more brilliant performance in Welles's next movie, *The Magnificent Ambersons*.) Moorehead's Mary Kane might almost have stepped out of a tale by Hawthorne: stern, puritanical, joyless. She is a woman who found out too late that she has married a fool. Trapped, she will endure the humiliation of her marriage, but she will not subject her son to the same fate. In her mind, he is meant for better things, even if that means she must part with the only person she loves. Mrs. Kane is a woman of few words, but her determination is communicated by her steely stoicism, her decisive movements, her ramrod-straight back. This is not a lady to mess with.

Everett Sloane and Joseph Cotten are flawless as Bernstein and Leland. Bernstein's uncritical hero-worship of Kane establishes him as the less intelligent of the two, a man who—unlike Leland—puts friendship above principle. But the endearing Bernstein is something of a comic innocent, so blinded by loyalty that he is incapable of seeing Kane's flaws, much less his vices. As an old man, Bernstein is still funny, a successful businessman, but no shallow materialist. "It's no trick to make a lot of money," he scoffs, "if all you want is to make a lot

11–15. *Citizen Kane, with Dorothy Comingore.*

Comingore's brilliant performance as Susan provides considerable warmth to an otherwise cold and intellectual film. The few close-ups in the movie are reserved primarily for her, forcing us to become more involved with Susan's feelings. Like most of the major characters, she is a study in contradiction, screechy and pitiful at the same time. She can also be very funny. "A person can go crazy in this dump," she complains in her typical whining monotone. "Nobody to talk to, nobody to have any fun with. Forty-nine thousand acres of nothing but scenery and statues." But Susan also has Soul: She endures great suffering and spiritual anguish, all in the name of love. She is one of the few characters capable of forgiveness. After the reporter Thompson listens to her sad tale of humiliation and loneliness, he says: "You know, all the same I feel kind of sorry for Mr. Kane." Susan's reply: "Don't you think I do?" *(RKO)* of money." He recognizes that Kane's motives ran deeper than the crassly entrepreneurial. He is still awed by the mysterious depths of Kane's inner spirit. And perhaps a bit saddened by the contrast with his own ordinary soul.

Welles's performance as Kane was lavishly praised. John O'Hara, reviewing the movie for *Newsweek,* said: "There has never been a better actor than Orson Welles." D. W. Griffith described it as the greatest film performance he had ever seen. Tall and imposing, with a deep, flexible voice capable of a wide spectrum of nuances, Welles is an astonishing technician, equally convincing as a brash young man, a rigid autocrat in middle years, and a burned-out, hulking septegenarian. At twenty-five, Kane is charming and charismatic, with an insolent skepticism toward all forms of authority. Indeed, he is so charming that we hardly notice some of his questionable methods, his insistence on having everything his way. As a middle-aged man, Kane is more somber. The element of threat is more brazenly paraded. He no longer argues that the end justifies the means—he automatically assumes it, expecting others to acquiesce to his views. As an old man, Kane is among the walking wounded, a man who has repeatedly fought and lost.

Drama

The live theater was Welles's first love. As a youth he attended a progressive prep school where he directed and acted in over thirty plays. Shakespeare was his favorite dramatist. In 1930, at the age of fifteen, Welles left school perma-

11–16. Artist's rendering of the interior set of Xanadu for *Citizen Kane*.
In the area of set design and décor, Welles was fortunate in his choice of studio, for RKO's art director, Van Nest Polglase, was among the best in the industry. Perry Ferguson, who actually designed the sets under Polglase's general supervision, shared his boss's preference for monumental sets with unusual sources of lighting and richly textured details. *(RKO)*

nently. With money left from an inheritance, he traveled to Europe, where he bluffed his way into the Gate Theatre in Dublin, claiming to be a well-known Broadway star. The managers didn't believe him but were impressed nonetheless, and they hired him. For about a year, Welles directed and acted in many stage classics, mostly of the Elizabethan period.

When he returned to America in 1933, he finagled an acting job touring with Katherine Cornell, one of the major stage stars of that era. They performed mostly Shakespeare and Shaw. In 1935 in New York, Welles joined forces with the aspiring theatrical producer (and later actor and director) John Houseman, under the aegis of the Federal Theatre Project, one of many WPA programs of the New Deal. The live theater of the 1930s was intensely political and **left-wing** in its leanings. Welles, a lifelong liberal, was a Roosevelt enthusiast and, like most intellectuals of that era, was strongly pro-New Deal in his sympathies. Welles helped write several of President Roosevelt's radio speeches.

In 1937, Welles and Houseman formed their own company, The Mercury Theatre. Several of their productions were hailed for their brilliance, most notably a modern-dress, antifascist production of *Julius Caesar*. Welles not only starred and directed but also designed the sets, costumes, and lighting. The influential theater critic John Mason Brown pronounced it "a production of genius." Critic Elliot Norton described it as "the most compelling Shakespeare of this generation."

Welles financed his theater with his earnings as a radio star. During his halcyon years in the late 1930s, he was earning about $3,000 per week in radio, two thirds of which was plowed back into the Mercury Theatre. The company

11–17. Exterior set of Xanadu for *Citizen Kane*.

The mist-shrouded tropic setting groans under the weight of the sprawling, towering Xanadu, unfinished and already beginning to decay, like a rotting mausoleum from the pages of Edgar Allan Poe. Although the palm trees sway as the wisps of fog drift past dreamily, the set was actually a matte painting, only a few feet high. *(RKO)* was a shoestring operation, constantly on the brink of collapsing. In 1939, after its first flop, the Mercury Theatre folded. Welles originally went to Hollywood with the intention of earning some quick cash so he could return to New York and revive the Mercury.

Welles's experience in the live theater proved invaluable when he turned to making movies. He regarded film as essentially a dramatic rather than literary medium. As we have seen, the lighting style of *Citizen Kane* is more indebted to the stage than the screen, and Welles's use of **lengthy takes** is similarly derived from the need in the live theater to stage the action in a unified space.

In the area of art direction too, Welles was able to save hundreds of thousands of dollars by showing only parts of sets rather than entire rooms. For example, the office set consists only of a desk and two walls, yet we seem to be in a huge luxurious office (11–9). Similarly, in the Xanadu scenes, Welles spotlights an oversized piece of furniture, a sculpture, or a fireplace, leaving the rest of the room in darkness—as though it were too enormous to be adequately illuminated. (The rooms are actually sparsely furnished.) When these techniques were insufficient, Welles was able to count on the RKO special effects department to create an **epic** canvas through such techniques as **animation, matte shots,** and **miniatures.**

Edward Stevenson's costumes adhere closely to the actual styles of each period. Since the movie traverses nearly seventy years and the events are not chronologically presented, the costumes had to be instantly recognizable in order for the audience to know the period of each scene. Kane's childhood has a nineteenth-century flavor—a cross between Charles Dickens and Mark Twain.

11–18. Three photos of Orson Welles as Charles Foster Kane at various periods in his life.
Welles was required to age about fifty years during the course of the story. Thanks in part to the makeup artistry of Maurice Seiderman, Welles is completely convincing, whether playing Kane at twenty-five, forty-five, or seventy-five. As Kane grows older, his hair grays and recedes, his jowls sag, his cheeks grow puffier, and the bags beneath his eyes grow more pouchy. Seiderman created a synthetic rubber body suit to suggest the increasingly flabby torso of an older man. *(RKO)*

(a) (b) (c)

The former can be seen in Thatcher's stiff collar and stovepipe hat; the latter in the plain frontier simplicity of the clothes of Mary and Jim Kane.

Costumes are symbolic as well as functional. As a crusading young publisher, Kane favors whites. He often removes his jacket and tie while working. Later in life, he is almost always in black business suits and ties. Emily's clothes look expensive, but with an understated elegance. She always looks like a well-bred young matron—fashionable, modest, and feminine. Susan favors simple clothes before meeting Kane. After meeting him, she is generally dressed in ritzy patterned dresses, sometimes sprinkled with sequins—like an aging showgirl parading her loot.

The following is an analysis of Susan's opera costume (11–19), a triumph of irony and wit:

1. *Period.* Ostensibly nineteenth century, though in fact an amusing pastiche of various periods and "Oriental" influences.

2. *Class.* Royalty. The costume is profusely festooned with pearls, precious jewels, and other queenly niceties.

3. *Sex.* Female, with an emphasis on curved, swaying lines and peekaboo slits in the skirt. Only the turban provides a masculine touch, though it is whimsically inflected with fluffy white feathers.

11–19. Publicity photo of Dorothy Comingore in opera costume for *Citizen Kane*.

Bernard Herrmann composed the film's opera, *Salommbô,* in the style of nineteenth-century French "Oriental" operas. Edward Stevenson's costumes are in this same campy style of mockery. For example, Susan's outlandish regalia is a send-up of what the well-dressed French-Oriental opera queen might wear while suffering the agonies of unrequited love, torment, and despair.   *(RKO)*

4. *Age.* The costume is designed for a woman in her twenties, at the peak of her physical attractiveness.

5. *Fabric.* Silks, beaded ornamentation encrusted with jewels.

6. *Accessories.* Turban, pearl strands, incongruous Joan Crawford–style ankle-strap shoes.

7. *Color.* The film is in black and white, but most of the fabric has a metallic sheen, suggesting gold and ebony.

8. *Body exposure.* The costume reveals and highlights such erotic areas as the breasts, midriff, and legs.

9. *Function.* The costume is totally without utility, difficult even to walk in. It is intended for a person who does not work, but is displayed.

10. *Image.* Every inch the opera queen.

Story

The differences between story and plot can be best illustrated by comparing the narrative in chronological order with the restructured sequence of the plot. When Herman Mankiewicz approached Welles with the idea of the story, Welles was concerned that the materials would be too sprawling, too unfocused. In order to sharpen the storyline and infuse it with more dramatic urgency, he suggested scrambling the chronology of events through a series of **flashbacks,** each narrated from the point of view of the person telling the story. Welles had used this multiple flashback technique in a number of his radio dramas.

11–20. *Citizen Kane.*
Like a number of Welles's other movies, *Kane* begins with the end—the death of its protagonist when he is about seventy-five. In his final moments of life, the old man holds a small crystal ball containing a miniature scene that flurries with artificial snow when shaken. With his last dying breath, he utters the word "Rosebud." Then the glass ball crashes to the floor, splintering into a thousand fragments. The plot of the movie is structured like a search—for the meaning of this final utterance. *(RKO)*

He and Mankiewicz also introduced a note of suspense. In his final moments of life, Kane mumbles the word "Rosebud" (11–20). No one seems to know what it means, and its significance piques the curiosity of a newspaper reporter, Thompson, who spends the remainder of the movie questioning Kane's former associates about this mystery, which he hopes contains the key to Kane's conflicting character.

Welles claimed that the Rosebud **motif** was merely a plot gimmick, intended to hook the audience on a dramatic question that's really a wild goose chase. But the gimmick works. Like the hopeful reporter, we too think that Rosebud will unlock Kane's ambiguous personality. Without this gimmick, the story would have remained rambling and unfocused. The search for the meaning of Rosebud shapes the narrative, providing it with a forward thrust, with a dramatic question we all want answered. This is what foreign critics mean by the American genius for storytelling.

The flashback structure of *Citizen Kane* allows Welles to leap through time and space, cutting to various periods of Kane's life without having to adhere to a strict chronology. To provide the audience with an overview, Welles introduces most of the major events and people of Kane's life in a brief newsreel shown early in the film. These events and people are explored in more depth in the individual flashbacks that follow.

Many critics have marvelled at the intricate, jigsaw-puzzle structure of the movie, with its interlocking pieces that don't click together until the final scene. The following plot outline sets forth the main structural units of the film and the principal characters and events of each:

1. *Prologue.* Xanadu. Kane's death. "Rosebud."
2. *Newsreel.* Death of Kane. Enormous wealth and decadent lifestyle. Contradictory political image. Marriage to Emily Norton. Exposé of "love nest." Divorce. Marriage to Susan Alexander, "singer." Political campaign. Opera career. The Great Depression and Kane's financial decline. Lonely, secluded old age in Xanadu.
3. *Premise.* Thompson is instructed by his editor (11–2) to discover the mystery of Rosebud by questioning Kane's former associates. "It will probably be a very simple thing." False step: Susan refuses to speak to Thompson.
4. *Flashback: The Memoirs of Walter P. Thatcher.* Kane's childhood. Thatcher becomes guardian. Kane's first newspaper: *The Inquirer.* Introduction of Bernstein and Leland. Newspaper crusading years. Kane's financial decline in the 1930s.
5. *Flashback: Bernstein.* Early days at *The Inquirer.* "Declaration of Principles." Building a publishing empire. Engagement to Emily Norton.
6. *Flashback: Jed Leland.* Disintegration of marriage to Emily. Kane meets Susan. Political campaign in 1918. Exposé, divorce, remarriage. Susan's opera career. Final break between Kane and Jed.
7. *Flashback: Susan Alexander Kane.* Opera debut and career. Suicide attempt. Years of semiseclusion with Kane at Xanadu. Susan leaves Kane.
8. *Flashback: Raymond, butler at Xanadu.* Kane's final days. "Rosebud."

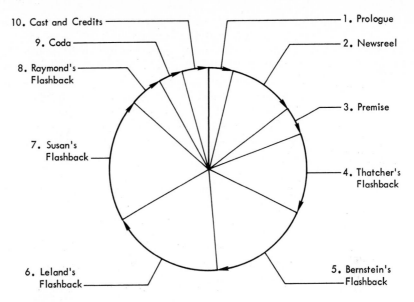

10. Cast and Credits
9. Coda
8. Raymond's Flashback
7. Susan's Flashback
6. Leland's Flashback

1. Prologue
2. Newsreel
3. Premise
4. Thatcher's Flashback
5. Bernstein's Flashback

11–21. *Citizen Kane.* Approximate proportion of each plot unit.

9. *Coda.* Revelation of Rosebud. Reverse of opening Prologue, producing closure.

10. *Cast and Credits.*

The ten sections of the film vary in length. A diagram charting the approximate proportion of each section is shown in Figure 11–21.

Literature

Citizen Kane is often singled out for the excellence of its screenplay—its wit, its taut construction, its thematic complexity. The script's authorship provoked considerable controversy, both at the time of the movie's release and again in the 1970s, when critic Pauline Kael contended that Welles merely added a few polishing touches to Herman Mankiewicz's finished product. Mankiewicz was a Hollywood regular, a notorious drunk—charming, witty, and almost totally unreliable. When he approached Welles with the original idea for *American* (it was later called *John Citizen, U.S.A.*, and finally *Citizen Kane*), Welles asked his former partner, John Houseman, to help Mankiewicz write the screenplay, preferably in an isolated place, far removed from temptation.

Welles made extensive revisions on the first few drafts of the screenplay— so extensive that Mankiewicz denounced the movie because it departed radically from his scenario. Nor did he want Welles's name to appear on the screenplay credit, and he took his case to the Writers Guild. At this time, a director was not allowed any writing credit unless he contributed 50 percent or more of the screenplay. In a compromise gesture, the guild allowed both of them credit, only with Mankiewicz receiving top billing.

When the controversy resurfaced in the 1970s, the American scholar Robert L. Carringer settled the case once and for all. He examined the seven principal drafts of the screenplay, plus many last-minute revision memoranda and additional sources. Carringer's conclusion: The early Mankiewicz drafts contain "dozens of pages of dull, plodding material that will eventually be discarded or replaced altogether. And, most tellingly, there is virtually nothing in them of that stylistic wit and fluidity that is the most engaging trait of the film itself." In short, Mankiewicz provided the raw material; Welles provided the genius.

The script sparkles with surprises. The main characters are a far cry from the tired stereotypes of most movies of this era. Only Thatcher seems conventional, a variation of the 1930s tycoon. The writing is often tersely funny. During Kane's noisy marriage to Susan, for example, the couple is surrounded by pushy reporters. When asked what he's going to do now, Kane replies: "We're going to be a great opera star." Susan chimes in: "Charlie said if I didn't, he'd build me an opera house." The gallant Kane demurs: "That won't be necessary." Cut to a newspaper headline: "KANE BUILDS OPERA HOUSE."

There are also moments of pure poetry, like Bernstein's surprising reply to Thompson after the reporter scoffs at Bernstein's suggestion that Rosebud might be a long-lost love. "You take me," the old retainer explains. "One day, back in 1896, I was crossing over to Jersey on the ferry, and as we pulled out, there was another ferry pulling in, and on it there was a girl waiting to get off. A white dress she had on. She was carrying a white parasol. I only saw her for one second. She didn't see me at all, but I'll bet a month hasn't gone by since, that I haven't thought of that girl." Welles always loved that speech—and wished that he had written it.

Thematically, *Kane* is so complex that only a brief itemizing of some of its themes is possible within these few pages. Like most of Welles's other movies, *Citizen Kane* might well be entitled *The Arrogance of Power*. He was attracted to themes traditionally associated with classical tragedy and the epic: the downfall of a public figure because of arrogance and pride. Power and wealth are corrupting, and the corrupt devour themselves. The innocent usually survive, but they are severely scarred. "All of the characters I've played are various forms of Faust," Welles stated. All have bartered their souls and lost.

Welles's sense of evil is mature and complex, seldom conventionalized. He was one of the few American filmmakers of his generation to explore the darker side of the human condition without resorting to a simplified psychology or to moralistic clichés. Though his universe is essentially doomed, it's shot through with ambiguities, contradictions, and moments of transient beauty. Welles considered himself a moralist, but his movies are never priggish or sanctimonious. Instead of facile condemnations, *Kane* laments the loss of innocence: "Almost all serious stories in the world are stories of a failure with a death in it," Welles stated. "But there is more lost paradise in them than defeat. To me that's the central theme in Western culture, the lost paradise."

When a story isn't told in a straightforward, chronological manner, something is lost and something is gained. What's lost is the suspense of any conventionally told tale, which usually asks, What does the protagonist want and how is

11–22. Production photo of Orson Welles (in middle-aged makeup) and Gregg Toland lining up a shot for the post-election scene between Kane and Jed Leland.
Welles uses low-angle shots as a motif throughout the picture, especially to emphasize the awesome power of the protagonist. In this scene, the angle is so low that the floorboards of the set had to be torn away to allow for the camera's placement. Combined with the perspective-distorting wide-angle lens, such low-angle shots portray Kane as a towering colossus, capable of crushing anything that gets in his way.   *(RKO)*

he or she going to get it? In *Citizen Kane*, the protagonist is dead almost from the start. We are forced to piece together his life from the points of view of others. This technique of multiple narration forces us to gauge the biases and prejudices of each narrator. *Citizen Kane* is their story too.

There are five different storytellers, and each tells a different story. Even when the events overlap, we view them from a different perspective. For example, Leland's account of Susan's operatic debut is colored by his condescending attitude toward her. Her performance is viewed primarily from the audience, where Leland is sitting. When Susan recounts the same event, the camera is primarily on stage, and the tone of the sequence is no longer comic but agonized.

Welles's narrative strategy is something like a prism: The newsreel and the five interviewees each offer a unique view of the same man. The newsreel offers us a quick tour of the highlights of Kane's public life. Thatcher's account is tainted by his absolute confidence in the moral superiority of the rich and powerful. Bernstein's story is steeped in the gratitude and loyalty he felt for Kane when they were young. Leland offers a more rigorous perspective: He judges Kane by what he actually does, rather than what he says. Susan is the most victimized of the storytellers. Yet she is also the most compassionate and sensitive. Raymond, the butler, pretends to know a lot more than he does. His brief flashback merely concludes Thompson's investigation.

There are literally dozens of symbolic motifs in the movie. Some of them are technical, such as the film's predominantly **low camera angles** (11–22). Others are more content oriented, such as the series of fences the camera must penetrate before we are able to see Kane. There are also persistent motifs of stillness, decay, old age, and death. The two most important motifs in the movie are Rosebud and the fragmentation motif.

Rosebud turns out to be a favorite childhood possession. Scholars and critics have argued about Rosebud for decades. Welles himself described it as "dollar-book Freud"—that is, a convenient symbol of childhood innocence. The ideas of Freud gained wide currency in the American cinema of the 1940s, especially the centrality of a child's prepubescent life in determining his later character.

But Rosebud is also a more generalized symbol of loss. Consider: Kane is a man who lost his parents when he was a child. He was brought up by a bank. He lost his youthful idealism as a publisher. He lost in his bid to be governor. He lost his first wife and son. He lost in his efforts to make Susan an opera star. He lost Susan. Because it's much more than a mere object, more even than a symbol of Edenic innocence, the revelation of Rosebud to the audience delivers a powerful emotional impact.

The fragmentation motif acts as a foil to the simple-minded notion that any

11–23. *Citizen Kane, with William Alland and Paul Stewart.*
Near the end of the movie, Thompson (Alland) admits defeat. He never does find out what "Rosebud" means, and he describes his investigation as "playing with a jigsaw puzzle," while the camera cranes back and up, revealing thousands of crates of artwork, memorabilia, and personal effects—the fragmented artifacts of a person's life. "I don't think any word can explain a man's life," Thompson continues. "No, I guess Rosebud is just a piece in a jigsaw puzzle, a missing piece." *(RKO)*

single word could "explain" a complex personality. Throughout the movie, we are presented with images that suggest multiplicity, repetition, and fragments of a larger whole. Examples of this motif are the jigsaw puzzles, the profusion of crates, boxes, and artwork. The very structure of the movie is fragmented, with each narrator providing us with only a partial picture. In Raymond's flashback at the end of the film, the elderly Kane mutters "Rosebud" when he discovers a glass globe. Dazed, he walks down a corridor, the globe in his hand. As he passes a set of facing mirrors, we see his image multiplied into infinity. All of them are Kane.

Theory

Citizen Kane is a masterpiece of formalism. True, there are some realistic elements in the film—its basis in fact, the newsreel sequence, the deep-focus photography that was so highly praised by realist critics like André Bazin. For the most part, however, it's the bravura sequences that are most memorable in the movie. Welles was one of the great **lyricists** of the cinema, and his stylistic rapture is best illustrated by the ornate visuals, the dazzling traveling shots, the richly textured soundtrack, the kaleidoscopic editing style, the highly fragmented narrative, and the profusion of symbolic motifs. The movie is brazen in its technical audacity.

Kane is the work of an indisputable *auteur*. Welles not only produced the film, he also coauthored its script, selected the cast and crew, starred in its leading role, and directed the entire production without interference. The movie is also typical in that it explores a complex of characteristic Wellesian themes, and is executed in a showy style that became a virtual signature of its author. Welles was always generous in his praise of his co-workers, especially actors and cinematographers, but there is no question that he was totally in command during the production of this film.

Marxist critics have long admired the movie, especially in Europe, where Welles was regarded almost as a semi-deity. Although *Citizen Kane* is not explicitly Marxist, its ideological underpinnings are clearly left-wing: (1) The movie can be regarded as a tool for social change, a critique of the abuses of capitalism; (2) it attacks the status quo of the socioeconomic system in America during the first four decades of this century; (3) it demystifies power and demonstrates the enormous influence of the media in shaping public opinion; (4) it shows how wealth and power go hand in hand, virtually disenfranchising those individuals in the lower social echelons; (5) its sympathies are on the side of the oppressed and victimized, especially women; (6) it demonstrates how environment largely determines human behavior—if Kane had not inherited a fortune, he might not have become morally corrupted by his power; (7) religion and the supernatural play no significant role in the film, which is strictly materialistic in its assumptions; (8) the characters are treated as equals in terms of their potential worth—the coarse, low-born Susan is accorded the same respect as the elegant Leland, who was born rich; (9) the film is dialectically structured, pitting thesis against antithesis in terms of Kane's contradictory character, and arriving finally at a synthesis: The truth about Kane is that he is both good and evil, progressive and reactionary,

11–24. *Citizen Kane,* with Joseph Cotten and Everett Sloane.
Kane's rampant consumerism is best illustrated by his mania for collecting European art treasures. Not because he enjoys art—indeed, he scarcely ever mentions it—but because of its value as a status symbol. His conspicuous consumption becomes a habit rather than a passionate interest. After a while, no one even bothers to uncrate his purchases—they're simply stored away with all his other possessions.   *(RKO)*

sensitive and callous. As the French critic Maurice Bessy noted: "In Welles' universe, truth is not, after all, either good or beautiful, but, in its own fashion, it is truth."

The commercial and critical history of *Citizen Kane* is a fascinating story in its own right. Shortly after the collapse of the Mercury Theatre, RKO offered the twenty-four-year-old Welles an unheard of contract: He was to be paid $150,000 per picture, plus 25 percent of the gross receipts. He could produce, direct, write, or star in any of his films, or function in all four capacities if he wished. He was granted total artistic control, answerable only to George Schaefer, the enlightened head of the studio.

RKO was in financial distress, as it had been throughout most of its brief span. The studio was founded in 1928 by the financier Joseph P. Kennedy (the father of the later President) and by David Sarnoff, the head of RCA and later NBC. Sarnoff hoped that the studio would become an "NBC with pictures." Kennedy soon withdrew, with a profit of some $5 million. After a promising start, RKO fell on hard times, primarily because of the constant reshuffling of management, which gave it no continuity. Unlike the other majors, RKO had no consistent identity or characteristic style.

11–25. *The Magnificent Ambersons* **(U.S.A., 1942),** *with Tim Holt, Ray Collins, and Richard Bennett; directed by Orson Welles.*
Like most of Welles's movies, this, his favorite work, deals with the theme of a lost paradise. Unlike *Kane,* however, the tone is warm and nostalgic, the images more softly lyrical. Welles does not appear in the film, though he does narrate the story off screen. He concludes with a shot of a microphone on a swinging boom, accompanied by his spoken credit: "I wrote the picture and directed it. My name is Orson Welles."   *(RKO)*

Sarnoff and his new partner, Nelson Rockefeller, wanted RKO to produce sophisticated and progressive films, but they discovered that artistic worth and box-office success were not easily united. Rockefeller and Sarnoff were pleased with Schaefer's idea to hire Welles, for they reasoned that if anyone could produce quality movies that also made profits, surely it was the boy genius, fresh from his Broadway and radio triumphs.

When Welles arrived in Hollywood in 1939, the resentment against him was immense. Most directors considered themselves lucky if they were permitted to direct an **A-film** before they were thirty-five, yet here was a mere stripling, an outsider at that, who was given total autonomy on his first time out. "This is the biggest electric train a boy ever had," he quipped when he saw the production facilities at RKO. The flamboyant Welles was regarded as arty, supercilious, and arrogant by most industry regulars. He didn't help matters by openly sneering at the film community: "Hollywood is a golden suburb, perfect for golfers, gardeners, mediocre men, and complacent starlets," he announced with obvious amusement. He was an incorrigible smartass. He paid dearly for the flippant wit of his youth.

Almost from the start, the production of *Citizen Kane* was sparked by

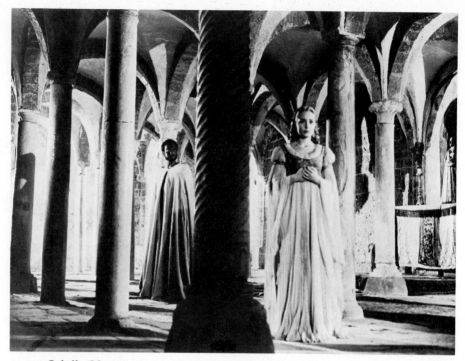

11–26. *Othello* **(Morocco, 1951),** *with Orson Welles and Suzanne Cloutier, directed by Welles.*
In 1948, Welles, discouraged by a string of box-office failures, left for Europe and Africa
where he hoped to work as an independent **producer–director.** His first movie was this
adaptation of Shakespeare. The project was a nightmare. It was over three years in the
shooting, and Welles had to interrupt production many times to seek additional funding. He
lost several players in the process. There were three Desdemonas, four Iagos. Sequences had
to be reshot time and again. But finally the movie was finished. On the Continent it was
enthusiastically praised and swept the Grand Prix at the Cannes Film Festival. But British
and American critics complained of its crude sound track. This was to be the pattern of
virtually all his subsequent work outside America.   *(United Artists)*

controversy. A master publicist, Welles had the film colony buzzing with specula-
tion. The movie was shot in "absolute secrecy." Rumors were rife about the
identity of the leading character, and when the syndicated Hearst gossip colum-
nist, Louella Parsons, heard that the picture was to deal with her boss's private
life, a campaign against the movie was launched by La Parsons, with Hearst's
blessings and full cooperation.

As the film neared completion, Hearst's campaign got ferocious. He threatened the industry with a series of scandals and exposés unless the picture was
destroyed before release. His stooge, MGM's Louis B. Mayer, the most powerful man in the industry, offered to reimburse RKO's costs, plus a tidy profit, if
the studio would destroy the negative. Hearst pressured the other studios to
refuse to book the film in their theaters. His newspapers attacked Welles as a
Communist, and suggested he was a draft-dodger. (Welles was rejected for
military service for medical reasons.) RKO stalled, paralyzed with indecision.

Welles threatened to sue unless the movie was released. Finally, the studio decided to take the risk.

With only a few exceptions, *Citizen Kane* received rave reviews. Bosley Crowther of the *New York Times* called it "one of the greatest (if not the greatest) films in history." It won the New York Film Critics Award as best picture of 1941, which was a very good year for American movies. It received nine Academy Award nominations, but at the ceremonies, Welles was booed whenever his name was mentioned. Significantly, the only Oscar that the movie won was for its screenplay. Pauline Kael suggested that this was intended as a gesture of support for Mankiewicz, the Hollywood regular, and as a rebuke to Welles, the upstart, who lost out on the acting, directing, and best picture awards.

Incredibly, *Citizen Kane* failed at the box office. It was the beginning of the end for Welles in Hollywood. When it failed to please several sneak-preview audiences, his next masterpiece, *The Magnificent Ambersons* (1942), was cut by RKO from its 131-minute length to 88 minutes, and a phony happy ending was

11–27. *Chimes at Midnight* (**Spain/Switzerland, 1965**), *with Orson Welles, directed by Welles.*

This film, also known as *Falstaff,* was the fulfillment of an old dream—an adaptation of five of Shakespeare's plays: *Richard II; Henry IV, Parts I* and *II; Henry V;* and *The Merry Wives of Windsor.* "I believe you must say something new about a book," he said, "otherwise it is better not to touch it." The adaptation, in short, should reflect more of the adaptor's vision than that of the original author. He compared his Shakespearean adaptations to the operas of Verdi. Significantly, Verdi's three operas based on Shakespearean materials focus on the same three protagonists as Welles's movies: Macbeth, Othello, and Falstaff. *(Peppercorn-Wormser)*

tacked on. It too failed at the box office. Shortly afterwards, there was a management shuffle at RKO and both Welles and Schaefer were ousted.

Welles was always a favorite with critics, especially in France. As early as the 1950s, excerpts from his scripts appeared in such journals as *Image et Son* and *Cinéma d'Aujourd'hui*. Welles was an idolized source of inspiration for the critics at *Cahiers du Cinéma*, who spearheaded the French **New Wave**. "All of us will always owe him everything," gushed Jean-Luc Godard. Truffaut claimed that *Citizen Kane* inspired the largest number of French filmmakers to begin their own careers, and he included a tender tribute to this famous movie in *La Nuit Américaine* (literally, "The American Night," but released in the United States as *Day for Night*).

Welles's critical reputation continued to rise. In the year of his death, 1985, three books were published about him. In a poll of international film critics, conducted every ten years by the prestigious British journal *Sight and Sound*, *Citizen Kane* has topped the list of the ten greatest films of all time. The filmmaker who consistently receives the most votes as the greatest director in the history of the cinema: Orson Welles.

FURTHER READING

BAZIN, ANDRÉ, *Orson Welles: A Critical View* (New York: Harper & Row, 1978). Critical study by France's greatest film critic.

BESSY, MAURICE, ed., *Orson Welles* (New York: Crown Publishers, 1971). A collection of critical articles and script excerpts from *Cinéma d'Aujourd'hui*. Filmography, selected bibliography.

CARRINGER, ROBERT L., *The Making of Citizen Kane* (Berkeley: University of California Press, 1985). Definitive.

GOTTESMAN, RONALD, ed., *Focus on Orson Welles* (Englewood Cliffs, N. J.: Prentice-Hall, 1976). A collection of critical essays, filmography, and bibliography. See also Gottesman's *Focus on Citizen Kane* (Englewood Cliffs, N.J.: Prentice-Hall, 1971). Two excellent anthologies.

HIGHAM, CHARLES, *The Films of Orson Welles* (Berkeley: University of California Press, 1970). Critical study and psychobiography. Very well illustrated. See also Higham's

Orson Welles: The Rise and Fall of an American Genius (New York: St. Martin's Press, 1985).

KAEL, PAULINE, *The Citizen Kane Book* (Boston: Little, Brown, 1971). Reading version and a cutting continuity of *Kane*, prefaced by Kael's controversial essay on the authorship of the script.

LASKY, BETTY, *RKO: The Biggest Little Major of Them All* (Englewood Cliffs: N.J.: Prentice-Hall, 1984). Studio history.

LEAMING, BARBARA, *Orson Welles: A Biography* (New York: Viking, 1985). Extensive interviews with Welles; somewhat idolatrous.

McBRIDE, JOSEPH, *Orson Welles* (New York: Viking, 1972). A perceptive critical study. Filmography. Stage, radio, television, acting credits.

NAREMORE, JAMES, *The Magic World of Orson Welles* (New York: Oxford University Press, 1978). Critical study.

GLOSSARY

actor star. See *star.*

aerial shot (T). Essentially a variation of the *crane shot,* though restricted to exterior locations. Usually taken from a helicopter.

aesthetic distance (C). Viewers's ability to distinguish between an artistic reality and external reality—their realization that the events of a fiction film are simulated.

A-film (I). An American studio era term signifying a major production, usually with important stars and a generous budget. Shown as the main feature on double bills.

aleatory techniques (C). Techniques of filmmaking that depend on the element of chance. Images are not planned out in advance, but must be composed on the spot by the camera operator. Usually employed in documentary situations.

allegory (C). A symbolic technique in which stylized characters and situations represent rather obvious ideas, such as Justice, Death, Religion, Society, and so on.

allusion (C). A reference to an event, person, or work of art, usually well-known.

angle (G). The camera's angle of view relative to the subject being photographed. A high angle shot is photographed from above, a low angle from below the subject.

animation (G). A form of filmmaking characterized by photographing inanimate objects or individual drawings *frame* by frame, with each frame differing minutely from its predecessor. When such images are projected at the standard speed of 24 frames per second, the result is that the objects or drawings appear to move, and hence seem "animated."

anticipatory camera, anticipatory setup (C). The placement of the camera in such a manner as to anticipate the movement of an action before it occurs. Such setups often suggest predestination.

archetype (C). An original model or type after which similar things are patterned. Arche types can be well-known story patterns, universal experiences, or personality types. Myths, fairy tales, *genres,* and cultural heroes are generally archetypal, as are the basic cycles of life and nature.

art director (G). The individual responsible for designing and overseeing the construction of sets for a movie, and sometimes its interior decoration and overall visual style.

aspect ratio (T). The ratio between the horizontal and vertical dimensions of the screen.

auteur theory (C). A theory of film popularized by the critics of the French journal *Cahiers du Cinéma* in the 1950s. The theory emphasizes the director as the major creator of film art, stamping the material with his or her own personal vision, style, and thematic obsessions.

available lighting (G). The use of only that light that actually exists on location, either natural (the sun) or artificial (house lamps). When available lighting is used in interior locations, generally a sensitive *fast film stock* must also be used.

avant-garde (C). From the French, meaning "in the front ranks." Those minority artists whose works are characterized by an unconventional daring and by obscure, controversial, or highly personal ideas.

backlighting (G). When the lights for a shot derive from the rear of the set, thus throwing the foreground figures into semidarkness or silhouette.

back lot (I). During the studio era, standing exterior sets of such common locales as a turn-of-the-century city block, a frontier town, a European village, and so on.

B-film (G). A low budget movie usually shown as the second feature during the big studio era in America. B-films rarely included important stars, and took the form of popular *genres,* like thrillers, westerns, horror films, etc. The major studios used them as testing grounds for the raw talent under contract.

bird's-eye view (G). A shot in which the camera photographs a scene from directly overhead.

blimp (T). A soundproof camera housing that muffles the noise of the camera's motor so that sound can be clearly recorded on the set.

blocking (T). The movements of the actors within a given playing area.

boom, mike boom (T). An overhead telescoping pole that carries a microphone, permitting the *synchronous* recording of sound without restricting the movements of the actors.

cels, also **cells (T).** Transparent plastic sheets that are superimposed in layers by *animators* to give the illusion of depth and volume to their drawings.

cinematographer, also **director of photography** or **D.P. (G).** The artist or technician responsible for the lighting of a shot and the quality of the photography.

cinéma vérité, also **direct cinema (C).** A method of documentary filming using *aleatory* methods that don't interfere with the way events take place in reality. Such movies are made with a minimum of equipment, usually a hand-held camera and portable sound apparatus.

classical cinema, classical paradigm (C). A vague but convenient term used to designate the style of mainstream fiction films produced in America, roughly from the midteens until the late 1960s. The classical paradigm is a movie strong in *story, star,* and *production values,* with a high level of technical achievement, and edited according to conventions of *classical cutting.* The visual style is functional and rarely distracts from the characters in action. Movies in this form are structured narratively, with a clearly defined conflict, complications that intensify to a rising climax, and a resolution that emphasizes formal closure.

classical cutting (C). A style of editing developed by D.W. Griffith, in which a sequence of shots is determined by a scene's dramatic and emotional emphases rather than by physical action alone. The sequence of shots represents the breakdown of the event into its psychological as well as logical components.

closed forms (C). A visual style that inclines toward self-conscious designs and carefully harmonized compositions. The *frame* is exploited to suggest a self-sufficient universe which encloses all the necessary visual information, usually in an aesthetically appealing manner.

close-up, close shot (G). A detailed view of a person or object. A close-up of an actor usually includes only his head.

continuity (T). The kind of logic implied between edited shots, their principle of coherence. *Cutting to continuity* emphasizes smooth transitions between shots, in which time and space are unobtrusively condensed. More complex, *classical cutting* is the linking of shots according to an event's psychological as well as logical breakdown. In *thematic montage,* the continuity is determined by the symbolic association of ideas between shots, rather than any literal connections in time and space.

convention (C). An implied agreement between the viewer and artist to accept certain artificialities as real in a work of art. In movies, editing (or the juxtaposition of shots) is accepted as "logical" even though a viewer's perception of reality is continuous and unfragmented.

coverage, covering shots, cover shots (T). Extra shots of a scene that can be used to bridge transitions in case the planned footage fails to edit as planned. Usually *long shots* that preserve the overall continuity of a scene.

crane shot (T). A shot taken from a special device called a crane, which resembles a huge mechanical arm. The crane carries the camera and the *cinematographer,* and can move in virtually any direction.

creative producer (I). A producer who supervises the making of a movie in such detail that he is virtually its artistic creator. During the studio era in America, the most famous creative producers were David O. Selznick and Walt Disney.

cross-cutting (G). The alternating of shots from two sequences, often in different locales, suggesting that they are taking place at the same time.

cutting to continuity (T). A type of editing in which the shots are arranged to preserve the fluidity of an action without showing all of it. An unobtrusive condensation of a continuous action.

day-for-night shooting (T). Scenes that are filmed in daytime with special *filters* to suggest night-time settings in the movie image.

deep-focus shot (T). A technique of photography that permits all distance planes to remain clearly in focus, from close-up ranges to infinity.

dialectical, dialectics (C). An analytical methodology, derived from Hegel and Marx, that juxtaposes pairs of opposites—a thesis and antithesis—in order to arrive at a synthesis of ideas.

dissolve, lap dissolve (T). The slow fading out of one shot and the gradual fading in of its successor, with a superimposition of images, usually at the midpoint.

distributor (I). Those individuals who serve as middlemen in the film industry, who arrange to book the product in theaters.

dolly shot, tracking shot, trucking shot (T). A shot taken from a moving vehicle. Originally tracks were laid on the set to permit a smoother movement of the camera.

dominant contrast, dominant (C). That area of the film image that compels the viewer's most immediate attention, usually because of a prominent visual contrast.

double exposure (T). The superimposition of two literally unrelated images on film. See also *multiple exposure.*

dubbing (T). The addition of sound after the visuals have been photographed. Dubbing can be either *synchronous* with an image or *nonsynchronous.* Foreign language movies are often dubbed in English for release in this country.

editing (G). The joining of one shot (strip of film) with another. The shots can picture events and objects in different places at different times. In Europe, editing is called *montage.*

epic (C). A film *genre* characterized by bold and sweeping themes, usually in heroic proportions. The protagonist is an ideal representative of a culture—national, religious, or regional. The tone of most epics is dignified, the treatment larger-than-life. The western is the most popular epic genre in the U.S.A.

establishing shot (T). Usually an *extreme long* or *long shot* offered at the beginning of a scene, providing the viewer with the context of the subsequent closer shots.

expressionism (C). A style of filmmaking emphasizing extreme distortion, *lyricism,* and artistic self-expression at the expense of objectivity.

extreme close-up (G). A minutely detailed view of an object or person. An extreme close-up of an actor generally includes only his eyes or mouth.

extreme long shot (G). A panoramic view of an exterior location, photographed from a great distance, often as far as a quarter-mile away.

eye-level shot (T). The placement of the camera approximately five to six feet from the ground, corresponding to the height of an observer on the scene.

fade (T). The fade-out is the snuffing of an image from normal brightness to a black screen. A fade-in is the opposite.

faithful adaptation (C). A film based on a literary original which captures the essence of the original, often by using cinematic equivalents for specific literary techniques.

fast motion (T). Shots of a subject photographed at a slower rate than 24 fps, which, when projected at the standard rate, conveys motion that is jerky and slightly comical, seemingly out of control.

fast stock, fast film (T). Film stock that's highly sensitive to light and generally produces a grainy image. Often used by documentarists who wish to shoot only with *available lighting.*

film noir (C). A French term—literally, black cinema—referring to a kind of urban American *genre* that sprang up after World War II, emphasizing a fatalistic, despairing universe where there is no escape from mean city streets, loneliness, and death. Stylistically, *noir* emphasizes *low-key* and *high-contrast* lighting, complex compositions, and a strong atmosphere of dread and paranoia.

filters (T). Pieces of glass or plastic placed in front of the camera lens, which distort the quality of light entering the camera, and hence the movie image.

final cut, also **release print (I).** The sequence of shots in a movie as it will be released to the public.

first cut, also **rough cut (I).** The initial sequence of shots in a movie, often constructed by the director.

first-person point of view. See *point-of-view shot.*

flashback (G). An editing technique that suggests the interruption of the present by a shot or series of shots representing the past.

flash-forward (G). An editing technique that suggests the interruption of the present by a shot or series of shots representing the future.

focus (T). The degree of acceptable sharpness in a film image. "Out of focus" means the images are blurred and lack acceptable linear definition.

footage (T). Exposed film *stock.*

foregrounding (C). When a critic isolates and heightens one aspect of a work of art from its context in order to analyze that characteristic in greater depth.

formalist, formalism (C). A style of filmmaking in which aesthetic forms take precedence over the subject matter as content. Time and space as ordinarily perceived are often distorted. Emphasis is placed on the essential, symbolic characteristics of objects and people, not necessarily on their superficial appearance. Formalists are often *lyrical,* self-consciously heightening their style in order to call attention to it as a value for its own sake.

frame (T). The dividing line between the edges of the screen image and the enclosing darkness of the theater. Can also refer to a single photograph from the filmstrip.

freeze frame, freeze shot (T). A shot composed of a single *frame* that is reprinted a number of times on the filmstrip; when projected, it gives the illusion of a still photograph.

f-stop (T). The measurement of the size of the lens opening in the camera, indicating the amount of light that's admitted.

full shot (T). A type of *long shot* which includes the human body in full, with the head near the top of the *frame* and the feet near the bottom.

gauge (T). The width of the filmstrip, expressed in millimeters (mm). The wider the gauge, the better the quality of the image. The standard theatrical gauge is 35 mm.

genre (C). A recognizable type of movie, characterized by certain preestablished conventions. Some common American genres are westerns, thrillers, sci-fi movies, etc. A ready-made narrative form.

high-angle shot (T). A shot in which the subject is photographed from above.

high contrast (T). A style of lighting emphasizing harsh shafts and dramatic streaks of lights and darks. Often used in thrillers and melodramas.

high key (T). A style of lighting emphasizing bright, even illumination, with few conspicuous shadows. Used mostly in comedies, musicals, and light entertainment films.

homage (C). A direct or indirect reference within a movie to another movie, filmmaker, or cinematic style. A respectful and affectionate tribute.

iconography (C). The use of a well-known cultural symbol or complex of symbols in an artistic representation. In movies, iconography can involve a star's *persona,* the preestablished conventions of a *genre* (like the shootout in a western), the use of *archetypal* characters and situations, and such stylistic features as lighting, settings, costuming, props, and so on.

independent producer (G). A producer not affiliated with a studio or large commercial firm. Many stars and directors have been independent producers to insure their artistic control.

intercut (T). See *cross-cutting.*

intrinsic interest (C). An unobtrusive area of the film image that nonetheless compels our most immediate attention because of its dramatic or contextual importance.

iris (T). A *masking* device that blacks out portions of the screen, permitting only a part of the image to be seen. Usually the iris is circular or oval in shape and can be expanded or contracted.

jump-cut (T). An abrupt transition between shots, sometimes deliberate, which is disorienting in terms of the continuity of space and time.

key light (T). The main source of illumination for a shot.

kinetic (C). Pertaining to motion and movement.

leftist, left-wing (C). A political term used to describe the acceptance, at least in part, of the economic, social, and philosophical ideas of Karl Marx.

lengthy take, long take (C). A shot of lengthy duration.

lens (T). A ground or molded piece of glass, plastic, or other transparent material through which light rays are refracted so that they converge or diverge to form the photographic image within the camera.

literal adaptation (C). A movie based on a stage play, in which the dialogue and actions are preserved more or less intact.

long shot (G). A shot that includes an area within the image that roughly corresponds to the audience's view of the area within the proscenium arch in the live theater.

loose adaptation (C). A movie based on another medium in which only a superficial resemblance exists between the two versions.

loose framing (C). Usually in longer shots. The *mise en scène* is so spaciously distributed within the confines of the framed image that

the people photographed have considerable freedom of movement.

low-angle shot (T). A shot in which the subject is photographed from below.

low key (T). A style of lighting that emphasizes diffused shadows and atmospheric pools of light. Often used in mysteries and thrillers.

lyrical (C). A stylistic exuberance and subjectivity, emphasizing the sensuous beauty of the medium, and producing an intense outpouring of emotion.

majors (I). The principle production studios of a given era. In the golden age of the Hollywood studio system—roughly the 1930s and 1940s—the majors consisted of MGM, Warner Brothers, RKO, Paramount Pictures, and Twentieth Century–Fox.

Marxist (C). A person who subscribes to the economic, social, political, and philosophical theories of Karl Marx. Any artistic work reflecting these values.

masking (T). A technique whereby a portion of the movie image is blocked out, thus temporarily altering the dimensions of the screen's *aspect ratio.*

master shot (T). An uninterrupted shot, usually taken from a *long* or *full shot* range, that contains an entire scene. The closer shots are photographed later, and an *edited* sequence, composed of a variety of shots, is constructed on the editor's bench.

matte shot (T). A process of combining two separate shots on one print, resulting in an image that looks as though it had been photographed normally. Used mostly for special effects, such as combining a human figure with giant dinosaurs, etc.

medium shot (G). A relatively close shot, revealing the human figure from the knees or waist up.

metaphor (C). An implied comparison between two otherwise unlike elements, meaningful in a figurative rather than literal sense.

metteur en scène (C). The artist or technician who creates the *mise en scène*—that is, the director.

mickeymousing (T). A type of film music that is purely descriptive and attempts to mimic the visual action with musical equivalents. Often used in cartoons.

miniatures, also **model** or **miniature shots (T).** Small-scale models photographed to give the illusion that they are full-scale objects. For example, ships sinking at sea, giant dinosaurs, airplanes colliding, etc.

minimalism (C). A style of filmmaking characterized by austerity and restraint, in which cinematic elements are reduced to the barest minimum of information.

mise en scène (C). The arrangement of visual weights and movements within a given space. In the live theater, the space is usually defined by the proscenium arch; in movies, it is defined by the *frame* that encloses the images. Cinematic mise en scène encompasses both the staging of the action and the way that it's photographed.

mix (T). The process of combining separately recorded sounds from individual soundtracks onto a master track.

montage (T). Transitional sequences of rapidly edited images, used to suggest the lapse of time or the passing of events. Often employs *dissolves* and *multiple exposures.* In Europe, montage means the art of editing.

motif (C). Any unobtrusive technique, object, or thematic idea that's systematically repeated throughout a film.

multiple exposure (T). A special effect produced by the *optical printer,* which permits the superimposition of many images simultaneously.

negative image (T). The reversal of lights and darks of the subject photographed: blacks are white, whites are black.

neorealism (C). An Italian film movement that produced its best works between 1945 and 1955. Strongly *realistic* in its techniques, neorealism emphasized documentary aspects of film art, stressing loose episodic plots, unextraordinary events and characters, natural lighting, actual location settings, nonprofessional actors, a preoccupation with poverty and social problems, and an emphasis on humanistic and democratic ideals. The term has also been used to describe other films that reflect the technical and stylistic biases of Italian neorealism.

New Wave, nouvelle vague (C). A group of young French directors who came to prominence during the late 1950s. The most widely known are François Truffaut, Jean-Luc Godard, and Alain Resnais.

nonsynchronous sound (T). Sound and image that are not recorded simultaneously, or sound that is detached from its source in the film image. Music is usually nonsynchronous in a movie, providing background atmosphere.

oblique angle, tilt shot (T). A shot photographed by a tilted camera. When the image is projected on the screen, the subject itself seems to be tilted on a diagonal.

oeuvre (C). From the French, "work." The complete works of an artist, viewed as a whole.

omniscient point of view (C). An all-knowing narrator who provides the spectator with all the necessary information.

open forms (C). Used primarily by *realist* filmmakers, these techniques are likely to be unobtrusive, with an emphasis on informal compositions and apparently haphazard designs. The *frame* is exploited to suggest a temporary masking, a window which arbitrarily cuts off part of the action.

optical printer (T). An elaborate machine used to create special effects in movies. For example, *fades, dissolves, multiple exposures,* etc.

outtakes (I). Shots or pieces of shots that are not used in the final cut of a film. Leftover footage.

overexposure (T). Too much light enters the aperture of a camera lens, bleaching out the image. Useful for fantasy and nightmare scenes.

pan, panning shot (T). Short for panorama, this is a revolving horizontal movement of the camera from left to right or vice versa.

parallel editing. See *cross-cutting.*

persona (C). From the Latin, "mask." An actor's public image, based on his or her previous roles, and often incorporating elements from their actual personalities as well.

personality star. See *star.*

pixillation, also **stop-motion photography (T).** An *animation* technique involving the photographing of live actors *frame* by frame. When the sequence is projected at the standard speed of 24 fps, the actors move abruptly and jerkily, like cartoon figures.

point-of-view shot, also **pov shot, first-person camera, subjective camera (T).** Any shot that is taken from the vantage point of a character in the film, showing what the character sees.

process shot, also **rear projection (T).** A technique in which a background scene is projected onto a translucent screen behind the actors so it appears that the actors are on location in the final image.

producer (G). An ambiguous term referring to the individual or company that controls the financing of a film, and often the way it's made. The producer can concern himself solely with business matters, or with putting together a package deal (such as script, stars, and director), or he can function as an expeditor, smoothing over problems during production.

producer–director (I). A filmmaker who finances projects independently, to allow maximum creative freedom.

production values (I). The box-office appeal of the physical mounting of a film, such as sets, costumes, props, etc.

prop (T). Any movable item which is included in a movie: tables, guns, books, etc.

property (I). Anything with a profit-making potential in movies, though generally used to describe a story of some kind: a screenplay, novel, short story, etc.

proxemic patterns (C). The spatial relationships among characters within the *mise en scène,* and the apparent distance of the camera from the subject photographed.

pull-back dolly (T). Withdrawing the camera from a scene to reveal an object or character that was previously out of *frame.*

rack focusing, selective focusing (T). The blurring of focal planes in sequence, forcing the viewer's eyes to travel with those areas of an image that remain in sharp focus.

reaction shot (T). A cut to a shot of a character's reaction to the contents of the preceding shot.

realism (G). A style of filmmaking that attempts to duplicate the look of objective reality as it's commonly perceived, with emphasis on authentic locations and details, *long shots, lengthy takes,* and a minimum of distorting techniques.

reestablishing shot (T). A return to an initial *establishing shot* within a scene, acting as a reminder of the physical context of the closer shots.

reprinting (T). A special effects technique in which two or more separately photographed images are rephotographed onto one strip of film.

reverse angle shot (T). A shot taken from an angle 180° opposed to the previous shot. That is, the camera is placed opposite its previous position.

reverse motion (T). A series of images are photographed with the film reversed. When projected normally, the effect is to suggest backward movement—an egg "returning" to its shell, for example.

rough cut (T). The crudely edited footage of a movie before the editor has tightened up the slackness between shots. A kind of rough draft.

rushes, dailies (I). The selected footage of the previous day's shooting, which is usually evaluated by the director and *cinematographer* before the start of the next day's shooting.

scene (G). An imprecise unit of film, composed of a number of interrelated *shots,* unified usually by a central concern—a location, an incident, or a minor dramatic climax.

script, screenplay, scenario (G). A written description of a movie's dialogue and action, which occasionally includes camera directions.

selective focus. See *rack focusing.*

sequence shot, also *plan-séquence (C).* A single lengthy shot, usually involving complex staging and camera movements.

setup (T). The positioning of the camera and lights for a specific shot.

shooting ratio (I). The amount of film stock used in photographing a movie in relation to what's finally included in the finished product. A shooting ratio of 20:1 means that twenty feet of film were shot for every one used in the *final cut.*

shooting script (I). A written breakdown of a movie story into its individual shots, often containing technical instructions. Used by the director and his or her staff during the production.

short lens. See *wide-angle lens.*

shot (G). Those images that are recorded continuously from the time the camera starts to the time it stops. That is, an unedited strip of film.

slow motion (T). Shots of a subject photographed at a faster rate than 24 fps, which when projected at the standard rate produce a dreamy dancelike slowness of action.

slow stock, slow film (T). Film stocks that are relatively insensitive to light and produce crisp images and a sharpness of detail. When used in interior settings, these stocks generally require considerable artificial illumination.

soft focus (T). The blurring out of focus of all except one desired distance range. Can also refer to a glamorizing technique which softens the sharpness of definition so that facial wrinkles can be smoothed over and even eliminated.

star (G). A film actor or actress of great popularity. A *personality star* tends to play only those roles that fit a preconceived public image, which constitutes his or her *persona*. An *actor star* can play roles of greater range and variety. Barbra Streisand is a personality star; Robert De Niro is an actor star.

star system (G). The technique of exploiting the charisma of popular performers to enhance the box-office appeal of films. The star system was developed in America and has been the backbone of the American film industry since the mid-1910s.

star vehicle (G). A movie especially designed to showcase the talents and charms of a specific star.

stock (T). Unexposed film. There are many types of movie stocks, including those highly sensitive to light (*fast stocks*) and those relatively insensitive to light (*slow stocks*).

storyboard, storyboarding (T). A pre-visualization technique in which shots are sketched in advance and in sequence, like a comic strip, thus allowing the filmmaker to outline the *mise en scène* and construct the *editing* continuity before production begins.

story values (I). The narrative appeal of a movie, which can reside in the popularity of an adapted *property*, the high craftsmanship of a script, or both.

studio (G). A large corporation specializing in the production of movies, such as Paramount, Warner Brothers, and so on; any physical facility equipped for the production of films.

subjective camera. See *point-of-view shot.*

subsidiary contrast (C). A subordinated element of the film image, complementing or contrasting with the *dominant contrast.*

subtext (C). A term used in drama and film to signify the dramatic implications beneath the language of a play or movie. Often the subtext concerns ideas and emotions that are totally independent of the language of a text.

surrealism (C). An avant-garde movement in the arts stressing Freudian and Marxist ideas, unconscious elements, irrationalism, and the symbolic association of ideas. Surrealist movies were produced roughly from 1924 to 1931, primarily in France, though there are surrealistic elements in the works of many directors, and especially in music videos.

swish pan, also flash or zip pan (T). A horizontal movement of the camera at such a rapid rate that the subject photographed blurs on the screen.

synchronous sound (T). The agreement or correspondence between image and sound, which are recorded simultaneously, or seem so in the finished print. Synchronous sounds appear to derive from an obvious source in the visuals.

symbol, symbolic (C). A figurative device in which an object, event, or cinematic technique has significance beyond its literal meaning. Symbolism is always determined by the dramatic context.

take (T). A variation of a specific shot. The final shot is often selected from a number of possible takes.

telephoto lens, long lens (T). A lens that acts as a telescope, magnifying the size of objects at a great distance. A side effect is its tendency to flatten perspective.

thematic montage (C). A type of *editing* propounded by the Soviet filmmaker Eisenstein, in which separate shots are linked together not by their literal continuity in reality, but by symbolic association. A shot of a preening braggart might be linked to a shot of a toy peacock, for example. Most commonly used in documentaries, in which shots are connected in accordance to the filmmaker's thesis.

three shot (T). A *medium shot*, featuring three actors.

tight framing (C). Usually in close shots. The *mise en scène* is so carefully balanced and harmonized that the people photographed have little or no freedom of movement.

tilt, tilt shot (T). See *oblique angle.*

tracking shot, trucking shot. See *dolly shot.*

two shot (T). A *medium shot* featuring two actors.

vertical integration (I). A system in which the production, distribution, and exhibition of movies are all controlled by the same corporation. In America the practice was declared illegal in the late 1940s.

viewfinder (T). An eyepiece on the camera which

defines the playing area and the *framing* of the action to be photographed.

voice-over (T). A *nonsynchronous* spoken commentary in a movie, often used to convey a character's thoughts or memories.

wide-angle lens, short lens (T). A lens that permits the camera to photograph a wider area than a normal lens. A side effect is its tendency to exaggerate perspective. Also used for *deep-focus* photography.

widescreen, also **CinemaScope, scope (G).** A movie image that has an *aspect ratio* of approximately 5:3, though some widescreens possess horizontal dimensions that extend as wide as 2.5 times the vertical dimension of the screen.

wipe (T). An *editing* device, usually a line that travels across the screen, "pushing off" one image and revealing another.

zoom lens, zoom shot (T). A lens of variable focal length that permits the cinematographer to change from *wide-angle* to *telephoto shots* (and vice versa) in one continuous movement, often plunging the viewer in or out of a scene rapidly.

INDEX